TEXAS PRISONS

THE LARGEST HOTEL CHAIN IN TEXAS

TEXAS PRISONS

The Largest Hotel Chain in Texas

Lon Bennett Glenn
WARDEN II-RETIRED

EAKIN PRESS  Austin, Texas

For CIP information,
please access:
www.loc.gov

FIRST EDITION
Copyright © 2001
By Lon Bennett Glenn
Published in the United States of America
By Eakin Press
A Division of Sunbelt Media, Inc.
P.O. Drawer 90159 ◻ Austin, Texas 78709-0159
email: eakinpub@sig.net
◻ website: www.eakinpress.com ◻
ALL RIGHTS RESERVED.
    2   3   4   5   6   7   8   9
ISBN 1-57168-522-7

DEDICATION

To the officers of the Texas Department of Criminal Justice-Institutional Division, who bravely walk the hallways and cell-block runs of our state prisons. To those infinitely patient men and women who devote their lives to working in a violent environment, largely forgotten by the public and trapped between the federal courts and the convicts in a never-ending battle for survival. To you who must trust in your own common sense, tempered by experience and professionalism borne of necessity, each officer faithfully watching his fellow officer's back while striving to make it through another day. I salute your integrity, your devotion to duty, and your historical dedication to service on behalf of all law-abiding citizens of Texas.

CONTENTS

A good read by someone who has actually accomplished something, has the intelligence to understand it, the talent to write about it, and most of all the courage to tell the truth, is rare. This is a personal story, not one of those pompous and self-serving monuments to ego. It is bawdy, violent, funny, sad, and filled with insight and wisdom that only come when intelligence and learning are shaped on the grindstone of experience. It is very human, and that, too, is rare these days.

History is hard to know, because of all the revisionist propaganda being written these days, mostly by people who weren't there. The author, my friend Warden Lon Bennett Glenn (retired TDCJ, 1995) was there for more than thirty years. He lived in state-employee housing on four Texas prison units in Brazoria County for twenty-two years. Lon worked for six Texas governors, six Texas Prison System directors, four Southern Regional directors, and fourteen unit wardens. He saw it all while working his way through the ranks at every job there was to work, on five prison units (one twice), and he spent twenty-five of his thirty years working with close-custody, maximum-security-classified inmates. He's worked with killers, ex–death row inmates, gang members, armed robbers, transsexuals, sexual predators, arsonists, the insane, con artists, dope dealers, and various other societal rejects.

Three and a half decades ago in the mid-1960s, the Texas Prison System was coming to the end of an era. The old guard force was mostly made up of men with modest education, rooted in agriculture. They were ex-farmers, ex–World War II and Korean War veterans. They had been hired because of their ability to farm and ranch by hand, using an inmate workforce, hand tools, mules, and a few tractors. These skills were important in those days, because the stated goal of each prison unit was to be as self-sufficient as possible.

Having come through the Depression and a couple of world wars, these loyal employees valued their jobs, but they were getting old. There was a new generation of young, intelligent, and highly motivated officers coming into the prison workforce. These young officers looked at their jobs as more than just a way to make a living; for them it was a noble calling. This was the Vietnam War era, and many of these young officers saw themselves as soldiers in a fight against the dark forces of evil. There was a fantastic sense that whatever we were doing was right, and that we were going to win. It was the sense of inevitable victory over the dark side that drove us forward. We felt that if we could just stay the course, our energy and our youth would simply prevail. We had the momentum; we had the full support of the Texas Legislature; and we were on a never-ending winning streak, backed by the righteous, taxpaying citizens of Texas.

In those days, the Texas Prison System had an excellent reputation and did what the people of Texas wanted it to do. The criminals were locked up and secure, which made the general public feel safe. The convicts worked in order to offset much of the cost of feeding, clothing, and housing them. Convict labor was even used to construct new prisons. The prisons were kept clean and the convicts well-disciplined. There were minimal rehabilitation and educational program opportunities for inmates, and clearly the priority was placed on hard labor. The general thinking was that anyone who spent a few years picking cotton, gathering sugarcane, and raising garden crops by hand on the Gulf Coast of Texas would surely be rehabilitated enough to not want to repeat the experience.

The inmates who worked hard, stayed out of trouble, and did what they were told were given the best inmate prison jobs. They were also allowed some oversight privileges over the other inmates. This arrangement was called the building-tender system. It was approved by lawmakers in Austin and had been used effectively for many years, resulting in Texas having not only an extremely efficient prison operation, but also the lowest inmate-per-day cost of any prison system in the nation.

The citizens of Texas could drive down any of several state highways that passed by or through prison units and watch the inmate workforce and their tax dollars at work. The prison system kept a low profile, and rarely was anything seen in the news media regarding prisons or prisoners. Of course, in those days a unit warden completely controlled access to his unit. News reporters were allowed by invitation only. All incoming and outgoing mail was censored, and inmate phone calls were limited to one monitored call every ninety days. This was at a time when nationally recognized penal experts, almost without exception, publicly stated that the Texas Prison System was one of the best, perhaps *the* best-run prison system in the nation.

All of that was before a few nonelected, activist federal judges, the ACLU, and a group of out-of-state lawyers decided that the Texas Prison System was in need of drastic change. Unfortunately, the federal courts and lawyers generally feed on our shortcomings, not our virtues. They are, after all, prisoners of their own lust to win. In the ensuing battle over who would control Texas prisons, the state politicians and the taxpaying citizens they represented quickly found out that they had no chance to win in federal court. The wants and needs of taxpaying citizens made little difference to a federal district court judge.

So began a battle of wills that would last for more than thirty years and cost Texas taxpayers billions of dollars—and it is still going on today. The Texas Prison System grew from a relatively small 14,000-inmate population distributed on twelve small farm units in only five counties to a multibillion-dollar growth industry with more than 160,000 inmates inhabiting more than a hundred TDCJ units statewide. Our society declared war on drugs and became more ethnically diverse; more women gained emancipation through work; and above all, we got politically correct. When the *Ruiz* court case was originally filed in 1972, the taxpayers of Texas were paying about $3.00 per day for each inmate in the prison system. Today it costs the taxpayers of Texas from $43.00 to $63.00 per day, depending on the custody class and medical status of each inmate in the prison system.

There are some, again mostly those who weren't there, who will say that the old system was rotten to the core and that all the employees were corrupt and brutal men. The truth is, some of these modern-day revisionists are just telling lies. I am here to tell you that there were some corrupt and brutal men employed by the system in those days, but they were the rare exception, not the rule. There were many, many more employees whom I was proud to work with, men of strong moral fiber who had a strong sense of personal integrity and held the highest ethical standards. I have made many friends over the years that any man would be proud to ride the river with. I rode the same plowed fields as the author for many years.

In a business where self-preservation is your first priority and a man's reputation is his most valuable asset, the betrayal of trust is perhaps the most serious offense. Even during the darkest, most vulnerable moments of my career, I was fortunate to have never been betrayed by a friend. Many others were not so fortunate. I am proud of what was accomplished when we all worked for the people of Texas instead of the federal courts. If that no longer counts for anything, I figure that's their shortcoming, not ours. I am satisfied that we did our best.

Texas prisons are in an undisputed mess today, with operational expenses and the inmate population spiraling out of control. We have gotten away from the basics. At the risk of sounding simplistic, I'll say this: It's not rocket science, folks. A lot of people who should know better have forgotten what the people of Texas want their prison system to do, and isn't that what a democracy is supposed to be about? Shouldn't these elected officials and federal judges be striving to represent the interests of the law-abiding, taxpaying public? Most of the bureaucrats on the nine-member Texas Board of Criminal Justice have little if any experience in penology. None of them has ever worn a correctional-officer's uniform. There is massive employee turnover, due in part to a thriving state economy that has bypassed a correctional staff that hasn't received a meaningful pay raise in years.

In a 1999 poll by a national magazine ranking the least-respected jobs in America, "Texas prison guard" was in the "nightmare job" category. With an annual salary of $25,524, TDCJ Officer ranks second on the list, just below "sewer-pipe cleaner" at $26,780. Also in the same category were porn shop janitor, fish-head trimmers, packing-plant slaughterers, zoo cage cleaners, and embalmers.

Another significant reason for the large employee turnover is the ever-growing absence of inmate control and the retirements of many of the more experienced personnel; the average TDCJ security supervisor and rank-and-file employee has been on the job less than five years. Another factor affecting turnover is that correctional officers are being assaulted by inmates on a daily basis, because there is little deterrent to stop them from doing so.

We are in this mess because a few years ago we allowed some former governors and state attorneys to agree to the conditions crafted by a federal judge and the convict's attorneys in the *Ruiz* case. The bottom line is that we, as a state, lacked the backbone to fight it out in federal court. Unless the people of Texas begin to pressure their politicians to get these federal judges out of our business, an ongoing tragedy is going to get much worse. Texas can and must do better. We can make prisons more than just violent warehouses, but we must give the unit-level administrators the tools and the authority that they need.

I hope that the public will read this book and become a little more enlightened as to where we have been in the area of corrections in Texas. Most importantly, if we are to avoid further tragic results, we must look at where we are headed.

This book is not intended to be an all-encompassing history of prisons in Texas. It does have a little history, a little past and some present. The author's concern is for the future safety and security of the citizens of Texas, especially those unappreciated employees who sacrifice daily to protect the general public. There have been serious problems in the past, but nothing like the Texas Department of Criminal Justice-Institutional Division faces today. The criminal-justice system eventually touches all the citizens of Texas in one way or another and will continue to do so for generations to come. Make no mistake about it. We all have a stake in who controls the Texas Department of Criminal Justice, because it is and will continue to be an integral part of our lives and those of future generations of Texans.

LARRY A. JOHNS
Senior Warden (Retired 2000)
Michael Unit, TDCJ-ID

INTRODUCTION

WHAT IS A CORRECTIONAL OFFICER?

Correctional officers are human beings, contrary to what the media may project, just like folks in the rest of our society. They come in both sexes, all races, and all sizes. Correctional officers can always count on four things: being understaffed, unprotected, underpaid, and underappreciated.

Correctional officers are found in all areas of a prison unit. It is their duty to protect, defend, secure, enforce, prevent, and serve. They know the environment is dangerous, but historically, they have always been there when the chips were down.

Correctional officers deliver chow, instructions, and bad news. They are required to have the wisdom of Solomon, the disposition of a lamb, and muscles of steel, and they are often accused of having hearts of stone. They are the ones who swallow hard and announce, "Your mother just died," then spend the rest of the shift wondering why they ever took this job.

In the media, correctional officers are portrayed as abusive, vile, and "on the take." In reality they are required to be compassionate, firm but fair, and most of all, pure as the driven snow. In spite of all their efforts, the general public gives them less respect than any other profession, with the possible exception of lawyers—and lawyers usually don't deserve respect.

If a correctional officer writes an offense report on some inmate rule violator, he is a monster; if he doesn't, he's intimidated. If he drives a new car, it's because "He sold out." If he drives an old car, the reaction is, "Who's he trying to kid?" When a correctional officer does something exceptional, "He's doing what we pay him to do." When he makes a mistake, he gets ten days' suspension without pay, and/or multiple lawsuits.

Some correctional officers have homes covered with ivy, but most of them are covered with mortgages. Their credit is usually good, thank God, because their salaries aren't.

A correctional officer sees more trouble, misery, and bloodshed than the average lawman. Prisons are always open, day and night, in all kinds of weather, seven days a week, on holidays and weekends, 365 days a year. An officer's shift and unit assignments can change more often than most people change socks, but his general outlook must remain the same; he must go on thinking, hoping, *If I can just get through this shift, tomorrow will be better.*

Correctional officers get citations and promotions for saving lives, stopping riots, and disarming dangerous convicts. On occasion, their widows or other family members receive the citation for them. Sometimes, the most rewarding moment comes when after some small kindness to an inmate, an officer looks into a grateful eye and hears, "Thanks, man."

CHAPTER ONE

LOOKING FOR WORK

"It's a dirty job, but somebody has to do it."
—UNKNOWN

The beginning has always been a mystery. Why would an otherwise sane person voluntarily embark on a thirty-year career that would require him to work around some of the most dangerous convicts in Texas? There is an old cliché: "It's a dirty job, but somebody has to do it." I can't say that's the reason I took the job. The simple truth is, I was just looking for steady work, anywhere away from Temple, Texas.

It was the mid-1960s. In Temple, gas was 30 cents a gallon, a hamburger was 35 cents, and a Coke (the liquid kind) cost a dime. I was a twenty-year-old, six-foot-two white boy with barely a high-school education, and I was about to begin an adventure. If one hoped to have any real future in Temple, Texas, there were two choices: work for the railroad or one of the four major hospitals in town. Everything else paid minimum wage, $1.25 per hour, with endless competition from thousands of others. It meant living paycheck to paycheck with no benefits or hope for advancement.

I'd heard about a new job opportunity that paid $315.00 per month with free uniforms and free room and board. In mid-July 1966, I rode a bus to Huntsville and back, four hours each way. We stopped at every one-mule town along the way. Finally, after taking an "IQ test" and suffering through an interview with Dr. Gates,

TDC psychiatrist, I was pronounced sane enough to work for the Texas Prison System.

It was in Dr. Gates' office that I met my first real live convict. His name was James Cross, and he was working as Gates' secretary when I walked in for my employment interview. I recognized him from his picture, which only a few months before had been plastered on the front of every newspaper in the country. In late 1965, Cross was found guilty of the rape and killing of two coeds at the University of Texas. The case received extra coverage on all the news stations in Central Texas, and Cross was known nationwide as an infamous killer. A job interview at the Walls Unit in Huntsville, Texas, was no doubt a unique experience. There's nothing quite like having a convicted multiple killer in the outer office to put a prospective job applicant at ease.

My interview with Dr. Gates consisted of one question. He asked me, "What is the shortest number of words that you can use to create a sentence?"

I answered, "A subject and a verb." That concluded my psychiatric evaluation, interview, everything. I later found out that based on that less than in-depth observation, he wrote in my personnel file: "Ninety-eight percent potential, two percent active."

I don't remember ever seeing a prison before my bus trip to Huntsville. As anyone who has ever been in a prison, even as a visitor, will tell you, that first time the barred door to the outside slams shuts behind you, there is a noticeable tightening in the pit of your stomach. Over the next thirty years of working in criminal justice, I never completely lost that feeling.

I reported to the Ferguson Unit Training School on the following Monday morning in a new khaki uniform with a dark brown stripe down the side. We lived in one end of the old double-bunked dormitory and went to class in the other end. Built with convict labor, the small barrack-style building was constructed from the same red brick that all TDC buildings were made from in those days. The red brick was made by convicts at the old Harlem Unit Brick Plant, now known as the Jester Unit, near Sugarland, Texas.

This was a paramilitary school with uniform inspections and by-the-book training from no-nonsense instructors. The first few days, the sergeants and lieutenants tried to break us, just to see who was in it for the long haul, but then we settled into a fairly calm routine. We learned a little prison history, mostly from the telling of "war stories" by our instructors. There was also a slide-show presentation about some of the more infamous prisoners and their crimes. One of the first and more interesting Texas out-laws to be incarcerated was John Wesley Hardin.

The Man with Forty Notches on His Gun

Arguably the most notorious man ever to serve time in a Texas prison, John Westley Hardin, the son of a Methodist preacher, was from Bonham, in Fannin County, Texas. Although unveri-fied, estimates based mostly on folklore are that Hardin mur-dered forty men. The real number is probably closer to twenty, both inside and outside of the penitentiary.

His criminal career began when the teenage Hardin killed an ex-slave in a fight and then killed two or three federal soldiers when they came to arrest him for the crime. After this incident, Hardin's life became a series of barroom brawls and gunfights. Later, while in Abilene, Kansas, Hardin socialized with Wild Bill Hickock and Ben Thompson, both well-known deadly gunfighters. During this time, Hardin gained a reputation for murder at the least provocation, killing one man who happened to be in the next room at the American House Hotel in Abilene for snoring too loud.

After several more killings, Hardin drew the attention of the Texas Rangers. His final two victims, so far as is known, were slain after a poker game in Mobile, Alabama, after they objected to him winning $3,500. Hardin changed his name and moved to Florida, hiding out under the alias J. H. Swain. His disguise worked so well that he was even asked to help a local police office round up some suspected criminals. He was safe until his brother-in-law wrote to family in Texas telling them of their location.

On July 23, 1877, Hardin was cornered in the smoking car of a train at Pensacola Junction, Florida. As Texas Ranger John Armstrong and deputies rushed him from both ends of the rail-car, Hardin's pistol caught in his suspenders, giving the rangers an opportunity to subdue him. After a Texas Ranger escort back to his home state, the so-called meanest man in Texas was found guilty of second-degree murder, and at the age of twenty-five,

John Wesley Hardin became prisoner #7109. He began serving his twenty-five-year sentence on October 5, 1878.

John Wesley was hardly a model prisoner. He tried to escape several times and was punished severely each time. His punishment consisted of lashes with a broad, heavy leather whip called "the bat." That was often followed by several weeks in a small, dark solitary cell called "the hole." While in solitary, he had to live on a diet of bread and water. He finally settled into prison life, however, and even wrote letters to his children urging them to live lives that the family could be proud of. Hardin wrote his autobiography while at Huntsville, claiming, "I never killed a man who didn't need killing."

While in prison, Hardin was given a job in the boot factory and seemed proud of his newly acquired skills. He became active in religious programs and was named superintendent of the Sunday school. On March 16, 1894, Governor James Hogg pardoned Hardin for "behaving in an orderly manner." He had served fifteen years, five months, with time off for good behavior. His wife had died only a short time before he was released.

Hardin studied law while in prison and soon after his release was admitted to the bar. He opened a law office in El Paso, Texas, but passed more time arguing in saloons than in court. Finally, after several stormy encounters with local factions, on August 19, 1895, a part-time policeman named John Selman stepped into the Acme Saloon and found Hardin gambling with a friend. Selman calmly walked up behind Hardin and shot him in the back of the head.

The next day, Hardin's body was laid out so that the citizens of El Paso could see the man with forty notches on his gun. According to a newpaper account at the time, one observer noted, "'Side from being dead, he never looked better." Selman's killing of Hardin was an act of coldblooded, back-shooting murder, but the jury acquitted him anyway, apparently in gratitude for his having rid Texas of a major menace.

TEXAS-PRISON TRIVIA

The early days of the Texas Prison System were filled with colorful times and even more colorful people. Established in 1848, the first prison in Texas held Indian chiefs, Civil War prisoners, and many infamous outlaws. Among these were Santana and Big Tree—Kiowa Indian chiefs convicted of murder. They entered the penitentiary in 1871 and were released by Governor Davis in 1873 upon the recommendation of President U. S. Grant. Santana violated the conditions of his release, however, and was returned by Lt. Gen. Philip Sheridan on November 8, 1874.

Santana served another two years before deciding that he could no longer tolerate the white man's prison. He committed suicide by jumping from the second floor of the hospital building. Santana was buried in the prison cemetery and remained there until the Kiowa tribe moved his remains in recent times.

Jesse Evans, a partner in crime with Billy the Kid, served one year and five months on a thirty-year sentence for murder and robbery before he escaped in 1882 and was never captured again.

In the 1800s, cattle or horse theft was considered a much greater crime than murder insofar as prison sentences were concerned. In one East Texas county, a man received four months for murder, whereas another received five years for cattle theft.

The first woman convict sentenced to a Texas prison was Elizabeth Huffman, in 1854. She was sentenced to one year for infanticide.

The shortest sentence on record was one hour, for William Saunders from Dallas, served on November 15, 1870.

The youngest convict ever received at the penitentiary was a nine-year-old Afro-American boy sentenced in 1887 to five years for robbery.

The youngest girl ever received at the penitentiary was a mulatto, eleven years of age, sentenced to three years for administering poison. She arrived in 1884 and served two years and eight months.

The youngest murderer to enter the penitentiary was an Afro-American boy, twelve years of age, sentenced to ten years for second-degree murder. He served eight years.

It was during the building of the Walls Prison Unit in 1848 that a chain gang was first employed. This was considered the only safe way to prevent the convicts from running away. The chains were later used in the fields for security purposes. Although chain gangs were utilized during construction of the prison, convicts were not numbered until the arrival of the first "chain" at the state penitentiary. Prisoner #1 was William G. Sansom, fifty-eight years of age, from Fayette County, sentenced to three years for cattle theft. He arrived in Huntsville on October 1, 1849, and served eleven months before being pardoned by Governor Bell on September 14, 1850. Prisoner #2 was Stephen P. Terry, thirty-seven years of age, sentenced to ten years from Jefferson County for murder. He arrived at the penitentiary on November 4, 1849. Less than a year later, Terry died of gunshot wounds inflicted by guards during an escape attempt.

Later on, the list of infamous names would include Clyde Barrow, Raymond Hamilton, and Joe "Cowboy" Palmer. As interesting as this trivia was, hearing it did not do much toward preparing us to be effective correctional officers. We had a lot of questions, but our instructors didn't give us many direct answers. We were issued employee rulebooks, but they were vague and didn't begin to cover any specific situations. Whenever we asked questions that began with, "What if...", we were told, "Look, we are going to tell you what policy and procedure says, but when you are assigned to a unit, do whatever they say, because each unit is different and each warden does things his own way."

WELCOME TO CLEMENS

The following Monday, in late August or early September 1966, I reported with my classmate, Slick, to the Clemens Unit, in Brazoria County. I don't remember Slick's real name, but he was about fifty and bald, hence the other trainees' nickname for him. The training instructors told us to choose three "preferred units" that we would want to be assigned to. Of course, they gave absolutely no consideration to our selected preferences. Although I had no idea where the Clemens Unit was, I was advised that it was going to be my new home.

Little did I know, but Clemens was the furthermost unit from Huntsville and therefore the one that received the least attention from the powers that be. That meant fewer inspections and less political correctness. It also meant that when a supply truck left Huntsville to make deliveries to the units, Clemens received whatever the other units didn't take off the truck.

As Slick and I passed through the small, historic town of Brazoria, Texas, on Highway 36, we knew we were getting close to the Clemens Unit. There were tall live-oak trees lining the highway in those days, and the 8,000-acre Clemens Unit began where the trees parted. The manicured, cultivated row crops began, and for as far as you could see there was lush green, row after row of cotton, corn, maize, and all variety of vegetables.

As we drove along the highway toward the main unit, Slick said, "What is that cloud of dust out there?" I looked in the direction in which he was pointing, but I couldn't tell what it was. We stopped the car on the side of the road. As we stepped out of the air-conditioned car, the moist heat hit us, and we stood there sweating on the side of the road transfixed by this mysterious cloud of rolling dust off in the distance. Slick said, "Isn't that the prettiest thing you ever saw?" There were some scattered summer thunderheads hanging in the sky, but Slick was still pointing at a low dust cloud being generated at ground level by some unseen force way off in the distance.

As we stood there, I finally realized what we were watching. I said, "Slick, you know what that is, don't you?" He looked at me with a puzzled expression on his face. "That's the inmate workforce out there, that's what's making your cloud." We stood there in silence for several minutes taking in a sight that few people have ever seen. It was one of those 101-degree Gulf Coast days when the wind doesn't blow and the humidity makes it hard to breathe. My shirt was sticking to my body from the sweat after being out of the car for only a few minutes. One could only imagine what it was like under that cloud of dust.

Slick and I went to the personnel office to report in. We were then escorted in to see Warden Scott Valentine. He appeared to be about fifty, with a light complexion and red hair. He chain-smoked and seemed very nervous when telling us what he expected, which basically boiled down to blind loyalty. The following paragraph was taped to the front of his desk:

LOYALTY

If you work for a man, in Heaven's name work for him. Speak well of him and stand by the institution he represents. Remember an ounce of loyalty is worth a pound of cleverness. If you must growl, condemn, and eternally find fault, why—resign your position, and when you are on the outside, damn to your heart's content. But as long as you are part of this institution, do not condemn it. If you do, the first high wind that comes along will blow you away, and probably you will never know why.

This "Loyalty Oath" was also on the first page of the Employee Rules and Regulations Manual. Warden Valentine told us that he was a graduate of the University of Arizona. I got the feeling that he didn't leave his office much. He wore black suits and ties in both winter and summer. I couldn't see him spending much time outside of an air-conditioned room in those clothes. Judging by the number of phone calls he answered while we were in his office, I got the impression that he did most of his business over the phone. We spent about thirty minutes with the warden, and when our audience was over, we hadn't learned any more about the prison business or the Clemens Unit than we knew when we went in.

FIRST REAL WARDEN

We were then escorted into the main building, down a short hallway that took us past the six open "tanks," upstairs and down, where the inmates lived. We were led through an outer office, where a convict bookkeeper looked us over, before being invited into the assistant warden's office. There we met Assistant Warden Grady H. "Dick" Stricklin and Building Captain T. J. Sparkman.

The captain did most of the talking—straight from the hip: "Treat these inmates fair but firm, and don't make exceptions to the rules. If you don't know, ask—be here on time—don't abuse your sick leave or time off—keep your hair cut short—no beards—or mustaches."

While the captain was talking, Warden Stricklin just sat there looking right through us. He appeared to be in his early fifties, and the years of experience in his eyes told me a lot about who he was. Before I even heard him say a word, I could tell instinctively that this guy knew his business. This was the man the warden delegated the day-to-day operational decisions to. Warden Valentine could sleep well at night because even if he didn't know what he was doing, Dick Stricklin did. Warden Valentine knew that whatever problem came up, it would be handled before he could even get there. This lessened the need for "the big warden" to make any decisions, except on those rare occasions when he wanted to remind folks that he was still the man in charge.

Warden Stricklin could tell what the inmates were going to do in advance. It didn't take me long to find out that you didn't have to physically see him to know whether he was in the building or not. You could tell by how quiet the inmates were. They posted lookouts, or "jiggers," for him. He had started at the bottom and earned his reputation as an honest, fair-minded man who would go the extra mile to help you if you were in the right, but if you were in the wrong, shame on you. He had worked his way up from field-squad officer to dog sergeant and eventually to captain, major, and assistant warden. He knew how to raise a crop with men and hand tools, and not much else. He had worked the pickets and the hallways both day and night and knew every inch of the Clemens Farm and all the land for miles around, from the Brazos to the San Bernard rivers.

I was given a free room in the Bachelor Officer's Quarters (BOQ). I had an inmate porter named Francis, who cleaned my room, changed the sheets, took my clothes to the laundry, prepared a clean uniform for me each morning, and ran various other errands as needed. I ate most meals free of charge in the Officer's Dining Room (ODR). The meals were not restaurant-quality, except breakfast, which was excellent. I was finding out that there were definite perks to this job. If a man wanted to save money, all he had to do was stay on the unit and bank his paycheck, as there were no living expenses. That first year, I bought a new car and made the two-hundred-mile trip to Temple to visit my parents about once a month. I was making $342.00 per month and feeling quite prosperous.

My first assignment was relief picket officer for the first and second shift. This meant I worked for the regular assigned picket officers on their days off. We worked eight-hour shifts, twelve days on and three days off. There were only four pickets at this time, three outside towers and one inside "swing picket" where the officer could oversee the "tanks."

The tanks consisted of double-bunked inmate dorms with the swing-picket officer controlling the doors with a system of levers. There were inmate turnkeys on duty twenty-four hours a day, 365 days a year. Each turnkey carried a set of brass keys that fit the doors under his control. Part of the turnkeys' job was key and door control, but their primary function was to ensure that the only inmates allowed to pass through "their doors" were the convicts the officer in the swing picket approved.

All the pickets were employee-staffed at all times. The picket assignments were rotated after the officers scheduled days off, except for the radio-picket post. The consistency of expertise required to successfully operate the unit's main line of communication was deemed more valuable than officer rotation. This officer not only had to operate the unit's base radio, he had to be able to identify by sight all persons who entered or exited through the front gate of the unit. The rotation of the other picket officers was an attempt to keep the picket officers from getting bored. After working eight hours on a picket, watching the same fence for twelve days in a row, most officers were ready for a change. I know I was.

MY FIRST RIOT

It was a Friday night in late September 1966. I had just been relieved from second-shift picket duty and was enjoying a hot shower in the BOQ when the call came in. There was a problem in the building. With only two weeks' time on the unit, I didn't know what to do or where to go. It was about 10:45 P.M., and there were only two other officers in the BOQ. I followed them through the back gate into the compound and up to the solid-steel back door of the main building. The old turnkey, Ginny, peered at us through the small glass window in the middle of the steel door before turning the key and allowing us into the building. Sergeant Moore, the night building sergeant, met us at the bottom of the stairs in front of the lower tanks.

We could hear some yelling and shouting coming from number-three tank, but the convicts had knocked out all the lights, so it was difficult to see more than a few feet into the living area. Sergeant Moore, an elderly man about sixty years of age, didn't seem overly excited. He said, "They've been drinking some of that old chock [homemade alcohol], boys, and they want to fight."

The four number-three-tank building tenders and the barber, "Old Ripper," were backed up behind the barber chair with their backs to the hallway bars. The rest of the number-three-tank convicts were about ten feet away, taunting, cursing, and generally telling the building tenders what they intended to do to them. A few of them had weapons, including homemade knives and clubs.

This stand-off had been going on for about ten minutes, and the drunk convicts were getting steadily more aggressive. The odds were about 105 to 5 against the building tenders. I was not at all sure about what was going to happen, but I didn't share in the sergeant's easygoing carriage of confidence. There was a total of five officers standing in that hallway, including the sergeant, when Ginny let Warden Stricklin and Field Major Eddie Breen through the back door.

Warden Stricklin took charge immediately, telling Major Breen, "Go out there and tell old Ponce to open up and get ready to do some business." The old outdoor solitary only had twelve cells, but the convicts called it "The Heartbreak Hotel." The cells were eight-by-four-foot concrete, with a hole in the floor for a toilet. Each cell had an outer solid-steel door and a barred inner door. The convicts got three full meals every third day. The rest of the time they got one slice of bread and one cup of water at mealtime.

The convict who was assigned to work the solitary building was named Ponce de Leon. He was Afro-American, about forty-five years old, six-foot-six, with long muscular arms, and when he walked he kind of stooped, giving the appearance that his knuckles were going to drag the ground. Warden Stricklin said Ponce had been a bare-knuckles prizefighter in his younger days. Part of Ponce's job was to fix the meal trays for the inmates in solitary. He liked that part of his job and enjoyed adding "seasoning" with generous amounts of salt, pepper, onions, Tabasco, and so forth. An eight-inch steam pipe ran through the back of each of the solitary cells, and it was used for heat when Ponce could remember to turn it on. Occasionally, Ponce turned the heat on in the summertime, creating the impression of an indoor sauna, and on cool mornings the rising steam from the old building gave off the appearance of a slow-burning inferno.

Warden Stricklin ordered Ginny to "Call all the day-shift BTs down here—and tell 'em to come packing." He was speaking in a calm, normal tone of voice, as if this was just another day at the office. Within three minutes, there were ten building tenders standing under the swing picket in center hall, and they were ready for battle. They had cut-off baseball bats, slapjacks, axe handles, links of trace chain, and various other implements of destruction. I even saw one set of brass knuckles. The building tenders inside number-three tank were getting nervous now, and about the only thing keeping the drunk convicts at bay was Old Ripper's razor. He was in the middle of the group waving his straight razor around, just daring anyone in the crowd to come within his range. His adversaries were drunk, but not drunk enough to be the first to take on a straight razor.

Warden Stricklin had a brief, quiet talk with the assembled building tenders. Once his instructions were given, he stepped back and told Ginny, "Open number-three tank." The building tenders went through the tank door and waded in among the drunken rioters. The first seven or eight fell under the coordinated blows from the building tenders and were dragged back to the door of the tank. As the building tenders held their ground, four or five of them started a shuttle service, dragging the wounded out of the tank.

My job was to escort the building tenders as they ushered the stumbling drunks toward the back gate and the old twelve-cell Heartbreak Hotel. We delivered them to the solitary building and into the waiting arms of old Ponce, who unceremoniously stripped them and deposited them into a waiting cell. There were some bumps, bruises, minor cuts, abrasions, and even a couple of missing teeth, but I saw nothing approaching a life-threatening injury. When it was over, only one of the building tenders needed any medical treatment, due to a cut ear, and that only required a few stitches.

I found the building tenders to be a very effective force. It took less than an hour to remove the 105 drunken convicts from number-three tank and secure them in the twelve-cell solitary. They averaged eleven inmates to a cell, and there were still three empty cells left over after everyone was locked up. The drunken convicts were all butt-naked inside the cells and didn't have room to sit or lie down. By 1:00 A.M. I was back in the BOQ getting ready for bed.

In the two and a half years (1966–69) that I was assigned to the Clemens Unit, I never saw the old twelve-cell solitary completely full of inmates. Ponce claimed he had put more than 200 convicts into the twelve cells at the same time on at least three occasions. I don't know if that was true or not, but after watching him put 105 drunk convicts into nine cells, I had no reason to doubt him. He assured me that if he had to, he could pack at least 20 convicts into each cell.

The following day, we found the remnants of some of the chock they'd been drinking in some rubber work boots inside their standup metal locker boxes. A good chock maker, if he has the right ingredients and knows what he's doing, can make alcohol that is as potent as anything legally sold on the street. A tank full of drunken convicts high on good chock is a sight to behold. After a while, they begin to believe that they're nine feet tall, invisible, and bullet-proof.

After having them stand naked, eleven to a cell, for two days, Warden Stricklin and Major Breen went out to the old solitary to see if the number-three-tank convicts had sobered up sufficiently to be released. Amazingly enough, almost all of them had seen the error of their ways and were looking forward to proving they could do better. Major Breen offered each and every one of them a chance to work in the line workforce as a penance and a show of good faith. After they agreed to terms, clothes were brought to the solitary and issued to them as they went out to get on the line trailers to go to work.

It would be a while before this incident was forgotten, and the convicts knew that they had screwed up. They also knew that the way to redemption was to do as they were told and to not further aggravate the situation. The day would come when they could ask for another job or some favor, but this was not the day.

This riot was not reported in the print media or on TV. There were no state representatives, senators, prison reformers, lawyers, or federal-court judges to investigate the quality of the methods utilized in resolving this riot. The outgoing mail was appropriately screened to avoid any undue publicity. Warden Valentine didn't even find it necessary to come into the building to bless Warden Stricklin's method of handling the situation.

This was no doubt a simpler, less complicated time in our state. Some would argue that this antiquated way of doing business, without the intrusion of lawyers, judges, and the media, is preferable to what we have today. I can't give a definitive answer to that question, because the answer depends on what we, as individual taxpayers, want from our prison system. I can say in hindsight that I've seen the job done both ways, and as politically incorrect as it may sound, the old methods clearly had some advantages.

Choices Versus Responsibility

The recidivism rate in 1967 was a relatively low 13 percent, which looks great compared to today's 48-percent rate. However, one must not jump to any conclusions about the reasons for the low recidivism rates of the time. For instance, any success enjoyed in the sixties cannot be attributed to the quality of educational standards in place at the time. My observation was that the inmate instructors spent more time trying to just keep their students awake than actually teaching. The vocational classes were somewhat more successful, mainly because the convicts could see that there was a tangible skill to be learned, and as a result, there was always a waiting list to get in. I used to interview the inmates for placement in the various classes, and as part of the process they had to state their reasons for wanting to attend. Without exception the reason was always: "To learn a skill so I can stay out of the penitentiary."

In hindsight, I can't say that I've seen any rehabilitation program, educational program, or religious program that has had any direct impact on keeping inmates from committing future crimes. In fact, the evidence continues to mount that despite our best efforts, these programs have little or no measurable impact on recidivism rates.

Every politician since the turn of the century has promised to be tough on crime and rehabilitate criminals through education. It's hard to blame them for saying it, because the public always buys it and it wins elections. The fact is, the national recidivism rate have floated between 40 and 60 percent for the past thirty years, according to the U.S. Department of Justice. Contrary to every politician's promise, it has become irrefutably clear that sending convicts to school, especially repeat offenders, has not kept anyone from committing additional crimes, and never will.

Even already-educated convicts can't be expected to mend their ways. While at the Clemens Unit, I became acquainted with two of the inmate instructors, Floyd Bennett Coolwater and Donald Dumont, both of whom had degrees. I had many discussions with them about their futures. Both were doing time for narcotics offenses. Dumont had been convicted in Dallas for possession, not sale, of a "penny matchbox full of marijuana" and given a life sentence, even though it was his first offense. Coolwater was a three-time loser from San Antonio who had received a fifty-year sentence for possession of a small amount of heroin. Dumont was in his late twenties and Coolwater in his late forties. In expressing their views on the future, neither would exclude the possibility of the future use of narcotics. Coolwater, perhaps because of his advanced age, was a little more realistic. He said, "The first thing I am going to do when I get back to San Antonio is get me some heroin. It's what I do; it's who I am. Some people like to chase women or gamble, I like heroin."

I have heard similar statements from many inmates over the years, and I believe there is a message here for the social scientist. Despite the rhetoric, crimes are committed by people who make a conscious choice to do so. It serves no useful purpose to blame a poor economy, poverty, or high unemployment rates. These things occur in all societies, but do not, in and of themselves, cause crime. In the past forty years, none of the unpleasant social or demographic facts about Texas have changed. High-school dropout rates remain at about 20 percent, and Texas ranks fourth among the states in the percentage of the population living in poverty, 19.1 percent in 1995. But poverty doesn't cause crime; if anything, crime causes poverty and economic decay.

One major reason for the success of the Texas criminal-justice system of the sixties was the message of personal accountability, the fact that criminals were held responsible for their actions. Regardless of social and moral conditions, lower crime rates require a credible justice system that treats criminals as fully responsible for the harm they do and that exacts a proportionate price from those who do that harm. If there is one single thing that can be identified as having been effective in the past that is not being done in today's prisons, it is that today there is no standard of personal responsibility being enforced.

In the sixties, the prison system did not give inmates options. Mandatory attendance meant mandatory attendance, whether it was work, school, shower, or chow. Inmates were required to be at work, on time, without exception, and if an inmate didn't meet the standard, punishment, and in some cases physical penalties, were imposed in order to remind the inmate that his decision-making process was not acceptable.

In our modern institutions, everything is optional and there are almost unlimited excuses for failure. In today's Texas prison, there is no physical deterrent, and the disciplinary process has been reduced to a mountain of endless written reports that lead inmates to believe that there are no consequences associated with negative behavior. After all, if discipline is reduced to "recreation restriction," meaning that instead of playing basketball or volleyball the inmate may only play dominoes or watch TV, where is the deterrent? There is a fifteen-day limit on what is laughingly referred to as "solitary confinement," during which inmates receive the same meals as the general-population inmates. In addition, during solitary, guards are required to hand-deliver a convict's meals and legal mail and escort spiritual advisors directly to his cell. Also, medical personnel are required to hand-deliver each convict's medication directly to his cell, sometimes several times a day. These deliveries to the inmates by staff must be made even if the inmate is spitting or throwing blood, urine, or other body fluids at them.

One need not look any further to see why the current system is not effecting change in the behavior of the criminals. In most cases, prison life is a step up in status from the one a criminal leaves behind on the street. After all, if you're living on the street, sleeping under a bridge, what do you have to fear from a Texas prison?

WHEN TEXAS PRISONS MEANT BUSINESS

In the sixties, the prison system meant business. The inmate workforce was awakened at 3:00 A.M. for breakfast. The last man was served at 5:45 A.M. No inmates were allowed to eat after that time. The field force turned out for work at 7:00 A.M., winter and summer. In 1966–69, when a taxpaying citizen of Brazoria County, Texas, drove by the Clemens Unit on Highway 36, he didn't have to look hard to see his tax dollars at work. All he had to do was look for the cloud of dust the inmate line force created as it worked.

In those days, you didn't see any Johnson grass or other weeds sticking up through the cotton, corn, or vegetables growing in the fields. The ends of the rows were scraped clean, and the turnrows, the rows between the fields, were always flat-weeded by the convict hoe squads. The ditches between the fields were always clean and open so that water could flow freely when it rained or when the fields were irrigated. The rows and rows of vegetables, tomatoes, and fruit trees were clean, and many a passing citizen was unable to resist the temptation to stop and pick something. After all, as they figured things, it was their tax dollars at work.

Questions of prisoners' civil rights had not been raised. Phone calls were only rarely allowed, and they were always monitored by an employee and of short duration. All correspondence was censored, both incoming and outgoing. If attempts were made to write the media, the courts, or politicians regarding what appeared to be frivolous complaints, the letters were simply denied. Inmates were instructed to "Limit their letters to matters of personal interest to friends and relatives. Other inmates or institutional personnel shall not be discussed, and the letters shall not carry any institutional gossip or rumors." Furthermore, inmates were not allowed to assist other inmates with legal matters. Any liberties an inmate enjoyed were earned by him.

The more I found out about Texas prisons, the more impressed I was with the absolute control the staff had over this group of allegedly dangerous convicts. Nowadays it is fashionable to say that the control was due to the building tenders, and they were undeniably a factor, but in addition to them were these no-

nonsense employees who utilized and enforced a very basic standard of justice that everybody could see and understand. There were definite and in most cases immediate consequences for one's actions. After observing this system up close for a while, I came to realize an undeniable truth—that swift and sure punishment is much more effective than any form of justice delayed. The absolute certain reality of punishment is more important than any other single element of the criminal-justice system.

There were many perks for those employees who demonstrated absolute loyalty to the warden. He could give them merit raises, free food, free housing, free laundry service, haircuts and shaves for $2.00 per month, shoeshines, and yard service. For sergeants and above, a houseboy, in the form of a convict servant, could be assigned. A houseboy's job description varied depending on what the employee wanted the inmate to do. Some were hired as cooks, waiters, and yard hands, or to do the laundry for the family of an employee. They were always on call and had to be ready to serve at the beck and call of the employee. The inmates prized these jobs, and many inmates worked for the same families for generations, developing close personal relationships.

The loyalty of some of these inmate servants was remarkable. An incident involving the houseboy of Warden I. K. Kelly (1920–52) illustrates the closeness of some of these relationships. One day in 1930, while the warden was gone, the houseboy was at the warden's house with the warden's wife and small children preparing lunch. He was standing at the kitchen sink, looking out of the window, when he saw a squad of inmates working about five hundred yards away. The houseboy observed one of the inmates in the squad hit the squad officer with his hoe and knock him off his horse. In his attempt to escape, the inmate jumped on the officer's horse and started to ride down the road that passed by the warden's house.

The houseboy, seeing what was happening, yelled at the warden's wife, "Where is the gun, ma'am? Where is the gun?" The warden's wife was so trusting of the houseboy that she did not ask why he needed the gun; she just pointed to the closet where the shotgun was kept. The houseboy quickly grabbed the shotgun and ran out into the yard, and just as the escaping inmate rode by the house, he fired both barrels into the air. The startled horse bucked like champion rodeo stock when it heard the shotgun. The escapee, not being a real cowboy, was immediately thrown over the horse's head, hitting the ground so hard that he lay unconscious until some officers finally came to pick him up.

Unfortunately for both the warden's family and the Good Samaritan convict, the houseboy had to be transferred to another unit for his own protection. It was no longer safe for him to go into the main building.

AN OLD-SCHOOL PHILOSOPHY

Most inmates, however, did not enjoy the freedom of the house-boys. The trust that they enjoyed was built over time, based on quality job performance and personal compatibility with the employee and his family. The other inmates were cut off from the outside world.

During the directorship of Dr. George Beto (1962–72), the control over the inmates was absolute and ensured by the use of informants, enforcers, and carefully selected inmates called building tenders. These building tenders were required to demonstrate their loyalty to staff by acting as unpaid guards. In return for their services, these inmates were extended privileges that were not afforded to those less fortunate. State lawmakers were well aware of the practice and prided themselves on being able to say that they succeeded in running a safe, secure prison system, at a cost lower than in any other state. Of course, the only way they could maintain the low cost was by using inmates as surrogate security officers, instead of hiring guards. This prac-tice continued well into the 1980s, until the federal courts finally forced the Texas Legislature to allocate funding for officers to replace the building tenders.

The only remotely serious effort on the part of the Legislature to even acknowledge that there may have been a problem with the building tenders came in 1973, when House Bill 1056 was passed. The bill was vague and didn't address what a building tender *could* do under the supervision of an officer. It basically said that inmates could *not* supervise or discipline other inmates. The Legislature did not outlaw building tenders, as has been alleged by some. The only major change in the way business was conducted was that we stopped using the term "building tender" and created a new job title, "Support Service Inmate" or SSI. Apart from the job title, there was no other fundamental change from the old building tenders' job description. There was certainly no increase in employee staffing to compensate for the absence of the building tenders. If the Legislature had in fact intended to replace the building tenders, all they had to do was triple the number of officers working at the time the bill was passed. The reality is that they had no intention of doing so. The building tenders were simply an inexpensive way to control the inmate population.

Each warden determined how much power he wanted the building tenders to possess on his unit. In the hands of a righteous, fair-minded warden like Dick Stricklin, the building tenders served as a valuable extension of the warden's authority. In the hands of a few misguided despots, the building tenders were instruments of destruction, loose cannons wreaking havoc on the helpless.

The building tenders were allowed to possess, and on occasion use, weapons to enforce the rules and to maintain order. The only inmates who whined about this were the ones who could not or would not conduct themselves in a manner consistent with the social norm. For the most part, building tenders were respected, as long as they were supported by an unofficial group of back-watchers who assisted them in their attempts at maintaining order.

The inmate living areas were all segregated by race, so there were no significant racial problems while the inmate population was inside the building. The field workforce was partially segregated, but there were still occasional clashes between hoe squads. The line squads were usually too tired from work to do much fighting.

The line hoe squads were sometimes segregated by race. There were all-white squads, all-black squads, and all-Hispanic squads. This was done as much to create competition between the squads, for production purposes, as for any other reason. Open warfare between the races was rare, because as much as they may have disliked each other, the thought of having to spend time in the old twelve-cell Heartbreak Hotel was always in the back of their minds.

Even with his unprecedented amount of power, a warden had to ensure that the building tenders enforced the rules and maintained order in a way that was fair and that reflected the standard of justice that he wanted to project. During the 1960s and 1970s, each unit took on the personality of the individual unit warden. The more the system transferred the wardens around to different units, the more uncertainty there was.

Inmates need to know what to expect; if not, they will continually test the line of authority to see exactly where the line is. It has been said that familiarity breeds not contempt, but contentment. I'm not sure that's entirely true, but if there's any truth in it, it's because there's no mystery as to what happens when clear lines of authority are *not* established. The wardens, and there were only a few, who misused their power were not successful over the long term and were generally despised by their peers. It is one thing to cultivate a reputation as powerful and to be feared because of it. It is quite another to be powerful, but also to be respected as fair but firm.

The successful wardens wanted to ensure that the building tenders were an extension of a philosophy that was based on the fair-but-firm concept. Warden Grady H. Stricklin and Major Eddie Breen had a clear policy of control based on that concept, and because the inmates perceived it as fair to all, there were very few problems. Inmate violence was almost nonexistent, the staff was safe from assault, and the work got done in a timely manner.

A high degree of security was maintained, and because of the intense work ethic that all offenders were made to adhere to, the recidivism rate remained very low. In fact, the work-first-and-rehabilitate-second approach was successful. Once having experienced a summer picking cotton on the Texas Gulf Coast, few wanted to repeat the experience. There are those who would say that there are no cotton fields in downtown Dallas or in Houston, and we should not require inmates to do work that is not readily available to them in their home environment. Ridiculous! I believe and the record demonstrates that hard work, swift discipline, and rehabilitation programs—only in that order—are the most effective deterrents to criminal activity. I do not allege that work and discipline "rehabilitate" anyone, but if used appropriately, the work sends a clear message of what society expects from its citizens, and the disclipline acts as a long-lasting deterrent. In the absence of work and discipline, rehabilitation programs amount to an extreme waste of time and taxpayer money. Research does show that most criminals eventually reform, but through personality changes that seldom can be linked to any rehabilitation program. Until those changes take place, a system of control must be in place.

There are some widely held liberal ideas that must be called into serious question. One is that criminal behavior is a "disease" that will respond to a prescribed therapy. Another is that a criminal has more chance of reforming outside of prison than inside. It is gratifying at least to hear some sociologists and "correctional experts" finally come around to the point of view that a large segment of the public has held all along. While the rest of society spent a decade experimenting with the rehabilitation of criminals, Texas had them doing something that worked—hard labor.

The evidence is accumulating that no one really knows how to reform a lawbreaker, but one thing is clear: There is no appreciable difference between the later behavior of convicted offenders who are provided with rehabilitation programs and the future behavior of those who are not. There are far too many offenders enjoying freedom due to the mistaken assumption that excusing them from punishment for breaking the law has increased their chances for rehabilitation. This attitude has corrupted the meaning of our laws and perverted the principle of justice. As a result of this philosophy, in many parts of Texas today, it is the law-abiding citizen who is behind locked doors, protecting himself from the criminal in the streets.

The end result of the highly predictable and stable prison environment of the 1960s and 1970s was that the Texas prison system was the envy of other states throughout the country. While Texas enjoyed the low cost, peace, and tranquility of an absolutely controlled inmate population, prison systems in other states suffered through troubled times. The correctional community nationwide praised Texas as a "model of efficiency."

Dr. Beto recognized the merit in agricultural inmate work programs, but he also understood the dual benefits of prison industries. First, the agency could better achieve its legislative mandate of self-sufficiency. Second, but no less important, inmates could be kept busy. The nationally renowned penal expert Austin MacCormick, who had been critical of the system in earlier times, visited TDC in the mid-1960s during the height of the building-tender period and concluded that the TDC was "in the top half-dozen systems in the country."

TEXAS TAXPAYERS LOSE TO THE REFORMERS

The reformers were not to be ignored, however, and with the aid of the Supreme Court, in 1961 they opened the door to litigation, allowing some persistent legal activists bent on bringing the Texas Prison System to its knees to succeed in their efforts. They began a movement that is still going on today. It has resulted in the absolute abdication of control by the people of Texas, handing what was once their prison system to the federal courts. The civilian Board of Criminal Justice has been reduced to a political-correctness monitor for a Legislature that runs for cover every time a federal judge even hints that some convict may not be receiving his court-mandated gym class.

The taxpayers of Texas are at the mercy of the reformers, activist attorneys, federal district courts, and the Supreme Court, which have all demonstrated time and time again that a convict's rights come before those of the victimized taxpaying citizen. By 1998, in the post–federal court intervention era, the annual cost of maintaining a convict in prison reached nearly $20,000. There is no hope of reducing that cost. The reformers are too numerous, and they have the support of the federal courts. We, the taxpayers, get much less for our money now than we once did. There was a time, not so long ago, when we had a state-controlled prison system with low costs. There was a time when Texas convicts knew that they were actually in a prison. Nowadays, it's more like a summer camp or a college campus, with a price tag to match, but none of that matters to the inmate attorneys who receive their pay from State of Texas taxpayers, by order of an nonelected federal court judge.

Reformers like to argue that federal control is necessary because prison guards cannot be trusted. The public is often taken in by this argument, due to the popular image of the prison guard as derived from old prison movies, in which they are portrayed as lazy, unscrupulous, stupid, brutal, and underpaid. In the late sixties, I not only worked at the Clemens Unit, but also ate there and slept there. It was my world, and I knew it well. In my experience, I did not find any of the sterotypes of prison guards to be true, except for the underpaid part. I can only speak for the officers I knew on the Clemens and Retrieve units between 1966 and the late 1970s, and that was before the system began to actively recruit employees who represented a more ethnically diverse, educated, and urban workforce.

There is no doubt that many fine employees who represented the State of Texas well are being slandered and treated unjustly by contemporary pseudointellectual writers. In their attempts to take the moral high ground, these wannabe journalists have not given credit to what was a very effective, professional, moral, and ethically sound correctional staff. These officers provided valuable service at personal sacrifice to the State of Texas, and that has not been acknowledged. In many cases, these men were superior in terms of devotion to duty, character, and honor to many of today's employees. This fact becomes glaringly evident when their years of spotless service are compared to the now-rampant TDCJ scandals so often reported in the media.

MOTIVATION TO REPENT

I was fortunate to be trained by men who had a deep and abiding respect for the fundamental fair treatment of the inmates placed in their care. That is not to say that these men were not willing to correct a problem in the quickest, most practical way possible. But employee misbehavior was not tolerated. The method of punishment for an employee who committed a serious violation was generally termination. If the violation was not particularly serious, he might receive a few days off without pay.

(I say "he" because there were no female correctional officers, except on the one female unit, Goree, at this time. The only female allowed on male units was the warden's secretary, and she stayed in the front office, which was located safely outside the fenced compound.)

Inmate violations were also not tolerated. During the mid-1960s, inmate disciplinary procedures were notably unsophisticated. If an inmate cussed a boss or was found to be lazy or an agitator, he could receive a disciplinary penalty requiring that he shell from one to four gallons of peanuts. A repeat offender, or one who showed that he was less than satisfied with a designated choice of minor punishment, might get to spend a few days in the Heartbreak Hotel. Since there was no time limit on solitary confinement in those days, the length of time spent living on bread and water was purely determined by the mood of security staff and the attitude of the inmate.

When the warden, major, or captain made his daily rounds, each solitary cell door was opened. If the confined convict stood up and answered, "Yes, sir" or "No, sir" to the questions he was asked, there was a small chance that he would be released back into the population. However, if he didn't stand up and respectfully address the officer, the solid door would remain closed until the next day's rounds were made.

It was Warden Stricklin's practice to wait a few more days after the convict began standing up and acting respectful before he actually let them out. He would say, "Well, I'm glad your attitude is improving, and I see you're ready to get out; now all we need is for me to get ready to let you out." Having said that, he would close the door until the next day, when the ritual was repeated. Warden Stricklin was never one to make any hasty decisions. By the time he finally decided to let a convict out of solitary, something loosely defined as short-term rehabilitation had usually been achieved. Once allowed back out into daylight, there was no hurry on the part of any inmate to do anything that might result in a return trip.

There were many minor offenses for which an inmate could be punished. It was, for example, an offense for an inmate to fail to remove his hat in the presence of an officer. Inmates were required to walk inside lines painted two feet from the hallway walls. Stepping over the line was an offense, because the center of the hall was reserved for staff only. If an inmate was not working as diligently as the officer supervising him thought him capable of, the slow-bucking convict could receive four hours on the rail.

The rail was a ten-foot-long two-by-four, with the edge turned up and positioned six inches off the floor. An inmate found guilty of a minor offense could be compelled to stand on the rail for up to four hours without falling off. If the inmate lost his balance or stepped off the rail for any reason without first obtaining permission, his time on the rail started over again.

If an inmate failed to pick an appropriate amount of cotton, he could be required to stand on a fifty-five-gallon barrel for four or five hours. Three or four convicts were usually placed on a single barrel. If any or all of them fell off, their time on the barrel began again.

Another common punishment involved being handcuffed by the wrist to the hallway bars located in front of the inmate dining room. In this position, both the swing picket officer and inmates in the inmate dining room could observe him. This was designed as a public object lesson for those contemplating a rules violation. Convicts were compelled to hold their arms as high as possible overhead. Handcuffs were placed through the bars and onto each wrist. Inmates were compelled to stand facing the bars with their toes, but not their heels, touching the floor for several hours, sometimes all night. I never observed anyone suffering any permanent injury from any of these disciplinary measures, and the notable absence of repeat offenders served as ample evidence that these methods did in fact offer clear incentives to repent.

–CHAPTER TWO–

FIELD BOSS

"Remember, boy, keep your feet deep in those stirrups—
a man without a horse is 'a foot.'"
—FIELD CAPTAIN OTIS REEVES, Clemens Unit, 1968

In the late summer of 1968, after working in the Education and
Recreation department for almost a year, I was offered a job as a
field officer. It was strange, because these jobs didn't turn over
very often, and officers sometimes waited for months or years for
their chance to join the ranks of the "mulligans." Field Major
Eddie Breen (*aka* Fast Eddie) presented his job offer to me in a
way that sounded as if I could choose to remain in my present
assignment or go with him as a field officer. In reality, Warden
Valentine would never have allowed me to decline the offer. In
mid-1968, I became a twenty-two-year-old hoe-squad officer at
the Clemens Unit.

The first day, Major Breen ordered Officer Phil Johnson to
allow me to ride along with him as he supervised number-two
hoe squad. I was given a huge blaze-faced sorrel to ride. Now, I
was not completely new to horseback riding, as I had done the
usual amount of recreational riding most boys did while growing
up in Central Texas in the early sixties, but this was not recreational riding. This was nine, ten, or eleven hours a day in the
saddle, with one hour off for lunch. After the first half-day
observing Officer Johnson carry his squad, the major advised me
that I would be carrying number-seven hoe squad when the line
squads turned out after lunch. My training period to be a field
officer had lasted about four-and-a-half hours.

When we turned out after lunch, the convicts in number-

27

seven hoe were at least as confused as I was. I was supposed to be telling them when and how to scrape the grass out from under a fence line. However, if convicts sense that you don't really know what you're doing, they have a tendency to forget everything they knew only the day before. After about two hours of my doing a lot of yelling and the convicts giving me these confused looks and mostly just standing around, Major Breen and Captain Otis Reeves rode over to check on my progress. The major didn't say much, but what he did say was short and to the point: "Either those convicts are going to carry you, or you are going to carry them. If you are going to let them carry you, then I don't need you out here." Having said that, he rode off, not waiting for a response.

Captain Reeves didn't say anything right away, but he remained there next to me sitting on his horse. He was smoking a cigarette and offered me one. I was nervous enough to accept. I only smoked periodically at the time, mostly small cigars, in an effort to appear as rustic as possible. He finally said, "Glenn, are you gonna let those convicts hog you? Are you gonna let those convicts get your job? You've got to let them know that it's you or them, and leave no doubt in their minds that it's not going to be you that is jobless when this is over. If you buy that hog they're trying to sell you, then they win—are you gonna let them do that?" He wasn't mad, and he spoke quietly so that the inmates couldn't hear. "Good luck, son," he said as he turned his horse and rode off.

I turned my attention back to my squad, twenty-five convicts looking at me as if asking, "Well, what are you going to do now?" The lead row, the first man in the hoe squad and the one who is supposed to set the pace for the rest to follow, was a big black inmate named Baker. He was in his early twenties, strong, stout, and proud. I called him away from the others, where they couldn't hear, and I told him to put his hoe down. He approached cautiously, to within ten feet of my horse. I whispered to him, "It's painfully obvious that I don't know what I'm doing, but you do. Now, I want you to go back to that squad and go to work, doing what you know you are supposed to do. If you don't, I'm going to tell that major that you are the only reason this squad isn't working. Do you understand?"

"Yes, sir," was his response. He kind of smiled and returned to the fence line and began to work. The others stood and watched him, as if he were an alien, for what seemed like twenty minutes, but it was really only one or two. Then, slowly, in groups of three or four, they gradually went to the fence and began to halfheartedly follow Baker. I then instructed the rest of them to follow the lead row and to do everything he did. I also advised them, "All y'all that want to eat and do well in that building this evening better make an effort to keep up with that lead row." As visions of handcuffs, rails, and fifty-five-gallon barrels raced through their heads, they began to work. They followed "Ol' Baker," as I began to call him, like twenty-five shadows. It seemed that Baker was afraid to disobey me, and the rest were afraid to not follow him. And so we had reached a clear understanding, and just as in most other human interaction, a clear understanding is the basis for a long-lasting relationship.

Later, when we reached a point on the fence line where the major and captain were observing from a distance, I told the squad, "All y'all that don't want to see that major at quittin' time better go to work!" They were throwing grass and mud fifteen to twenty feet behind them as the squad passed by. Captain Reeves rode over by me and whispered, "Damn, Glenn, what did you do to them?"

I just told him that we had reached an understanding. I lit one of my little cigars and handed him one. He had a bewildered look on his face as I said, "Thanks, Captain," tipped my hat, and rode off to catch up with my high-rolling squad.

That first day I spent about ten hours out of eleven actually in the saddle. When we finally reached the building and turned the convicts in through the back gate, I stepped off my horse and had to grab the fence in order to remain standing. My knees were so weak that I couldn't straighten them. It took a moment for me to regain the use of my legs.

I met my squad on the yard where the field officers strip-searched each inmate in their squad. All inmates were strip-searched each time they returned from an outside work assignment before being allowed to enter the building. For the line force, that meant a strip search at lunch and again during the evening turn-in. Each squad lined up in single file on the yard in front of the shower room, which was outside the main building. Each inmate stood totally naked while waiting his turn to approach his squad officer with his clothes in one hand and his shoes in the other. At the officer's command, the next inmate in line stepped forward and handed his clothes to the officer who physically searched them and threw them into one of the laundry carts. Once out of the showers, each squad was counted back into the main building, and my first day as a field mulligan was over.

ASSAULT ON AN OFFICER

I don't remember much about the rest of that first week in the field, except that I was tired and sore all the time. It was a little embarrassing, because I was the youngest of the field officers.

I had only been in the field a short time when (in 1968) two inmates who normally worked in number-one hoe escaped. Number-one hoe squad was reserved for the inmates who had proven to be disciplinary problems and security risks. One morning, two black inmates decided to jump squads and turn out in one of the garden squads that they knew had been working by itself. No one noticed that the inmates turned out in the wrong squad. After they got to the field and knew that the only officer with them did not have a radio or a highrider, they rushed him, knocking him off of his horse with their hoes. When the poor man hit the ground, they almost beat him to death. They would have killed him, except some of the older inmates got between the escapees and the officer and told them, "Look, y'all got his pistol—go on, we won't say nothing." After grabbing the officer's pistol, the two desperate convicts ran toward the Brazos River.

No one even knew that there had been an escape. There was nothing to keep the rest of the twenty-five convicts in the squad from escaping also, but for some partially unexplained reason, an unusual thing occurred. The remaining inmates in the garden squad picked up the unconscious officer, put him across his saddle, being very careful to not further injure him, and then led the horse to the Clemens Unit back gate. The whole garden squad was following along behind the officer's horse when they arrived. One of them, Bonny O'Henry, was serving a 199-year sentence for a murder/rape conviction. Another, Milford Griffin, was also doing a substantial amount of time. There were others involved in saving the officer's life, but I don't remember their names.

TDC Director Dr. George Beto wrote a favorable letter of recommendation for each of the inmates' central files for consideration by the parole board.

When the back-gate officer saw the lone squad walking up the dirt turnrow with the critically injured officer draped across his saddle, he ran over himself calling for help. The radio call came quickly, and we brought the line force to the building at a dead run. Sergeant Robinson was called to bring the dogs to the garden area where the assault and escape had occurred. Warden Stricklin had one of Sergeant Robinson's dogboys saddle a horse for him, as he always kept his own saddle at the dog pens, just in case. He and Sergeant Robinson went with the number-one pack of dogs and began to drag for the inmates' track. As soon as the line force was turned in, Major Breen caught up and joined them. Captain Reeves put the rest of us on standby at the back gate until the direction of the escapees' travel could be determined.

After securing the line-force inmates in the building, we waited for further instructions at the back gate. Warden Scott Valentine drove up in his white Ford warden's car with Captain T. J. Sparkman riding shotgun.

Warden Valentine usually worked hard at appearing cool under fire. He prided himself on being a calm professional, an educated man, reserved at all times. On this occasion, he didn't fit that profile. Valentine bailed out of the car all excited and ordered the number-two picket officer to lower two shotguns and two pistols. The picket officer got a little excited himself and attempted to lower all the weapons at the same time on a rope attached to a three-pronged metal hook. He managed to lower the weapons almost to the end of the rope, to a point just above Warden Valentine's head. Just then, the officer's nerve gave out, and he jiggled the rope, causing one of the shotguns to discharge, blowing chips of red brick off the side of the picket about a foot above Warden Valentine's head.

Valentine turned bright red from the ears up, but didn't say a word. He slowly walked back to the car and got in. A moment later, Captain Sparkman got out, walked around the car, and carefully removed the guns from the rope-hook. Captain Sparkman returned to the car, and they drove off without ever saying anything to the picket officer or anyone else.

It wasn't long before the dogs picked up the inmates' scent. All of the local landowners were notified that there had been an escape and were given descriptions.

A chase is always more dangerous when you know that the escapees are armed, as they were in this case. Warden Stricklin, Major Breen, and Sergeant Robinson had to cut most of the fences between the Clemens Unit and the Brazos River just to try to stay up with the dogs. This was a fresh track, an hour old, and the dogs were running flat-out. We could hear them in the distance when they howled, as good track dogs will do. The sound is useful in the woods or at night when you are trying to find the pack. It doesn't serve much of a purpose to have tracking dogs you can't find.

In this instance we were lucky. One of the landowners near the Brazos River saw the two escapees coming across the field, and when the convicts climbed through one of the stock pens behind his house, he threw down on them with a double-barreled .12-gauge shotgun. The farmer was smart enough to keep his distance. He just held them at gunpoint until Warden Stricklin, Major Breen, and Sergeant Robinson rode up. Unfortunately, or fortunately, depending on one's perspective, the dogs got there first and did some degree of damage to the escapees before Sergeant Robinson could pop them off with his eight-plait bullwhip. The convicts had the pistol they had taken from the fallen officer, but, typical cowards, when it came time to use it, they didn't have the stomach for it.

When the escapees were returned to the unit, I didn't detect any great outpouring of sympathy for them. They were brought back to the building and placed in the old outdoor twelve-cell solitary. Officer O'Banion was the name of the squad officer whom the escapees almost killed. He was in his late fifties, was well-liked by all the employees, and had been at the Clemens Unit for almost twenty years. He spent several weeks in the hospital before he could go home. The doctors told his family that he would never be able to work again.

Warden Stricklin, Major Breen, Captain Reeves, and once in a while Sergeant Robinson would go out to the solitary building and talk to those escapees about Officer O'Banion. Now, I wasn't a direct witness, and I can't say exactly what it was that they talked about, but I do know that after each visit it seemed to take those convicts longer and longer to heal up. About four months passed before they were physically well enough to be transferred to another unit. Old Ponce escorted them from their cells out to the waiting chain bus, and the look on their faces demonstrated that they were mighty glad to be leaving the Clemens Unit.

THE COTTON PICKERS

It was said, and I believe, that Major Breen could make the blind see and the lame walk with that old twelve-cell solitary. The Clemens Unit had an inmate population of about six hundred at the time. I did see the major, Captain Reeves, and Ponce put twenty-eight inmates in two cells late one afternoon after they failed to pick a respectable amount of cotton.

We had received about thirty new inmates in on the chain bus all in one week, and they claimed that they did not know how to pick cotton. Most of our line inmates could pick at least 150 pounds per day. Many could pick as much as 405 pounds per day, but the minimum weight for a new man was 75 pounds per day for the first week. This was informally referred to by the convicts as "the hog law," which basically meant that if an inmate couldn't or wouldn't pick the minimum amount of cotton, he could look forward to spending his evenings in the Heartbreak Hotel.

Well, the new inmates were only picking thirty or forty pounds, and much of the cotton they picked was not clean—it had leaves and dirt in it. When the squads turned in for the evening, Major Breen saved the sacks of cotton that the new inmates had been picking into and put them out on the yard by the laundry.

When Ponce and the major put the twenty-eight inmates in solitary, they only used two cells. Ponce helped each convict remove his clothes and escorted them to the cells. They had to stand up, as there was no room to sit down. The major had to grab the bars on each side of the last cell door and use his foot to squeeze the last two into the cell.

The next morning at approximately 3:00 A.M., Major Breen called the night sergeant and told him to get those inmates out of the two solitary cells and have them clean their sacks of cotton before 7:00 A.M. turn-out time. When I say clean the cotton, I mean they had to pick every dirt clod, cottonseed, leaf, and burr out, leaving only pure white cotton in the sack. At about 6:00 A.M. Major Breen came to the building and inspected the cotton cleaners' progress. He was not pleased. He told them to continue cleaning the cotton until the 7:00 A.M. turn-out time. Before the first squad was called, Major Breen asked the reluctant cotton pickers, "Do y'all think you can do better today?" When no one spoke up, the major grabbed one in the front row by his shirt and asked again, "Do you think you can pick more than a hundred pounds of cotton out there today?"

One of the new inmates, who had obviously seen the light, answered, "If it's out there, Boss, I can pick it."

When turn-out time came, Major Breen turned out the new inmate cotton cleaners without sleep or breakfast. A most amazing thing happened. By noon each one of the new inmates had more than seventy-five pounds of clean cotton in his sack. Inmates who only the day before couldn't pick seventy-five pounds of cotton in ten hours could now pick more than that in half the time. It seemed that these men did not realize their own capabilities until Major Breen and Old Ponce explained it to them in terms they could understand.

There was one inmate who stayed in the old solitary that whole first summer I was in the field. He told the major that he wasn't lazy and that he could do any kind of work, but he said he had made a promise to his mother that he would never pick any cotton, and he kept his promise. After about ninety days of old Ponce's food and steam-bath accommodations, the guy was almost thin enough to pull between the bars. He was transferred to the "real" hospital at the Walls Unit for a "psychiatric exam." He was the only inmate I observed during my time at Clemens who was not completely cured of his "ailment" through the use of the old solitary. Of course, all that changed when the federal courts took over the system in later years.

Shortly after the O'Banion incident, Sergeant Robinson died of heart failure, and the sergeant who was in charge of the hog-breeding operations was moved to the dog sergeant's position. His name was Nelson Gladys Sparks. He was about forty, stood six-foot-four, and was already a ten-year veteran of the Clemens Unit. He was a native of East Texas and so "country" he could drop a bucket down a fifty-foot well without making a ripple. He didn't believe that anything that had happened in the past twenty years was good for anybody. He preferred the company of his dogs to most people, saying, "They don't talk back and they don't question everything you do."

I guess I got along with Sparks about as well as anybody, and in later years he liked to tell people that he "raised me." In fact, I did spend much of my off-duty time with him, when he would let me ride on practice tracks with him. I learned to keep my mouth shut and to listen to his stories of people and events that he chose to share with me.

FIRST CHASE

The first chase that I was directly involved in occurred on July 26, 1967. The line force was hoeing cotton next to the "free world" on the Jones Creek side of the farm when the one hoe boss, Fred McDougald, followed his squad out of the field at the end of a set of rows and met the water wagon on the turnrow. He instructed the convicts, "Get water if you want it and smoke 'em if you got 'em!"

The convicts all gathered around the water wagon, and one of the water boys took a pitcher of water to Boss McDougald. While he was getting a drink, an eighteen-year-old black convict named Robert Earl Johnson, serving twenty years for armed robbery, was on the other side of the water wagon. Johnson crawled under the barbed-wire fence that separated the Clemens Unit from free-world pastureland and lay down in some tall grass. When Boss McDougald instructed his squad to leave the water wagon and to "'catch' another set of rows," he didn't notice the convict who had been left behind.

One of the first rules a new field officer learns is to count the convicts as continuously as possible, especially when the squad moves from one place to another. Boss McDougald had violated that rule and did not realize his mistake for about ten minutes. Meanwhile, the now-escaping inmate was in one of the irrigation drainage ditches that cross the unit and was running east toward

Jones Creek. Ten minutes doesn't sound very long, but a young man in good condition can run almost two miles in that amount of time. In this case, the highrider did not see the escapee, because of the ditch and the tall grass. When Boss McDougald did discover that he had a convict missing, the squad was about halfway through the next set of rows, and you could hear McDougald yelling all over the field: "One gone! Major, got one gone here!"

We had more than two hundred inmates out there that day, and they had to be escorted back to the building before the field officers could get involved in the chase. While we were escorting the rest of the line force back to the building, Dog Sergeant Sparks and Major Breen unleashed the dogs and began dragging for the escapee's track. Boss McDougald advised Major Breen that in hindsight he thought he had lost him at the water wagon.

The dogs picked up the trail and howled to let everybody know they were on the track. The chase was on. Breen and Sparks had to ride flat-out to stay up with the dogs. They first ran toward Highway 36, then parallel to the highway toward Jones Creek and Freeport. It is about four miles to the first houses outside of Jones Creek, and by the time the convict got to the first set of houses, he knew the dogs were not far behind. A nineteen-year-old woman who heard her dogs barking came outside to investigate. She quickly became the convict's captive. After making sure she was alone, he took her back inside the house and tied her up. "Why did you have to come outside?" he asked her. "The next time, you'll know better, won't you?"

He found a butcher knife and asked for a pistol, but there wasn't one in the house. The woman saw guards and dogs searching for Johnson outside as she lay bound and gagged on her bed. The officers passed by the house without stopping. Johnson changed into some of the woman's six-foot-two husband's clothes, which dwarfed the short convict. The guards and dogs headed back toward Highway 36. Johnson took the woman's house keys, $10.00, and her 1954 Chevrolet. He was running about ninety-five through the middle of downtown Jones Creek when he passed a DPS officer going the opposite direction. The officer made a U-turn and gave chase. The convict left the highway, and not being familiar with the area, drove onto a shell road in a trailer park that was a dead-end street. There was a canal at the end of that street, and I'm sure that the convict didn't know it was there. He didn't even slow down as he went through the dead-end road barrier and ended up about midway across the canal, where the car sank with only the roof sticking out of the water.

The DPS officer stopped on the bridge overlooking the canal, and with his gun drawn ordered the convict to come out of the water to the highway with his hands up. Johnson did as he was told until he reached the bank of the canal, where waist-high broom weeds were growing. He walked two or three steps into the weeds and then dropped down and started crawling toward the nearby woods. The DPS officer fired three or four times, but the convict was gone and running through the woods.

Sergeant Sparks and Major Breen tracked the convict to the house in Jones Creek, then loaded the dogs in the trailer and proceeded down Highway 36 to the place where the DPS officer had shot at the inmate. The dogs had been very close to catching him at the house in Jones Creek, and when they unloaded at the woods, they were very close again. It was about three or four miles from the highway to the Brazos River, and at that time there were no houses in the immediate area.

Sergeant Sparks was getting more confident, because he knew that the escapee would have to cross the river to have any chance of getting away. All the law-enforcement agencies and adjoining prison units had been notified, and officers were being posted on all the nearby roads. The Retrieve Unit had a pack of dogs on the other side of the river just in case he managed to get across. The river was higher and swifter than normal because of the above-average Central Texas rainfall runoff. It was very unlikely that anybody, except maybe an Olympic swimmer, could swim that swollen, log-filled, whirlpool-infested river.

When Sergeant Sparks reached the river with the dogs, he could plainly see where the inmate had entered the river. There were muddy tracks up and down the bank, so it appeared that the convict had been indecisive about what to do. Sergeant Sparks worked the dogs up and down the riverbank and could not find any sign of Johnson coming back out of the river on the side where he had entered it. Sergeant Louis Nichols, dog sergeant from the Retrieve Unit, was ready with a pack of dogs on the other side; there was no sign that the convict had made it across.

My assignment post during this chase was at the end of a fishing pier on the Brazos River near the location where Sergeant Sparks thought the inmate had entered the river. There was no relief and no thought of giving up until we knew for certain what had happened to that convict. I spent the next forty-eight hours on that pier eating ham sandwiches and swatting mosquitoes. On the second day, one of the officers found a shirt the convict was thought to have been wearing, which had washed up on the riverbank. Near dark on the second day, I noticed a bundle of sticks floating near the pier and called for one of the boats to check it out. It was soon confirmed that a TDC-issue belt had been tied around the sticks. The theory now was that the inmate had been waiting in the river, using the sticks to hold himself up, either until he thought the time was right or until he could build up enough courage to swim or float across the river.

On the third day at about 11:00 A.M., an officer in one of the boats saw the inmate's body as it floated to the surface. After two and a half days in that river, the only identifying characteristic on him were his inmate-issue boxer shorts. When some of the local media saw what the crabs and two and a half days in the water had done to the body, a rumor was circulated that some TDC officer had shot the escapee. Later on, the autopsy report proved he had died as a result of drowning. The warden returned the stolen money to the woman and had the car cleaned and repaired. In December of that same year, the woman moved into the village of Jones Creek, a little farther from the prison. She said the move was prompted in part by the hostage incident. These events rarely occur these days, but escapes are a hazard for those living near a prison.

SAM EDWARD EAGLIN

I had been moved from number-seven hoe squad to number-five. Just as I was getting a handle on number-five, Major Breen decided to move me to number-two hoe squad. This was the laziest bunch of malingering misfits ever put in one group. They were young, inept, and did not know how to work, nor did they want to learn. I asked Major Breen what I was supposed to do with them, and he grinned. "Do with them what you did with seven-hoe and five-hoe."

Most of number-two were repetitious disciplinary problems. There was heavy peer-group pressure on any convict who attempted to assume the lead-row position. The few good workers in the squad were afraid. If I couldn't find an inmate leader, someone they had respect for, I wasn't going to be able to break through this impasse. I couldn't get anything out of them for the first week.

About that time, one of the other field officers fired his push-row for "cussing him." I knew that the convict was a good worker but was also somewhat of a malcontent. The other squad officer said he was through with him and told me he didn't want him back in his squad under any circumstances. I asked Major Breen if I could have him. The major clearly didn't like the idea, but he knew I was desperate for a lead row and said he would think about it. A day or two later, after watching number-two hoe drag around behind the other squads, the major said I could go talk to him in solitary. He had been in solitary for about two weeks, and the major warned me, "Be careful, 'cause he is a real turd and he'll probably kill you if he gets a chance."

I said, "I need a lead row, and whatever else his faults are, at least I know he's not lazy."

I walked back to the last cell in the old outside solitary and told Ponce to open the solid outer door. When the door opened, the light blinded the convict, and he retreated into the darkness at the back of the cell. I couldn't tell where he began and the darkness ended as he stood against the back wall avoiding the glare. "What's your name?" I asked.

"Who wants to know?" was the quiet response.

"I'm the guy who can get you out of here if we can agree on a couple of things."

He raised his voice a little. "Yeah, well I ain't no snitch, I ain't no suckass, and I ain't gon' be nobody's nigger—now what else you want?"

I said, "Now that you told me what you're *not* going to do, let me tell you what I need. I need a man that's not lazy, that will work and can keep his mouth shut and set the pace for what is going to be the best hoe squad in the field. I'll handle all the disputes, arguments, and name-calling, and I'll never ask you to snitch on anybody."

I could see his teeth in the darkness as he kind of grinned and moved closer to the barred door. "I'm Sam Edward Eaglin," he said. "If you can do what you say, I'll give it a shot."

The next morning, he turned out with my squad. Major Breen was looking at me sideways as Sam led the squad out the gate. Even though he had been locked up in solitary and had been living off old Ponce's diet of bread and water for a couple of weeks, he was still able to work faster than the rest of number-two hoe squad wanted to go.

That was the beginning of a relationship that would last for more than thirty years. I grew to respect Sam on a personal level. As a man, he was an honest, hard worker who never lied to me, as long as I didn't ask him the wrong questions. He was a respected leader within the inmate population, and without compromising his own brand of integrity, we probably kept some people from getting hurt over the years.

DEADLY USE OF FORCE

I could hear a lot of grumbling in the line as they flat-weeded the ditch, but I didn't observe any outright challenge to the pace Sam was setting until about 3:00 in the afternoon. A tall white convict named Rainey was working near the end of the line. He was about twenty-three years old and mean as a snake, and he had blood in his eyes when he jumped out of the line and ran up the other side of the ditch. He was now up on top looking down on the rest of the squad, still standing in the bottom of the ditch. He drew his hoe back like a home-run hitter and said to Sam Eaglin, who was looking up at him, "Nigger, I'm gon' cut your head off."

I fired a warning shot into the ground, getting Rainey's attention long enough for him to notice that I had my state-issue, chrome-plated .38-caliber Smith and Wesson leveled at him. I said, in an even tone of voice, "If you swing that hoe, I'm going to try to blow the top of your head off."

The other inmates, standing in line with Eaglin, parted like Moses had waved his hand over the Red Sea. Rainey stood there for what seemed like eternity thinking about what he would do next. Eaglin stood like a rock below the threatening convict. He did not show fear and he did not speak, and I knew that in that moment his life was in my hands. I mentally made note of the fact that if Rainey did swing his hoe at Eaglin, I was going to fire to stop the attack.

All the theories one hears about these situations, such as only firing warning shots or shooting to disable, were not realistic options. I knew without a shadow of a doubt that one swing of that hoe was all Rainey would need to kill Eaglin. Finally, Rainey dropped his hoe. I told him, "You're gonna need that hoe. Pick it up, get back in line, and go to work." He looked at me strangely. I am sure he expected to be taken to the building and placed in solitary immediately, which is what normally would have happened in such circumstances. He picked up his hoe and went back to work. I called Sam back to my horse and told him not to say anything to Rainey and not to seek revenge on him for what he'd tried to do.

Sam nodded, saying that he would not make the first move, but added, "I'm not going to back down from anyone." Major Breen was watching from a distance and sent Captain Reeves over to see if I needed help. I told the captain I really didn't think that Rainey was a threat to Eaglin, but I was not sure if he had enough sense to keep his mouth shut.

The captain advised me to put Rainey on tail row, as that would keep him away from Eaglin and put peer pressure on him to work with the other inmates. "If he doesn't work or if he refuses," Captain Reeves said, "I'll let him live with old Ponce until he gets some religion back in his heart."

In the thirty years that I worked for the Texas Department of Criminal Justice, I don't think I ever came any closer than that incident to actually having to kill an inmate. I broke up many fights during my career and had to use a weapon in the performance of duty many times, but I don't remember any occasion when the choice between life and death was quite as clear or as immediate as it was in this instance.

I have thought about that event many times and wondered what would have happened if I had been forced to pull that trigger. In all likelihood, in 1968, it would have been considered a "justifiable homicide" by an officer in the legal performance of his duty. Today there would be an internal-affairs investigation, in which my version of the events would be tested against each of the inmate witnesses in the squad. There would be polygraph tests. There would be media inquiries alleging gross negligence and brutality, and a Grand Jury hearing during which my motives and personal integrity would be questioned.

I feel today as I felt then, that I would have been justified if I'd pulled that trigger. The question is, what would or should today's officer do? There are all kinds of rules relating to the "authorized use of deadly force." None of those rules allow an officer to fire his weapon without first taking a series of "reasonable actions" designed to mitigate the need for force "where possible." In order to understand, you have to put yourself in that place; if you're a correctional officer in charge of a crew of inmates with tools in their possession, you know that they're fully capable of killing each other with the tools that they carry. What would you do, should that situation occur?

The federally mandated "Use of Major/Deadly Force Policy" was written by lawyers, for lawyers, and leaves correctional employees with no legal protection. The present use-of-force policy was specifically written so that the Internal Affairs Division and senior TDC administrators can hide behind rank-and-file employees, conveniently disciplining or terminating them, or pleading ignorance of their actions, so that the officers, not the administration, can be held liable. A prudent employee, after reading the use-of-force plan, may very well choose not to take action, even if such action is necessary, due to the likelihood that he or she will be prosecuted regardless of whether the action was justified. In today's system, the correctional officer has become the potential victim, not only of the inmates, but of the very criminal-justice system to which he has pledged loyalty. Officers have become prey to not only physical assault by inmates, but also criminal and civil litigation against which they have little defense.

HAZARDS OF ESCAPE

We were into the winter months now, and the rules governing what kind of weather conditions inmates could or could not work under grew more vague with each passing day. Supposedly, if the temperature got down to 42 degrees or below, the line was not to turn out, due to inclement weather, but that decision was left to the discretion of the captain or the major, and it was not uncommon to turn out when it was below freezing. In mid-December, we were flat-weeding the high levee in the Brazos River bottom with a strong twenty-mile-an-hour wind blowing in off the river. I had to yell at the top of my lungs just so the squad could hear me.

I'd pretty much lost my voice by 9:30 A.M., and as the morning wore on, I began to notice icicles hanging from my rain slicker. I swore to myself, *If the major rings that turn-out bell after lunch, I'm going to see if I can find a different line of work.* At about 11:00, there was a minor fight in the squad, and the captain and lieutenant came over to investigate. It was just one of those slapping contests, where one of them was scared and the other one was glad of it, so it didn't last long. They were both yelling threats at each other, so the captain decided to send the aggressor to the building in order to avoid having to split them up again. He told me to ride in the pickup with Lieutenant Rupert Thompson (*aka* "Big Red") to escort the fighter to lockup, and that he would carry my squad while I was gone.

Just as the inmate was securely placed in old Ponce's twelve-cell hotel, we heard several shots being fired from the direction of the front of the building. The lieutenant and I jumped in the pickup and hurried around to the front construction yard, where a crew of about two hundred convicts was working on the new addition to the main building. It was a hectic scene. One of the inmate dump-truck drivers had decided to drive his truck through the front security gate in an attempt to reach Highway 36. The problem was, the road was muddy from the morning rain, and the escapee had failed to negotiate the S curve just outside the gate. He broke through the gate and the security cable all right, but the truck slid to a halt in a ditch about halfway between the two security-guard towers. When we arrived, all three pickets were shooting at the dump truck. The officers blew out the windshield, the tires, and the back and side windows, but they couldn't hit the convict, who was hunkered down inside.

When the pickets quit firing, this little five-foot-four-inch, twenty-two-year-old white convict thought the officers were out of ammunition, so he crawled out of the driver's side window and started running. The picket officers began firing again, but they still couldn't hit the now zigzagging convict. He crossed Highway 36 and ran into the ankle-deep muddy field. He got about 200 yards into the field and was at least 450 yards from the construction yard when one of the back picket officers fired his M-I carbine and hit the convict. An M-I carbine isn't supposed to have that kind of range, but the bullet went through his left hand and lodged in the back of his upper left thigh. The convict dropped like a sack of potatoes.

We stopped on the edge of the highway, walked out, picked him up, and carried him back to the truck. With the wounded escapee in the back of the pickup, we drove around to the back gate, arriving just in time to see the line-force trailers coming up the road for lunch. Lieutenant Thompson got out of the truck and told Ponce, "Put him on the fence until after the line comes through, then take him to the hospital—he may need a little medical attention." Ponce helped the convict limp over to the fence by the turn-in gate and handcuffed him as high as he could reach, with his toes barely touching the ground.

So there he hung, limp and bleeding, on the fence, as the line-force squads all looked him over as they went through the back gate. The leg wound was apparent, as there was enough blood on his lower left leg to attest to the picket officer's marksmanship. It was an effective, but unspoken, object lesson on the hazards of escape. The message was clear: Escape is an option, but there is a price to pay for those who don't make it. As Ponce assisted the limping convict off to the infirmary, we all went into the ODR for lunch. After all, it was just another day on the Clemens Unit, TDC.

A few weeks later, number-one hoe squad boss Phil Johnson and I were advised by Major Breen to accompany him on a spur-of-the-moment trip to Warden Valentine's office. He went with us, but wouldn't tell us why we were going. Once there, we sat in the outer office while the major went in. I noticed two other men whom I had not seen before with Warden Valentine. After about ten minutes, they called us in, and we were introduced to Warden Bob Cousins of the Darrington Unit and Warden Eli

Rushing of the Retrieve Unit. It seemed that they were each in need of field lieutenants, and we were being considered for the jobs. At that time, you did not apply for a promotion or send in a résumé. The wardens made all decisions as to who worked on their units.

After a short group interview, Warden Cousins chose Phil Johnson as his lieutenant and Warden Rushing chose me. Phil Johnson was about thirty and was an experienced field officer. He had been on Clemens for at least six years and was familiar with all the crop cycles and the other unique methods of TDC farming. He was selected on the strength of his experience and his proven ability to handle inmates. I, on the other hand, was selected because Warden Rushing needed someone to keep track of the field officer's time book. He said the only other ranking field officer he had who could keep the time book was his field captain, and it took up too much of his time. As a lieutenant's job represented a considerable increase in salary and came with a house, although I wasn't married, I did not hesitate to accept. The interview had been on Friday morning, and I was told to report to the Retrieve Unit on the following Monday.

A REAL CONVICT FARM

I arrived at the Retrieve Unit on a Monday morning in September 1969. I had just turned twenty-three years old and had a total time with the TDC of about two years—and only six months in the field. I reported to the Retrieve Unit as the youngest and least-experienced field lieutenant in the system.

The field major, Don Garner, was sixty-seven and looked every day of it. The field captain, Sam Lanham, was in his late fifties but was fit and had a military presence about him. The warden, Eli Rushing, was an A&M graduate with the most laid-back attitude of anyone I had met up until that time in TDC. This man didn't get excited about anything. The assistant warden, Bobby Morgan, was an impressive, plainspoken man about six-feet-three-inches tall. He was also very easygoing, but you got the feeling that nobody wanted to see him lose his temper. He had worked in the agriculture department on the Ellis Unit outside of Huntsville before coming to Retrieve.

The Retrieve Unit convicts were all three-, four-, five-, or six-time losers, most over thirty years old. I was used to "holding school" with the seventeen- to twenty-five-year-olds at Clemens Unit. They didn't know how to work and had to be shown through repetitious demonstration. Most of Retrieve's convicts had grown up in prisons, and they not only knew how to work, they also knew the rules better than the officers did. Just because most of them had no more than a third-grade education was not a reason to underestimate their ability to con an officer. Many of them had lived by their wits on the streets and had survival skills that most refined "citizens" don't possess. They prided themselves on being called "convicts," not "inmates," because: "A convict does his own time and an inmate does everybody else's."

The officers were equally "old school." With the exception of three field officers, all of them were forty or older. Many had been on that same unit for more than twenty-five years. There was a garden-squad officer named Frank Lofton who had worked on every farm in the Southern Region. He was sixty-five in 1969 and had been a boss for more than forty-four years. His father had been a farm manager at the turn of the century, and Frank was raised on a prison farm until he was old enough to go to work on one. It was like walking around in a history class to hear them talk about "the old days."

The highrider's name was John L. Nichols (*aka* "Eat 'em Up"). He was about fifty-five, and he was assigned as the highrider because he had demonstrated less-than-civilized methods of attempting to carry a hoe squad. The wardens had standing instructions that John L. was not to carry a squad under any circumstances. He had been a sergeant in earlier times, before TDC became a more civilized agency. John L. had been fired several times by old Zan Harrelson, the Retrieve warden from 1951 to 1967. Warden Harrelson always hired him back, though, which was the reason Harrelson was about the only thing John L. had any respect for. John L. could not read or write, which was a common trait among the older Retrieve Unit officers of that time. His personality was something akin to someone dragging fingernails across a blackboard. He was a crusty, cantankerous old bag of wind who didn't even like himself, but he was a rare, one-of-a-kind character. Being around John L. was like watching a burning building; you knew it was a bad thing, but you still couldn't take your eyes off him for fear that you'd miss something. In John L.'s opinion, the whole world was going to hell in a hand-basket, and the TDC leadership was leading the charge.

Warden Harrelson had helped the Retrieve Unit earn the name "The Burning Hell." All the older convicts referred to him as either "Red Devil" or "Big Devil." The convicts all felt like they had been given a vacation since Harrelson had been transferred to the Eastham Unit after being at Retrieve for more than twenty-five years. Many of the old Retrieve bosses quit or retired when Harrelson left. Old Captain "Red Dick" Robinson retired after thirty-five-plus years at Retrieve. The field lieutenant, King, transferred to one of the northern units when Harrelson left, leaving the opportunity for my promotion into his old job. In those days, ranking staff positions did not generally change unless someone died or got fired.

The new warden, Eli Rushing, could be found almost every evening in one of the lower inmate tanks playing dominoes with the convicts. He would laugh and slam dominoes just like the convicts did. With the door locked behind him, he would wait his turn at the table and pass his readyroll cigarettes around freely. The convicts were glad to have him in the game. Warden Morgan didn't like the situation at all, but realized his limited ability to do anything about it. His response was, "Yeah, I know what he's doing. I'd like to know how I'm supposed to maintain building security around here when he keeps volunteering himself as a hostage." The first time I saw Warden Rushing playing dominoes with the convicts, I got the feeling that one way or another, there would be an administrative change in the near future. As it turned out, I was right.

CHAPTER THREE

RETRIEVE

The Burning Hell
"Lord, grant me the serenity to accept the things I cannot change, the courage to change the things I can, and the wisdom to hide the bodies of those people I had to kill because they pissed me off."
—JACK BROWN

In 1967, when a Texas convict arrived at the back gate of the Retrieve Unit on old "Black Betty," the transport van, he knew he'd reached the end of the line. The seven-thousand-acre prison farm was once part of the Retrieve Plantation, established in 1838 by Major Abner Jackson as part of Stephen F. Austin's original Old Three Hundred land grants. Retrieve was originally part of the Jared E. Groce land grant and was one of the finest plantations of the time. Major Jackson came from South Carolina and

> built a brick mansion about a mile south on the banks of Oyster Creek from where the present buildings are, near a lone oak tree on the east side of the creek. It had a two-story brick residence, brick cabins, a large brick sugarhouse with a double set of kettles, and a large brick oven to cook for the slaves. It was a well-equipped sugar plantation. Major Jackson owned three sugar plantations, seventy thousand acres of land and over three hundred slaves. His stock of cattle branded annually ran over five thousand calves. He sold a half interest in the Retrieve Plantation to General James Hamilton of South Carolina, who made this his permanent home as long as he was in Texas. General Hamilton was killed in 1857 when his ship went down off the coast of

Florida. Major T. Lynch resided on the Retrieve Plantation for many years, and like many others, he lost his plantation home during the era of inflation and corruption that followed the Civil War. (From *Old Plantations and Their Owners* by Abner J. Strobel)

The Retrieve Plantation had a steamboat landing and was a prime destination for the surrounding plantations' cotton and sugar until well after the turn of the century, when other forms of transportation became more economical. There is still a place on the Retrieve Unit today, below the current "garden house" location on Oyster Creek, called Steamboat Landing. After the end of the Civil War, the large sugar and cotton plantations could not operate successfully without slave labor. When the State of Texas began leasing inmates, they were taken to Brazoria County in the 1870s and utilized on the Retrieve, Clemens, Darrington, and Masterson (now the Ramsey Unit) plantations.

In 1884 J. E. Williams Jr. came to Brazoria County, where he was a captain at the Retrieve Prison Farm. According to county records, he married Lizzie I. Jamison. Dr. Josiah Green Smith practiced medicine in Angleton and Velasco, and served as physician for the prison farms. He also managed the Surfside Hotel.

On September 6, 1900, a massive hurricane struck Galveston, Texas, killing more than 6,000 people. The Lowood Plantation, now part of the Clemens Unit, reported fourteen convicts killed as a result of the storm. The Retrieve Plantation was "lightly damaged," with damage estimates of about $2,000.00. The Retrieve Plantation manager, Mr. Westall, thought that "While the cane had been blown down, it was not greatly damaged."

CONVICTS REPLACE SLAVES ON THE PLANTATIONS

This was a particularly brutal time for inmates in Texas. In those days the word *brutality* didn't mean an absence of TVs or recreational facilities, or denial of access to the unit law library. During the lease period, there was little or no oversight, escapes occurred on a regular basis, and inmate deaths were common. Records of the lease period are vague, but according to the State Board of Labor records, in 1876 there were 382 escapes and 62 inmate deaths. As late as 1909, the number of escapes was seventy and the number of inmate deaths was reported at sixty-one.

The main reason the lease period lasted for more than forty years was that it did provide a source of revenue for the State of Texas, whose citizens did not want to spend tax dollars on prisons.

In 1867, 150 state prisoners were contracted to the Brazos Branch Railroad at $12.50 per month per man. This contract lasted only a few months, because too many of the prisoners escaped or were killed or wounded in attempted escapes. In 1871 the state leased the Huntsville State Prison and all of the prisoners to Ward, Dewey & Company of Galveston for a fifteen-year period. The prison conditions improved during the first few years of this lease and then began to decline. The following is an excerpt from a report to the Texas Legislature titled, "1874–1876 Report on the Conditions of the Texas Penitentiary":

> At Lake Jackson plantation [Retrieve], in September, 1874, I [Inspector J.K.P. Campbell] found sixty-five sick convicts confined in the prison out of a force of one hundred and eighty-five, some of whom were quite sick. These men at the time had no medical attention. There was a hospital steward on the place who had some knowledge of medicine, coupled with some experience as a nurse, but he was very ill himself, and unable to give any attention to the sick. I at once made the Sergeant send for a physician who visited the camp the next day. He found the most essential medicines were not at the camp, and the Sergeant had to send to Houston for them . . . The sick occupied the same building with the well convicts, and the attention required of the sick prevented the other men from obtaining that sleep which laboring men need.

The report continued:

> At the Lake Jackson Plantation, which I visited in September of 1874, I found three trusty convicts whose backs were cut to pieces in a most shocking manner. The only offense, so far as I could learn, committed by these brutally treated men, was, they had taken some flour and exchanged it for whisky, and returned to camp intoxicated . . . The Sergeant, who had been on the place for sixteen months, informed me the convicts had not changed their clothing for ten weeks, and that the lower extrem-

ities of some of them were naked . . . The Assistant Inspector reports that the night he left, some clothing was put off at the landing [Steamboat Landing on Oyster Creek] for this camp.

Here is a report to the Legislature, December 1876, by Inspector J. T. Gains:

Huntsville, Texas, December 20, 1876
Lake Jackson, Sergeant Shaw
9th of December
No. in ranks 37 . . . Trustees 22, died 3, Total Number 62.
Day guards 7, Night guards 2.
#5352 Frank Furlow died in stocks, a written report of which accompanies this report.
#5359 Wiley Wilson convict was killed on the 9th while attempting to make his escape by C. E. Witten, guard. On an investigation of this killing I formed the same facts as stated in the accompanying written statement. The convict had got in the standing cane some distance when he was shot.
#5312 Jas Taylor died Nov. 1, from natural causes.

In an 1876 report to the governor, Frank Furlow, the inmate who died in the stocks, is listed on page 21 as convict #535:

He was a black male, seventeen years of age, from Anderson County who was convicted of theft of a mare and mule and sentenced to 10 years. He was received at Huntsville on June 22, 1876. No records could be found on when he arrived at Lake Jackson.

In an additional report by J. T. Gains, assistant inspector, dated January 26, 1877, on file in the Texas State Archives, the following observations regarding the death of Frank Furlow were made:

Convict Furlow had failed to work to satisfy the guard when upon ordered him in the stocks; he being placed in the stocks by another convict 'Hill.' This squad of men was at work in the field; when the stocking took place. I refer you to statement made by the darkies who witnessed the stocking. I do not regard this case more unfortunate than others that have happened on other farms, but shows clearly how cautious men ought to be when observing . . . a convict . . .

Statement of witnesses to the death of Frank Furlow in 1876:

> I heard Mr. Sumner tell Frank Furlow to get on the stocks which Frank Furlow did. Mr. Sumner told a George Hill to stock the said Furlow which the said George Hill did: He raised the said Furlow until he stood on the balls of his feet he stood in the stocks about five minutes he then let him down. The said Furlow was not concerned; he then commanded the said George Hill to put him in the stocks again, which the said Negro did. After he was put in the second time, he jumped and flayed about to a considerable extent he stayed in the stocks about five minutes and was taken out and found to be dead.
>
> L. E. WHITTEN AND WILLIAM LURMEN

Wiley Wilson, #542, is also listed on page 21 along with Frank Furlow in the 1876 report. Wiley was fifteen years old, was born in South Carolina, and was convicted of theft in Harris County and sentenced to two years.

State Inspector's report of March 3, 1877, at Lake Jackson:

> Lake Jackson Force, February 24, A. O. Shaw, Sergeant
> Prison in tolerably good conditions. Men get enough to eat but are dirty looking fellows but look very stout and hearty. Clothing needed badly. Shoes only tolerably good. None sick. None complain of bad treatment. Bedding scant and dirty. In ranks 30, Trustees 14, Pardons 1, Discharged 1, Transferred to McNeals 13, Escaped 1, Now in camp 49. Day guards 7, Night guards 1.

The state revoked this lease in 1877 and took back control of the prisoners.

Abner Strobel described a scenario that involved subleases:

> In 1875 Edward H. Cunningham, a veteran of the Civil War and wealthy farmer and rancher in Bexar County, while looking for favorable investments, became interested in the sugar plantations in Fort Bend County. He entered into a partnership with Col. Littleberry A. Ellis. The purpose of the partnership was to lease the entire convict population, which they would then sublease to other plantation owners. Their lease contract included the Huntsville Prison, and for each prisoner they were to pay the state $3.01 per month. In 1880 more than half of the convicts in the system were being used in Fort Bend and Brazoria counties. In

that year, Ellis and Cunningham between them worked 365 convicts, and Cunningham had seven on his Bexar County Ranch..."

In the *Biennial Reports of the Directors and Superintendent of the Texas State Penitentiary . . . with the Report of the Prison Physician . . . 1878–1880,* the following is found on page 21:

No one will attempt to deny that the system is an evil, the true reason of which is because of the large mortality attending, the facilities afforded for escapes, and because under it there is little or no chance for reform. It can only be defended on two grounds: necessity, and because it is a source of revenue.

In 1882 *The Biennial Reports* reported that 1,040 prisoners were contracted out in groups to individuals for $15.00 per month. The lessee had to furnish housing, food, and guards. Lessees were entitled to ten hours of work per day per prisoner. The report listed the Darrington Plantation with twenty-eight convicts and the Lake Jackson Plantation with thirty-six. In 1884 1,128 prisoners were leased to private individuals or farms. In addition, 176 inmates worked on railroad construction crews.

On page 7 of the *Report on Conditions of the State Penitentiary For The Year 1884,* the following information is listed:

Under the contract entered into between ex-Governor Davis, on the part of the State, and Managers Ward, Dewey & Company, the present lessees, the labor and general management of the convicts passes from the State to those gentleman, subject, however, to the supervisory control of the Board of Directors and myself [Inspector J. K.P. Campbell].

In the various industries in and around
the prison proper 676
In agriculture and brick making on the Lake Jackson
and Patton Plantations, in Brazoria County 314
In agriculture on the Alston farm, in Walker County 77
At the Prison Tannery, in Walker County 131
On various railroads 255

Most of those employed in agricultural pursuits are the Negro convicts, and I have visited all the detachments at a distance from the Penitentiary regularly, and made a thorough inspection of the labor required of convicts and in no case have I found onerous or excessive tasks imposed, and, but for the prison garb, there is no observable difference between them and free men engaged in the same kind of labor, except that the convict seems better clothed, fed, and in better health.

In the official records, the last listing for convicts at the Lake Jackson Plantation was for November 1, 1884, with a total of thirty-three convicts.

> By 1892, the State leased 1,039 prisoners and was getting $17.00 per month per prisoner on sugar plantations, $16.50 for prisoners on sugar and cotton, and $15.50 for cotton and corn . . . In 1886, the State bought the Harlem Plantation in Fort Bend County to be run as a prison farm using convict labor. In 1899 the State acquired 5,527 acres in Brazoria County and acquired the adjoining land of the Lowood Plantation with 2,685.47 acres to establish the Clemens Prison. The Lowood Plantation was the largest sugar producer in Brazoria County for several years before the Civil War and had some of the finest land in the Brazos River valley . . . (Walker, 1988)

The state continued to gradually acquire land as the lease system continued off and on until 1912. By 1914 all leases had expired and state inmates were all placed on state-owned property and under the supervision of state employees. This removal from the public market of access to forced labor brought about the decline of sugar production in Texas. The main reason that the lease period lasted until 1914 was that it did provide a source of revenue for the state, which did not want to spend tax dollars on prisons.

The State of Texas had been working inmates in Brazoria County since 1871 on the lease system, although the first state prison unit, in Brazoria County, was not officially purchased until the Clemens Unit in 1899. The Ramsey I and II units were purchased in 1908, and the Retrieve and Darrington units followed in 1918. The Brazoria County prisons were run like farm labor camps with little investment by the state until the 1930s. The first manager at the Retrieve Farm, after formal purchase by the state in 1918, was John Henry Weems. In the beginning, the state sent its most desperate criminals to Retrieve, and its reputation among the inmates as the "Devil's Island" of Texas prisons was well-earned.

CLUB LAKE

On October 10, 1919, the 18th Amendment, named the Volstead Act, was passed by Congress, mandating that "No person shall manufacture, sell, barter, transport, import, export, deliver, furnish or possess intoxicating liquor except as authorized by this act." The act was ratified by thirty-six states, and after allowing for "a year's adjustment period," America went "dry" on January 17, 1921. During the next twelve years, ten months, and nineteen days, America—and Texas in particular—entered an era of corruption, scandal, gangsters, smuggling, wealth, and violence that was unprecedented. Prohibition, not unlike the present-day "War on Drugs," did not work in America.

At the Retrieve Unit today, there is a lake that most of the locals call "Horseshoe Lake," but on the official maps of Texas and Brazoria County it is labeled "Club Lake." The name Club Lake originated during Prohibition, when a gathering place, some say a speakeasy, known as "The Retrieve Hunting Club" was located there. I. K. Kelly Jr., who was raised on the Retrieve farm, said there were large gatherings almost every weekend, weather permitting. His father, the Retrieve Unit warden during Prohibition, wouldn't allow young I. K. to go down to the club after dark. The dirt roads were only accessible by horse or wagon. The remote location of the prison farm made it an ideal place for those Brazoria County citizens who were perhaps a little less politically correct than those who voted for Prohibition.

The Hunting Club was a two-story wooden building with an attached boat dock and fishing pier. There were six rooms on the second floor of the L-shaped wooden structure. One room was large enough for gambling tables, and the small rooms attached at the rear were reserved for overnight guests. Guests, both male and female, attended gatherings during good weather, and they sometimes stayed for days at a time. The older Retrieve guards, Frank Lofton and Louis Nichols, remembered earlier guards speaking with reverence about The Hunting Club and its still, which produced some of "the best sugar-cane sour-mash whiskey ever made." It was always ready for those who didn't take the Volstead Act too seriously. There were always plenty of ducks, deer, and other game to hunt, and fish were plentiful to catch in those days. It was no doubt a simpler time, when civilization was miles away and folks were inclined to mind their own business.

The Hunting Club was in uninterrupted service until the spring of 1933, when Franklin D. Roosevelt made "real beer" exempt from the 18th Amendment. By December 5, 1933, the 21st Amendment was passed, repealing the Volstead Act, and alcohol once again became legal. Prohibition had been created with the intention of providing a healthier, happier, safer, and more productive America. It didn't work out that way. After Prohibition was repealed, the old "Hunting Club" faded out, mainly because there was no longer any demand for still whiskey, especially when you had to cross seven miles of bad dirt road to get to it.

LEE SIMMONS

Mr. Lee Simmons became the prison-system manager in March 1930 after Governor Dan Moody inspected some of the prison units and pronounced them "not fit for a dog." His goal was to end the prisons' reputation as brutal and inhumane. Lee Simmons began the first Prison Rodeo in 1930, and it became an immediate source of pride. In later years, it became a source of income that helped pay for educational materials and rehabilitation programs. Many celebrities attended the rodeo, and it became known worldwide.

Incidents of escapes were rampant during the 1920s, and one of the main challenges for Lee Simmons was to find a way to stop them. The following is an eyewitness account of a mass escape. According to Clemens Unit officer J. P. Hicks,

> On June 19, 1928, forty inmates escaped. An inmate named Joe Willis had a gun slipped in to him. He drew the gun on Boss "Squirlhead" Moore, the picket officer, and made him give up his weapons. There were only two other employees on the unit at that time and they were unarmed. The inmates with the guns opened the doors and forty of them escaped. They took the employees with them, crossed the river, and then three of the inmates took the guards' clothes, made the guards dress in convict uniforms. When the employees got back to the building several hours later, they were still wearing the convict uniforms. The majority of the

inmates were apprehended the first two days after the escape. It took a week to catch some of the stragglers. The "big captain" got a whipping order and whipped thirty-six of the inmates in one night.

Lee Simmons brought to the position of prison-system manager a thorough understanding of the prison system and its problems. He then wanted to improve the treatment of convicts; he gathered all the farm managers together and told them, "From this time on, every prisoner is some mother's son, some woman's husband, some sister's brother. I expect you to treat them as human beings."

Lee Simmons was hired as a reformer, but he believed in corporal punishment, which was being used liberally during this time in the form of "the bat." The bat was a twenty-four-inch-long leather strap, four inches wide, attached to a wooden handle. Monthly reports were sent in to Huntsville from the units telling how many inmates received lashes and for what disciplinary offenses.

Although the following report is dated prior to Mr. Simmons' tenure as general manager, it is representative of "whipping orders" issued during this time period. It was evidently required by law to report the whippings to the local District Judge:

July 18, 1927, Huntsville, Texas
Honorable Carl T. Harper
District Judge
Madisonville, Texas

Dear Sir:
As required by law, we are forwarding you herewith the list of whipping orders executed on the Ferguson State Farm, located in Madison County, also the Huntsville Prison, located in Walker County, for the period from January 1, 1927 to June 30, 1927.

It is hoped that these reports are in proper form and meet with your approval.

Yours very truly,
Secretary to Acting General Manager
Mattie Anders, Secretary

STATEMENT OF WHIPPING ORDERS EXECUTED DURING THE PERIOD OF January 1, 1927 to June 30, 1927

FERGUSON STATE FARM

Date	Number & Name	Offense	Lashes
Jan. 26	53933-Marion Allgood	Beating up another Convict	12
Jan. 7	39064-Wesley Boatwright	Hitting another convict over the head with a hammer.	11
"	39058-Jack Satterwhite	Ditto	11
"	54166-Roy Bickle	Escaping as unapproved Trusty. Stealing Winchester and six shooter, also shooting guard and killing horse.	20
"	528443-E. L. Hazelwood	Ditto	20
March 15	49730- Arthur Pace	Trying to smuggle out letters to get a gun.	20
"	52727-Lloyd Waddell	Laziness	20
March 25	53965-Glayitor Hammer	Throwing brick-bat at mule and hitting convict Bill McDonald and knocking out four teeth.	9
April 16	50000-E. A. Silas	Refusing to get on barrel.	15
"	51692-Clarence Bayless	" " "	8
"	53119-S. L. Irvin	Refusing to get on barrel and refusing to work.	20
"	52506-Ted Davis	Refusing to get on barrel	20
May 25	55346-Dewey Moran	Hitting convict in head with Single-tree.	20

**STATEMENT OF WHIPPING ORDERS EXECUTED DURING THE PERIOD OF
January 1, 1927 to June 30, 1927**

HUNTSVILLE PRISON

Date	Number & Name	Offense	Lashes
Jan. 27	32477-John Osgood	Fighting fellow Prisoner And Cursing Guards.	20
Mar 27	49623-C. E. Bailey	Escaping as unapproved Trusty.	16
May 27	55758-Frank Burk	Escaping as unapproved Trusty and taking Dr. Mallett's car.	15

The concept of prison reform has changed significantly between time of Lee Simmons and Austin MacCormick and present-day federal judge William Wayne Justice. Lee Simmons was called to testify and give his opinion on proposed legislation to end the use of "the bat." The State of Texas' leading "prison reformer" said:

Gentlemen, it's just like using spurs. You get on an old cow horse without spurs—and you can't head even a milking-pen cow; but when you've got your spurs on, the old horse will do the job, and you don't have to use the spurs, because all he needs is to know that the spurs are there. It's the same with us and "the bat." The record shows we seldom have to use it. But the boys all know it is there. The hellraiser fears nothing more than the bat. When I was in charge he got it. Generally, after five lashes, the rebel raised his hand and cried, "That's enough; I'll behave." I saw only a very few take the full twenty.

A more enlightened administration was to follow Mr. Simmons during the late 1930s and in 1941 did find it necessary to outlaw the use of the bat. Mr. Simmons said that this unnecessary step was the action of "misguided and ill-informed humanitarians."

According to Warden C. L. McAdams:

One morning in 1938, an officer who was drunk got too close to the squad and they mugged him. They cut the officer all to pieces with knives. Eight of the inmates got his guns and left. Officers from all the surrounding units were called to Eastham to help apprehend the escapees. I got there about 10:00. After the inmates left, the dogs were put on their trails, and soon afterwards, two of the inmates were cornered and killed. The next day the bodies of two more inmates were found floating in the Trinity River. A Negro told officers that two men had passed by with a guard up front. The next day they found two more inmates who had been killed. Eight ran and six got killed. A drunk officer was the cause of it all.

In 1929, the year before Lee Simmons became the prison-system manager, the number of escapes had averaged 12 percent of the total inmate population. In the first year of Mr. Simmons' administration, escapes dropped to 3 percent of the population and remained at that level through his last year, 1935. The fact that the overall escape rate was lower under his administration than his predecessors' was not widely known, because of one infamous escape that occurred at the Eastham Unit in 1934. The Eastham Prison escape turned out to be a fatal error for the Clyde Barrow gang and Raymond Hamilton. Lee Simmons was so enraged over the killing of one of his guards that he persuaded Frank Hamer, a legendary ex–Texas Ranger, to come out of retirement and track down Bonnie Parker and Clyde Barrow. The escape also brought Henry Methvin into the gang. Fearing for his son's life, Henry's father made a deal with Lee Simmons to sell out Bonnie and Clyde in exchange for a full pardon for Henry for crimes he had committed in Texas and Louisiana.

On January 16, 1934, five prisoners, Raymond Hamilton, Joe Palmer, Henry Methvin, Hilton Bybee, and J. B. French escaped from the field workforce at the Eastham Unit near Waldo, Texas. Clyde Barrow, Bonnie Parker, and James Mullen, who had planted automatic weapons in the field for the escaping inmates, made the escape possible. Clyde and his brother Ivan "Buck" Barrow had both served time in the early 1930s in Texas prisons, where Clyde had two of his toes from his left foot chopped off in an effort to avoid having to pick cotton. Clyde was very familiar with the inmate workforce routine. The escaping prisoners shot two guards with the .45-caliber automatic pistols, which had been previously concealed in a ditch by the Barrow gang. TDC officer Major Crowson was killed in the initial gunfire from Raymond Hamilton and Joe Palmer. As the prisoners ran, Barrow and Mullen covered their retreat with bursts of BAR. (Browning Automatic Rifle, 30.06 caliber) machine-gun fire. The inmates who were not involved all hit the ground in order to avoid the gunfire. Witnesses said Officer B. B. Bullard was instrumental in preventing further escapes by telling the inmates to lie down while gunfire was exchanged with the Barrow gang. Although this escape was successful, Clyde Barrow and Bonnie Parker were killed only four months later on May 23, 1934, when a task force involving Texas Ranger Frank Hamer, a Texas Prison officer, Louisiana Police, and federal agents ambushed the couple at a rural roadside near Sailes, Louisiana. At the time of their deaths, Bonnie and Clyde were wanted for numerous automobile thefts, burglaries, bank robberies, kidnapping, and at least thirteen murders. They are known to have killed eight police officers, one prison guard, and four civilians.

Raymond Hamilton and Joe Palmer were both captured and sent to the electric chair in 1935 for the murder of Major Crowson. Henry Methvin received his pardon from Texas as promised; however, he did get arrested in Oklahoma for murder, for which he received a life sentence.

RETRIEVE, 1934

In 1934 the construction of the "new building" began, and in 1937 the "modern" version of the Retrieve Unit opened. The old wooden barracks and the warden's house located on the right side of the road on a curve of Oyster Creek about a half-mile from the entrance, was torn down. The new "fireproof brick dormitory" was originally designed "To hold white prisoners who have served one or more previous prison terms and who have been segregated from the incorrigibles on other units." The inmate population grew at such a rate that by the early 1950s the unit was composed almost entirely of multirecidivist black inmates who had been classified "incorrigible." The building was designed to house, double-bunked, 450 inmates.

COLUMBIA TAP STEAM LOCOMOTIVE BURIED AT RETRIEVE

A couple of years before moving into the new building, in 1932 or 1933, the old "Columbia Tap Railroad" spur that ran off of the main line to the old unit was taken up. The warden used some of the railroad track to secure the windows and doors of the old rapidly deteriorating wooden-barn-like prison. The rusty old steam locomotive was pushed out to the end of the spur track where the convicts dug a huge hole. The train engine was pushed into the hole and buried there. It is still there today. Over the years, I have talked to several eyewitnesses to this event. Captain Maulden, who was the medical officer at the time, and Mr. I. K. Kelly Jr., who was a child of nine in 1932, but lived on the unit, verified the location of the buried train engine. Kelly said that he personally watched as the convicts dug the hole. For years the railcars had been used to haul trash and everything else that wouldn't burn to the landfills alongside the old spur line. Items such as bottles, mule harnesses, plow blades, tools, toothbrushes, silverware, plates, trace chains, and many other items considered trash at the time were buried. During interviews in the last years of his life, ex–Retrieve inmate Clyde Thompson verified that during the early 1930s he was working in a hoe squad involved in the digging of a hole for the purpose of burying "a steam locomotive."

CLYDE THOMPSON, 1930S

He was an unlikely combination—a preacher's kid who killed four men! Clyde Thompson was a living legend down where they grow legends by the yard. Like John Wesley Hardin before him, in his prime, Clyde Thompson was called "the Meanest Man in Texas." That may have been an understatement. He was possibly the meanest man anywhere.

He was born in Oklahoma in 1910. Clyde's father was a Church of Christ preacher. As he was a circuit-riding preacher, the family moved often, and Clyde's schooling suffered. In the fourth grade, at age fourteen, he quit. When he told the story in later year, he said, "I was the oldest and dumbest kid in my class."

By this time, Clyde was packing a pistol. As fate would have it, two men challenged Clyde, a friend named Tom, and a juvenile to a fight. When the two men attempted to use a powder horn and a tree limb as weapons, Clyde pulled his pistol and killed both men. A claim of self-defense seemed less than credible to a jury of his peers, so Clyde and his friend Tom both received the death penalty. Upon arrival at the Walls Unit, Clyde became death-row prisoner #83. He was nineteen years old, the youngest person to have been sentenced to death row at that time. Errors in a trial transcript led to a second trial for both men. Clyde again received the death penalty, because he admitted that he had been the one who fired the gun, but his friend Tom got a five-year suspended sentence.

On March 2, 1931, Clyde was transported to death row. He had sixty days to live. On the last day, when he was six hours from execution and had turned down his last meal, Governor Ross Sterling commuted Clyde's sentence to life. Clyde was transferred from death row to the Retrieve Unit. Clyde said later in his book, "It was better than death, but not much." There were eighteen men in number-one hoe squad on Clyde's first day at work. The number-one hoe boss had the squad dig a huge hole in which to bury a rusting steam locomotive that was beyond repair. The old engine stood at the end of a railroad spur line that ran into the farm. The spur was used to transport crops grown on the farm to the main track about a mile away.

In January 1933, Clyde tried his first flight for freedom, scampering off when a guard's attention was diverted by a falling tree. However, one of his cohorts had tipped off the guards that an escape was imminent. The guard yelled, "Stop!" Clyde and three others, not knowing it was a setup, kept running. The guard fired, and one prisoner fell, hit in the back with a load of buckshot. Loping along on his horse, the guard caught up to Clyde and cocked his gun. He could have killed Clyde easily, but fired a warning shot instead.

For that escape attempt, Clyde's punishment was the Coke box: he had to stand on a wooden Coca-Cola box stood up on its end, every night, all night. Some men would stand there until they just keeled off the box, or they would have to step down to get the circulation going in their legs. Clyde also suffered the bat. Made of rawhide with a wooden handle, it was a leather strap, thirty-nine inches long and two-and-a-half inches wide. Clyde said he was often beaten twice a day for some real or imagined infraction of the rules.

A few weeks later, Clyde and another convict killed the informer who had squealed on their escape. Two and a half years later, in July 1935, Clyde killed another inmate during a knife fight. In the trials that followed these killings, Clyde pled self-defense. The only thing that saved him from the death penalty, on both occasions, was that Clyde convinced the jury that he had been warding off convicts who were attempting to homosexually rape him.

After four more years marked by numerous escape attempts, Clyde was transferred to the Eastham Unit, sixteen miles north of Huntsville. He was placed in an allegedly escape-proof cellblock. Clyde, Roy Thornton, and two other convicts began planning an escape. They planned to take over the unit arsenal and "give guns to everyone who would shoot one." As the break unfolded, two guards and their pistols were captured. Using the guards as shields, the prisoners attempted to climb to the second floor of the arsenal. A gunfight erupted, and Clyde was shot through the shoulder with a .30-30 Winchester slug. In the exchange of fire, one of the four prisoners was killed. Clyde kept shooting until his gun clicked empty. Out of ammunition, he had to surrender.

Thirty days after being shot, he was back at work in the hoe squad. Eight months later another convict was knifed to death. Although Clyde swore he didn't do it, he was charged for his third prison killing and indicted for the fifth time for murder. Clyde said he knew who did it, as did most of the other convicts, but nobody would tell, least of all Clyde. The day before the trial for the fatal knifing, the case against Clyde Thompson was dismissed for lack of evidence. Clyde said, "In those days if they could have found two false witnesses to testify against me, I wouldn't be here today, but I was with men who'd have died rather than tell the prison officials anything."

After the Eastham Unit knifing incident Clyde refused to work in the fields, fearing the guards might just shoot him for revenge. He was transferred to the Walls Unit and placed in the East Building solitary cellblock called "the morgue," located behind the old death-row cellblock.

Now, locked in total isolation, the only thing he had left to occupy his time was a Bible. He began to read and eventually claimed to have had a religious conversion. He was permitted to enroll in Lee College's two-year correspondence Bible and journalism courses.

Finally, after spending a quarter of a century in penitentiaries, Clyde was released in November 1955. He would never again return to prison, except to preach. He used to tell the hard-cases, "If I made it, you can make it, too, with the help of the Lord."

THE BALLAD OF REDWINE

Violence has and always will be a part of the Texas prison system, but on December 15, 1948, there was a particularly violent homicide at the Retrieve Unit. According to Warden I. K. Kelly, inmate Clarence Redwine, age thirty-eight, was decapitated in the inmate dining room by inmate Earnest "Cleave" Jones, age thirty-three. Earnest Jones and two other inmates saved the apricots they had been served for breakfast and took them to the tank, where they turned it into homemade whiskey. Redwine bought a pint of whiskey for $5.00, and after drinking it, he asked Jones to sell him another pint on credit. Jones told him he did cash business only. This led to a fistfight in which Jones apparently whipped Redwine. Jones was afraid of Redwine, and all the time he was whipping him, he was apologizing. Redwine told Jones that he had better get a knife and be prepared the next time they met.

When the line squads went to the dining room for supper that night, Jones tried to talk with Redwine, but Redwine told him that they were enemies and that it would do no good to talk. Jones, who worked in the food-service department, went to the kitchen vegetable room, obtained a long "cane knife," and returned to the inmate dining room. He waited for Redwine to come into the room to eat. After Redwine received his tray of food from the inmate serving line, he went to one of the eight-man tables and sat down. Earnest Jones quickly walked up behind Redwine and with one blow decapitated him. Redwine's head fell onto the table in front of him. His body remained in an upright position, only now it was gushing blood from the stump where Redwine's head had once been.

Several convict witnesses said there was a black inmate, nicknamed "Tarzan," sitting across the table from Redwine when the decapitation took place. According to the witness statements to Warden Kelly, Tarzan didn't even stop eating when Redwine's head hit the table. When the other inmates jumped up from the table, Tarzan slid down the bench a little and continued eating until he had finished his meal.

Earnest Jones pled guilty to the killing and received an additional five-year sentence. In one of the several crime-scene photographs taken after the incident, there was at least one staged photograph showing Redwine's upright headless body with a burning cigarette located between the fingers of his left hand. The photo with the cigarette was obviously staged, because in those days there were no cameras readily available immediately after the homicide. (I. K Kelly Jr., Warden I. K. Kelly's son, provided many of the original photos.)

BEAR TRACKS

After the Retrieve Unit beheading incident in 1948, a real fire-breathing convict tamer was sent to "the Burning Hell." C. L. "Bear Tracks" McAdams was appointed as the new Retrieve Unit warden. He was until the day he retired the most feared warden in the system. The nickname "Bear Tracks" came from a convict who said McAdams was "Big as a bear and leaves tracks in every prison where he goes." He was white, rough-looking, with little formal education, and his legend transcended Texas borders. One convict who had served more than twenty years under McAdams said, "If you keep your business straight, you have nothing to fear from McAdams. If you don't, he is the last warden you would want over you." McAdams had spent his career troubleshooting in the toughest of the Texas prisons. He said, "I got one philosophy: you treat them firm, but fair, and you treat them all alike, and you keep them working, because idleness is the devil's workshop."

The third day after arriving at Retrieve, the inmates went on "strike" in the mess hall and demanded to negotiate with Warden McAdams. He strode into the hall and didn't say a word, but picked up the nearest inmate by the scruff of the shirt and dragged him out into the corridor alone and demanded to know what his grievance was. One by one he took the inmates out, not allowing them to negotiate as a group, but isolating them, separating them, until he had found the leaders and thrown them into solitary.

After that incident, you could not have melted and poured those convicts into a strike. One convict who was involved in the strike later said, "Old Bear Tracks knows us so well that there is almost no difference between us. He can look down into that cellblock or tank and tell you what you're thinking. Bear Tracks would make a perfect convict." McAdams said, "Those that don't like me, don't like me because I don't let them do what they want."

RED DEVIL

Warden Zan Harrelson, *aka* "Red Devil," followed Bear Tracks, becoming warden of the Retrieve Unit in 1951. He had begun his career as a guard in 1936 and worked his way through the ranks as a food-service steward, assistant warden, and warden. The Retrieve Unit would continue its reputation as the graduate school for every bad-ass convict who didn't want to follow the rules on other units. The officers who survived under Harrelson gave him absolute obedient service. Most had little education and had held their jobs since coming out of the Depression in East Texas. They revered Warden Harrelson as a mostly benevolent father figure who could ensure their futures—or end their careers. The language of the Harrelson era was crude. The "bosses," as officers were called, referred to the convicts as "nig-guhs," "old thangs," or worse. If a black convict appeared less dark than his peers, he was called a "high-yella" and his ancestry was questioned.

Officer John L. Nichols, who had worked for Harrelson since the early fifties related one such example of ancestral inquiry to me. He said old Captain Robinson (*aka* "Captain Smooth Mouth" or "Captain Red Dick") would interview new inmates before they were assigned to a squad. If a "high yella" came in, the interview might go something like this:

Captain: What's your name, boy?
Convict: John Doe.

Captain: How old are you?

Convict: Thirty-six.

Captain: Can't you say "sir," boy? Damn, was you raised in a barn?

Convict: Yes suh!

Captain: What did you do for a livin on the streets, besides steal?

Convict: I work mostly with my hands, suh.

Captain: Hard labor, huh? Well, don't worry, you'll be right at home here.

Convict: Yes suh.

Captain: What are you doing time for?

Convict: Car theft, suh.

Captain: Where you from, boy?

Convict: Dallas, suh.

Captain: South Dallas?

Convict: Yes suh.

Captain: I've never seen a nigguh, much less a high-yella from South Dallas, that was worth a damn. What kind of car did you steal?

Convict: It was a red Ford truck, suh.

Captain: Why you son-of-a-bitch, my old grandmother lives in Dallas, and she had a red Ford truck, until some low-bred bastard stole it.

Convict: Naw suh, naw suh, it wasn't yore family truck, suh—

Captain: I know what you did on the streets, you yeller South Dallas bastard. You one of them "gals" ain't you, you shoe shinin' bastard? You suck dicks and shine shoes for a livin', don't you, boy?

Convict: Naw suh, naw suh.

Captain: You don't even know who your momma is, do you?

Convict: She dead, suh.

Captain: Bullshit, you never knew who your mama was. Quit lying to me, nigguh!

Convict: Yes suh . . .

Captain: You catch number-one hoe in the mornin', and I better not see nothin' but elbows and assholes from yo' goat-smellin' ass, either. I'm gon' check with my ol' granmaw 'bout that red truck. If it turns out a yellar nigguh stole it, shame on your ass, boy. Now git out of my office.

Convict: Yes, suh, yes, suh, boss.

Of course it didn't matter where the inmate was from or what he was doing time for. Before he left the office the captain would have him convinced that he had something personal against him.

CAPTAIN "RED DICK" ROBINSON

Captain William E. Robinson acquired the nickname "Red Dick" because of a favorite game he liked to play on the new inmates assigned to hoe squads. When an officer couldn't get all the work out of a new inmate that he thought him capable of, he would call the captain. The captain would threaten the inmate with dire consequences if he didn't improve, but inevitably, whatever the inmate did was not quite good enough. Eventually, the captain would have to come back to the squad and talk to the inmate: "You just ain't gon' work, are you? You just gon' lag around and eat my groceries and take advantage of me, ain't you? You just get your ass out to that turnrow, and we'll see about this."

Once on the turnrow, the convict would be handcuffed to one of the line or cotton trailers with his back to the workforce. The captain would then dismount and start talking to the handcuffed convict loudly enough for all to hear: "Well, if you ain't gon' work, I need to know, what else are you good for? You gon' have to understand that I just can't allow no nigguh to hog me. That warden won't let me keep my job if I let y'all ride my hoss. Naw suh, if I'm gon' feed you, I'm gon' get somethin' for my trouble." Then the captain would use his pocketknife to cut the inmate's belt so that his pants would fall to his knees. He'd then jerk the poor convict's boxer shorts down so that the whole line force could see him naked from the waist down. The captain would then take out his penis and parade up and down the turnrow behind the bare-assed convict and talk some more. "You know if you ain't gon' work, I might as well make you my woman. At least then folks wouldn't say you was gettin' over on me. I'm plumb ashamed of the way you are treatin' me by not doin' your fair share of the work—people are gon' thank we related or somethin'." By now the convict was usually making all kinds of promises to work harder and to not be such a burden on the captain. I could not find a witness to verify him actually ever having followed through with his threat to have sex with a convict, but he did play this little charade often enough to have the story repeated by numerous witnesses; hence the nickname "Red Dick."

The TDC administration used to give guided tours of the Huntsville (Walls) Unit for 25 cents. A visitor could see the license-plate plant, where the guide would say, "Now here is where we teach the men a useful trade." The officials made sure that the visitors saw only what they wanted them to see: a well-lighted plant, a few spotless cells, and kitchens serving hot food to the convicts. To complete the tour, everybody got the opportunity to sit in the electric chair and hear the guide say, "Now here is where Raymond Hamilton died..."

There were no guided tours being given at the Retrieve Unit or at any of the other farm units. The Walls Unit was the showplace of the system, and as far as most people knew "Huntsville" was where all the state prison–system inmates were housed. At Retrieve, the inmates had to walk as far as two miles just to get to the work site, work all day, then walk the same two miles back.

Once back at the building, if the inmate survived the disciplinary process and wasn't handcuffed to the bars, standing on the "rail" or a "barrel" or shelling four or five gallons of peanuts as punishment, there were still other dangers to consider. Occasionally, the outside picket officers would shoot out a window or shoot at the building, just to remind the inmates that they were still out there. The walls of the inmate tanks were littered with bullet holes, and inmates were hit by "stray" bullets on several occasions. The food in the inmate dining room on most of the units was from time to time inedible. There were weevils in the bread, dirt in the unwashed vegetables, worms in the meat and beans, and the biscuits were described as "too hard to break with your hands, let alone bite into."

Captain Emit "Foots" Franklin

The conditions varied from unit to unit depending on the philosophy of the individual unit warden. A warden who believed in feeding his men had the means to do so. On the other hand, a warden who was not interested in having a healthy, well-fed inmate population allowed his men to suffer and eat poorly, if at all. Warden Zan Harrelson, Retrieve, hired Captain Emit "Foots" Franklin to be his food-service steward in the early fifties, and from that time on the food at Retrieve was known throughout the system as among the best. The inmates called the captain "Foots," but not to his face. Franklin wore a size-thirteen shoe and kind of shuffled his feet when he walked, which gave him the appearance of being on skis.

As hard as he tried not to show it, Franklin cared about the convicts. He made sure that each meal was prepared properly, and the standing rule was that each inmate could have as much food as he wanted, with the exceptions of meat and dessert. There was a small catch to the "take all the food you want" rule, though. Convicts weren't allowed to waste food and had to eat everything they put on their tray. Shame on the poor convict who got caught throwing away food. Captain "Foots" was known for putting his size-thirteen shoe in a wasteful convict's butt while unceremoniously escorting him out to the old solitary building. Captain Foots would then feed him "special seasoned meals" for a few days until the appropriate amount of rehabilitation was achieved.

Warden Harrelson had been a food-service steward during his rise through the ranks, and he knew the importance of having a well-fed inmate population. He taught his philosophy to Captain Franklin and made sure that the inmates had plenty to eat. That is not to say that the food was prepared to gourmet standards. This was plain farm food, with fresh milk that came in daily from the unit's dairy herd. There were fresh vegetables in season, and Captain Franklin did not believe in opening a can if he could get produce out of the field. There were fish and crabs from Oyster Creek, and if a convict caught a rabbit, possum, squirrel, or armadillo and brought it to the kitchen, Captain "Foots" would have it cleaned and served as an "optional entrée."

At the end of a particularly good harvest, Warden Harrelson might, as a reward for their hard work and for making him look good, give the inmates a special meal. This usually consisted of part wild game, deer, raccoon, or fish, or perhaps one of the older bulls or a lame cow would have an accident and have to be destroyed. It was a rare occasion when inmates received a piece of beef large enough to stick a fork into, but at these "reward dinners," each convict in the workforce got a steak with potatoes, vegetables, and home-churned ice cream. It is important to note that only the working inmates got the special meal. Those directly involved in the gathering of the crop, the food-service workers, and the building tenders also received the special meal, but all others were excluded, and for one day, and one day only, the convicts in the line force were in an enviable position.

O. B. ELLIS

Mr. O. B. Ellis became the manager of the Texas Prison System on January 1, 1948. He was responsible for many fiscal improvements in the system's infrastructure. New cellblocks and farm equipment were added, and low-cost employee housing was built so that the employees could live on the units where they worked. This added an additional measure of security to the farm units. Bachelor Officers' Quarters were constructed on all the units for the single officers to live in at no cost to the employee. These "perks" were approved by the Texas Legislature in order to enhance prison security by providing employees with an incentive to live on prison property and as part of the officer's salary, which was intended to attract a better-quality employee.

The average prison guard during Mr. Ellis' tenure had a modest education, and many were illiterate. Most of the employees were sincere, honest men who made every effort to do the best they could with the materials and equipment they had at hand. Small minorities of the officers were brutal sadists who were lower on the evolutionary scale than the criminals they were hired to guard. Many of today's overeducated elite, using the benefit of 20-20 hindsight, have tried to make the case that an absence of highly educated employees contributed to the brutality of the era. Nothing could be further from the truth. A man's education has little to do with his ability to be fair and humane with the inmate population. To say that a person without a formal education is not capable of treating inmates other than brutally does a great disservice to a large segment of the

American populace of the 1940s and 1950s. In my experience, many of the new prep-school employees in today's system come to the job with so many preconceived notions about what they think a prison ought to be that they are largely ineffective.

The degree to which abuse was allowed to occur depended on the individual warden at the unit level. One has to remember that during this time a Texas prison warden was a godlike figure and was the absolute power on his unit. The cliché "Absolute power corrupts absolutely" no doubt applied to some of these wardens. Some units were fair and humane places; others could have just as easily been called hell. On some units there were overcrowded living areas, convict unrest, extensive sexual perversion, brutal guards, and food unfit for human consumption. On the other hand, some of the prison farms could have been called model units, with good living conditions and fair and equitable treatment of their inmate populations. Attempting to judge the entire prison system by looking at one or two units is like trying to judge a brick building by looking at one brick.

DR. "WALKING" GEORGE BETO

The prison system was operating without major interruption when on November 12, 1961, O. B. Ellis died while attending a board meeting. On January 8, 1962, Dr. George J. ("Walking George") Beto was appointed to the new position of director of corrections. Prior to his appointment, the head of the department was titled prison manager. Dr. Beto was instrumental in changing the name of the department from the Texas Prison System to the Texas Department of Corrections. In addition to his duties as director, Dr. Beto was also asked to serve concurrently as chief of chaplains. Dr. Beto received his MA and Ph.D. degrees at the University of Texas, and his doctoral work was done in the area of educational administration. He was nationally recognized as a penologist. In the year before his appointment he had made a study of the major penal institutions of Europe and was a member of the Board of Corrections.

Dr. Beto believed in hands-on management, and he quickly earned the nickname "Walking George" by visiting units unannounced, walking with and talking to inmates and staff. One of the first things he did was to appoint a committee to study the uniformity of punishment and rewards throughout the system. As a result, a revised set of rules governing inmate punishment was implemented in May 1962.

At the Retrieve Unit, some of the old guards worried that their jobs were in jeopardy. For the first time, actual written offense reports would be required prior to the punishment of any inmate. Zan Harrelson was still the warden at Retrieve, and he still had absolute control over the inmates and staff, but there was now a system in place that required some degree of accountability from unit staff. This had never been the case before. Dr. Beto supported his wardens, but he made it clear that there would be consistent application of his policy of fair-but-firm treatment of all inmates. He believed that inmates should work, go to church, attend school, and be afforded the opportunity to participate in rehabilitation programs—in that order. In Dr. Beto's prison, if an inmate refused to work, he forfeited the right to participate in any other program.

Like all new employees, Dr. Beto was tested shortly after becoming director. A group of inmates refused to work at the old Harlem II Unit. He quickly demonstrated that his philosophy of requiring all inmates to work was not some lightly stated, politically correct platitude intended to pacify the conservative working public of Texas. He first attempted to talk to the inmates who had refused to work, to find out if they had a legitimate grievance, but when they refused to answer his questions, Beto did not hesitate to use force in order to compel them to work. He ordered some of the assembled wardens to arm themselves with wet rope, ax handles, hydraulic hoses, eight-plait bullwhips, and so forth, and to use "whatever force necessary to put the inmates to work." The wardens did as instructed, for if they had not, they would no longer have been wardens. The inmates went to work—they had no choice.

The story of the way that first "work buck" was solved spread through the inmate grapevine, and by the next day both employees and inmates knew who George Beto was. When the convicts repeated the story, it went, "That preacher came down here with a baseball bat in one hand and a Bible in the other." Unlike years past, when officer-on-inmate force was often unprovoked or indiscriminate, the message being passed here was clear and direct: Inmates would be required to work to support the prison system. Dr. Beto later said, "I think what we did was right and proper. If we hadn't done it, we would have had bucks or strikes all over the system. As it was, we never had another one until years later on the Eastham Unit, when a generation arose that knew no Joseph. It was settled without force. A show of force, but no use of force." I did not work for the TDC when this incident occurred, but in hindsight, regardless of the philosophy mandated by the federal courts and the hands-off-the-convicts, kinder, gentler requirements of today's system, I know he was right.

I firmly believe that every taxpaying citizen of Texas should be offended that in today's system convicts are allowed to refuse to work with impunity. In today's prison system, inmates cannot be physically compelled to work. We have become too civilized for such crude treatment of our convicts, but that civilization comes at the ever-growing expense of our taxpaying citizens. Texas taxpayers are federally mandated—forced—to pay for the convicts' food, gymnasiums, educational classes, healthcare, dental work, postage, law books, and much more. In many cases, the taxpayers can't afford such things for themselves. Meanwhile, in many parts of Texas, those same taxpayers are reluctant to come out of their houses for fear of the criminal element.

CHAPTER FOUR

RIDING FOR THE BRAND

"If it ain't broke, fix it 'til it is."

—ANONYMOUS

In 1969 the Texas Department of Corrections was widely known as the best prison system in the nation. It did what a prison is supposed to do. It protected the state's law-abiding citizens, and the prison units were relatively safe, clean, and cheap to operate. Texas had one of the lowest recidivism rates in the country. The Texas prison system operated without the intrusive intervention of activist federal judges, the ACLU, or multitudes of California lawyers. It was an era of pay-as-you-go common sense.

The taxpayers of the state had the peculiar notion that their prison system should be, so far as humanly possible, self-supporting, and the prison system reflected the taxpayers' wishes. The vast majority of prison employees remembered who they worked for— and it wasn't the federal courts, the lawyers, the ACLU, or even the politicians. Loyalty was ultimately reserved for the people of Texas. The old field bosses had a name for it. They called it "riding for the brand," a simple philosophy based on the idea that when a man puts on a badge, he does the job he's being paid to do.

The brand was in the shape of the state of Texas, and it was burned onto the rear of every horse and cow the state prison system owned. That Texas-shaped brand represented the taxpaying citizens of the state. It stood for common-cause loyalty, common-sense solutions, and the honor of giving a good day's work for a day's pay in the service of and for the citizens of Texas. Like most other TDC employees of the time, I was proud to ride for the brand.

MY FIRST WORK BUCK

It was the end of May 1969, just before Memorial Day, a traditional holiday for state employees, and the inmates were all looking forward to a lay-in from work. However, the decision was made to work the line force on Memorial Day in order to make up for some of the many work days that had been lost due to an extended rainy season.

There hadn't been any work bucks when Warden Harrelson was in charge, at least not any that didn't result in the use of whatever immediate physical force was necessary to compel the convicts to return to work. The convicts knew Harrelson was not going to negotiate on any level with them, but this new warden had set a bad precedent by negotiating with the convicts, by playing "let's make a deal." The field captain, Sam Lanham (*aka* "Crazy Man"), said that the last time the convicts had "sat down," before I was transferred to Retrieve, Warden Rushing gave them all a special meal to get them to go back to work. The time before that, he had given them an extra day off. This occasion would be different, because the convicts had made a serious error in the timing of their work strike. Warden Rushing, their savior, was gone on vacation.

We turned out at the regular time, and the convicts all came out as usual, got their hoes and loaded on the trailers for the ride to the field. The young corn was about knee-high and was in a fight for survival with the weeds and Johnson grass that were trying to take over. About two hundred convicts turned out that morning, divided into eight squads. When we arrived at the work site and instructed the squads to unload, the first four squads refused to get off the trailers. The last four squads unloaded and went to work as usual. The number-four hoe squad acted as if they didn't know what they wanted to do. At first they got off the trailers, but when they looked up and saw number-one, -two, and -three hoe still sitting on the trailers staring at them, they quickly jumped back on the trailers. We had half of them hoeing corn and the other half sitting on the trailers refusing to work. Captain Sam

Lanham rode up and down the line of trailers trying to talk to the convicts: "What are you doing? Why are you bucking?" He called them by name and instructed them one by one to get off the trailers and go to work. He got no response to his questions or orders. The only response finally came from the lead row in number-one hoe: "We want to see the warden." Major Don Garner, in his late sixties at the time, had driven his Lincoln Continental to the field that day and was sitting about two hundred yards away with his driver's-side door leaning open. He had his foot propped up in the door opening and was listening to the good-time radio. Captain Lanham rode over and told him what the inmates had said. The major didn't get excited, because he had seen this scene played out several times before. He got on the field radio and notified the radio picket, "We need the warden out here."

I sat on my horse next to the captain, and we waited, not saying anything for about ten minutes, until the old white Dodge drove up behind the line trailers. Assistant Warden Bobby Morgan was alone, and after Captain Lanham explained the situation, he slowly walked up and down the line of trailers and tried to talk to the inmates, saying, "Why are you sitting on those trailers? What is your problem?" The only answer Morgan got was, "Why are you asking me? I'm just one in a crowd."

After about five minutes of trying to get a straight answer out of them, with no success, Morgan raised his voice loud enough for everyone to hear: "Well, I'll tell you what I'm going to do. I'm going to go back to that building and get whatever it'll take to unload your asses, and I'll be right back." With that said, Morgan got back in the Dodge and drove off, leaving a large cloud of dust trailing behind as he went. This was not the type of "negotiation" the convicts had anticipated. Just as Morgan's car reached the unit, but before the plume of dust had settled on the turnrow, suddenly, all the bucking convicts decided it was time to go to work. They bailed over the sides of the line trailers, gathered around the tool wagon, and desperately reached in for the hoes they had refused to pick up only moments before. The squad officers directed them toward the cornfield, and within a few minutes they were all at work with the rest of the inmates.

Just in case the inmates thought that Warden Morgan had been bluffing, he did return about twenty minutes later.

Following close behind Morgan was Johnny Kibby, the unit maintenance supervisor, in his pickup with the pipe rack on top. On top of the pipe rack was a belt-fed, .50-caliber machine gun. Captain Lanham and I rode over and told Warden Morgan that all the convicts had gone to work not long after he drove off. Morgan opened the back of the warden's car to reveal a trunk-load of ax handles, grubbing-hoe handles, and heavy-duty hydraulic steel-mesh rubber hoses cut into six-foot lengths. We looked at the implements and took some of them out of the trunk. Warden Morgan advised that we keep them handy and to let him know immediately if the inmates refused to work again. He told Mr. Kibby to stay out there with the .50-caliber for the rest of the day, "just in case." The inmates had learned one thing that morning: Warden Morgan wasn't buying any hogs.

The inmates worked well for the rest of the week, and we heard that word of the way Warden Morgan had handled the work buck had reached Huntsville. The powers that be were not pleased with the almost constant reports of Warden Rushing's lax management style. The following week, Warden Rushing was demoted to assistant warden and transferred to the Diagnostic Unit in Huntsville. Being demoted and transferred on short notice was about the most embarrassing thing that could happen to a warden, short of being fired. All the older bosses at Retrieve were glad to see Rushing go. The simple truth was, Retrieve needed a warden who would let the convicts know who was in control. Even though Warden Rushing's demotion was welcomed, there was real apprehension about the nature of his replacement. Nothing seems to worry TDC employees as much as change.

HAL "HOOKIN' BULL" HUSBANDS

We didn't have long to wait. Rushing hadn't even had a chance to move off the unit when early on a Monday morning the new warden showed up on the back loading dock of the unit's kitchen. Warden Hal H. Husbands (*aka* "Hookin' Bull"), from the Central Unit, had arrived. He called for the field major, captain, and lieutenant to join him on the dock. The field officers were on their horses waiting for the squads to turn out. When the bell rang and the first squad came through the turnout door,

Husbands motioned for the convicts to gather around the loading dock in front of him. When all the squads had come out of the building and gathered around, he said, "I understand that you men like to talk about a work buck." It got real quiet. "Well, I'm here to talk about a buck. My name is Hal Husbands, and I'm your new warden. If you have a problem, you can stand up on your hind legs and tell me what it is. If you do that, I'll give you an answer. It may not be the answer you want, but I promise you I'll give you an answer. If you don't hear anything else I say, understand this: I'm not going to talk to a swinging dick that's sitting on his ass. If you sit down and refuse to work, don't expect me to come and talk to you. These men here (he pointed to the major, captain, and me) have got my standing orders to put your asses to work. Are there any questions?" There were none. His last words to them were, "Go to work."

(It was out of character for Warden Husbands to use even mild profanity. He'd been sent to Retrieve to put the inmates to work, and I think it was his intent to ensure that the inmates took him seriously.)

From that day until the last day that he was on the Retrieve Unit, there was not even a hint of a work buck. Warden Husbands had been sent to Retrieve by Dr. George Beto, with specific instructions to put the inmates to work and to keep them working. He had the full support of the administration and the Board of Corrections. This is a good example of the top-to-bottom cooperation that existed in those days. Every effort was made to ensure that the prison system was doing everything possible to be self-supporting. This philosophy was enforced on all the units during Dr. Beto's era.

Warden Husbands was a graduate of Rice University and had been with the prison system since the days of O. B. Ellis. Although college-educated, he was definitely from the "old school," and he supported Dr. Beto's philosophy 100 percent. He was one of the wardens who helped Dr. Beto put the inmates to work at the old Harlem II Unit shortly after Beto became director. Unlike Warden Harrelson, Warden Husbands didn't allow his staff to use profane or crude language, and it was very important to him that the perception of fairness be maintained.

A REAL MANHUNTER

Sergeant Louis Nichols (*aka* "Buzzard") was the Retrieve Unit dog sergeant, and he was an unimpressive figure. He was around sixty-five years old, stood all of five-foot-eight with his boots on, and weighed about 150 pounds. He had been at Retrieve longer than anyone could remember and was a throwback to another age. Louis was illiterate and didn't think anything that had happened since World War II was "worth a damn." Appearances are sometimes deceiving, though. The world had long ago passed him by, but Louis was, bar none, the most competent, knowledgeable dog man I ever saw or worked with in thirty years in TDCJ.

Not long after I arrived at Retrieve, I was introduced to Louis. He barely spoke and expressed no interest in carrying our new relationship further than a casual handshake. I guess I was skeptical of Sergeant Nichols' ability because of his slight appearance and his age. He just didn't look like I thought an honest-to-God manhunter ought to. He was a scrawny man with a buzzard's neck and a buzzard's beak for a nose. I asked the other old-timers if he was really good at his job. They all said he was the best. He had never lost a convict out of the field, and his dogs were well-regarded by all the law-enforcement agencies. Louis bred his own dogs and trained them with the help of his inmate "dogboys," Ol' Skinny, Butler, and Ragmouth.

Cautiously, I approached Louis Nichols under the pretense of wanting him to be my mentor. I wanted to learn about the profession of manhunting with dogs, and I wanted to learn from the best.

Nichols' bright blue, predatory eyes let the world know he wasn't going to take much agitation from anyone. Louis let me know in no uncertain terms that he didn't want me or anybody else around him when he was working. He was afraid that if he taught what he knew to anyone else, he would be in danger of losing his job. He resisted taking me on a track at first, but Major Lanham intervened and ordered Louis to schedule a once-a-week track for me to observe. The first one was a night track, and I am sure Louis did that on purpose in hopes of discouraging me.

I met Louis at the dog pens at about 8:00 P.M. It was pitch-black dark as we rode a mile or so across the railroad tracks into Bailey's Prairie. The dogboy, Skinny, had been sent on a track about four hours earlier, and now we were supposedly going to use the dogs to go and find him. There was no moon, and although I could feel the brush and weeds on my stirrups, I could not see the ground or anything around me. I could feel my horse under me, and I could see the shadow that was Louis riding beside me. I had to keep reminding myself that he was sixty-five years old. He didn't talk at all, and if I tried to ask any questions he would say, "You can't hear the dogs if you're talking."

He stepped down from his horse and unchained the eight dogs so that they could run free. When he remounted, he began calling the dogs by name and directing them to the left or right by moving his horse toward the area in which he wanted them to search. It wasn't long before they picked up the scent—a howl that let the other dogs know that the track had been found. The other dogs ran to the one that had found the track, and the chase was on.

Louis just sat there for two or three minutes listening to them run and howl. He then put a large plug of Red Man chewing tobacco in his jaw, pulled his hat down tight, and rode in the direction of the howling dogs. Now, I don't mean that he carefully guided his horse after the dogs. He broke that mare into a stretched-out gallop across the prairie that lasted for at least a mile. The only way I could stay anywhere close to him was to position my horse directly behind his and to try to follow his horse. We crossed ditches half-filled with water; we went through fifteen-foot-tall thornbriars and through brush and trees that tested the thickness of my chaps. After a while, he pulled up to listen for the dogs. We could hear them at what sounded to be three or four hundred yards away. He mumbled, "They're headed back toward Dow Reservoir," and he was off again. In my mind, I was forgetting any questions I had entertained about this old man's ability to do this job.

My quarter-horse mare was a little winded from the run across Bailey's Prairie, and I had to prod her hard with the spurs to keep up with the old dog sergeant. Even on this moonless night, Louis knew where every ditch, fence, and tree was. He stopped and dismounted to open a pasture gate and to dig a fresh pack of chewing tobacco out of his saddlebags. As he settled back into his saddle, he looked back at me with mock concern and said, "You gon' be able to keep up, boy?" The old man's expression was set, hard as stone.

I said, "I'll be all right," not believing for a minute that he had any real concern for my welfare. With no further conversation, Louis spurred his horse into the darkness. Once again, I did my best to stay with him.

After crossing several more water-filled ditches, we came to a high levee. In the darkness, I thought it was just another bank of another ditch we were going to cross. We were getting closer to the dogs, and as we rode down the levee I could hear them splash when they entered the water. All of a sudden, Louis pulled up. My horse was in full gallop as I passed him. The last thing I saw, before I went under, was my mare's head disappearing into the black water. There was no bottom to this ditch. I tried to stay in the saddle, but the mare couldn't get her head above water. As I rolled out of the saddle and grabbed for an overhanging limb, the mare's nostrils broke the surface, blowing water. My chaps were soaked, and my boots were filled with water. I held tight to the limb, knowing that the weight of all that soaked leather wouldn't allow me to swim the thirty yards back to the bank.

There I was, about to drown, and I see Louis throwing a rope in the direction of my flailing mare. As I clutched at the limb and hung on for dear life, Louis' rope found the mare's head. He pulled the mare to safety, and once he had her back on dry land, he dismounted and retrieved the rope from around her head. Then he turned his attention toward me.

Louis finally threw the rope in my direction. I grabbed for it, and as he was pulling me back toward the bank I said, "Damn, I'm glad you finally decided to help me out."

In a matter-of-fact tone of voice, Louis said, "A good horse is hard to replace. I can get another field lieutenant anywhere."

At first I was angry, but then I thought, Louis couldn't help being Louis. I had invaded his world without an invitation. He didn't owe me anything. He wasn't being exceptionally cruel in saving the horse first; that act was just a simple indication that Louis had a different set of priorities. In the world of Louis Nichols, a good horse was at least as valuable as a man, especially an inexperienced man who was dumb enough to ride his horse off into Buffalo Bayou with his chaps, boots, and spurs on.

He didn't wait long after dragging me back to the bank to say, "Well, I've still got a convict to find, are you coming?"

I was soaking wet, I'd lost my hat, and my horse was still shaking water off, but I answered, "You're damned right I'm coming."

Thankfully, we didn't have much farther to ride before we came upon Ol' Skinny waiting in a tree. The dogs had found him during my unexpected swimming adventure. The dogs were all howling and trying to climb the tree after him. Louis gave Skinny the signal to jump down from the tree. With a switch in each hand, Skinny fought the dogs as if to try and get away from them. He was very skillful at fighting the dogs, and it was obvious that he had done this many times; he had begun training them as puppies.

This was the part of the chase that the dogs liked the most. They got to catch what they were chasing. In later years, TDC would find out that if you don't let the dogs catch and fight, they soon lose interest in the chase. Skinny fought the dogs for about four or five minutes, and just as the dogs were about to win, Louis popped his eight-plait bullwhip, causing them to immediately stop. Skinny was good at his job, but no one man could fight off a pack of eight bloodhounds and stay on the ground. The dogs don't quit, and they get more aggressive the more their prey tries to fight back.

When Louis popped his whip, the dogs scattered and then gradually regrouped behind his horse. Louis offered no conversation regarding the evening's events. He didn't look stressed or any worse for the wear. It was just business as usual. I had been on tracks with Sergeants Robinson and Sparks at the Clemens Unit, and believe me when I say that they did not have anything on this old man.

Over time, after he figured out I wasn't after his job, Louis actually began to like me some. He told me many stories about the old days that helped give me insight into what it took to survive in the early days of the Retrieve Unit.

Louis had gotten his nickname, "Buzzard," during a multiple-escape attempt in the mid-fifties. The line force had been working on the edge of the Retrieve Unit property line, clearing brush and trees in the fifty-four pasture. Louis was highriding, sitting horseback in the edge of the free-world trees. He had positioned a pack of dogs and a dogboy about seventy-five yards down the fence line. Hidden by the smoke from one of the burning brush piles, three inmates slipped away from their squad officer. Louis said he didn't see the inmates at first, but Ol' Skinny did, and he waved his bandanna until he got Louis' attention.

When Louis saw the fleeing inmates, they were already at the property line trying to crawl through a barbed-wire fence. The three convicts were about ninety yards away, and one was holding the wire while the others went through. Louis yelled, "Halt!" and fired a warning shot, but they began to run. Louis fired twice with his Smith and Wesson revolver, a .38-caliber pistol with a six-inch barrel. The first bullet hit one of the convicts in the back of the head and he fell graveyard dead in the fence line. The second bullet hit another of the inmates square in the back, and he fell in the edge of the woods.

Skinny had the dogs unchained and ready to run by the time Louis got to the fence. As Louis used his wire cutters on the fence, Skinny unchained the dogs. The dogs didn't have to run far before they treed the other convict, who gave up and was brought back alive. In under twenty minutes, Louis had killed one escapee, wounded another and tracked down a third. This all happened in full view of the inmate workforce. Thereafter, the inmates referred to Louis as "that old Buzzard who just sits out there waiting to kill somethin'."

After verifying the story with other officers who witnessed this event, I asked Louis if the ninety-yard shot that hit the convict in the back of the head was luck, or if he hit what he was aiming at.

He said, "It was damn unlucky for the convict. I was just doing my job." Sergeant Louis Nichols may not have been the most formally educated man I've ever met; in fact, he had his dogboys read his mail to him, but he did the job he was hired to do as well or better than any dog sergeants before or since. I grew to have a healthy respect for Louis and the way he went about his business. His favorite phrase when he saw someone do or say something that he didn't agree with was, "He ain't got sense enough to pour piss out of a boot!" I began to notice that on most occasions when he made that observation, he was right.

In January 1973, Warden Husbands accepted a position as

head of the Harris County jail system. Our new warden, Bobby Taylor, was a former schoolteacher who had worked his way through the ranks to senior warden. Bobby Taylor was very likable on a personal level, but he didn't have the people skills or the years of practical experience that Warden Husbands had used so effectively.

Taylor was impulsive and quick-tempered and showed little patience with those who did not readily accept his style of management. No doubt some of the old-time wardens had similar management styles, but they had the experience to make it work for them. Warden Taylor had no such experience, and the older convicts at Retrieve could smell the newness on him. Retrieve's older convicts were just waiting for the appropriate chance to try him, just as they would have tested the mettle of any new employee. We could all see it coming; it was just a question of whether or not he would meet the challenge.

The methods employed so successfully by Dr. Beto at the old Harlem II Unit a decade earlier would now be tested again. This event would ultimately determine the manner in which TDC would conduct future business. As the publicity mounted, prison employees throughout the state held their collective breath and the rest of Texas watched.

THE FATHER'S DAY MASSACRE

It had been raining for weeks, and due to standing water, the machines couldn't get into the fields to harvest sweet corn. There were several hundred acres of sweet corn that were ripe and beginning to harden. When sweet corn gets ripe, there are only a limited few days available to get it to the cannery before the corn is unacceptable to can. The head of the TDC edible crops division, Paul Newton Sr., had surveyed the crop and recommended that the line force be utilized in order to save the loss of the entire sweet corn harvest. Newton, Retrieve Unit Farm Manager Obie Harmon, and Warden Taylor met in the warden's office and discussed the possibility of working the inmates on the first dry day in order to save at least some of the crop. Warden Taylor called the director's office and obtained Mr. Estelle's permission to work the inmates on a weekend if necessary, with the intent of repaying a day off to the convicts who had to work.

On Saturday, June 18, 1973, Father's Day, there was a light rain in the morning, but by noon the sun was out, and the forecast was for clearing skies. The major, the captain, and I went into the building and talked to the inmates. They were advised that although the line force was going to work on Sunday, those who worked would be compensated with time off for the time worked. They were advised that no visits would be cancelled and that church services and A.A. meetings would be held in the evenings. The convicts were generally agreeable to the instructions given, and there was no display of dissension at this time.

On Sunday, the Retrieve Unit inmate workforce was ordered to work. There were 274 inmates scheduled to work that morning. The major and captain took the line force to the field while I went into the building to find out why ten inmates didn't report for work. Walking cell to cell, it took a while to locate them. The reasons they offered for refusing to work varied from, "I don't work on Sundays," to "It's my day off," to "This is a joke, right?" None of the inmates had a valid excuse for not reporting to work.

They had no common reason, and there was evidently no organization behind their refusals. They were of varying races, white, black, Hispanic—even one American Indian/Cajun. Each of these convicted felons, for his own reasons, believed that we, as representatives of the State of Texas, did not have the right to require them to work on a Sunday.

After interviewing each inmate, I returned to the field, where the line force was busy loading four large trailer trucks with sweet corn bound for the Central I Unit Cannery. (The cannery had advised that they could not handle more than four truckloads per day.) I explained the situation regarding the ten inmates' refusal to work to Major Lanham. We continued to gather corn until the four trucks were loaded, and then at approximately 11:00 A.M. we returned the line force to the building for the day. The intent was to turn out again the following morning and load four more trucks. We could load about one truck an hour and still have the inmates back to the building by noon, thereby not creating a hardship on anyone.

When the line turned in at 11:00 A.M. on Sunday, the major and I went to the warden's office to discuss the ten inmates' who refused to work. After a brief discussion, Warden Taylor agreed that we should handle this as a routine matter, as this did not appear to be a planned and organized "work buck." Disciplinary reports were written on each inmate, and the ten convicts were placed in individual pre-hearing detention cells pending their disciplinary review date. They were advised that they would be given the opportunity to turn out for work the following day. According to the building officers who monitored the convict conversation during the night, the inmates, hereafter known as the "Texas Ten," yelled obscenities from their cells on the bottom row of the three-tier-high cellblock to the inmates on the upper rows. They called the other convicts "Uncle Toms" for "gathering that white man's corn." They challenged their manhood by saying, "Anyone who turns out tomorrow ain't got a hair in their ass!" The Hispanic convict called the ones who turned out for work *"putos"* and tried to get others to join them in their refusal to work.

The yelling went on most of the night, but the next morning, all of the line force turned out except for the same "Texas Ten" who had refused the day before. Again their refusal to work was documented in the form of an offense report, and we gathered two loads of sweet corn with the line force. We had turned out late that morning, as the trucks hadn't made it back from the central cannery in time to complete four loads that day. At about 11:00 A.M., we turned in with the intention of going back for the other two loads after lunch.

Warden Taylor called the major, the captain, and me to his office. When we got there, the farm manager was already in the office. Warden Taylor was waiting on a call from the TDC director, James Estelle. While waiting for the call, Warden Taylor expressed the view that we were in danger of having a major incident if we continued to allow the ten convicts to agitate the others into not working. The warden said that the "inmate grapevine," which meant the building tenders, had already indicated that many more inmates intended to join them if some action wasn't taken. There hadn't been a work strike at Retrieve since the days of Eli Rushing, and Warden Taylor didn't intend for one to happen on his watch. He wasn't particularly concerned with the fact that ten convicts had refused to work. The much larger problem was the possibility that the rest of the line force was going to join them. Taylor did not want a confrontational situation involving the entire workforce.

When Mr. Estelle's call came in, the conversation was short. The one-sided phone conversation went, "Well, Boss, what do you think? . . . Yeah, I believe that if we don't do something to put them to work, the rest are going to join them. It's just a matter of time. . . . Okay, I just wanted to make sure you concur. I'll let you know how it turns out."

The phone call was the smartest thing Warden Taylor could have done in that circumstance, because it put the director of TDC in the position of preapproving whatever happened. Any future repercussions would have to begin in the director's office, as a matter of policy; TDC would have to present a united front.

When he hung up the phone, Taylor looked at Major Lanham and said, "Turn out the line and then go down there and give them one more chance to go to work. If they refuse to go to work again, I want you to put them to work using whatever force you have to use to get it done. I want them gathering corn this afternoon." The major turned to me and said, "We'll send Bobby [Captain Crawford] with the line. You go and round up some help—six or eight should be enough."

I went to the back gate and advised Ralph Brister, the livestock supervisor, of what was about to happen. Remembering Warden Morgan's previous example, I advised Brister that I could use some six-foot lengths of hydraulic hose just in case it was needed. I was leaning on the back end of Brister's pickup when I observed a piece of an old oak axhandle about two feet long. He had been using it for his pickup jack handle. I asked him if I could borrow it. He said I could.

Following the line-force turnout, we went back into the building after the Texas Ten. The five officers who accepted this assignment were Victor Huntsman, building lieutenant; Gene Langham, livestock officer; Kerry Bice, building officer; and Obie Harman, the unit farm manager. John L. Nichols, the field-force highrider, was also armed, but he remained mounted on his horse at the back gate. At one point, I observed Warden Taylor standing on the outside yard, as the inmates were coming out, but he was not armed. (When I say "armed," I am referring to axhandles, baseball bats, riot batons, or similar implements. Firearms were never taken inside the compound fence.)

After the line turned out, I walked with Major Lanham to

number-four-wing cellblock, where the "Texas Ten" was housed in individual cells. The only officers who entered the cellblock were the major, Lieutenant Huntsman, and me; the rest of the officers either stayed in the main hall or out on the turnout yard between the main building and the back gate.

The major approached the first cell and called out, "Work time!" A big Hispanic convict in the first cell was sitting there in his shorts. The major calmly told him, "Get dressed—you're going to work!" The convict smiled and just sat there. Major Lanham caught him between the eyes with the riot baton. The convict stood up as if to fight, then lowered his head and came charging out of the cell like an out-of-control bull. The major stepped aside as the convict went by, his own weight carrying him into the windows across from the cells. The big convict weighed around 250 pounds, and as he came off the windows, the major jabbed him in the short ribs with the riot baton, telling him to go on down the hall to work.

I was ahead of him near the cellblock door. There are stairs at the front of the cellblock that lead to the upper cellblock rows. When the big convict got to the stairs, he turned as if to go upstairs. I instructed him to go on down the hall to the turnout door. He took a half-hearted swing at me and continued to go up the stairs. I used the axhandle to hit him on the shinbone. When he bent over to grab his leg, I hit him two or three times about the head and shoulders until he changed direction and started down the hall toward the turnout door. The other officers ensured that he did not change direction before he got to the line trailers.

Major Lanham continued, opening each cell door and repeating the instructions to "Go to work." He found very little resistance. After the first two went out of the cellblock, the rest were dressed and waiting when the major got to their cells. The small (150 pounds) part-Indian, part-Cajun convict in the last cell cussed and raised Cain, but he didn't put up much of a fight. The major dragged him out of his cell by his shirt and shoved him ahead down the hall as we went. At the back gate, I had to hit the little Indian once with the axhandle to keep him from jumping off of the line trailers. We were now outside the compound fence, and if he had jumped off the trailer, John L. might very well have shot him as an escapee.

The trailer ride with John L. and me following on horseback lasted about fifteen minutes. We stopped short of where the rest of the line force was working, but close enough so that they could see that the Texas Ten agitators were working. A few of them needed some encouragement to get off the trailer before they began gathering corn, but after it was explained to them in terms that they could understand, they each got a sack and began to work. The big Hispanic was still in his shorts, but he was gathering corn. The little Indian was still not caught up in the idea of gathering corn, but he, too, was working.

There was one older inmate who was out of shape and out of breath. He wasn't injured; he was just older than the rest and was allowed to walk along behind the others carrying the empty sacks. After about twenty minutes, Warden Taylor drove up and asked how they were doing. I advised him that his instructions to have them gather corn that afternoon had been carried out with a minimum amount of force. I advised him that there were two inmates who would probably need medical attention. The warden then decided to take the older convict and the big Hispanic in his car to the building for medical attention. We worked the other eight until the trucks were loaded and then boarded the trailers to go back to the building. When we arrived back at the building, the major had each of the remaining Texas Ten inmates evaluated for possible injuries and medical attention. All injuries were documented in the medical record.

Just as Dr. Beto had been tested a decade earlier at the old Harlem II Unit, Mr. Estelle and Warden Taylor received their test in the form of the "Texas Ten Father's Day Massacre," as some of our more liberal media pundits labeled the incident. It seems that one of the inmates involved in the incident was an ex-political activist whose family contacted a lawyer, who contacted the media, who contacted local congressional representatives. Unlike Dr. Beto's incident in 1962, which received almost no publicity outside of the system, by the end of the week the "Texas Ten" story was a statewide news headline. The Joint Committee on Prison Reform was calling for public hearings on the matter, and lawsuits were filed. Mr. Estelle and Warden Taylor were under fire to defend both their actions and ours. We had made our point with the convicts, and they were all working, but the question now became; how much support would we get from the board of corrections and the Legislature? Would the people of Texas support us?

Two Trials

I was about to receive an education in the intricacies of the federal judicial process. I spent the next three years going back and forth to federal court in both criminal and civil trials as a defendant. Various inmates' attorneys and the FBI repetitiously interviewed me on numerous occasions. The U.S. Department of Justice attorneys, the Citizens' Committee for Prison Reform, and several lawyers from the Texas Attorney General's office also spent time repeatedly taking our depositions. We were all advised by the attorney general's office not to worry about any self-incrimination issues or attorney–client privilege, because as state employees our statements would be considered "public information." In other words, we were supposed to answer any question put to us, no matter how stupid or irrelevant.

By the time we got to the criminal trial held at the federal courthouse in Houston, the lead attorney for the Department of Justice, Ms. James, had several depositions from each of us. She would lay out the depositions on the table in front of her and begin asking questions. As the depositions told the same story, but were not carbon copies, they varied in wording and response depending on how the questions were asked. She would ask the same questions several different ways in hopes of getting a slightly different answer. If we witnesses did not repeat word for word what was in the deposition, she would jump up and declare that we were either lying now or that we had lied in the deposition.

My advice to any correctional employee who may find him- or herself in a similar situation (accused of a crime, a civil-rights violation, or brutality) is to not make any statements without your attorney present. If you do make a statement, even in the presence of your attorney, require that you receive a written copy for your own records. Don't give interviews or depositions to anyone, not the press, politicians, reform committees, internal affairs, or your mother unless the above conditions are met.

The Joint Legislative Committee on Prison Reform set up in

the Brazoria County Courthouse and began to call witnesses. The committee, chaired by State Rep. Mickey Leland of Houston, Texas, was made of what Senator Walter Mengden Jr. called "The most grotesque collection of radical activists ever put together under one roof." By anyone's description, they were, to say the least, representative of the most liberal-minded minority members of the Texas Legislature.

The reform committee had about a dozen microphones in front of the witness chair, and there were more radio, TV, and press reporters there than members of the general public. The Texas Ten inmates were called to testify first, and then they called any employee who had been implicated by the inmates, to refute whatever allegation they had made. I was the lead story on the six o'clock evening news every day for more than a week.

The reform committee wasn't really looking for answers. As politicians, they were much more interested in getting a favorable sound bite on the evening news. Neither Major Lanham nor I denied using force to put the convicts to work on June 18, 1973. I testified truthfully that this was the first time in my seven-year TDC career that I had used force on an inmate in a mutinous situation. The major and I had acted on direct orders from the Retrieve Unit warden and the director of the Texas Department of Corrections, Mr. James Estelle.

Years later, Steve Martin, a lawyer who had been the general counsel for TDCJ during the infamous *Ruiz* lawsuit, wrote a generally self-serving book that described the demise of the Texas prison system. At the time, Martin had (and may still have) aspirations of becoming the director of the Texas Department of Criminal Justice. His job as general counsel for TDC was to defend the State of Texas, its interests, and its employees. It was on his watch that the State of Texas lost the *Ruiz* case, arguably the single most important prison litigation in American penal history. In his book, Martin cheerfully praises the jailhouse lawyers and applauds the state's complete abdication of control over Texas prisons to a bunch of convicts and the federal courts. He even dedicates his book to one of the inmate attorneys and to the infamous trial court judge, "The Czar of Texas," William Wayne Justice.

In his book he quoted my testimony to the reform committee and published his conclusions about my answers, alleging that I was less than truthful in my responses to the committee's questions. I have been unable to respond publicly until now, due to my ongoing employment with the department. There are others, some long dead and a few still employed by the department, who also haven't been able to respond publicly to some of the absolute drivel that has been published about them. It has never been my wish to bring any discredit upon the TDCJ. As I respond now to Mr. Martin's remarks, which I believe reflect negatively on not only myself, but also on some of my fellow employees, I want to make it clear that I hold no animosity toward any of the TDCJ administrations for whom I've worked. Although Mr. Martin quoted my testimony accurately, his conclusions drawn from what I said couldn't be further from the truth. The excerpts of my testimony to the Joint Committee on Prison Reform are as follows:

Q. If the inmate continued to refuse to go to work, what force would you use to cause him to go to work?

A. That force that was necessary to effect that change.

Q. In other words, if you were to go into a cell to give an order to move—to go to work—and he continued to refuse to go to work.

A. Yes.

Q. Would you continue to hit that inmate if the inmate continued to refuse to go to work?

A. Yes.

Q. At what time would you stop hitting the inmate?

A. When he went to work.

Martin stated in his book that I had "developed a moral order that took precedence over the law." I submit that what we did was not only lawful under the rules that existed at the time, but that what we did was no different than what Dr. George Beto had done a decade earlier at the old Harlem II Unit when the inmates refused to work. Eighteen months after the "Father's Day Massacre," the federal grand jury that heard all the evidence and criminal charges against us agreed that our actions were "lawful" when they voted to "no bill" and chose not to even indict one of the employee participants in the "Texas Ten" incident. I believe in the First Amendment, and I guess Mr. Martin is entitled to his opinion, but one cannot, especially if he is a lawyer and wishes to maintain credibility, judge events that occurred in 1973, after the fact, by present-day William Wayne Justice *"Ruiz"* standards.

After the federal grand jury refused to indict anyone on any criminal charges, we then went to federal civil court charged with the violation of the inmates' civil rights. This hearing was before a judge, not a jury. After a protracted trial, hearing the same evidence used in the first trial, the attorneys agreed to a compromise settlement in the case. We, the defendants, denied all liability for any of the plaintiffs' claims, but said we were settling the case in order to avoid the inconvenience and expense of further litigation. The State of Texas, not the individual employees, would pay a minimum amount of liability. None of the defendants involved in the "Texas Ten" incident ever admitted to any violation of law. None of the Texas Ten defendants pled guilty to anything. As part of the agreement, the judge in the case did make a finding of liability against Warden Bobby Taylor, Major Sam Lanham, and me in the amount of $11,246.00, which was paid to the inmates by the State of Texas. The inmates' attorneys received $17,072.00 in legal fees awarded by the court. As anyone with walking-around sense can readily see, the legal fees were mounting significantly faster than any potential liability claim by the inmates. It seemed prudent of the attorneys representing the State of Texas to settle as long as no one pled guilty to any violation of law.

In addition to accusing me of brutality, Martin also accused me of either using racial epithets or having knowledge of the widespread use of them. He quoted the following excerpt from my testimony to the committee:

Q. Have you at any time used the term "nigger" in referring to a black inmate?

A. No, sir, not only have I not used the term, abusive language is not tolerated within the TDC and is not used by officers therein.

Q. Do you have any knowledge of any of the guards or prison officials using this kind of terminology in relating to prisoners within TDC?

A. I do not have knowledge of that.

In 1973 I had been employed by TDC for seven years and had worked on two units, Clemens and Retrieve. From the first day that I entered the TDC training academy, through the time spent at the Clemens and Retrieve units, every instructor, supervisor, and warden I had worked with had emphasized that the use of profanity or racial epithets was against the rules and would not be tolerated. Men like Assistant Wardens Dick Stricklin and Bobby Morgan, Major Eddie Breen, Captain Otis Reeves, Warden Hal Husbands, Major Sam Lanham, and Captain Bobby Crawford did not allow it. Sure, I'd heard some tales about things that happened before my time, but the TDC had changed a lot before I began my career. I couldn't speak for what happened on other units, either.

Now, I don't personally know this book-writing lawyer, but I understand that he began his career in TDC in the early 1970s, as a building officer at the Ellis Unit, north of Huntsville. I'll give him the benefit of the doubt and say that his frame of reference is different from mine. I don't know anything about the Ellis Unit. I never worked there. For all I know, it could have been the practice on the Ellis Unit in 1970 to use racial epithets and curse convicts on a daily basis. Unfortunately, in the *Ruiz* case, the entire TDC was dismantled due to problems that, if they existed, were not system-wide.

I am here to tell you that racially biased language and abusive language were not allowed on Clemens and Retrieve units at any time while I worked there. I can say, without fear of contradiction, I have never cursed or used a racial epithet directed at any inmate during my entire thirty-year career with TDC. Furthermore, in thirty years of working with convicts, I don't ever recall being cursed by an inmate during a face-to-face confrontation. I have worked with thousands of inmates over the years, and some of them did not like me for whatever reason, but I don't think any of them will say I cursed them or used racial epithets toward them. If they do, they are being less than truthful.

In order to follow this lawyer's reasoning, one would have to believe that I got on the witness stand in front of the world and admitted to hitting convicts with an axhandle and then lied when I denied the use of profane language. His reasoning not only defies logic, but also demeans the many fine officers whom I worked with in the early years. Many of these employees represented the State of Texas well and to the highest standards of the time. Unlike Mr. Martin, who champions the cause of these parasitic jailhouse lawyers, I have a deep and respectful memory of all those officers who possessed a strong work ethic, high moral fiber, and personal loyalty to a common purpose. Yes, some of them did have a modest education, but that in no way detracted from their ability to successfully do the job and to make the TDC of that day "the best in the nation." The vast majority of men who served the State of Texas during the Beto–Estelle era were honorable men. I did not say anything derogatory about them in 1973; I will not do so now.

The single most important factor in our being "no billed" in the criminal-indictment stage of the "Texas Ten" Grand Jury hearing was the fact that Jim Estelle testified on behalf of all the employees involved. He personally supported Warden Taylor's decision to "put the convicts to work." During one of the many days spent at the federal courthouse in Houston, Texas, I had an opportunity to talk to Mr. Estelle one on one. I asked, "What would you have done if the officers in this case had refused to follow the orders to put those convicts to work?"

He said, "I would have fired them."

Then he said, "I have a question for you."

I said, "Okay."

He asked, "If I have to give that order again, will you carry it out?"

I answered, "As long as you are the director, the answer to that question is 'Yes, sir.'"

Jim Estelle was the last director of the TDC who would give an order and then have the authority, personal integrity, and plain old *cojones* to back up what he'd said, no matter what criticism was mounted against him. He demonstrated through his actions over and over again that he was true to his priorities, the protection of the public, the security of the institutions, and the well-being of his employees. He was a man of his word in an era when that meant something. James Estelle clearly earned the respect and loyalty of this employee, and there is no doubt in my mind that the loss of such men from the Texas Department of Criminal Justice has diminished us all.

—CHAPTER FIVE—

A FEW GOOD OLD BOYS

"The enemy is anybody who's going to get you killed,
no matter which side he/she is on."
—JOSEPH HELLER in his novel *Catch 22*

A few months after the "Texas Ten" incident, Warden Taylor's personal problems escalated, but it had little to do with inmates. The Brazoria County Fair, second in size only to the Texas State Fair in Dallas, comes every year during the first week of October. This was the major social event of the year, and the local prison units all participated by putting up a TDC booth, displaying vegetables, and supplying inmate labor to get the fairgrounds ready for the public. The Retrieve Unit had a precision inmate drill team called "The High Rollers," which was allowed to put on shows at the fair pavilion twice daily. This was very popular with the public, and the inmates were allowed to keep the money that was thrown at them during their performance. The money was counted, divided evenly, and placed in their individual accounts in the unit commissary.

Warden Taylor and a personal friend from the Retrieve Unit agricultural staff chose to participate in the charity livestock auction. By the time they got through bidding, they had bought a calf, a couple of pigs, and various other animals. Warden Taylor got caught up in the moment, and under the pretense of obtaining good publicity for the unit, spent more than $2,500.00 of the Retrieve Unit employees' barber fund. The barber-fund money was supposed to be kept in a separate bank account, theoretically controlled by a committee of unit employees. In addition to barber supplies, the employee committee would occasionally approve expenditures for a gift rewarding a retiring employee, flowers for the ill, or perhaps refreshments for a unit employee function. The money was always supposed to be spent "on employees or for employees." Obviously, the purchase of farm animals by the unit warden did not fall within the description of approved expenditures, especially since the barber-fund committee didn't know anything about it.

About a week after the auction, TDC Director James Estelle found out about it from a Retrieve employee who was not at all happy about the way his money was being spent. Mr. Estelle, after verifying the animal-buying fiasco, instructed Warden Taylor to immediately repay the money. He also demoted Bobby Taylor from senior warden to a livestock supervisor and transferred him to one of the northern units. Within a couple of days, TDC had a moving truck in front of the warden's house, and by the end of the week Bobby Taylor was gone. So ended 1973. I had been with TDC for a little more than seven years, and I was about to work for my fifth warden.

SUNDOWN SLIM SAVAGE

Our new warden, Oscar Savage, (*aka* "Sundown Slim") was a longtime TDC veteran who had worked his way through the ranks. He had been a field major at the Ellis Unit, which like Retrieve was classified as a multirecidivist unit. His reputation was that of a "convict warden," which I hoped was accurate. The last thing the Retrieve Unit needed was an academically arrogant experimenter. The Retrieve Unit needed stability during this time of prison-reformer activism. We got it from Warden Savage.

Savage was plainspoken, and he meant what he said. He didn't go out of his way to harass convicts over small matters, and he let the building tenders know where the line was. Warden Savage walked and talked with the convicts, and everybody had a clear understanding of what "the law" was. No one doubted the fact that he was in charge. Savage always seemed to know how to adjust a convict's attitude just enough to obtain the appropriate amount of respect, yet still leave him with his dignity and his will to survive.

In many ways, Warden Savage was cast into the eye of the

storm after Warden Taylor's departure. The news media, the Prison Reform Committee, and the inmates' attorneys besieged the unit, sometimes without notice. Savage handled it well. He would sometimes make them wait at the highway gate for hours when they showed up without prior notice. This always resulted in the standard threats: "You don't know who you're dealing with!" "This is discriminatory!" and my personal favorite— "We're going to get your job for this."

James Estelle still had a lot of support in the Legislature, mainly because politicians in those days were a lot like they are today. They made a lot of noise around election time, but they really didn't want to get involved in the hands-on, day-to-day operations of the prison system. When the "Recommendations Report" from the Joint Committee on Prison Reform reached the floor of the State Senate, Senator Walter Mengden succeeded in having many of their proposed reform measures rejected. On a recommendation by the committee to "Ban discrimination within the prison system because of political beliefs," Senator Mengden stated: "For political beliefs don't read Republican or Democrat, read Communist, Black Panther, Symbionese Liberation Army and other subversive philosophies whose objectives are to destroy our society. I think it extremely important that such radicals be identified and kept under close scrutiny." The proposal by the committee that "all inmates receive a reasonable wage for their labor while in prison" was also defeated. The senator referred to the Reform Committee's proposals by saying, "If fully implemented [the recommendations] would cause the greatest crime wave in the history of the world because every person would have a tremendous incentive to want to go to prison in order that he could enjoy all the benefits in it." This was not an isolated view at the time. It seemed that neither the politicians nor the people of Texas were yet ready for radical prison reform.

When the prison-reform group failed in their legislative attempt to liberalize the TDC, they began to look for a new champion. They found him in the radical, politically activist judge named William Wayne Justice. Justice had been a boyhood friend of liberal U.S. Senator Ralph Yarborough, who lobbied his friend President Lyndon Baines Johnson to appoint Justice to the federal bench. This was one of Johnson's last appointments, and his name has been taken in vain by his fellow Texans on numerous occasions because of it.

On one occasion, ten thousand of Justice's own hometown residents signed petitions calling for his impeachment. Judge Justice had accepted a lawsuit filed by jailhouse lawyer David Ruiz claiming that the TDC was a less-than-"constitutional" prison system. The *Ruiz* case was filed, by design, in the most liberal federal court district in Texas. One of the many bumper stickers popular at the time read, "Will Rogers never met Judge Justice."

We at the unit level were largely unaffected by all this talk about pending litigation by a bunch of whining convicts. As anyone who has ever worked around a prison will tell you, it is not uncommon to be threatened with a lawsuit several times a day, especially if you do your job by the book and enforce the rules.

Oscar Savage, the Retrieve Unit warden 1973–75, was replaced by Edward Turner (*aka* "The Arm") as warden, 1975–77. Warden Turner's nickname derived from the fact that he was a weightlifter whose forearms measured fourteen to sixteen inches around.

Savage and Turner were similar in their management styles, and the unit ran as smooth as glass during their administrations. Warden Turner, like Savage, had come up through the ranks and clearly had the people skills to promote loyalty and respect within his staff and compliance from the convicts.

It took several months for the media frenzy over the Texas Ten fiasco to subside. The members of the Joint Committee on Prison Reform all became mildly famous for a brief period, but most Texans recognized their agenda for what it was. The inmate attorneys who had been coming to the unit on almost a daily basis began to come less frequently when the media lost interest. I found out something about lawyers that I've never forgotten. It seems they are much less willing to do *pro bono* work when the cameras are absent and there are no reporters waiting at the press conference.

THE OLDEST FIELD BOSS

Frank E. Loftin was nearing seventy and had forty-four years in TDC service when he finally retired. He was born and raised on prison farms. Frank's father had been a farm manager at the Central Unit around the turn of the century, and he had later managed several other farms. Although Frank never rose above the rank of field officer, he had worked on every unit in the southern end of the prison system, including some that don't exist anymore. He worked at the Old Imperial Farm at Sugarland, Texas, the Blueridge Farm just south of Houston, and at the Darrington, Clemens, Ramsey, and Retrieve units.

Frank had gone through so many changes in his forty-four years that a new twenty-three-year-old lieutenant wasn't going to change his way of doing business. On the first day that I observed Frank carry his squad, I was mortified to see him ride his horse into the middle of his squad while wearing his pistol. As he corrected an inmate who had missed some weeds on his row, there were inmates carrying sharpened hoes all around him, within five or ten feet. I pointed out to Major Lanham what I perceived to be a severe breach of security and asked if this was the way Frank always carried his squad. The major didn't respond, so I persisted with, "I was taught at Clemens that a field officer should never turn his back on a squad or let an inmate within fifteen feet of him while he's carrying a weapon." The major seemed aggravated at my observation, but nevertheless he yelled, "Frank, come over here."

Frank rode over, and the major ordered him in a stern voice, "Hand me your pistol."

After spitting chewing tobacco all over the neck of his horse, Frank said, "Yes, sir, Major," and handed Lanham the pistol.

Without looking at the weapon, Major Lanham handed the weapon to me with the instruction, "Inspect this."

I could tell immediately that the pistol was old, very, very old. It was a single-action .44-caliber Colt, known as a "thumbbuster." With some difficulty, I opened the rust-encrusted cylinder and observed that the lead in the bullets had turned green from age and exposure to the weather. Each bullet was frozen in place, each in its own rust-covered tomb. I looked down the barrel, but couldn't see daylight because the barrel was blocked with rust. When I tried to cock the hammer, it would only go about halfway back. The pistol was obviously not capable of firing. If, by some accident, the pistol did fire, the shooter would have probably been killed from the explosion, rather than it harming anyone else.

I was confused as to why anyone would carry such an antiquated weapon and asked Frank, "How old is this pistol?" Frank smiled proudly and said, "I am the third generation of Loftins to carry it. My dad gave it to me somewhere around 1920. He got it from his father sometime after that unpleasantness between the states. I don't really know how old it is."

As I handed the antique pistol back to Frank, the major said, "Thanks, Frank, you can go on back to your squad now." After he rode off, the major asked, "Well, Lieutenant, are you still worried about some convict taking Frank's pistol away from him?"

"I guess not," I said. The major went on to say that Frank's eyesight wasn't what it used to be, and he felt safer when Frank didn't have a "real weapon."

If TDC could only be so fortunate as to find some future employees with the dedication, work ethic, and loyalty of Frank Loftin, the department would be well-served. Whatever deficiencies in education or eyesight Frank may have had, they were clearly eclipsed by his other qualities. I have no doubt that any supervisor I ever worked with, given a choice, would choose an employee with Frank's qualities over some of the pseudoeducated, lazy, substance-impaired, litigation-seeking employees coming out of the pre-service training programs these days.

DEATH IN THE AFTERNOON

The two old field bosses couldn't remember for sure, but finally agreed that the chase happened in the winter of 1951 or '52. Frank Loftin and John L. Nichols both participated in the chase, but they didn't brag as they told the story. It was like they wanted the facts to be told, but it wasn't something they were proud of.

It began when two black convicts knocked an officer named Williams off of his horse and beat him to death with their hoes. It wasn't at all unusual for an officer to be sent off alone with a squad. This was a time before handheld field radios or the later common practice of using highriders. Staff allocations didn't allow for such luxuries. Officer Williams was all alone when he was killed. The two convicts stripped the officer of a shotgun, a pistol, and extra ammunition and ran toward the southwest, across the railroad tracks onto Bailey's Prairie. Louis Nichols said they probably hoped to catch a ride on one of the passing trains. The other inmates in the squad just sat down on the turnrow and waited for someone to come by. An hour passed before one of the roving farm trucks came by to see why the squad hadn't come in for lunch.

Louis was called immediately, and within twenty minutes he was dragging with his dogs in the area where the officer had been killed. After picking up the scent, Louis tracked the escapees all afternoon. Bailey's Prairie was only partially cleared in those days, and it took some time for Louis to work his dogs through the brush and find the armed convicts. The other officers stayed out of his way and watched from a high point on the railroad track. When the convicts heard the dogs coming closer, they ran away from the railroad tracks and hid in a large brush pile about a mile out onto Bailey's Prairie.

Louis offered them a chance to give up, but he figured rightly that since they had already killed an officer, there would be no surrender. They were afraid to give up, fearing, with some justification, that they might not survive capture. They had gone too far to give up now. As the dogs closed in on their hiding place, the escapees used the shotgun to kill one of the dogs. Louis was careful to stay back out of range while using his eight-plait whip to pop the rest of the dogs off the track. Louis fired his pistol at the brush pile a couple of times, just to keep them pinned down. There was no real hurry; Louis knew they had no place to go.

It was almost dark when the other officers finally got there and began to work their way around the brush pile. Louis gathered up his dogs and began the ride back toward the unit. He didn't want to be a part of what was going to happen next. He said he could hear the gunfire in the distance as he rode back in. The gunfire lasted until after dark, when the convicts were down to their last few shells. One of the officers threw a torch into the brush pile, setting the dry brush on fire. As the fire got closer, one of the convicts came out shooting the officer's stolen pistol and was killed in a hail of bullets. When the fire got too hot and too close for the other escapee, he put the shotgun in his mouth and pulled the trigger. The officers had to wait for the fire to burn down before they could locate his body.

Today at Retrieve, there is a major turnrow that was named for the officer who was killed during that escape. The "Williams Turnrow" begins at the electrical power plant near the sight of the original unit and ends at the Retrieve Unit property line on the Dow Reservoir Bridge on Buffalo Camp Bayou.

Louis didn't like to talk about the fact that there had been at least three convicts (and probably several more) brought back from his chases dead. I'm sure that today's liberal pundits would say that Louis was an "inhumane dinosaur" and crucify him for his longstanding record of deadly apprehensions. Louis was not inhumane; he just did his job very efficiently in a time when political correctness was less important than getting the job done. Like Frank Loftin, after he retired, Louis lived less than a year.

THE HIGHRIDER

The highrider John L. Nichols had been at Retrieve since the late 1940s and had even been a field sergeant in earlier days. John L. was illiterate and crude-talking, and the warden had long since decided that for the safety of all concerned, John L. shouldn't come into close contact with inmates. John L. had emphysema and was prone to coughing spells that had on occasion cleared the entire officers' dining room, but that didn't keep him from chain-smoking Bull Durham cigarettes. When he was feeling frisky, John L. would even have a chaw of old *Brown Mule* chewing tobacco.

He drove a twenty-five-year-old, rusted-out pickup truck and carried ten or twelve homemade dog cages around in the back of it. John L. liked to stop on the side of the road and pick up stray dogs. He would then try to sell them as "Prime Hunting Dogs." He lived in an old wood-frame house on the outskirts of Angleton, and the house was not hard to identify. The whole front yard was full of old washers, dryers, stoves, broken-down cars, worn-out furniture, and other "antiques," as John L. liked to call them. The house had no electricity, air-conditioning, or other modern conveniences, as John L. believed them to be a waste of money. He was fond of saying, "A poor man has got poor ways." There were always a dozen or so dogs of dubious pedigree in and around John L.'s house. Once, one of his dogs had a litter of puppies under his living-room couch. John L. didn't even know the pups were there for almost three weeks, when they finally opened their eyes and started moving around.

John L. often bragged about his prowess with his .30-30 Winchester highrider rifle. He sounded like a coldblooded gunslinger when he promised that he could and would hit a "gnat's ass" at 200 yards. Well, as fate would have it, shortly after Warden Savage arrived in 1973, there was an unusually bold escape attempt out of the main-line workforce. The line and garden workforces were working together hoeing knee-high cotton in the East Field. It was probably three-quarters of a mile across open pasture to the nearest free-world property line and the relative cover of the free-world woods. Between the cotton field and pastureland, there were 400 yards of bright green rye grass growing about two inches high.

A young white convict named Dennis slipped away from the number-one hoe squad by crawling through the knee-high cotton to the end of his row. The squad officer, John Bennett, didn't see him right away, and when he finally did spot him, there were too many convicts between them for the officer to use his pistol. I saw the officer waving his pistol in the air and caught sight of the convict just as he stood up and began to run. Everybody saw him except for our less-than-observant highrider, John L. Nichols.

I rode to the top of the levee that separated the cotton field from the rye-grass pasture and fired a warning shot. The convict was only about twenty-five to thirty yards away when I fired, and it would have been easy to hit him, but he still had a long way to go to get to freedom. When John L. heard my warning shot, he was getting a drink of water from one of the inmate waterboys. John L. had the drinking cup in his hand when my pistol went off. He spilled water all over his horse, the waterboy, and himself as he yelled at the waterboy, "Get out of my way!" He tried to dismount and at the same time draw his Winchester .30-30 out of its scabbard. John L. got tangled up in one of his many raincoats on his way out of the saddle, and the only thing that kept him from landing in the barbed-wire fence was the convict waterboy. The waterboy, desperately trying to separate himself from John L., finally succeeded, got up, and headed back toward the water wagon.

John L. finally regained his balance, got his rifle, and leveled it at the running convict. It was a perfect, once-in-a-lifetime opportunity. John L. had a corner fence post to rest his rifle on; it was broad daylight, and in his white cotton clothing, the running convict looked like a rolling cue ball on a large green-felt pool table. John L. took careful aim, and at a distance of about sixty-five yards he fired. The inmate kept on running. John L. took aim again, and at a distance of about eighty-five yards, fired again. The inmate kept on running. That made two missed shots inside of 100 yards under what can only be described as ideal conditions. The convict was still running wide open as John L. leaned down for his third shot. Now he took his time and really concentrated on his target. The convict was running at a distance of about 120 yards. John L. fired—nothing. The convict never even ducked or slowed down. That made four shots, counting my warning shot, and the convict was still running like an Olympic sprinter.

There were two pasture gates about 250 yards apart. Major Lanham went through one gate, and I went through the other. I was riding a young, three-year-old, half-breed, Tennessee walker/Quarter horse mix named Deadman, and he wasn't happy about all this gunfire. His ears were up, and just as I flipped the latch open on the pasture gate, Deadman jumped through at a dead run and I had to grab the saddlehorn to stay mounted. The major and I had the angle on the running convict, and he was still a half-mile from the free-world woods.

Deadman was much faster than the major's horse, and I closed on the convict forty yards ahead of him. As we got closer, I tried to pull Deadman up, but the little horse was going way too fast to stop. It was all I could do to avoid running over the convict, but I did manage to catch him with my stirrup as we went by, causing him to tumble headfirst into the ground. About twenty-five yards later, I finally got Deadman turned around. The convict was lying on his belly looking up at me. I ordered him to get up and walk back toward the high levee turnrow. When we reached the turnrow, Warden Savage was waiting in the warden's car. He had been listening to the chase on his car radio. He told the convict to get on the hood and to "hold on." We watched them drive the turnrows for about thirty minutes before the warden decided to take him back to the building.

In hindsight, I really don't think that even John L. was that bad a shot. Although he would never admit to it, I always thought that he purposefully missed hitting that convict, giving him a break that day. The really embarrassing thing about it was, he had put on his non-shooting exhibition in front of the entire inmate workforce. His reputation as a killer highrider was gone forever.

One thing that is undeniable about these old-timers, they were not sophisticated men. The majority of the ones I knew were plain, soft-spoken men of modest education. This is not to imply that they were stupid. John L. Nichols was probably the most ill-mannered, crude, and generally obnoxious of all the older officers I worked with, but he was not stupid. He used his self-admitted deficiencies to gain an advantage over those who would underestimate his ability to adapt. Men such as John L. Nichols, Louis Nichols, and Frank Loftin were very resourceful and comfortable in their own environment. In my experience, based on the men I knew and worked with, as a group they were no more or less ethically or morally corrupt than today's modern correctional staff. Of course, defending them is difficult because most of them are dead and have a hard time speaking for them selves.

WILLIE NELSON

In 1976 Willie Nelson visited the Retrieve Unit. His ex-drummer, Sam Coleman, was doing a little time for some misunderstanding with the authorities and had been sent to the Retrieve Unit. Sam wrote Willie a letter and asked him if he would bring his band by the unit the next time he was playing in the area. Willie said he would, if the warden would grant permission for a concert for the entire inmate population. I went with Sam to see Warden Turner about the request. At first Warden Turner thought it was a joke, but Sam showed him Willie's letter. Warden Turner looked at me and said, "What do you think, Glenn?"

I said, "I don't see why we couldn't set up a couple of flatbed cotton trailers and run some extension cords out of the BOQ for electricity. The convicts would have to sit on the ground, but I don't see a problem with it."

The warden told Sam to write Willie back and tell him the warden approved, but needed at least two weeks' notice. The visit was scheduled for a Saturday afternoon in early October when Willie was scheduled to play at the Brazoria County Fairgrounds. Two big "Silver Eagle" tour buses pulled up at the back gate, and Willie got out asking if he was in the right place. The warden took Willie and his band into the ODR for something to eat while a couple of Willie's equipment people and a few building tenders set up the instruments. This wasn't the first time Willie had stood in front of a bunch of convicts on a cotton trailer. He had been performing at the Huntsville Rodeo, "The Wildest Show on Earth," for years.

We announced a concert by Willie Nelson to the inmate population, and although many of them had never heard of him, they all came to the yard to see what was going on. It was sort of like being at Willie's Fourth of July Picnic, except everybody was drinking red Kool-Aid instead of beer. The first thing Willie did was get Sam Coleman onstage to play drums with the band. Sam gained a lot of respect that day from those who thought his stories of traveling the highway with Willie Nelson were just so much convict talk. Willie talked to the convicts between songs, and before long even the black inmates were clapping and singing along. The group played for about an hour and a half, then signed autographs for everyone who wanted one.

I don't want to pretend that I understand what makes a guy like Willie Nelson tick, but there is one thing I can tell you about the man from observing him up close that day. He enjoyed being with those convicts as much as they enjoyed being with him. They knew he didn't have to be there. He wasn't getting paid, and he didn't ask for anything special. He was there partly for his friend Sam Coleman, but I got the feeling that he would have played regardless of where the invitation came from. The convicts talked about that concert for months afterward. It was like everyone who had attended was part of a special club.

A TRUE NIGHTMARE

The director, Jim Estelle, was speaking to the San Antonio Rotary Club on July 24, 1974, when at 1:30 P.M. he was interrupted and called to the phone. He returned to the luncheon meeting in a hurry and apologized with the comment that he would have to leave because an emergency was calling him back to the main TDC unit in Huntsville.

All Mr. Estelle knew was that an inmate named Fred Gomez Carrasco had somehow smuggled guns into the Walls Unit prison and now held several employees and some inmates hostage. What was to become the longest attempted escape in American penal history had begun. By the time Jim Estelle drove the three hours from San Antonio to Huntsville, his worst fears had become a reality. Three inmates, Fred Gomez Carrasco, Rudolfo Dominguez, and Ignacio Cuevas had guns, ammunition, and sixteen hostages. They were holding the hostages in a fortress-like, two-story brick library building in the center of the Walls Unit complex. At the time, this was one of the few areas in the TDC where female employees were allowed to work in direct contact with convicts. Most of the hostages were female prison schoolteachers and librarians.

The siege ended after eleven days of tense negotiation between the convicts and prison officials. Finally, with twelve hostages surrounding a "Trojan Horse," a homemade box containing the three convicts and three hostages, they attempted to reach an armored car that had been parked on the main yard. A team of thirteen officers, including two Texas Rangers, Captain G. W. Burks, Captain John F. "Pete" Rogers, and FBI Agent Bob Wyatt led the assault on the Trojan Horse. As the convicts attempted to come down the library's second-floor ramp in their makeshift box with the hostages, the assault team hit them with high-pressure water hoses, knocking the Trojan Horse over. A TDC officer ran in and cut the rope that held the outer ring of hostages, and the officers yelled for the convicts to surrender. The only response from behind the shield was gunfire, approximately eleven shots. The lawmen returned fire for less than a minute with thirty or forty shots. The shattered wooden box that had once shielded those inside now rolled down the ramp in front of the library, leaving the convicts and handcuffed hostages exposed. About ten minutes later, some ten more shots were fired. "It was Cuevas firing his pistol and our officers returning fire," prison spokesman Ron Taylor said. Amazingly, convict

Ignacio Cuevas was captured without sustaining any wound. Cuevas shot Father Joseph O'Brien once in the back, wounding him critically.

Carrasco and Dominguez shot the two women hostages to death. Dominguez shot Mrs. Julia Standley four times, killing her at point-blank range. Carrasco killed Mrs. Elizabeth Beseda with a shot to the chest. All the inmates were firing hollow-point bullets. Carrasco and Dominguez were killed sometime during the exchange of gunfire. The Walker County justice of the peace, J. W. Beeler, issued a ruling of murder-suicide in the aftermath of the shootout. "The two women were shot to death by the two inmates," Beeler said. He ruled suicide in the deaths of convicts Fred Gomez Carrasco and Rudolfo Dominguez, but did not say that they turned guns on themselves. He said he considered their deaths suicides because they "chose to go ahead and fall into this volley of fire" from the officers' guns. Cuevas, the inmate who survived, was tried, convicted of capital murder, and sentenced to death. Years later, after three trials and seventeen years of appeals Cuevas' execution date approached. I couldn't help thinking that it was a shame that those Texas Rangers couldn't have saved the taxpayers of Texas all that time, trouble, and trial expense years ago on that ramp in front of the prison library.

Immediately after the incident, the vice-chairman of the Joint Legislative Committee on Prison Reform, Mickey Leland, was very critical of the way law enforcement handled this event and announced that the committee intended "to investigate to make sure that the convicts' civil rights had not been violated." This announcement by the minority state representative from Houston was immediately and profoundly offensive to the rank-and-file employees of the TDC. His misplaced loyalty to some killer convicts at a time when the TDC family had just lost two of its own was unforgivable. The House Administration Committee, which controls the money for such inquiries, told Leland to "keep out of the Huntsville shootout investigation." Leland was also told to appear before the House Administration to "explain some of his recent statements." Leland accused Lieutenant Governor Bill Hobby of "delaying, harassing and interfering with the Prison Reform Committee." The House Administration stated that if Leland refused to appear before them, they would cut off all money to the reform group. It seemed many of the ranking members of the Legislature had come to believe that the Prison Reform Committee had served its purpose. It became increasingly clear that the house members were now weary of the reform committee's attempts to run the prison system.

As he sat in his office on the Sunday after the siege ended, Jim Estelle looked worn and frazzled, but he tried to answer questions from the television reporters and other news media gathered around him. He reviewed the events of the past twelve days and talked about the future. "For years we have been trying to obtain a budget that would allow the Board of Corrections to compensate employees for the dangers they are exposed to every day. Next January we will go to the Legislature with a budget proposal that will hopefully get officers out of a salary bracket where they must supplement the necessities of life with the use of food stamps. There will be some operational changes at the prison unit, but it is too early to determine what they will include. Certainly some remodeling of the prison library will take place."

Then an interviewer struck a sensitive note. Estelle was asked, "What about the presence of women in the system exposed to the dangers which left two of them dead Saturday night?"

Estelle stared down at his office floor, sniffed back a tear, and said, "I just can't handle that one right now."

CHAPTER SIX

ESCAPES, POLITICS, AND GANGS

"Packs are composed mostly of cowards who are frightened of being ostracized themselves—people who are neither fascinating nor original. I wouldn't want to belong to any club that would accept me as a member."

—GROUCHO MARX

In late September 1976, three young white convicts escaped from the Clemens Unit. They were all state-approved outside trusties and had been planning their move for months. Two of them were assigned to the tractor shop as mechanics, and the third was a dump truck driver. The mechanics had been assigned to a job of fixing an antiquated dump truck, which they had been working on for weeks. After considerable difficulty, they got the old truck running and convinced the tractor-shop supervisor to allow them to take it on a test drive, delivering some parts to a stalled tractor at the back of the unit. According to their plan, they would use the truck to block a small bridge on County Road 400 to stop a free-world car for further use in their escape. County Road 400 runs through the very back of the Clemens Unit, parallel to the Brazos River.

In late afternoon, as Mrs. Washington drove home from work along County Road 400, her car was the first one to approach the narrow bridge. She was a young married woman, driving along minding her own business. By the time she saw the big truck pull across the road in front of her, it was too late to stop. She tried to drive around the truck. This wasn't in the convicts' plan, and in order to stop her they had to use the truck to push her car into a roadside ditch. The convicts tried to use the dump truck to pull the car out of the ditch, but ended up getting the dump truck stuck also. Their plan was quickly going to hell.

They were all on foot. Mrs. Washington, now a hostage, had injured her ankle in the collision with the truck. It was starting to get dark, and the convicts had to move fast in order to avoid the dogs they knew would be coming. Paranoia began to set in, and they figured County Road 400 was probably blocked at both ends already. They would have to swim the Brazos River—it was their only hope of evading the dogs. The convicts were young strong swimmers, but their hostage wasn't. The Brazos is a swift, dangerous, and unforgiving river, and more than one convict has drowned after making a hasty decision to try to cross it. Once in the river there is no choice but to swim, swim or die.

It took all the strength the three convicts had to get Mrs. Washington across to the other side. They lost their shoes and most of their clothing in the river. When they got to the other side, they found the woods between the Brazos and FM 332 to be one of the most mosquito- and snake-infested swamps this side of Louisiana.

By the time the four of them climbed breathlessly out onto the riverbank and into the woods, they could hear the dogs from the Clemens Unit. Sergeant Nelson Sparks and Field Major Dickie Stricklin (the son of Assistant Warden G. H. Stricklin) were riding behind the dogs trying to pick up scent from the area around the stuck dump truck. It didn't take long for the dogs to run the track to the bank of the Brazos River.

Darkness was closing in as all the southern regional units responded to Clemens' call for assistance in capturing their escapees. The hostage, Mrs. Washington, was living in her own personal nightmare as she was being pushed, shoved, and dragged through the dense woods by desperate convicts trying to stay ahead of the dogs. The Retrieve Unit was the first unit to arrive in response to Clemens' call. We arrived with officers, farm trucks, horses, and dogs. As we neared the Brazos River sandpit on FM 332, we could hear the Clemens dogs howling in the woods. We could tell that the dogs were running something by the way they howled, but we couldn't see them.

We spread our officers out on FM 332 about thirty yards

apart. There were several private free-world residences located across FM 332, and one of our immediate goals was to keep the convicts from crossing the road. The sheriff's department had boats in the river, and the DPS had one of their bubble-cockpit helicopters flying at treetop level, shining a huge spotlight down into the trees. The Darrington, Ramsey I and II, and Central units also sent officers and dogs, and within an hour of receiving Clemens' request for help, they began to arrive. We had about six square miles of wooded swamp blocked off on all four sides. The Clemens Unit dogs were getting louder now, and at one point we could hear Sergeant Sparks' voice saying, "Could be running a deer!" He could have been right; sometimes when dogs run real hot and fast, it's an indication that they're running a fresh animal track, but in this case he was mistaken. They were running convicts, and they were steadily gaining on their prey.

Between the dogs and the line of officers, the convicts were in a bind. When the convicts, with their hostage, stumbled through the brush to the edge of FM 332, they watched the officers out on the road. There was no way to get across the road without getting killed or captured. On the other hand, if they didn't do something quick, the dogs, which were closing in fast, were going to catch them on the ground.

They made their decision. The hostage was threatened and forced to run out onto FM 332. As she did so, the convicts climbed trees and watched, hoping the dogs would follow the scent of the hostage. As she stumbled out onto the road yelling, "Don't shoot! Don't shoot!", the dogs came out of the woods behind her. Luckily, the officers got to her ahead of the dogs, which no doubt kept the already injured woman from being bitten. A sheriff's deputy put her in his patrol car for a quick trip to the local hospital. The hard part was over; we had gotten our hostage back with only minor injuries. The convicts had gone back into the woods and climbed trees.

About 9:00 P.M., an early-season cold front blew in, dropping temperatures from the high 60s to the upper 30s. We quickly received a two-inch rain, followed by a twenty-five-mile-an-hour wind, all within about thirty minutes. This turn of events was a definite advantage for the convicts. Wherever there had been a trail before, it would be gone now. As long as the convicts didn't move, we wouldn't be able to track them in the woods. It became a waiting game. They had nothing except time on their side. If we got tired or if they could hold out until our resources became too expensive to maintain, then they had a chance. We set up our perimeter, and the dogs began dragging for scent every half-hour. We did this for three straight days and nights while Warden Turner ran back and forth to the unit for supplies. We ate cold sandwiches and slept in the backs of pickups, in horse trailer, or in the saddle. Whatever hardships we had to endure, the convicts had to endure, except they had no food, water, or extra clothing. The convicts would have to have some hard bark on them to win this battle.

The ex-hostage, Mrs. Washington, told us about the trip across the river and the fact that the only remaining clothes the convicts had were their shorts and that they didn't have shoes. During one of our perimeter drags, we found a shirt belonging to one of the convicts hanging from a tree, but they had moved on. It was about 35 degrees, and the more I thought about them swimming that cold river, the less likely I thought it was that anyone, even a desperate convict, would do it again.

We had some of the most experienced dog sergeants and the very best dogs in the system on this chase. Sergeants Jim Taylor, Central Unit; Johnny Mansker, Retrieve Unit; Homer Heron, Darrington Unit; and Nelson Sparks, Clemens Unit were all experienced men with well-trained dogs. We had to keep dragging, searching, trying to do the things that would make the escapees move so we could get a starting point for the dogs. Toward the end of the third day, driven out by hunger and thirst, one of them came to a break in the trees to see if the officers were still on FM 332. A Retrieve Unit officer assigned to the area didn't see the convict, but he heard him making noise in the woods. The closest pack of dogs belonged to the Darrington Unit, and Sergeant Homer Heron. The sergeant and his assistant unloaded their dogs, took off the neck chains, and began dragging in the area where the officer said he had heard the sounds. Many times these "tips" come from overanxious officers who hear or see "buggers"—things that don't exist. Every dog sergeant hates these wild bugger hunts. It's usually a waste of time and precious energy, but at the same time the information can't be ignored, because one never knows when it might be real.

In this case, the tip was right on. Homer's dogs didn't drag a hundred yards before the lead red-bone hound howled, letting everybody know that he had found them. The three convicts took off through the woods and ran about 300 yards to a small hay barn that had been searched several times before. The eight-dog pack was scratching at the barn, barking and howling when Sergeant Heron got there. He yelled, "Come on out, now! Don't make me come in there after you!" There was no response. Homer fired three shots through the top of the barn with his .38 revolver and repeated, "Come out now!"

The side door of the barn opened, and all three of them walked out with their hands up. Homer tried to call off his dogs, but one of the convicts kicked at them, and what followed can only be described as a one-round fight with the decision going to the dogs. All things considered, the three convicts were in surprisingly good physical condition, given the amount of exposure and low temperatures they had undergone in the woods, without any food or water. Of course, they were charged with escape and kidnapping, which caused them to end up with considerably more time than they had originally started out with. They were also sent to units where, instead of being trusties, they got to see a lot of bricks and bars along with the rest of the escape-risks. When asked if he enjoyed his three days of freedom, one of the escapees wryly remarked, "Naw, man, I didn't enjoy it." He would enjoy the remainder of his time in TDC even less.

A TIME TO PARTY

A month or so after the Clemens escape, Warden Turner called the field supervisors to his office. He said that all those who participated in the hunt for the escapees were invited to a "get-together" at the Clemens Unit. The function was for the purpose of thanking all those who had assisted in the apprehension of the escapees. These little soirées, held several times each year, were always entertaining, and it was an honor to be invited. Most all of the ranking local law-enforcement staff, southern regional wardens, Huntsville dignitaries, TDC agricultural staff, and a few politicians would be in attendance.

I arrived just as it was getting dark. The Clemens Unit dairy barn had been converted into a party pavilion with picnic tables and decorations. There were half a dozen barbeque pits with convict cooks busy cooking brisket, fajitas, and mountain oysters (calf fries). The lower farms had been working cattle for the past couple of months, so it was prime mountain-oyster season. There was an open bar, several kegs of beer, and poker and dice tables waiting on players yet to arrive. The Southern Region wardens were some of the first to arrive, and they mostly stood around the front door greeting the new arrivals. There were ranking representatives from the Texas Department of Public Safety, sheriffs from all the surrounding counties, three or four Texas Rangers, a half-dozen state senators, several members of the state House of Representatives, three or four members of the Board of Corrections. Many of the TDC's assistant-director-level department heads and the director, James Estelle, were there. Representatives from all the power base of the Texas law-enforcement community were present.

We rank-and-file unit employees had been invited to this gathering of the elite merely because we had participated in the chase. As it turned out, we were treated like semicelebrities and were real curiosities to some of the politicians and dignitaries in attendance. It was a sight to behold.

The high point of the evening came when one of the TDC's assistant directors from Huntsville made seven straight passes on the dice table, with the Brazoria County sheriff, Robert Gladny, betting against him. There were several hundred dollars of the sheriff's money on the table when the assistant director picked up the pile of cash and sheepishly stuffed it in his pockets. As he backed away from the table, he tentatively said, "I pass the dice."

The old sheriff's voice boomed across the room, "You what?"

The man from Huntsville, looking for some way to gracefully extricate himself from the situation, whispered quietly, "It's late, I have to be going, I pass the dice." The sheriff had every eye in the room on him. He was mad, and he was wearing a gun on his hip, and when he leaned across the dice table to speak it was so quiet you could have heard a rat pissing on cotton. In a voice cold and steady, the sheriff said, "Boy, you'd better be glad you're a guest in this county." The place erupted in nervous laughter, which the sheriff clearly did not appreciate. Mr. Estelle hastily escorted the assistant director to his car and gave him clear and specific direction on the fastest way to get out of Brazoria County.

When Mr. Estelle returned to the assembly, he looked relieved as he sat down at the table where most of the Retrieve Unit field officers had gathered. We set him up with a plate of mountain oysters and a cold beer. If a stranger had walked up and didn't know that Mr. Estelle was the highest-ranking prison official in Texas, they would have thought he was just another field mulligan. He was wearing blue jeans and a western hat and was obviously comfortable in this environment. We talked about hoe squads, convict trivia, escapes, and prison farm life in general. Jim Estelle was like that; he could have a good time just sitting there drinking a beer and listening to what some of his employees had to say. He was the last director in my experience to have had that kind of personal relationship with the employees.

They say that today the system is too large for such close relationships to exist between the boss and the common employees. I guess it's true. Today's prison directors don't even know the ranking staff, much less the rank-and-file employees. That's a shame, too, because the loyalty born in such relationships is everlasting. Those field officers sitting at that table with Mr. Estelle would have charged Hell with a bucket of water if he had asked them to. That kind of loyalty doesn't exist anymore and some say that's a good thing. I admit, I would have difficulty being loyal to some of the less-experienced wardens in today's Texas prison system, but with a man of Jim Estelle's stature and integrity it was not a problem, and I've never regretted following his leadership.

In 1977 the Retrieve Unit received its sixth warden in eight years. The winds of change were also sweeping through the rest of the system at this time. Older employees were leaving in record numbers as the daily battles with the federal courts became oppressive. Even Mr. Estelle said he felt he had become a political "lightning rod," attracting political criticism that reduced his credibility and hampered his ability to effectively operate the prison system.

KING DAVID

The new warden, David Christian (*aka* King David), was one of the new breed of young Sam Houston State College graduates who were gravitating through the ranks of the department. Warden Christian, in his mid-thirties, was by far the youngest warden I had worked for. He had worked his way through the security ranks on the units around Huntsville while he was in college and later worked as an assistant warden under the Ramsey I Unit warden J. V. Anderson (*aka* "Wildcat" or "The Cat").

To say that Warden Christian was proactive would be an understatement. In 1977 the Retrieve Unit was entirely too calm and peaceful for Warden Christian's tastes. Upon arrival, he immediately tripled the number of building tenders and had several building tenders of his own choosing imported from the Ramsey I Unit. These building tenders were real thugs, prone to expressing Warden Christian's philosophy of proactive inmate control physically, rather than waiting to be called upon for assistance by staff.

The building tenders readily began exercising their power with the support and direction of the new administration. There were several untouchable building tenders who were given privilege and power above that of ranking staff. When the old building major, Henry Johnson, didn't actively support this new management style, he was abruptly transferred to the Jester Unit. A previous subordinate of Warden Christian's, Robert "Little Man" Lawson, was brought in as Johnson's replacement. Lawson was about five-foot-nine-inches tall and took on the appearance of a Banty rooster when he got up in some convict's face and shouted orders, as he liked to do. Major Lawson was fiercely loyal to Warden Christian and quickly began to set up what he viewed as "his unit." Many of the longtime Retrieve Unit employees, who had been loyal to previous wardens and to Major Johnson, took exception to this new take-no-prisoners style of inmate management.

I was thankful, and more than a little lucky, to be working in the field. I didn't have to see or endure the daily battles between the out-of-control building tenders and the general-population convicts. The battle lines were drawn between bickering officers, the building tenders, the general inmate population and the new administrative regime. Several convicts resigned their building jobs in order to be assigned to the field, where they at least knew that some other convict wouldn't be trying to order them around. The building officers felt that they were in danger of losing their jobs, or at the very least being ostracized by those who supported Warden Christian. This was no small matter, as many of the older Retrieve employees were dependent on their jobs for their families' survival and future retirement. If you were a younger employee, the peer pressure to join in the building-tender-dominated environment was tremendous. After all, the warden had the power to promote, transfer, or terminate any employee. It was clearly career-threatening to oppose Warden Christian.

David Christian may not have intended for violence to occur, nor was he entirely responsible for it. There is no question, however, that his administrative style did give rise to very serious problems. An administrator cannot allow those under his authority to act with impunity. I am inclined to believe that Warden Christian simply let the building tenders and some of his imported security staff get out of control.

When a challenge (or a perceived challenge) to authority came, it was met with swift and brutal force that could not be recalled. From the time Warden Christian was assigned to Retrieve in 1977 until after the gang wars ended in 1986, the Retrieve Unit was in an almost constant state of war. Christian was eventually reassigned to the Darrington Unit in 1980 and was later terminated from system employment in 1983. The violence that began during his tenure did not end until all the verified gang members were eventually placed on permanent lockdown in administrative segregation.

Warden Christian's reputation for violence was well-deserved. Later, in federal court, Judge Justice described him by saying, "The violent propensities of Warden David Christian were repeatedly underscored by the evidence." One inmate stated, "Violence followed Warden Christian like a shadow"—an observation that was borne out by the record. Christian's protégé, Retrieve Unit Building Major Robert Lawson, was later (1983) fired from the system for "excessive use of force," but in 1977 he was the second-most-powerful man on the Retrieve Unit. Unlike previous unit administrations I had worked for, this warden and this major believed in daily demonstrations of administrative control through the high-profile use of their building tenders. It was like waving a red flag at a bunch of already-irritated bulls. The older convicts at Retrieve were not easily intimidated, and the population became openly contemptuous. The number of offense reports tripled, and many inmates refused to work; some inmates refused to cut their hair or shave. These problems had always been of a rare and minor nature. Now these incidents were occurring on almost a daily basis. The TDC had always made up for being grossly understaffed by using building tenders as a backup security force, but now they were being used to actively promote and enforce a warden's agenda.

THE RISE OF THE TEXAS PRISON GANGS

The building tenders, in an all-out fight for survival, had to become more aggressive, not only to maintain control of the inmate population, but to protect their hard-earned status as rulers of the damned. Inmate-control problems escalated, and more and more inmate assaults began to occur. Loss of inmate control was only a symptom of a much uglier problem that for the first time in the history of the TDC began to raise its ugly head. The prison gangs began to form.

There had never been a serious gang problem in the TDC before. Oh, there had been gang members in TDC for many years, but the only gangs that held any real authority were the building tenders; they represented the administration, and they didn't allow any competition. The difference between past and present was that now the convicts didn't see the building tenders as simply staff helpers or a standby force to be called upon only when things got out of hand. Now the convicts saw Warden Christian's enforcers as a predatory force that they felt a need to unite against in order to survive.

At first, they formed small groups along racial lines, or with friends from the old neighborhoods. In a pack of other convicts, they felt some degree of safety from the building tenders and their "hired help." All of a sudden, it became very fashionable to be in a gang. Gangs began to form representing every ethnic group. There were white, black, Hispanic, and even a few inter-racial groups.

Even though the building tenders had access to weapons, blackjacks, clubs, knives, et cetera, they were reluctant to challenge a group of convicts that presented a united front. The emergence of these new types of gangs caused alarm among prison authorities as well as outside law-enforcement agencies. Some of these groups demonstrated a remarkable ability to organize in comparison to their predecessors and were generally more ruthless and coldblooded.

The new gangs were very distinctive from past inmate cliques in that they demanded absolute obedience to the parent group. They obtained and enforced this obedience by compelling every potential member to make a "death oath" of allegiance to the group. The requirement in most groups is that once you join, you are in for life. There are some groups that don't strictly subscribe to this requirement, but in most of the larger cliques, death or serious injury is the only way out. This ensures that only those coldblooded, violent, and loyal enough to fight for the group are taken in as members. New members must be sponsored by current members, and in most cases they must demonstrate loyalty by smuggling drugs, donating money, or fulfilling a "hit" or "contract" on an enemy of the group. After a prospect has demonstrated his loyalty, a vote is taken to decide if he will be accepted.

Most inmate gangs form their rank structure along paramilitary or corporate structural lines. Prison gangs are also, with few exceptions, broken down along racial lines. They all have a symbol of some sort to distinguish them from others. This symbol is usually in the form of a "tattoo," patch, or "copia." They all have very specific rules or a "constitution" spelling out what the gang stands for. Some of the groups have very sophisticated secret codes used for communication. They promise their new members that the group will protect them, give them money, and take care of their families.

All gangs, to some degree, subscribe to the pack mentality. The strength of the pack is determined by the amount of peer pressure and leverage that can be directly applied to its membership. The tools of the trade are derived from the control of narcotics, prostitution, and the protection rackets within the institution and to a lesser degree on the free-world streets. The wannabes who desire gang membership are easily influenced to carry out violent acts demonstrating their aptitude for gang membership, and in many cases they are some of the most dangerous convicts in any prison. As they have not yet been confirmed as gang members by prison security, they may very well be in a minimum-security status. Their mindset is ruthless, because only their expressions of violence can pave their way into gang membership, and an inmate thinks gang association will enhance his individual control and power over his situation.

After all, once having received a long mandatory sentence, a convict's fear of the law is diminished. The way a convict looks at it, he has little to lose. The law can't take anything else away from him. The gang, on the other hand, literally has the power of life or death over him. Neither the law nor a prison administration can protect an inmate in general prison population. In some cases, the choice is to either join the gang or look forward to trying to do a life sentence in single-cell, protection status. If you only have a two- or three-year sentence, that might be an option, but if you have thirty or forty years of flat time to do, the choice can seem pretty clear. The gangs promise power to their members and death to their enemies. The bottom line is that once involved, they are all members of an organized criminal enterprise.

In the Texas Department of Criminal Justice, not all "gangs" are defined as "dangerous disruptive groups." The ones that have demonstrated a propensity for violence within the department are locked down in administrative segregation as threats to the security of the institution. The other known groups, street gangs, religious or political fanatics, biker gangs, racial supremacists, and just plain old thugs, are monitored and tracked on an individual basis, but unless they are involved in violence of some kind, they remain in general population.

The confirmed gang members in the TDCJ have never at any time represented more than 10 percent of the total inmate population. As of the year 2000, they represented approximately 6 percent of all inmates. Prior to 1977, the gangs were almost nonexistent. In 1982, faced with rising violence and threats from the federal court, Mr. Estelle went to the Texas Legislature with hat in hand and tried to obtain funding for additional staff and the construction of more high-security inmate housing. His request was denied. The Legislature acted on the public position of Governor Mark White, who was widely quoted saying, "The state cannot afford to build Cadillac Prisons." He wanted to put the inmates in tents and dormitories, which Estelle knew the courts would never allow.

On September 15, 1983, Mr. Estelle said he was resigning, in part because he was "frustrated with [his] lack of effectiveness in obtaining needed prison appropriations from the Legislature," and also because he opposed some prison-system changes proposed in court action. I can remember as a unit employee feeling a deep sense of loss when Estelle resigned. In the weeks and months after he left, that feeling turned to one of having lost control. Once Estelle was gone, there was an overall feeling by staff that there was no one left now to stand up for their rights. There was nothing now to stop the steamroller of federal courts and reformists from continuing the TDC's devolution from the best prison system anywhere to the doormat for every experimental wannabe penologist in the country.

The sudden increase in violence when Estelle resigned was alarming. In 1983, under Estelle, TDC had three gang-related inmate murders. In the two following years, 1984 and 1985, TDC had fifty-two inmate-on-inmate homicides. There were twenty-five homicides in 1984 and twenty-seven in 1985.

In the absence of James Estelle, the whole system seemed to move in slow motion just waiting for the next wave of negative influence to come. In the media every politician and self-styled prison expert had a plan to fix the problem in TDC. Those of us who had grown up in the old system and knew how effective it had been didn't feel like we were the problem. All of a sudden there were all these "experts" walking around our units telling us that what we had been doing all along was wrong. Of course, while they were telling us that, inmates were dying like flies, being killed by other inmates. We knew that none of this would have occurred under Jim Estelle, if the Legislature and Mark White had just fulfilled his request for staff. Even without the building tenders, Estelle would never have allowed the abdication of control forced on the system by the federal courts—if he had been given the staff and additional inmate housing he had asked for.

By 1986 it became necessary to lock all confirmed gang members into special housing areas called administrative segregation. The Board of Criminal Justice and the directors who followed Mr. Estelle's departure grossly underestimated the gangs' future growth and the problems they would cause. The first year after Estelle resigned, in addition to the many homicides, there were more than four hundred nonfatal inmate-on-inmate stabbings and assaults. Assaults on employees went up by 25 percent. Nineteen-eighty-five would be even worse.

CHAPTER SEVEN

TIMES THAT TRY MEN'S SOULS

"Integrity is doing the right thing, even if nobody is watching."
—JIM STOVALL

THE DEATH OF GUS FEIST

On the afternoon of October 24, 1979, I was scheduled to go to the Ramsey I firing range to qualify for sniper-team training. The department bought .270-caliber Seiko rifles with special scopes and matchpoint ammunition for each unit. As a member of the four-member unit sniper team, I had to qualify every two months. I was off the unit from 11:00 A.M. until about 4:30 P.M., and when I returned, I entered the compound through the back gate and went directly to the field office in south hall. The inmate bookkeeper, Robert "Shakey" Lawson, always nervous anyway due to being a self-admitted methamphetamine addict, was unusually pale. He said, "You missed it, Lieutenant, they beat old Gus Feist bad out there in that hallway, I mean they did him really bad."

Whatever had happened occurred about a half-hour before I returned to the unit. I walked up the hallway and met the building sergeant, Robert Shaw. I said, "I heard old Gus got into some trouble."

He nodded. "Yeah, well, he won't be getting in any more trouble."

I asked where Gus was, and he pointed to the infirmary. Just then two officers carrying Gus on a stretcher, followed by medical officer Captain Jennings and Major Lawson, came down the hall from the infirmary. They proceeded toward the back gate to a waiting ambulance. I waited until Captain Jennings returned to the building. He was walking alone, with his head down. I asked, "How bad is it?" He just shook his head from side to side and did not answer.

Gus Feist was a forty-eight-year-old black convict serving a twenty-year sentence for assault with intent to murder a police officer, from Beaumont, in Jefferson County, Texas. Gus was a Korean War veteran who was constantly in trouble with the law and had served time in both California and Texas. He was a prolific writ-writer, though few if any of his poorly written lawsuits actually made it into a courtroom. Old Gus never missed an opportunity to be an outspoken critic of the Texas prison system.

I had been one of his immediate supervisors for the past few years, as Gus was assigned to number-four garden squad. This was a "medical squad" set aside for inmates in their forties, fifties, and sixties who had minor health problems but were still capable of doing light work. I guess I knew Gus as well as any of the staff. He was no doubt very vocal about his dissatisfaction with various aspects of the prison system. He was always threatening to sue someone, including me, but he rarely followed through. He was the one in the squad who always wanted to voice his opinion, which was usually negative. He liked to hear himself talk.

I never viewed Gus Feist as a threat, and neither did the convicts who worked with him. He just wasn't a physically intimidating presence. I can only recall him getting into one minor fight the whole time I knew him. He played in the inmate chess tournaments, and although he was only a mediocre player, he relished the opportunity to give unsolicited advice to the other convicts.

On October 24, 1979, Gus Feist was beaten to death by several building tenders in the main hallway at the Retrieve Unit. The head building tender and leader in the assault was a white convict named Roy Melancon. Feist's death occurred just a week or two before he was scheduled to testify before U.S. District Judge William Wayne Justice in the *Ruiz* civil-rights lawsuit. His family was told that he hit his head on the concrete floor when a fight broke out between Gus and another inmate. After seeing

Gus' body at the hospital in Galveston, Gus' sister, Martha Feist Louis said, "They had beaten Gus so bad his head looked four times larger than it actually was. They ripped that boy up so bad he didn't even look like my brother. His mouth was all swollen, I said, 'This can't be Gus.'"

Following Gus' death, his parents filed a wrongful-death lawsuit, alleging that Warden David Christian had ordered a TDC guard and a gang of convicts to beat Feist for his unrelenting legal activity against the prison system. At the time of Gus' death, a federal grand jury in Corpus Christi, Texas, was investigating prison brutality. The Feist family attorney, Kenneth Lewis, said, "I had sworn testimony by deposition where they said the warden ordered he be punished. Of course, that warden was Christian."

The lawsuit filed by the family met stiff resistance by TDC officials and the attorney general's office. Inmate witnesses refused to testify before the Grand Jury because of intimidation, and some TDC officials pled the Fifth Amendment when asked to give depositions. Gus' family never got their day in court. "We were on the verge of going to trial when the state settled the case," Lewis said. He declined to discuss the settlement, but Gus' sister Martha said, "The family received $10,000 and our attorney received $8,000." Their lawsuit had originally requested more than a million dollars in damages. Lewis, who said the case would have been tough to win, still believes the facts surrounding Feist's death had an impact on lawyers in the attorney general's office, which was then headed by future-governor Mark White.

TDC had, just months previously, been involved in a controversial court report on building tenders, in which prison officials at the highest levels had denied all allegations of building-tender abuses. These statements made it particularly difficult to provide a credible defense for Warden David Christian, Major Robert Lawson, convict Roy Melancon, and the other building tenders. In addition to the civil-rights case brought by Gus Feist's parents, both Christian and Lawson were investigated by a federal grand jury. In a rare departure from using the state attorney general's legal staff to represent them, a well-known attorney, Richard "Racehorse" Haynes, was paid a flat fee of $10,000 by TDC for his services in their defense. Although no criminal responsibility was ever proven

in the Gus Feist case, Christian and Lawson were repeatedly implicated in charges of brutality throughout the *Ruiz* trial.

During the investigation into the death of Gus Feist, a
request was made to separate Warden Christian from any potential inmate witnesses. Since there were so many potential inmate
witnesses at the Retrieve Unit, the department chose to transfer
Warden Lloyd Hunt to Retrieve from the Darrington Unit and to
move Christian from Retrieve to Darrington. This move was made
early in 1980, and although they were not formally "outlawed" at
this time, this administrative move served to end the rule of the
building tenders at the Retrieve Unit.

Lloyd Hunt was a hard, fair-minded administrator who
believed in setting the standard during informal talks with his
supervisors and then delegating operations to the department
heads. He made it crystal clear that he did not believe in "a convict running anything." After three years under King David and
the rogue building tenders, the staff and the convicts welcomed
the change.

DEATH AT THE BACK GATE

In the early morning of August 19, 1980, I was sitting outside the
shakedown room at the Retrieve Unit back gate waiting for 7:30
A.M., the time when the line force would turn out. The outside
trusty squads were in the process of being counted, identified,
and turned out to their respective supervisors. The back-gate officer was turning out the tractor squad, the garden squad, the
dairy squad, the fencing squad, and all the other outside trusties
that it took to keep a prison unit up and running during the
1980s. When it came time for the outside maintenance squad to
pair up inside the two enclosed sally-port gates, the convicts filed
in and waited in front of the outside gate as they had done hundreds of times before. I casually watched them walk by. Some of
them were talking low, and some just called out their name and
number and went to stand in line. I did not notice anything
unusual.

There was a flurry of activity at the front of the line. From
my vantage point, approximately thirty feet away, it looked like
the beginning of a fistfight. A Mexican convict I knew as Arnulfo

Medina (*aka* "Pelon") was pushing and shoving a black inmate whom I didn't know into the chain-link fence near the turnout gate. The other convicts were just watching. I yelled for them to break it up, but to no avail. There was a rapid exchange of blows as I started to run toward the fight. As Medina backed away from the black inmate he had pinned against the fence, I saw a flash of steel in his right hand. When I got to Medina, his back was to me, and I grabbed him by his upper arms and pushed him into the gate. He looked over his shoulder to see who it was, but he didn't resist. I held Medina against the fence and searched him, finding a sharpened stainless-steel table knife in his right pants pocket.

Sometime during all this I noticed Joe Forgue, the maintenance supervisor, standing on the other side of the locked outside fence gate. He had been yelling at the fighting inmates, but I had only just then realized that he was there. I placed Medina face down on the concrete slab and struggled to put handcuffs on him. I looked up to see the black inmate holding his bloody shirt. It was clear that he had been stabbed several times. He had a look of confusion on his face and whispered to me, "Lieutenant, what do I do?"

I called for the back-gate officer to tell the medical department there was an emergency at the back gate and to bring a stretcher. The black inmate started to walk toward the entrance gate, but he didn't make it very far. He collapsed on the yard between the back gate and the building, where they picked him up with the stretcher. I found out later that he was pronounced dead shortly after his arrival in the unit medical department.

I testified at Medina's murder trial, as did Maintenance Supervisor Joe Forgue. Medina attempted to plead self-defense, but got an additional sixty-year sentence. Medina's lawyer didn't deny that his client murdered inmate John Louis Black, age thirty-three, who was serving a burglary sentence from Jefferson County. He claimed that Black was a homosexual and that he had made improper advances toward Medina on the previous day. The jury didn't believe a word of it. The fact that Medina was a self-admitted Texas Syndicate member did not come up at the trial. There was no evidence that the homicide was gang-related. Whatever it was that caused Medina to want to kill Black was personal business between the two of them. It took a long time to get the terrified face of that dying inmate out of my mind. On those rare occasions when I think about the past, I can still hear his voice whispering, "Lieutenant, what do I do?"

WAYNE SCOTT'S STAND

In October of 1981 there was a brief moment of clarity. It was one of those defining moments in one's career that deserves an occasional look back because of the pure majesty of the event. All employees who stay in the prison business long enough have such moments. These are the events that determine the quality and ultimately the success or failure of one's career. When reality and survival meet integrity and high ethical standards in the hallway of a prison unit, there are many who don't pass the test. The failure of an employee to meet the challenge does irreparable damage to his peers, because it lowers the standard for all of those who play by the rules. The problem was, during this time, in some areas there were no rules, and in other areas the rules were vague or changed so fast that no one could keep up with them.

The Retrieve Unit had been recently blessed with a new building major due to Major Robert Lawson being promoted to assistant warden on one of the northern units. The new major's name was Wayne Scott (he would later become the executive director of TDCJ). Scott came right out of the fashionable Sam Houston State College mold of TDC administrators, except his degree was in Business Administration instead of the usual Criminal Justice. He was a young, by-the-book, no-nonsense administrator. I worked with him for about a year, and although we were not personal friends, we had a good working relationship and I liked him. Wayne was idealistic, in the sense that he believed in the concept of a staff-controlled institution, but at that point in time it was virtually impossible, due to staff shortages, to manage a unit without some support from the building tenders. The ratio of security officers to inmates in Texas prisons was about 12 to 1 at the time, while the national average was around 6 to 1.

On October 1, 1981, at the Retrieve Unit, six building tenders assaulted Juan Garcia, #295857, in the main hallway during the noon meal. They caught him in front of the number-one-wing cellblock door as he came out to go to the inmate dining room. This was a bold, six-on-one attack at high noon, with clubs and nightsticks, and the victim was beaten until he fell unconscious on the hallway floor.

I was in the field major's office nearest the inmate dining room, located in the old building, when I heard the noise. I walked out into the main hallway, which was empty except for the first-shift lieutenant, who was standing at the crashgates while the six building tenders were busy beating on Garcia in front of number-one wing. Just as Garcia fell semi-conscious onto the floor, I heard this roar of noise from the direction of the inmate dining room, which was full of inmates eating the noon meal. Someone had yelled out, "They're beating 'El Rifle!'" ("The Rifle" was Juan Garcia's convict nickname.) The building tenders were still crowded around the fallen Garcia, who was not moving. I thought, *Oh no, not another Gus Feist incident.*

The Hispanic inmates were pouring out of the inmate dining room now and coming up the hall like a wave. They wanted to get to those building tenders bad. They ripped the four legs off the wooden inmate mailbox as they went by. The first-shift lieutenant was on the other side of the crashgates, and he locked them so the convicts couldn't get to him or the building tenders. He then opened the barred door into number-eight-wing dormitory and motioned for the building tenders to follow him inside. All the building tenders entered number-eight wing with the lieutenant following and locking the barred door from inside the dorm. His action left me standing in the hallway with about 125 of the most irritated Hispanic convicts I'd ever seen.

Just then, Major Wayne Scott entered the hallway from the main entrance by the control picket. I was never so glad to have company in my life. At first we tried verbally to get the inmates to return to their cells. They refused—they were angry and wanted to take it out on somebody.

I got an extra key from the control picket and opened the crashgate. We helped Garcia to his feet. He was bleeding badly, and we walked him into the major's office at center hall for some quick first-aid. He was only semiconscious, but after we got some of the blood off and cleaned him up some, he looked considerably better. I didn't want to call for medical personnel with all the angry Hispanic inmates controlling the hallway—and make no mistake about it, they had uncontested control of that hallway. Anybody who walked into the hall at that time was a potential hostage.

I asked Garcia if he would help us get control again by requesting that the inmates return to their cells so we could get him to the unit infirmary. He consented, and we helped him to the doorway where he spoke to the group in Spanish. He basically said, "I'm going to be all right. Go to your house before someone else gets hurt." Some of them grumbled a little, and a few windows were broken on their way down the hall toward the cell-blocks, but they returned to their cells without any further problems. We were able to get Garcia to the medical department, where he required several stitches and treatment for numerous cuts, bumps, and bruises.

Immediately after the incident, Major Scott convened an inmate disciplinary hearing in order to find out what happened. The committee of three consisted of chairman Major Scott, and members Lieutenant Larry Johns and me. The hearings were held in the inmate visiting room because it was not considered safe to have the building tenders in the main building at the time. All of the inmate hearings were recorded on Retrieve Disciplinary hearing tape number-twelve, side one. The incident and offense reports were filed in the appropriate inmate record. The following inmate building tenders were called before the committee:

Wright, Willie	#300551
Goodacre, Willie	#253843
Heywood, Earnest	#290406
Cauruthers, Kenneth	#Unknown
Lockett, Glenn	#286823
Thompson, Ben	#Unknown

All of the above-named building tenders called before the committee pled guilty on tape to assaulting inmate Juan Garcia. Each one interviewed separately said that the first-shift lieutenant both knew about and helped plan the attack on Garcia.

After the first two or three inmates were interviewed, during a moment when we were alone in the committee room, I raised the issue of future implications of what we were hearing with the other two committee members. I was particularly concerned about the actions of the first-shift lieutenant. Lieutenant Johns said, "If he did what they're all saying he did, it's not right."

After Larry voiced his opinion, I said, "I just want to make sure that we are in agreement, because this is not going to play well in Huntsville."

Major Scott said, "We are going to tell it like it is, and that's it." We looked at each other and nodded in agreement, and that's exactly what we did.

All six of the building tenders had to be transferred the same day for their own safety. Inmate Juan Garcia was not charged, nor did he report anything regarding this incident. Garcia didn't know of the first-shift lieutenant's involvement and thought that the reason for the assault was the fact that he had an argument with one of the building tenders the previous evening.

The following morning, when the inmates were released from their cells for work, they began breaking windows, barricading the cellblock doors, and refusing to return to their cells. The riot spread from number-three wing to number-two wing and went on for several hours. Finally the warden obtained permission to quell the disturbance, and riot teams were assembled. Three teams went in, one on the outside of the building and two on the inside. Assistant Warden M. D. Herklotz walked up to the door of number-three-wing cellblock with a bullhorn and announced: "You have five minutes to cease and desist and to tear down these barricades."

Several voices from the depths of the cellblock came back: "Fuck you." Herklotz didn't wait the five minutes. He turned to the officer with the CS gas pepperfog machine and said, "Gas 'em." We entered the cellblocks in riot teams after tearing down the barricades, and it was just a matter of herding them into the cells. CS gas is very effective in this type of situation, and I've never seen anyone who could tolerate it well enough to put up a fight (with the possible exception of a few who were on some type of psychotropic medication). The riot was over in less than an hour from the time the teams went in. There were no significant injuries, but there was major property damage. All of the windows in two cellblocks had to be replaced.

All things considered, it could have been much worse. After the inmate disciplinary hearings and subsequent investigation into the cause for the riot, Major Scott recommended employee disciplinary charges against the first-shift lieutenant for failure to communicate a potentially serious security risk and for allegedly having prior knowledge of the assault on Garcia by the building tenders. Major Scott went to the warden with the charge that the lieutenant was not only responsible for putting the building tenders in the hallway, but in fact may have encouraged the assault. The warden refused Scott's recommendation of disciplinary action against the lieutenant, and no formal disciplinary action was ever taken against him, except that he received an informal "letter of instruction" from the warden suggesting that he should have maintained better lines of communications with the administration regarding potential unit disturbances.

Major Scott advised the warden that as much as he detested the idea of ending his career in TDC, it was going to be either him or the first-shift lieutenant. He said if some form of disciplinary action was not taken against the lieutenant, then he would have to resign. His personal honor would not allow him to continue to work in an environment where such blatant injustice was allowed to go unpunished. The warden continued to refuse a recommendation for disciplinary against the lieutenant. Wayne Scott, true to his word, resigned his position as building major of the Retrieve Unit, TDC.

Director James Estelle did not find out about Wayne's resignation or the reasons for it until Wayne had already left state employment. Mr. Estelle called and set up a meeting with Wayne and attempted to rehire him, but he would not retract his resignation. I admired the fact that Wayne would not compromise his principles. This was the first time in fifteen years of working for TDC that I had seen someone challenge the system at the highest level over a point of simple justice, only to suffer the most severe consequences for essentially just trying to do the right thing. I was so disillusioned that I wanted to resign with him, but due to family responsibilities at that time in my career, resigning was not an option.

Lieutenant Johns and I talked about it. We basically decided that if we followed Wayne's course of action, the only change would be our unemployment and an even greater opportunity for rogue elements of the department to influence the system. We decided that if we were to have any chance to make a positive difference in the way things were done, it would have to be from the inside, not the outside. Someone said, "The only thing necessary for evil men to triumph is for good men to do nothing." Wayne Scott is a good man, the kind of man TDC needs badly, and in my view he did the only thing his conscience would allow him to do. Many at the time thought that his resignation was a futile gesture. To those I say, sometimes that's all there is.

THE DARRINGTON RIOT

Within a week of the Retrieve riot, turmoil spread to several other TDC units. Around 9:00 P.M. in mid-October 1981, I got a call from Warden L. D. Hunt. He said the Darrington Unit needed assistance due to an ongoing riot. I met Lieutenants Larry Johns and Charles Mask at the unit armory just as the second-shift officers were getting off duty. We held more than thirty-one officers for a double shift, put the oncoming shift workers on the bus, and headed for Darrington. Lieutenant Johns and I took my personal vehicle, and Warden Hunt followed the bus in the warden's car.

Upon arriving, we could see that all the perimeter fence lights and most of the building lights were out. Smoke was rising from several areas of the building. The officer on the radio picket was out on the catwalk, shotgun in hand. His voice sounded worried as he asked, "Did you bring some help?"

As Johns and I went through the bullpen gate, Larry said, "Help's on the way."

We found Warden David Christian, sitting alone in his office. This was the first time I'd seen him since his transfer from Retrieve during the Gus Feist investigation. It must have been a tough week for the warden; his face had broken commandments written all over it. He'd aged at least ten years in the few months since I'd last seen him.

I asked, "What have we got, Warden?" Christian looked up drearily and said, "To tell you the truth, Glenn, I don't know. I've got this office and the control picket. I think they've got the rest of it."

"I've got thirty-one officers and some extra gas coming. We can establish perimeter security as soon as they arrive."

Christian said, "Some of them have gotten out onto the tent yard, but it's hard to tell how many. The emergency generator's not working. We tried to gas them, but the gas didn't do any good."

Just then, I saw the lights from the Retrieve Unit bus coming into the parking lot. Larry and I met Warden Hunt in the parking lot, and I advised him of our conversation with Christian. Warden Hunt headed into the building as the Retrieve officers established perimeter security thirty yards apart around the Darrington Unit.

Johns and I arrived at the Darrington Unit back gate and put on our helmets and gas masks. We did a quick inventory of the gas shells; we had thirty short-range blast-dispersion shells, fifteen in each vest. I carried the .37 millimeter gas gun, and Lieutenant Johns carried the extra vest and a riot shield. There was a fire truck sitting inside the bullpen at the back gate, but it wasn't doing any good because every time the firemen attempted to get close enough to spray water on the fires, the convicts would throw glass and debris at them, forcing retreat. With Johns holding the shield to protect our approach, we managed to get back to back against one of the concrete pillars outside of the lower row of cellblock windows. The convicts were throwing all kinds of stuff at us and trying to spear us with sharpened broom handles. Lieutenant Johns used the shield to keep them off of us long enough for me to fire three or four rounds of gas into the first window. The gas didn't stop the attack, but it slowed them down some. I continued firing gas, emptying my vest within a few minutes, and backed off long enough to change vests with Johns. He kept warning me to not let them get behind us, but after the first fifteen or twenty gas shells, it was too smoky to see what was behind us.

By the time we reached the end of the cellblock, I was almost out of gas shells. We entered the building through the back of the laundry and discovered that the entire building was at least four inches deep in water due to inmate commode flooding. The water created an additional hazard of possible electrocution to anyone standing in the ankle-deep water. All an enterprising convict would have to do was drop a live wire into the water.

We met Warden Christian in the main hall. I could see convicts throwing things into the hallway from behind a massive barricade blocking the door to one of the cellblocks. Christian said, "See if you can get them off that door." I fired four rounds into the crowd, and they retreated to the back of the cellblock. The gas was doing its job, but I pointed out to Warden Christian that we had used almost all of the gas we'd brought from Retrieve. He said, "Reload those vests—it may be a long night."

Convicts in one of the cellblocks used weight bars (dumbbells) to beat out two of the barred windows, enabling them to get out onto the tent yard. They had also disabled many of the rolling cellblock-door mechanisms, releasing the convicts and rendering the cells useless. The tent yard looked like a small military camp with little fires going everywhere. The odd thing was, as much as they tried, they just couldn't get the tent material to burn.

Just then, an officer came running up to Warden Christian saying, "They're starting to burn in the dorms." The dormitory "tanks" were on the other end of the building and were supposed to house some of the better-behaved inmates. Christian turned to me and said, "Gas 'em." Lieutenant Johns and I headed for the other end of the building. Even before we got to the dorms, we could see the flames coming out from between the hallway bars.

It was a surreal sight. On one side of the hallway there were two dormitories full of convicts trying to burn and break everything in reach. Directly across the hall there were two more dorms, but inside there were the most peaceful-looking convicts I'd ever seen. They were all sitting on their beds, quietly observing the show coming from across the hall. I opened up with the gas gun, firing several rounds into the two troublesome tanks, and as the smoke began to clear, we turned on the fire hoses. Shining a spotlight into the tanks, we could see them all bunched up at the back of the dorms. They didn't want any more gas. Someone ordered them to get on their beds. After some grumbling, they complied. Finally, by around 2:30 A.M., enough reinforcements had arrived from the Ramsey units to start bringing the rioters in from the tent yard. The plan was simple: open the tent-yard gate, bring them onto the slab behind the laundry, and strip-search them before placing them into one of the remaining functional cellblocks. Of course, the remaining cellblocks already had at least two convicts per cell.

When we opened the tent-yard gates, a few of the rioters surrendered and came off the yard peacefully. Most didn't. Some of the convicts had converted some of the tent poles into clubs and weren't going to give up without a fight. We could get close enough to use the gas gun effectively now, and after ten or twelve rounds into the crowd, most of them lost interest in the fight.

As they staggered from the crowd a few at a time, we directed them toward the laundry door. All clothes were removed to ensure that no weapons made it back into the building. There was a small minority that actually tried to put up a fight, and that's where most of the injuries occurred. Some were taken down with riot batons, some ran kicking and screaming into the line of officers where they were forced to the ground and carried to the shakedown yard. The few who refused to disrobe had their clothes ripped unceremoniously from their bodies. The general consensus among staff was that order had to be restored. This civil disobedience had to end.

Owing partially to the way these convicts had behaved over the past twenty-four hours, the property damage, and the four hospitalized officers, none of the staff was in the mood to debate the political correctness of the situation. It was a question of priorities; first we would secure the unit, then we could discuss the merit of any alleged injustice. This was, after all, not a battle we could afford to lose. If those convicts had gained total control of that prison unit, which they very nearly did, there would've been significant loss of life, both inmates and staff. As they say in the South, "You've got to drain the swamp before you can deal with the alligators."

It took the rest of the night to get the inmates off of the tent yard and into the cellblocks and search and remove all the potential weapons from the living areas. I had fired sixty-one rounds of CS gas over a six-hour period. There had been some broken arms, legs, and ribs and a few missing teeth, but all things considered, we were fortunate not to have had loss of life, officer or inmate. The early property-damage estimates were between $350,000 and $400,000, but a riot creates many other costs. There are the medical bills for staff and inmates, staff overtime, the loss of inmate labor, and the extra expense of running a unit while everything is being repaired. For staff, there is the psychological toll of having to recover from the scary realization that at least for a time, the convicts were in control.

Mr. Estelle pointed out in his review of the Darrington riot that "From January 1973 to June 1981 TDC had six significant disturbances. From June of 1981 through Friday (the day of the riot) we have had 10—eight of those last 10 in the last 60 days." He said the lack of resolution in the *Ruiz* civil-rights suit, which was before the Fifth U.S. Circuit Court of Appeals, had "caused difficulty for both staff and inmates." As one warden put it, "We're like a rowboat that springs a leak; you can plug the leak, but you still know the bottom of the rowboat is rotten, and we've used everything we have to plug the leak. That's the kind of feeling we have. We're afloat, but for how long?"

IN THE LINE OF DUTY

On April 4, 1981, the TDC was dealt a devastating blow when Ellis Unit Warden Wallace Pack and Farm Manager Billy Max Moore were both killed by convict Elroy Brown. With this incident, what little positive employee morale we'd been hanging onto turned negative. Pack was the first Texas prison warden to be killed in the line of duty by an inmate in the state's history. Pack was drowned in a drainage ditch minutes after Moore was shot by Brown, who had obtained a pistol from the warden's car while being transported. Craig Washington, a controversial minority senator from Houston, Texas, defended the convict. He tried to characterize Pack as a brutal man through the testimony of several convict character witnesses. Washington put every convict who had ever had a grudge against the warden or TDC on the stand to cry and whine about how brutal the system had been to them. The first trial ended in a mistrial with the jury deadlocked 11 to 1 in favor of acquittal. Elroy Brown was acquitted of capital murder in the second trial when the jury concluded that a convict witness lied in his testimony that he saw Elroy Brown shoot the farm manager in the head at point-blank range. When the not-guilty verdict was read, TDC employees present, and the family members of the two prison officials, were visibly stunned. For those of us who understand the realities of the Texas prison system, this was a clear case of injustice. We were left knowing that a multiple-offender convict with a rap sheet a yard long had killed two good men and gotten away with it. It made me want to throw up.

CHAPTER EIGHT

A TIME TO DIE

". . .behold a pale horse: and his name that sat on him was
Death, and Hell followed with him."
—Revelation 6:8

Is a disaster any easier to live with when you know it's coming,
when you know that people are going to die, but can't do anything to stop it from happening? In my experience, the answer is
a definite no—it is not any easier. In fact, it is extremely frus-
trating.

THE CZAR OF TEXAS

"Will Rogers never met William Wayne Justice."
—Tyler, Texas, bumper sticker, 1982

I will not dwell on the intricacies of the never-ending *Ruiz* lawsuit. I leave the details of that subject to the lawyers, politicians,
and pundits who pretend to understand it. Suffice to say that as
a result of *Ruiz*, the federal court now dominates the Texas
Department of Criminal Justice. Any illusion that the governor of
Texas, the people, or their elected representatives had any
authority over the Texas prison system was pulled out by the
roots, by Judge William Wayne Justice.

The plain fact is that now a federal judge and convicts' attorneys can intervene at any time and take control of all or any part
of the Texas prison system. The next time you hear some politician get up and say he's going to be "tough on crime" and "lock
them up and throw the key away," or that he is "going to intro-

duce convicts to the joys of busting rocks," please remember: In the absence of federal-court approval, no Texas politician has the authority to back up such a promise.

THE BEST-KEPT SECRET IN TEXAS

In September 1981, Special Master Vincent Nathan accused prison officials of harassing and intimidating inmates who talked with staff from the special master's office. In October 1981, the special master reported that TDC officials were violating Judge Justice's prohibition against building tenders acting as correctional officers. In reality, the unit administrators had little choice but to use building tenders to support security staff, because the staff-to-inmate ratio was still running about one officer for every twelve inmates. No prison system, not even a minimum-security prison, can control an inmate population with staff ratios that far out of line.

Steve Martin, an attorney on the TDC headquarters staff, went to then–Attorney General Mark White, who was at the time in a dead-heat race with Bill Clements to be the next governor of Texas. According to Martin's book *The Walls Came Tumbling Down,* Martin advised Mark White of a real hush-hush secret: "General, the TDC has a sophisticated building-tender system under which serious abuses occur frequently, maybe daily."

"You mean," asked White, "we're using inmates as guards?"

"You are," replied Martin, "probably since the first day the lawsuit was filed."

"You mean, they've been lying to me all these years?"

This conversation demonstrates just how far out of touch our state government was with the realities of the Texas prison system. Given the well-documented figures showing an unworkable staff-to-inmate ratio, who did they think was running the state's prison system? Of course, the nine-member civilian Board of Corrections appointed by the governor acted like this was the best-kept secret ever and pled ignorance to the facts.

At the time, there were about 22,000 inmates and roughly 4,000 officers in TDC, all of whom clearly knew in graphic detail of the building-tender system. Nothing was kept secret. The claim that this fact was unknown to the highest elected officials in the state is, to say the least, disingenuous.

WELCOME TO RAMSEY

In August 1984, I was promoted to field major of the Ramsey I Unit. On the following Monday morning, I went directly to the warden's office and met an obviously tired Senior Warden Terry L. Terrell. He looked up at me over a cup of black coffee and said, "Welcome to the Ramsey farm, Glenn." Terrell advised that there had been a homicide the night before. Wilbur Jones, a black convict, had killed Richard J. Hord, twenty-nine, a white convict who was a member of the Aryan Brotherhood of Texas (ABT). Jones stabbed Hord to death at approximately 2:30 A.M. with a home-made "shank" by stabbing him once in the eye and cutting his throat. This homicide was believed to have been in retaliation for the stabbing of a black inmate "Seed"(a member of a black gang called "the Seeds"), Willis Jones (no relation to Wilbur) a couple of days before by an Aryan Brotherhood member.

About an hour after inmate Hord was fatally stabbed on number-nine wing, another white inmate, Fred G. Linthicum Jr., thirty-five, was stabbed several times by an unknown black assailant. Linthicum, an ABT member, also was believed to have been targeted by the Seeds in retaliation for the attack on Willis Jones. After treatment in a local hospital, Linthicum survived and was returned to the Ramsey I Unit to join the ever-growing numbers of convict gang members in segregation.

There were more than 150 known "patched" (identified by tattoo) gang members walking the hallways at the Ramsey I Unit when I arrived, and those were just the ones we knew about. There were at least that many more whose membership was suspected but couldn't be confirmed. The most active groups were the Texas Syndicate, Mexikamemi (*aka* Mexican Mafia), Aryan Brotherhood of Texas, The Texas Mafia, Mandingo Warriors, and the Seeds. An unofficial war had started between the ABT and the Seeds in June 1984 when the leader of the Seeds, Roy Lynn Boozer, twenty-seven, was killed in the inmate dining room by ABT member Gary Brown.

According to witnesses, Boozer, a large, loud-talking black convict, had walked by the inmate barber shop on the day of the slaying and pointed his finger at inmate barber Gary Brown, saying, "I'm going to get you, white boy." After making his threat,

Boozer walked on down the hall and into the inmate dining room for the noon meal.

Gary Brown took the threat seriously and didn't wait to see what would happen next. He got his homemade shank—almost every convict kept one nearby in those days—and followed Boozer to the dining room. He waited until Boozer was seated at one of the four-man tables and then casually walked up behind him. There were three other Seed members sitting at the table when Gary Brown stabbed Boozer several times in the back and then, just to be sure, cut his throat, nearly decapitating him. As Boozer lay slumped over the table bleeding to death, witnesses said, Brown asked the others sitting at the table if they had a "problem" with what he had done. None of them had anything to say. Brown, having accomplished what he wanted to do, walked to the door of the inmate dining room and handed the murder weapon to an officer.

After investigation by the sheriff's office, Gary Brown was indicted for the murder of Roy Lynn Boozer by a Brazoria County grand jury. At trial, several witnesses, including some of Brown's Aryan Brotherhood friends, testified that Boozer threatened Brown's life immediately prior to the homicide. As a result, Brown was subsequently found not guilty by reason of self-defense. It was hard to blame the jury for their verdict, because as they each placed themselves in Gary Brown's position, they could see from the crime-scene photographs that the threat of attack by other inmates in the TDC was a real fact of life. The jury did not find that Brown had a duty to retreat or go to prison officials for protection.

This court verdict encouraged several other convicts to use the same strategy in their homicide cases, some successfully, some not so successfully. To give the plea of self-defense credibility, a defendant would get his lawyer to call a bunch of his gang-member friends into court to say that the victim had threatened the defendant's life. Unfortunately, once in court, a convict's word is just as good as a taxpaying citizen's. The jury, of course, did not have a clue as to the manipulative capabilities of the convict gangs and felt obligated to give equal weight to their self-serving testimony.

Spring Cleaning

After the Hord killing, Warden Terrell had the building locked down, and he set about making some major changes in the way the Ramsey I Unit conducted its business. He said, "Glenn, don't worry about turning out the line force for a while. We have to get a handle on this place before we can even think about doing any work. I want you to use your field officers and organize some shakedown teams. We are going to shake this building down from one end to the other. I've got some dump trucks lined up, and they'll be at the turnout doors when you need them. I want to take everything but the fixtures out of those living areas. If it looks legal, store it in the furniture factory. If it's not legal, put it on one of those dump trucks to be destroyed."

I answered, "Yes, sir." Obviously, I had not been the only one who noticed the abundance of inmate property and the absence of control in the inmate living areas.

We worked twelve hours on, twelve hours off for the next three days and kept those dump trucks running. There were a lot of homeless roaches when we got through with the search. We found stashes of homemade alcohol, gambling paraphernalia, free-world clothes; $425.00 in cash; marijuana; cocaine; and a number-three washtub full of weapons. After the three-day shakedown, the pile of contraband looked like a small city. The fire burned for a week.

The convicts were in shock sitting in their cells without all of their amenities, and the grievances, lawsuits, and letters to the "special master's" office were flying. Warden Terrell had made up his mind that at least for as long as we were in charge, we were going to run the Ramsey I Unit by the book, and he didn't intend to lose any arguments with any convicts. He stressed the importance of documentation and kept meticulous records on anything that he thought might be a future problem area.

"The Pro"

After Mr. Estelle resigned in 1983, there was a quick succession of replacement directors who tried unsuccessfully to please the courts and their lawyer watchdogs. Mr. Estelle's assistant director, Dan V.

"Red" McKaskle, was appointed as "interim director" by the board until a search for a new director could be completed. They wanted Red to take the job on a permanent basis, but he was smart enough to know that there was no future in being director as long as Judge Justice was second-guessing every decision made.

The TDC board formed a search committee chaired by one of its members, Mr. Harry Whittington, to search far and wide to find a politically correct director. They finally came up with sixty-one-year-old Raymond K. "The Pro" Procunier, an out-of-state "expert" who had worked in prisons in California, Utah, and Virginia. He had most recently been the deputy director of the New Mexico prison system, since July of 1980, where he had been called in after a riot that left thirty-three dead. His first statement to the media, when asked, "What can the employees expect?" was, "They should expect a chief who knows what he wants and gets it—I don't expect any trouble."

The politicians, the TDC board, and even the convicts' attorneys applauded this guy as the answer to the Texas prison system's prayers. They could not have been more wrong.

His first day on the job was July 1, 1984. By October 1984, only five months into The Pro's administration, there had been twelve more inmate homicides, and even The Pro admitted he didn't have a clue as to how to stop the rising tide of violence. Governor Mark White would later respond when asked about Procunier, "Most of the time I don't think he knew where he was." This is the only time I ever remember actually agreeing with Mark White.

JOSEPH KEITH PRICE, PH.D.

The only person more reviled by rank-and-file TDC employees than attorney Steve Martin was the ex–security captain from the Eastham Unit, Keith Price, who had been appointed as the head of the new TDC Operational-Audits office. He was now investigating wardens, majors, captains, and other officers alleged to have violated federal court orders. Several high-ranking officers, including some wardens, were fired or demoted based on Price's investigative reports. As a result of his eat-your-own-kind persona, most TDC employees viewed him as somewhat of a Judas.

When he was an Eastham Unit security captain, Price had been called upon to testify in the *Ruiz* trial regarding the use of building tenders. He denied, under oath, having any knowledge of the illegal use of building tenders and further denied that there was any such abuse by the inmate guards. Later, in October 1986, after being rewarded for his work in the operational-audits office with a promotion to senior warden of the Darrington Unit, Price gave an interview to a national news magazine. Price showed that he may have committed perjury in the *Ruiz* trial by publicly admitting in that interview that he was not only aware of the use of building tenders, but that as a security captain at the Eastham Unit in November 1981, he was in command of a force of officers and building tenders that used "excessive force" in the quelling of a riot. In the national news publication, Price admitted that he witnessed a group of "about 150 building tenders carrying trash can lids, pipes, clubs, weight-lifting bars," preparing to do battle in the the riot in November 1981. Price was then working at the Eastham Unit for Warden Edward Turner, who called on Captain Price to command the suppression of the rebellion.

Price admitted in the article, "I liked action. I went to work waiting for it—almost hoping for it. Here I was a captain, a middle-management person. There was no reason to wear combat boots every day, but I wore them." When the time came to quell the riot, Captain Price admitted that he "led the charge" of about sixty officers into the riot zone. During that charge he said that the 150 building tenders, who had tied white rags around their heads to distinguish them from the other convicts, pursued "the rioters into a far corner of the yard." One building tender said afterward, "We had clubs, bats, chains, knives, and we formed what we called a 'whupping' line."

The rioters now had to run through a gauntlet of officers and building tenders to get to the safety of the gym. Witnesses said that as they staggered back into the building, "Some you couldn't recognize, and some were unconscious. We weren't sure if they were dead or alive." Price admitted, "It's a miracle that nobody was killed."

Price later said, "Some of the things I did had a high price, but they were morally right for the agency." He said he had since found God and contentment, that he was a changed man and a survivor.

Price then said something that really made me glad that he has found God, because with his ego he's going to need someone to talk to. Price said, "That's called surviving in the real world. It's why the dinosaurs didn't survive. Our organization evolved and I simply changed with it, which seems to me to be the only thing that a thinking man would do. It doesn't have anything to do with loyalty or how I feel about either model of inmate control. It's simply a matter of pragmatism." Referring to his fellow wardens, he continued, "They're the dinosaurs. I'm the new man."

The sheer arrogance of that speech was overwhelming. The man had turned on his own fellow employees, his own personal friends, causing several of them to lose their jobs or be demoted for simply being accused of doing the very same things that Price himself had admitted doing. I suspected that Price didn't change his values for any moral purpose, but simply in order to advance his career. Now he had the unmitigated gall to call his fellow wardens "dinosaurs" and announce that he had now somehow magically "evolved" onto a higher plane, giving him the moral right to pronounce judgements on his peers. Price said that it is simply a "matter of pragmatism" and "doesn't have anything to do with loyalty." After years of watching him step over the mangled bodies of his less-than-perfect fellow employees to get to where he is, I humbly submit that loyalty is indeed the question. If the opposite of the dinosaur is Dr. Keith Price, Ph.D., then call me a dinosaur. When the day comes that I become so "pragmatic" that I sacrifice my own fellow employees in order to worship at the alter of the likes of William Wayne Justice, I would prefer being a member of an extinct species. If Dr. Keith Price, Ph.D. is truly "the new man," then there are truly a lot of mice out there in serious training to be rats.

PSYCHOTIC AND DEADLY

The Texas Syndicate and the Mexican Mafia had a history of competing for recruits, and the battle was becoming even more intense. One Hispanic convict was especially in demand: Pablo Rios, a thirty-four-year-old bona fide psychopath serving a ninety-year sentence for aggravated rape from Harris County. The MM and TS had both been trying to recruit him because he had a reputation for being a coldblooded, don't-give-a-damn-about-the-consequences killer.

The problem with Pablo was that he woke up in a different world every morning. He had been sent to the treatment center for his ongoing psychiatric problems so often that it was difficult to tell whether he had consciously joined either gang. On return from his latest trip to the psychiatric center, he arrived at Ramsey I with copies of his inmate disciplinary offense reports for threatening to kill staff still in his shirt pocket.

The TDC psychiatric personnel were forever playing this game. If a convict was sent to them as somewhat out of touch with reality but nonviolent, passive, they would accept him as "psychiatrically impaired." If, on the other hand, the same convict was sent to them but took a swing at one of the doctors or bit a nurse, they would load him up on some pacifying drug and put him on the next thing smoking back to his original unit of assignment. He would arrive with a dazed look on his face and a note saying, "This inmate is a management problem." This was the medical staff's way of saying, we don't care if he's crazy or not—you deal with him. So, regardless of how many times Pablo Rios was sent to the treatment center, and despite his apparent psychiatric problems, the psychiatrists always sent him back just as soon as they figured out who he was.

A couple of days after his last trip, I talked to Pablo, and he had that faraway look in his eyes as he stood there answering voices that only he could hear. I referred him to the unit psychologist, who said he was taking his medication and that there was nothing else to be done. The next morning at about 4:00 A.M., when Pablo's cellblock was called for breakfast, he came out into the main hall. An officer who had long been suspected of running drugs for the Mexican Mafia was working traffic control in front of number-six wing. Pablo Rios took this opportunity to stab the officer in the back. When the officer turned around, Pablo stabbed him once again in the abdomen. The weapon was made from a carpenter's L-shaped tool; it had been sharpened on a grinder, and the handle had been wrapped by someone who had a lot more mental capabilities than Pablo Rios did. After being stabbed twice, the officer staggered toward the unit infirmary, where another officer helped him inside. When Pablo was confronted by Security Sergeant Pedro Soto and told to drop the knife, he did as the officer told him to do. Pablo was still carrying the offense reports from the psychiatric center in his pocket at the time of the stabbing.

The officer was taken by ambulance to Hermann Hospital in Houston, Texas, where he was listed in critical condition. At first, the motive for the stabbing was unknown, although we suspected gang involvement. Almost immediately, Pablo Rios began to receive money in his trust fund account from relatives of Texas Syndicate members. Convict informants alleged that the officer had been stabbed because he was a known mule for the Mexican Mafia. Informants said that Texas Syndicate members approached the officer and asked him to run drugs for them. He refused, saying that he only worked for the Mexican Mafia. While in the hospital, the officer received a get-well card signed by about twenty of the highest-ranking Mexican Mafia members in the prison system. The gang members all signed it and wished him a speedy recovery. The officer eventually recovered from his wounds, but did not return to duty as a correctional officer.

About a week after the officer had been assaulted by Pablo Rios in the Ramsey I Unit's main hallway, another young Hispanic officer came into my office with a note he said he had just received in the mail. I knew the officer to be a close friend of the officer who had been stabbed. As he held out the note to me, the fear in his eyes was apparent. It read, "You're not going to be as lucky as [the other officer]" and was signed, "TS."

The second officer was asking, "What should I do?" I walked with him to the warden's office, but I knew even before we got there that his career was over. He was shaking so badly that I knew there had to be more to the note than he was telling me. The warden advised that he could get a transfer to another unit, but also told him that if the TS really wanted to get him, a transfer would not provide much protection. He briefly thought about it and then resigned, refusing to even go back into the building for his personal belongings. I don't know if he was a mule or not, but the TS thought he was, and that was good enough for them. It was a tough lesson for our staff to learn, but at least for a while the drug traffic slowed down. There weren't as many officers anxious to do business with the Mexican Mafia, the TS, or the ABT. The cost associated with being in the drug business had gone up, but it wasn't too high yet; it had just been raised to another level.

THE LOWEST FORM OF LIFE IN PRISON

I hate officers who go bad. I don't care what their reason is; I hate them. They poison the profession and devalue the honorable contributions of all the other officers who wear the uniform. Texas corrections officers work for and represent the people of the State of Texas. The commodities that we trade in are the protection of the public, trust, loyalty, integrity, and credibility; without any one of them we are worthless.

There is a most important contract between the uniformed officer and the public. It is unwritten and unsigned, but very much understood. As someone who accepts that contract with the public and takes it seriously, it burns a hole right through my soul every time I hear about some officer who got caught smuggling drugs into a prison. It always ends up the same way: someone gets killed, ripped off, or sold out.

Prison-employee drug smugglers deserve a special place in Hell. I feel the same way about an officer who would knowingly allow another officer to sell or smuggle drugs without reporting it. An officer who witnesses this behavior but claims, "Hey, it's not any of my business," puts not only his own life in danger, but also risks the lives of every other officer and inmate in the prison. I've seen people get killed over a small matchbox full of marijuana that would sell for less than $20.00 on the street.

As far as I'm concerned, officers who trade their souls for prestige with the convict gangs or carry drugs for money are right down there with the baby rapist and child molesters on the evolutionary scale. At least convicts don't wear officer uniforms with the emblem of the State of Texas on their arm while pretending to be something they're not.

REVOLVING DARRINGTON WARDENS

In February 1984, Darrington Unit Warden David Christian was terminated for alleged or imagined violations of Judge William

Wayne Justice's court order. Christian wasn't "convicted" of any offense and eventually sued the TDC for wrongfully firing him. TDC settled the case by allowing Christian to draw his full retirement. Warden Christian's replacement as senior warden of the Darrington Unit was Willis M. Gilliam, a twelve-year TDC veteran.

On February 3, 1984, Warden Gilliam's first day at work, the Darrington Unit had a true "maximum custody" inmate population. The problem was that the unit did not have the physical plant, the trained staff, or the support from the TDC director's office to successfully manage the convicts.

The racial tension was running high. The Darrington Unit's inmate population was composed of 54 percent black inmates, 26 percent white inmates, and 20 percent Hispanic inmates when Warden Gilliam was assigned. The Hispanic inmates, although grossly outnumbered, were organized into gangs that held the balance of power. After months of almost-daily assaults by convicts on other convicts and officers, the guard force was ineffective, complacent, intimidated, and in many cases corrupt.

The daily stabbings and assaults on inmates and staff continued, finally culminating in the homicide of inmate David Paul Alto, twenty-six, serving eight years for a Harris County burglary. Alto, an outside trusty, was killed in the unit laundry/shower area by the Texas Syndicate on Sunday, October 14, 1984. At about the same time that Alto was being killed, a diversionary disturbance occurred in the main hallway, in which five inmates, all Hispanic, sustained minor stab wounds. Alto's dead body was found fully clothed in about five inches of water in one of the group shower areas. He had suffered multiple stab wounds to the head, chest and back, twenty-four wounds in all.

The investigators didn't say so at the time, but the Alto killing had all the earmarks of a well-planned TS hit. With the exception of Alto, all the injuries and suspects were Hispanic inmates. Most of them were known or suspected TS members. The big question was motive. As an outside trusty, Alto's access to the outside may have played a part in whatever problem he had with the TS.

The entire 1,900-inmate population at Darrington Unit was locked down immediately after the Alto killing, and in a search of the unit more than a hundred homemade weapons were found. A day or so later, Warden Gilliam announced that he intended to resign, saying, "There must be a better way to make a living." He had been warden for only nine months, and there had been four inmate homicides and numerous inmate and staff assaults. "I've been thinking I had to make a choice between my private life and being warden," said Gilliam. "Wardens should be paid more for all that grief they have to put up with." At the time, Gilliam was making $38,808 per year. His resignation became effective November 1, 1984.

A few days later, Timothy West, thirty-five, was named to replace Gilliam. He had been a warden over the medium-security, 620-bed Connor Correctional Center in Hominy, Oklahoma, since 1982. He had been deputy warden for operations at the Oklahoma State Penitentiary in McAlester, a maximum-security facility with 1,300 inmates, from 1980 to 1982. West began his corrections career in Texas in 1974 as an officer and worked his way through the ranks to lieutenant, before he left to work in Oklahoma.

So why would a thirty-five-year-old warden from Oklahoma want to move to Brazoria County and take over a prison where four convicts had been killed in the past year? "It's a challenge," West said at the time, "but I've been in this situation before. The first 12 days on the job in Oklahoma we had three inmates killed, but we worked things out. It's called communicating." When he worked in Texas in what he called the "old days," West said, "I was pretty naive about the way prisons worked. I never saw inmates being beaten up by guards, but if we had to remove an inmate holding a knife from his cell, we were as punitive as we were successful. It didn't bother you if you heard a crack as you forced his hands behind his back."

According to West, now that the system frowned on such measures, guards thought they had lost control of the inmates, when in fact they just hadn't adjusted to a new form of persuasion—mutual respect and dialogue. West believed that by paying attention to detail, the Darrington Unit could be transformed from the worst unit to the best. He said, "It's going to be a test. The inmates will test me, and I'll test them. If we both pass, we'll be in good shape."

By the end of the first week, Warden West had to communicate his way through a small riot that resulted in injuries to twenty-five inmates and four guards. Four inmates were hospitalized. The second week, forty-two convicts sawed through the hollow cell bars in one of the "maximum-security" cellblocks, escaping from their cells in order to fight with other convicts. By the third week, the 1,800 convicts at the maximum-security Darrington Unit had to be locked down and fed in their cells due to rampant rumors that guns had been smuggled into the unit.

In addition to unit staff, special operational-response teams (SORTs) were called in to search for the alleged hidden weapons. After an extensive search of the building and compound using staff, dogs, and metal detectors, a .25-caliber pistol and a box of ammunition were found inside a locker box. The locker was located in an inside storage area where four "trusties" were making craft items. In addition to the gun and ammunition, more than seventy pieces of metal that were being formed into knifes were found. Warden West speculated, "From the interviews we've conducted so far, we either spoiled an escape attempt or a gang-related killing."

The rumors of another gun were still strong and the search ongoing when an alleged "hit list" with five high-ranking prison officials on it was found. In private, the fear was that the gangs had organized in an effort to smuggle in weapons, take hostages, and take over the prison unit. The rumors were unsubstantiated, but they had to be taken seriously. The last time guns had been successfully smuggled into a Texas prison unit was in 1974 at the Walls Unit in Huntsville, where Fred Gomez Carrasco led an ill-fated escape attempt. Carrasco, another convict, and two employees died in a shoot-out with Texas Rangers, Department of Public Safety officers, and an FBI agent.

After being locked down for about a week, Warden West announced, "We plan to have a traditional Thanksgiving Day dinner. We'll see how it goes from there. If their attitude is good, we may start letting them out again." While Warden West was waiting for the inmates to develop a "good attitude," system-wide gang activity had reached unprecedented levels. By November of 1984, there had been 22 inmate homicides and 360 non-fatal stabbings. This had been the most violent year in TDC history.

At 8:30 A.M. on March 19, 1985, at the Darrington Unit an

illiterate, borderline mentally retarded convict, Calvin Massey, twenty-one, was hacked to death in an administrative segregation recreation room in full view of a video camera. Massey had tried unsuccessfully to join several of the inmate gangs, but they wouldn't take him, because of his unpredictable behavior. He had also cooperated with law enforcement by giving a statement during the investigation of a 1984 gang-related homicide at the Ellis II Unit. Vergil Barfield (*aka* "Midget"), age thirty, serving a nine-year sentence for a Harris County burglary, butchered Massey by chasing him around a dayroom and stabbing him forty-two times in front of a dozen inmate witnesses.

The officers in the area were armed with only a video camera. Although on the tape Massey can be heard yelling to the other convicts in the room for help, not one of them makes any attempt to intervene. As Massey finally weakens and falls to the floor, Barfield is seen going over and kneeling near him and stabbing him several more times. While Massey lies there bleeding to death, Barfield pulls out another weapon, secured to his thigh with a rubber band, and places it in the dying convict's hand. This was supposed to help Barfield in his later claim of self-defense. Barfield can be seen several times looking into the lens of the video camera. He knew he was being filmed while he was killing Massey, but he didn't care. He seemed to revel in his temporary "celebrity" status.

At the trial, Barfield claimed that he was "scared" of Massey and said he once heard him bragging about stabbing an inmate on another unit. However, the grim pictures were worth more than any number of words or witnesses. The videotape showing Barfield stabbing the victim forty-two times was shown several times, and his actions did not impress the jury as being motivated by self-defense. It only took the jury thirty minutes to agree that Barfield was guilty of murder. It took another seventeen minutes for them to give him a life sentence.

The final straw came on Monday, June 24, 1985, when two inmates who belonged to the Texas Mafia killed Brian Mimier, the same convict who had attempted escape a few months earlier and was now being held in the "high-security" administratiove segregation wing. At the time, the Texas Mafia was doing everything it could to enhance its reputation as the "baddest of the bad" of the prison gangs. In some cases, they worked with the ABT and other gangs to fulfill murder contracts in exchange for favors.

Marty Ray Sohn and Doyle Wayne Hill, two verified Texas Mafia members, fatally stabbed Mimier sixteen times in the face, neck, and chest while in a recreation area at the Darrington Unit. It was Brian Mimier's twenty-sixth birthday. TDC's Southern Regional director, Ron Angelone, and Warden Tim West both came out in the press at the time placing the blame for Mimier's death on correctional staff.

Angelone was quoted as saying, "Some people are either going to bite the bullet or go to work somewhere else. If we find out that people are just lazy and there is a breach in security, they're out. I know that they're under a lot of pressure handling inmates who would kill their own mothers for fun, but we're paying them money to do a job."

Warden West said, "There'll probably be some dismissals or charges filed. Some guards either didn't follow procedure or actually took the weapons out [to the yard]." That statement didn't help to instill confidence in the correctional staff at the Darrington Unit. The first change made was by the TDC director's office. Tim West was reassigned to an administrative job in Huntsville. It had become clear that his plan to "communicate and have a dialogue" with the Darrington convicts was not going to be enough to stop the violence.

At trial, Darrington Unit convict Marty Ray Sohn, twenty-eight, already serving thirty-five years for an attempted capital murder, pled guilty to the killing of Brian Mimier. Sohn, a confirmed Texas Mafia member, made a package deal with prosecutors in exchange for a twenty-year sentence. Sohn pled guilty to the homicides of Mimier and Donathan Steen, twenty-eight, who was serving thirty years for a Tarrant County aggravated robbery.

Sohn admitted to killing Steen at the Darrington Unit by stabbing him in the chest while on a recreation yard in front of fourteen inmates. The fourteen alleged witnesses told sheriff's-department investigators that they didn't see anything. Sohn also admitted to breaking the nose of an officer who refused to allow him to shower in June of 1984. The district attorney's office said they offered Sohn the twenty-year "plea bargain" because it would have cost at least $60,000 to conduct three separate trials.

As a result of this plea bargain, Sohn got less time for two homicides and an aggravated assault than he had received for his initial conviction for attempted capital murder, thirty-five years.

An Offer I Had to Refuse

A few days after the Brian Mimier homicide, the Ramsey III Unit Warden, Michael W. Moore, who also happened to be my next-door neighbor, knocked on my back door. I had known Mike ever since he had replaced Assistant Warden Grady Stricklin back at Retrieve. My wife and I had a friendly, casual relationship with the Moore family, so it was not that unusual for us to visit. I walked out onto the small patio, where we sat at a table over drinks while he made me a proposition.

Moore told me that he was going to be transferred to the Darrington Unit as the new warden. I expressed some surprise, because the general rumor had been that Warden Keith Price, Ph.D., was the likely candidate to replace Tim West. Moore went into great detail about how the Huntsville administration was willing to do anything to stop the killings and get control of the Darrington Unit. Then, when Moore went to great lengths to compliment my work as both field and building major at Ramsey I, I suspected that he had an ulterior motive.

There was no doubt about it, Warden Michael W. Moore was a rising star in the system. If he could get a handle on the Darrington Unit, the sky was virtually the limit for not only his career, but also anyone who was riding on his coattails. Mike Moore was almost as good a salesman as Jim Shaw, and he presented a compelling argument based on loyalty, integrity, and general team spirit. He beat around the bush for about forty-five minutes before formally asking if I would go to Darrington with him as his building major.

I didn't answer right away. I knew immediately that this was very likely going to be a turning point in my career. I reminded him of my respect and loyalty for both Warden Terry Terrell and Jim Shaw. I told him of the many unresolved problems still facing the Ramsey I Unit. We had just had another gang related homicide the week before. There had been almost as many stabbings at the Ramsey I as at Darrington. Then I sat up and looked him squarely in the face and said, "I'll go to Darrington with you under one condition."

He asked, "What's that?"

I said, "I want you to promise me that in a few months, when we have the Darrington Unit under control and you move on to the regional director's office, you won't leave me behind at Darrington working for Keith Price."

His chin dropped like I had spit in his drink. He said, "I can't do that."

I leaned back and said, "I understand, and with all due respect, I'll stay here with Warden Terrell at Ramsey I."

On July 1, 1985, Michael W. Moore became the fourth senior warden assigned to the Darrington Unit since February 1984. He took my old friend Larry Johns with him as his building major. I was happy that Larry was getting the opportunity and sure that he could do the job. I was more than a little dubious about whether Mike Moore would help him when it was over.

In hindsight, with the possible exception of my telling the Huntsville administration that I wasn't interested in any assignment outside of the southern region, when I turned down Mike Moore's offer, I probably turned down the single biggest opportunity of my career. I knew I had made the right decision, though, when only six months later in December 1985, Michael Moore replaced Ron Angelone as the Southern Regional director and Warden Keith Price, Ph.D., became the fifth senior warden assigned to the Darrington Unit within two years. My standard of personal ethics would not have allowed me to work for the doctor. If I'd been the building major at the Darrington Unit when Price arrived as the new warden, in all likelihood my career would have ended right there.

CHAPTER NINE

EMANCIPATED WOMEN

> "All job positions with TDC are now open to women on
> an equal basis with men."
> —From *Coble* consent decree

Prior to 1981, the only female employees allowed on most TDCJ units were the warden's secretary, a few mailroom employees, and medical staff. The warden's secretary and mailroom employees were both "non-contact" positions. Medical staff did have contact with inmates, but under the supervision of security staff.

On November 7, 1974, Ms. K. K. Coble, a white female, applied for a position as a correctional officer with the Texas Department of Corrections. She was ultimately denied employment in any capacity. As a result, Ms. Coble and Donna Beneze Riggs, also a white female who had been denied employment, filed what became a class-action lawsuit on behalf of all women under Title VII of the 1964 Civil Rights Act.

On December 20, 1982, Federal District Judge Norman Black ruled that TDC's policy of not hiring women to perform any correctional-officer function at male prison units could not be justified as due bona fide occupational qualification and was in violation of Title VII. The settlement called for TDC to actively recruit females for jobs on male units and to open 1,018 positions formerly held by male officers to women. Ms. Coble received $65,000, and Ms. Beneze received $5,000.

In 1984, TDC recorded 1,678 attacks on officers by inmates. The victims of those inmate-on-employee assaults were not limited to male employees. As more and more women began to work contact positions in Texas male prisons, they began to pay a high price for their emancipation.

Ellis I Unit convict Ramon Mata stabbed Minnie R. Houston, forty-one, to death on June 3, 1985. A six-year employee of the Texas Department of Corrections, Ms. Houston had only been working in contact positions for three months. The slain officer's mother, Irene Simmons, said she couldn't understand why her daughter was killed. "She was a good guard, and the other inmates and guards looked up to her," said Simmons. Houston had worked at the Goree Women's Unit in Huntsville until they moved all the female prisoners to units in the Gatesville, Texas, area in 1981. After transferring to the Ellis I men's unit in order to remain close to family and friends in the Huntsville area, she was assigned to work the picket towers that overlook the prison's fenced perimeter.

Ms. Houston had been commended on November 9 by the TDC for preventing two death row–assigned inmates from escaping. From her guard tower, Houston leveled a shotgun at them and held both convicts at bay until help arrived. Then Officer Houston was moved to the food-service department; her mother said of the kitchen assignment, "She didn't like that job at all. She liked the tower job and complained about working the other one." Ms. Houston had been transferred to the Ellis I kitchen staff because of "staffing increases at other parts of the prison," said then Ellis I Unit warden, Jerry Peterson.

Officer Houston was stabbed at least ten times in the chest with a fifteen-inch carving knife at about 9:30 P.M. on Monday night, June 3, 1985. After inmate Mata was seen leaving the area, six other inmates found her, still alive, but mortally wounded, in the kitchen bathroom. She died later, still at the scene.

Mata had been assigned to the kitchen detail after being promoted to State Approved Trusty Class II on May 10, 1984. "According to our new Classification Plan, there is nothing in there to indicate that Mata was a mean person," said Warden Peterson.

It seems that evidence concerning Mata's character was available, however. Former Pecos County District Attorney Bill Mason, who had prosecuted Mata in 1979, described him as "just plain mean. That guy's a coldblooded killer, and [prison officials] knew it. All that information went down there with him," Mason said, expressing surprise that a convicted murderer was given a job in the kitchen, where he had access to potential weapons. Bill Mason no doubt had a point.

Mata and another man, Ruben Hernandez, had been found guilty of murder in the June 1978 shooting deaths of Felix Rodriguez and Guadalupe Jimenez. Mata received a thirty-year sentence in a plea-bargain agreement, while Hernandez was sentenced to life in prison. Mason described the two Pecos County murders matter-of-factly: "They flat executed them," he said. The victims were taken to a field and their hands were tied behind their backs before they died. Mata and Hernandez were captured several days later in Arizona.

As for the murder of Ms. Houston, immediately after killing the officer, Mata tried to run by using his trusty status to get out to the employee parking lot, where he stole Houston's car. Sergeant Bobby Ennis, who was working the highway gate on the unit's exit road, captured him. Ennis testified at Mata's capital murder trial, "As we were taking him inside, [Mata] said it's too late to save her, that he knew what he was doing and that we might as well kill him right now." Mata told authorities at the time that he was in love with the officer and couldn't live without her. Dr. Jim C. Whitley testified that an autopsy showed Houston had had sexual intercourse just prior to her death, but Judge Jerry Sandel ruled that Whitley's testimony about the autopsy test could not be presented to the jury.

Defense attorneys tried to show that Mata and Houston had an intimate relationship. Dr. Whitley said, "The reason [Mata] gave for killing Ms. Houston was that a sudden rage overcame him connected to her statements that she was abandoning the relationship." The only physical evidence presented indicating that even a casual relationship existed between the two was a birthday card to Mata's eight-year-old daughter that was co-signed by Houston, reading: "Happy Birthday, with a lot of love."

Mata did not even look up during most of the trial testimony and remained hunched over a yellow legal pad at the defense table. Dr. Whitley said Mata—a longtime drug and alcohol user—started seeing hallucinations of Houston coming to his jail cell on nightly visits. Dr. Whitley ordered a change of the drugs Mata had been taking to treat a mental disorder. The hallucinations stopped only after his psychotropic medication prescription was changed. After finding Mata guilty of murder, the jury deliberated for about five hours in the punishment phase of the trial before giving him the death sentence.

In the aftermath of the Minnie Houston tragedy, there were a lot of people trying to place blame on everything from the inmate-classification system to management of prisons in general. One woman who spoke up at the time came as close to the truth as any—Molly Standley of Huntsville, Texas.

At the time of Minnie Houston's death, Molly Standley (no relation to Julia Standley, who died at the hands of convicts during the 1974 "Carracso Hostage Siege") had been working in one of TDC's administrative offices (a non-contract position) for eighteen years. She was obviously a preceptive woman, and I thought Molly's comments expressed a realistic view. She said: "The blame (if there should be any) should be placed on the courts that declared that TDC must hire a certain percentage of women officers to work inside men's penitentiaries. There are only X number of 'safe' posts for women inside the TDC. The courts say we must have a certain number of women officers. If we are going to have to furnish one male officer to guard every female officer who is assigned to guard a number of inmates, then you the taxpayer, are going to have to dig deeper into your pockets. The confines of a men's penitentiary is no place for a woman."

Warden Jerry Peterson, who eulogized Minnie Houston, said, "Her professional service and helping attitude could not be surpassed. The TDC has suffered an extreme loss." More than five hundred people, many of them TDC guards, attended the memorial ceremony inside the Trinity High School auditorium and at least fifty more stood outside and sweated in the 95-degree heat. Governor Mark White, who attended the forty-five-minute service, signed a resolution recognizing Houston for her outstanding services in the community and at the TDC. A female

TDC sergeant, Kathy Bahlman, who was not persuaded that women should not work inside the prisons, said the stabbing could have happened to any guard, not just a female. She was right, of course, it could have happened to any officer, but historically, there have not been very many lovesick convicts who have killed male officers over alleged personal relationships.

I didn't know Officer Minnie Houston personally, but from what I've read and what the people who knew her best said, she was not a card-carrying feminist. She had nothing to prove and was just trying to do her job when she was killed. No one can speak for Minnie Houston, but if she had been given her choice of work assignments, she would have (at least according to her mother) preferred the non-contact tower duty to the contact work in the prison unit's kitchen.

Unfortunately for Officer Houston, a federal judge, lawyers, and litigious feminists chose her work assignment for her. It is a true shame that some of those judges, lawyers, and feminists can't understand what Ms. Houston experienced at the mercy of that psychotic convict's knife. Perhaps if they could have stood in front of that fifteen-inch butcher knife, they would have seen the ramifications of the situation more clearly and made a more objective decision regarding the place of women in male prisons. For the feminist who is truly interested in a sane and rational approach to this issue, there is a moral lesson to be learned here: Be careful what you ask for, because you may very well get it.

FEMALE HOSTAGE

On August 3, 1984, Richard Joseph Sisto, thirty-five, serving a life sentence for a Dallas County aggravated rape, kidnapped a female officer at the Ramsey II Unit and held her at knife point in a locked medication-dispensing room. The convict obtained the knife by simply asking a male security officer to "borrow his pocketknife to cut up some sandwiches." The inmate entered the pill room when the woman opened the door to leave. He inserted the key into the security door lock and then broke it off inside, rendering the lock useless. Then he pulled the knife on the female officer. During the five-hour standoff, the white female officer, in her late twenties, was threatened and sexually assaulted. In an effort to buy himself some time alone with the woman, the inmate demanded to talk with TDC Director Raymond "The Pro" Procunier, who flew in from Huntsville to negotiate with the inmate. The director arranged for the convict to speak by phone to a Catholic priest and to his mother during the standoff. Procunier promised the convict that he would fly him back to Huntsville with him if he would release the woman.

Sisto did finally release her, and he was flown back to Huntsville in the director's plane. The convict said the female officer agreed to have sex with him and drank whiskey with him for five hours. Sisto said that he and the guard had staged a fake hostage incident to dramatize the lack of security at the Ramsey II Unit. The woman at first said that she was unharmed, then later she told authorities that she had been raped. After a Brazoria County grand jury indicted the convict on aggravated rape and aggravated kidnapping charges, the woman changed her mind and requested that the district attorney's office drop the charges.

The prosecutors wanted to try Sisto on both counts, but couldn't build a case against the convict without the woman's testimony, especially after she requested that the charges be dropped. The woman was reassigned to an outside (non-contact) picket post at another of TDC's Brazoria County prison units. The male officer who gave the convict the knife "to cut sandwiches" was fired. This incident caused TDC to draft a new rule that for the first time prohibited employees from carrying pocketknives while at work, unless it was required as part of their job description. The convict was not prosecuted for any offense. The source of the whiskey was never established, but it was storebought and clearly did not originate inside the unit. This incident was widely publicized and did not do anything to enhance the reputations or credibility of female correctional officers working within male TDC units.

One of the many frivolous arguments put forth in order to justify placing women in contact positions at the male prison units was that they would have a "mellowing effect" on the inmates. The lawyers said it would be a "Beauty and the Beast"–type phenomenon and would calm the savage inmates. They envisioned a kinder, gentler, more polite convict population that not only dressed more neatly, but also would no longer use profanity or act out in violent episodes. With the exception of the trusty camps and some of the minimum-custody units, this argument has proven to be patently false. The evidence is reflected in the number of employees raped, assaulted, and verbally abused. The ever-mounting evidence of assaultive inmate behavior demonstrates that in reality, convicts can and will be every bit as crude and violent in the presence of women officers as with men. Convicts are basically predators preying on the weak; the more vulnerable a target appears, the more likely an assault is to occur.

Looking for Love

Just when we thought that our working environment couldn't get any stranger, evidence began coming in that clearly demonstrated that some of our female employees were having consensual sexual relationships with convicts. In my experience, it first came to light during a drug-smuggling investigation at the Ramsey I Unit. We knew that a couple of convicts who worked in the inmate craft shop were receiving drugs on a regular basis. Shortly after a drug delivery had been received, a fairly reliable convict informant, who had been cut out of what he believed to be his rightful share of the narcotics, snitched as to how the drugs were coming in.

I found the informant's story hard to believe, but the subsequent investigation and additional informant tips allowed us to trace the dope back to a couple of enterprising female officers. We found out that the convicts had been paying them to mule in small amounts of liquor and marijuana in exchange for leather belts, purses, and other craft-shop items.

We set up a sting through one of our informants, who knew when the two Hispanic female officers were supposed to deliver. When the two drove into the unit parking lot, we were waiting for them. After a quick search with a drug dog, we had two very confrontational female officers and almost two ounces of marijuana. The two convicts who were expecting the marijuana were searched, and love letters, cards, and nude photographs of the two officers were found. When we confronted the officers with the evidence, they admitted to having consensual sexual contact with the convicts and smuggling drugs and liquor into the unit on several occasions over a period of several months. When we asked them why, they said that they were in love, and after resigning from their jobs, the only thing they wanted to know was, "Can we still be on their visiting list?"

There are very few secrets in the prison environment, and that is especially true when the subject involves sex, drugs, or money. If one convict thinks that another convict is getting something that he is not allowed to have, there is no way he's going to keep it secret. He may first try blackmail against the parties involved, but soon the circle of information grows and can no longer be contained.

As more and more informants began to flood my office with reports of these relationships, I began to wonder if any of the females were immune. I didn't have the staff to investigate the veracity of all the alleged indiscretions, but that didn't stop me from worrying about the potential consequences.

Not long after discovering the dope-smuggling plot at Ramsey I, a schoolteacher at the Darrington Unit got caught having consensual sex; she was found with one of her inmate students on top of her classroom desk. All the other units in the region were having similar problems. To some of these women, the concept of survival in a man's prison environment meant that they wouldn't hesitate to use all of their assets. Many of these would-be delicate flowers of womanhood, dressed coquettishly in their purposefully form-fitted correctional-officer uniforms, became so addicted to their own passionate desires that they ceased to function as employees of the state and simply became mules for "their convicts."

THE RN AND THE CONVICT

We got in a new director of nurses, an RN who was a second-generation TDC employee. She had grown up as the child of an employee on an East Texas prison farm. She was married to a sheriff's-department officer, and she was all business. The new RN seemed to be just what we needed. She organized the sick-call procedure and the doctor's clinics and did not waste any time treating the inmates and getting them back to work. Even the security staff was complimentary about her efficiency and no-nonsense approach to the practice of medicine.

Some mornings at around 6:00 A.M. I would see her having breakfast in the ODR. It was unusual for medical-department heads to be at work so early, but we just figured that she was dedicated to the cause.

One morning after breakfast, one of the black inmate waiters caught me in the hallway outside the ODR and said that the RN was having an affair with a white convict waiter who also worked in the ODR. I listened to him, because he'd been a credible informant in the past, but I had a real hard time believing this story. He said he had seen them early one morning at about 4:00 A.M. in a serious embrace, kissing in the hallway just outside the ODR. He said that the convict had his hand so far up her dress, she had to stand on one leg and hold onto the wall to keep from falling. I hoped that he was wrong, but as he told me the story, I couldn't help seeing visions of the Minnie Houston crime scene in my mind. I had to find out the truth, one way or another.

The inmate reported to be involved with the nurse was a three-time loser working on a life sentence. He was an old-school convict who had been around the block in some of the toughest prisons in the state. He was a borderline white supremacist with the appropriate tattoos up and down both arms, but compared to the general run-of-the-mill convict at Ramsey I, I kind of liked him. He stayed out of trouble, minded his own business, didn't snitch, and worked hard at his job.

From a practical standpoint, it's difficult to blame the convicts in these situations. After all, it is a "consensual relationship," and he is just doing what she allows him to do. No woman ever had more power over a man than a female has over a lovesick convict. She is the one who can come and go. She always knows where he is and what he is doing. She is pretty sure that if he fools around with other women she will soon know about it, because it will have to be another employee.

Soon after the informant reported the affair, the RN was promoted to the director-of-nursing position at the regional medical center at the just-completed Ramsey III Unit medical facility. I was hopeful that the change in unit assignment for the RN would end the alleged problem. At this point I didn't have any verified evidence of the relationship, and I really didn't want to have to pursue the matter.

The Ramsey III Unit is only about a mile down the road from the Ramsey I Unit. I started getting a feeling that made the hair stand up on the back of my neck when I saw the RN leaving the Ramsey I building early one morning. As I passed her, she waved and said she just came by to "say hello" to everyone she had worked with. I thought to myself, *No one gets up at 4:00 A.M. to go on a casual visit on a workday.* I checked in the ODR and sure enough, she had been on time for early breakfast, the three-time loser's shift. She had started showing up every morning for breakfast.

The next morning we met her when she entered the building and advised her that we thought it would be more appropriate if she ate her meals at Ramsey III. She got this hand-caught-in-the-cookie-jar look on her face and said, "I understand." We made no accusations, but she knew that we knew what had been going on. Evidently she did not wish to risk her professional status any further, because a day or two later she resigned her position as director of nurses at the regional medical facility. She filed for divorce from her husband, and a few months later, when her convict lover made parole, they got married. I received Christmas cards from them for several years, but I have no way of knowing if they stayed together. It was no doubt a strange match.

Of course, these relationships are generally of short duration and end badly. They rarely reach the marital stage, and even the ones that do are usually short-lived. I've seen many of these affairs over the years, and there are a couple of common threads that runs through them: 1. The affairs are based solely on impulse and emotion. 2. There is no correlation between levels of education. 3. An individual's attractiveness or lack thereof doesn't seem to matter. 4. Race doesn't matter. 5. Marital status is irrelevant. 6. Loyalty to the job, the State of Texas, or one's peers are of no consequence to employees who engage in these affairs.

WHY DOES IT HAPPEN?

There were many women in the mid-1980s who came to work every day, did their jobs by the book, and performed in a professional manner, within their physical limitations. I don't want to stereotype all women. I won't speculate as to the individual reasons that motivate women to want to work in male prisons, but I have heard the following reasons offered:

1. "It's the rush, the adrenaline. Until you do it, you can't really explain it."
2. "It's better than office work. I hate office work."
3. "This is the only job I've ever had where I get to give the orders."
4. "Well, I was working at fast-food joints before I got this job."
5. "My husband and I both work for the system. I didn't want to stay home by myself."
6. "It's not the money, it's the benefits. I like the insurance and retirement."
7. "Hey, it's steady—no lay-offs like in construction."
8. "'Cause I can work days and go to night school and get that degree—I want to promote."
9. "I'll be honest, I never been around so many good-looking officers in my life."
10. "I like the excitement of not knowing what these fools are going to do next."

Some of these are legitimate reasons; others are questionable. However, probably none of them outweighs the harsh, undeniable reality that the average woman who goes to work in a male prison is physically unable to defend herself in any one-on-one situation with a convict. Beyond that, and at least as important, she's not physically able to come to the aid of a fellow officer in confrontational situations. For example, even in the minimum-custody units, if a fight occurs between inmates in a fifty-man dormitory where a female officer is working, her only options are "verbal intervention" and screaming that there is a fight in progress. Then she has to wait until male officers arrive to separate the inmates. If a male officer finds himself in the same situation, he, too, is instructed to call for help before physically intervening in the fight. The critical difference is that at least when a male officer does arrive, he can physically help break up the fight and/or protect another officer while he is doing so. A female officer cannot.

In the maximum-security units, the women officers, regardless of their level of professionalism, are routinely the objects of obscene remarks and targets of physical abuse by the convicts. It is becoming an almost-daily occurrence for female officers to be physically assaulted by convicts. The on-duty job description of a correctional officer is becoming more hazardous by the day—I know female bull riders who haven't had their noses broken or their teeth knocked out as often as some of these female correctional officers.

When these violent attacks occur, a female officer's only recourse is to file a disciplinary report against the offending convict. At a disciplinary hearing, the most that can happen to the convict is loss of "goodtime" or fifteen days' solitary confinement. Most convicts in maximum custody don't have any earned goodtime anyway, and a fifteen-day stay in solitary only amounts to a quiet vacation away from the other idiots he's been living around. The convict sits in his solitary cell and laughs at the "gray slaves" who have to bring him his daily hot meals and medication and make sure that he receives his court-mandated hot shower in a timely manner. Convict attacks on staff are rarely prosecuted in courts of law unless the assault involves the use of a weapon and documented serious injuries. If the case is not an extremely flagrant violation, the local district-attorney's office will usually not take it, due to the time and expense involved in the prosecution of someone who is already incarcerated. Also, as DAs are fond of pointing out, "convicts don't vote."

Female officers are singled out, largely because of their sex, for special ridicule and obscenities. Convicts take a certain pleasure in getting to a female, especially if she is conscientious about her job and doesn't play favorites. The convicts know what they are doing and will try almost anything to intimidate the female until she gets scared enough to quit or to give them what they really want, which is either sex or for them to smuggle something in for them. Sometimes a female officer is naive enough to think that because she is female, convicts won't get physical with them. Then, a day or two later, after she's made a promise she doesn't intend to keep, some convict walks up and breaks her nose, and she learns that when a convict's money or livelihood is involved, the fact she is a female makes absolutely no difference.

THE DIFFERENCE BETWEEN POLICE, MILITARY, PRISONS

A female cop on the street is equipped with a gun and usually works with a partner who also has a gun. If she gets into trouble or if her partner gets in trouble, at least the guns they carry make them equally able to back each other up. In the military, female soldiers are armed when on the battlefield, and they rely on their fellow soldiers to back them up. Again, without the gun, she wouldn't have a fighting chance.

There are no guns or other weapons allowed inside TDC units. When a female TDC employee meets a convict one-on-one in a confrontational situation, it is the female who is at the mercy of the convict. Ninety-nine times out of a hundred, she will lose any physical altercation that occurs. In their efforts to be politically correct, the federal courts, the state and federal EEOC offices, and the lawyers in the state attorney general's office have so far been unwilling to recognize that reality. It is flawed policy that continues to put unarmed female prison employees in harm's way. I submit that anybody who will not acknowledge that simple fact is not living in the real world.

Unfortunately, female line officers pay the price for this artificially structured workforce, with their continuing daily risk of serious injury and the ever-rising possibility of death. Women, especially today's young women, have been programmed to win. Over the past twenty-five years they have been told since birth, over and over, that they can do anything. When placed in a one-on-one situation with a physically stronger convict who is not interested in playing by any of the rules that she has grown up with, the results can be deadly. She is defenseless. She can be verbally abused, pimp-slapped, physically assaulted, raped, or killed, and all the time, in her mind she's thinking, "This isn't supposed to be happening." According to everything she's been taught by our politically correct society, she is supposed to be able to handle this situation. It's tough when the rubber meets the road and reality raises its ugly head. The sad thing is that in most cases, when an inmate does injure a female officer, there is little that can be done. The convict is usually already doing more time than he can do, and it serves little purpose to add more time to his already infinite sentence.

When, not if, a takeover of a Texas prison occurs on the scale of the New Mexico or Attica, New York, riots, I suspect the policy regarding women working in contact positions will be reconsidered. I do not believe that most Texans are going to be willing to pay the price in terms of employee trauma, particularly to female victims, or for the unfortunate, but inevitable loss of life.

HARD TIME IN A TENDER TRAP

In 1981 the TDC moved the last of the female inmates from the old Goree Unit in Huntsville, to Gatesville, in Central Texas. When they began staffing the Mountain View Unit, the new "maximum security" unit for the "baddest of the bad" women convicts, I was recruited for a building captain's job. I was told that they needed a "family man of high moral fiber." I had never entertained thoughts of working in a women's prison, but I didn't want to be rude to those who believed I was somehow right for the job, so I went for the tour and interview.

I was familiar with the old red-brick Goree Unit, as I had visited that unit several times, but I was somewhat surprised to see that the new maximum-security unit was mostly made up of dormitories. It looked more like a small college campus than a prison. There was a large gym, with the only wooden floor I've ever seen in a TDC unit. There was a large, almost Olympic-size swimming pool.

The Mountain View Unit for "incorrigible" female convicts was truly a surreal environment. They still had female convicts acting as turnkeys, and dorm mothers. Everywhere we went, there were women convicts turning keys to let us in and out of the security doors.

There were male schoolteachers, laundry supervisors, psychologists, counselors, a priest, and a "religious advisor." At that time, the rank-and-file male correctional officers were still required to work in only "non-contact" positions, but there were exceptions. When I was escorted into the unit laundry, we had to go through three locked doors in order to get to the male supervisor's office. He was literally surrounded by about thirty female convict workers, and he was the only male in the department. It became apparent that there had not been much realistic forethought put into the feasibility of working male employees in such an environment.

This was before the days of DNA testing, and the current blood testing didn't really identify the paternity of a child to the exclusion of all others. TDC has averaged about one hundred women a year who give birth, and that number has been steadily rising. Although many of the women came into the system already pregnant, there were those occasions when employees and inmates were caught in the "throes of ecstasy" as it were, whereupon there would be an outrageous scandal lasting several days. The employee was usually, but not always, fired, and the convict received a disciplinary case. Of course, there was a steady stream of female convicts claiming to have undergone Immaculate Conception.

The dynamic relationships within female prisons are among the few things that are not exaggerated in the B-grade movies. It is true that many, if not most, female inmates take part in homosexual relationships while in prison. One female warden advised that in her experience, as much as 80 percent or more of her total female unit population was or had been involved in a lesbian relationship. She observed that "the nurturing instinct in females is very strong and the need to be held and touched is almost undeniable." This is usually a temporary phenomenon that reverses to heterosexuality upon release.

Unlike on male units, where the homosexuals pair up, or prostitue themselves after loneliness and desperation set in, the females form entire family units. The influence of the inmate family structure is more than most inmates can resist. When a new female convict arrives on the unit, she has about two days to decide which "family" she is going to join. Each family member has a role to play, from grandparent, parent, brother, sister, or children, to of course husbands, wives, and lovers. The strength of the family is determined by the size of membership and the assets it controls. The families are partly for protection and sometimes function as support groups, but they are also sexually predatory. The only way a general-population inmate can avoid the families is to do all of her time in protective segregation. Very few female inmates choose that option. The female segregation population has consistently averaged around 2 percent.

The "War on Drugs" has been particularly hard on women.

Violent female offenders account for only a fifth of the growth in the female prison population; drug offenders account for more than half of the total growth. The drug offenders have changed the dynamic in the prisons for the worse. When surveyed, more than half of the drug-dependent inmates said they had engaged in prostitution, compared to only 8 percent of the non–drug-dependent inmates. Once incarcerated, a career prostitute generally does not quit being a prostitute, she just looks for new customers among the female convicts or prison employees (male or female). Of course, in order to avoid conflicts, she must be sure to obtain the permission of her prison family first. On occasion, the family may actively promote her business enterprise and of course share in the rewards, which can vary from cash, to drugs, to weapons and all other forms of contraband. To a moderately attractive prostitute, sex is power and a means to an end. She looks for the weak link in the chain, determines what is required of her to accomplish her mission, and then makes her victim an offer he or she can't refuse.

One of the more lucrative ways that women make money while in prison is the promotion of mail-order romance. They will send pictures, not necessarily of themselves, and "hot letters" promising everything from everlasting love to exotic sexual escapades if the recipient will only assist them financially while they are incarcerated. Hundreds of thousands of dollars are sent to women prisoners on the misguided premise that upon release they will be everything the senders have dreamed of. Victims include the elderly, the lonely, and the desperate. Religious organizations especially fall prey to these convicts, who write convincing letters of repentance in exchange for continuing financial support. Religious volunteers are especially vulnerable to these convicts, who simply tell the gullible optimists whatever they want to hear. Male convicts attempt this kind of fraud also and have achieved some limited success, but somehow it just seems more sincere and believable coming from a female convict.

Some of the more successful convict schemes involve solicitation of money for the support of their children. They usually send pictures of small children, not necessarily their own, along with tragic letters of abuse attached to them requesting that money be sent to the inmate's trust-fund account. Law enforcement has made several cases of outright mail fraud against female convicts, but usually the victims are too ashamed to complain to the authorities. Even if the victims do complain, the convicts usually have no assets from which to reclaim any lost money.

According to TDC statistics, women generally come to prison for the following reasons:

Drug Offenses	46.4%
Property Offenses	33.4%
Violent Offenses	17.2%
Other	3.1%

Type of custody in Texas women's prisons:

Minimum	74.3%
Medium	2.2%
Close	1.2%
Maximum	2%
Special Status*	20.2%

*Newly received, unclassified, mentally impaired, pregnant

Children: About 80 percent of women in state prisons are mothers; two-thirds had at least one child under age eighteen when they entered prison; and 6 percent enter prison pregnant.

Mountain View is the home of women's death row. Due to the ongoing success of the women's movement, juries are becoming more and more willing to see women as equal to men when it comes time to pay for their crimes. Beginning in 1984, the newly emancipated TDC, in an effort to avoid the appearance of discrimination, began placing male officers in contact positions within female prisons. Of course, the female units have individual showers in the housing areas, with privacy doors. The male officers don't work the strip-search houses where the inmates are searched for contraband at turnout gates and visitation areas. There are none of the gang showers that are so common on all of the male units.

Male officers are assigned as security officers in the female-inmate housing areas. Interestingly, the problem of overt sexual exposure by inmates that is reported so frequently by female officers on the male units is rarely reported by male officers working in female units. As a couple of female wardens observed, there is no doubt that a high percentage of the female inmates routinely engage in openly physical lesbian relationships while in the presence of male officers. Although these consensual sexual contacts between inmates are an institutional-rules violation, they are rarely if ever reported by male security staff. The general consensus is that male officers generally don't find sexual conduct by the female inmates objectionable and perhaps even enjoy the spectacle. Imagine that!

There have been numerous incidents of male officers being disciplined or fired for sexual involvement with the female inmates; however, some of the female unit wardens report that there is an even more difficult problem for them to manage. There is an increasing incidence of jealous female officers getting into physical altercations with each other while at work. The source of the problem is usually the real or sometimes imagined alienation of affection by their inmate lovers. In many cases, the fights occur when a female officer catches her paramour trifling with another woman. It seems that female units are laced with lesbian female employees constantly competing for control of their own workplace environment, with the sex-charged male employees and the female inmates caught in the middle.

Male officers clearly have no business working contact positions inside women's prisons. It is just dumb. The best argument I've heard for having the male employees is that they do at least provide some measure of physical security, but even that asset is lost when they are placed in contact positions. The fact of the matter is that women inmates have all the weapons they need to bribe or test the integrity of the strongest male employee without ever offering him a dime. Even if his intentions begin as honorable, it's just a matter of time before the female officers or the inmates place him in a compromising position. The issue again is, or should be, security. As a matter of sound correctional practice, it's just as dumb to place male correctional officers in contact positions in women's prisons as it is to place female correctional officers in contact positions in men's prisons. The issue should not be gender, but rather the safety and security of staff and the inmate population.

As the female assistant warden of the Mountain View Unit and I neared the end of my tour, we sat down for a cup of coffee in the ODR. She was telling me that there was really nothing to the job and that I should have no problems. She said she spent a lot of time interviewing inmates and recommended that if I chose to take the job, I would need to always have a box of Kleenex handy. "Their first reaction to any problem is to cry," she said.

While we were sitting there discussing the intricacies of running a female prison unit, a bright-eyed inmate waitress came to the table. She was perhaps twenty-four or twenty-five years old and had a figure like you might have seen in the lingerie section of an old Sears & Roebuck catalog. She smiled and asked if there was anything she could get for me. I had a brief moment of clarity and knew without going any further that I was in the wrong place. As Clint Eastwood said in some movie I once saw, "A man has got to know his limitations." I told my tour guide to tell the warden thanks, but no thanks, and headed for the parking lot. As I drove back toward Brazoria County, I assured myself that I had done the right thing, not just for myself, but for my family and the department. The environment at the women's unit was all smoke and mirrors, with intrigue and deception around every corner. I had no interest in becoming a part of it. At least back in Brazoria County I knew where the danger was; it was real, you could feel it and it was in your face, but I was comfortable with it.

CHAPTER TEN

My Worst Day in TDCJ

"Negotiation involves no more than saying 'nice doggie,'
until you have the opportunity to pick up a stick."
—Anonymous

By 1985, we at the units weren't hearing much from the Huntsville administration. They were all too busy patting themselves on the backs over the alleged settlement of the *Ruiz* lawsuit to bother with our trivial unit problems. We had just come through 1984 with twenty-five inmate-on-inmate homicides and an additional 404 non-fatal stabbings, so that the year was now officially on record as the deadliest in TDC history. We were still in the middle of a raging gang war with no end in sight. Our director, Raymond "The Pro" Procunier, was still stumbling around trying to pacify or at least stall the federal courts into believing everything would be all right.

The chairman of the Board of Corrections, Robert Gunn, joined then–Attorney General Jim Mattox in signing the proposed prison-reform settlement and used the opportunity to make a speech regarding the quality of the TDC staff. He started by saying, "Raymond Procunier heads probably the finest prison staff of any prison in the country today, but there is a certain subversive element, held over from previous administrations. We've got a lot of people from the old school," Gunn said. "You know, kick their ass and whip 'em with the rubber hose and everything else, and that's the way they feel inmates should be treated." He said some employees had stonewalled the philosophy of reform.

"We've had a group of people working there that are more or less obstructionist, as far as I'm concerned. They're the kind of people that are saying, 'If we just put this off long enough, it's going to go away.' Well, I want to inform them that the war is over, that the side of reform has won and that we certainly hope that they will become cooperative." Asked to comment about Gunn's remarks, Steve Martin, TDC's general counsel, said, "We prefer not to talk about that."

When Gunn's remarks came out on the front page of the state section of the *Houston Chronicle*, I had to sit down and take stock. I not only didn't feel like I was a part of a team effort anymore; instead, I was beginning to believe that I was being drawn into an unsolicited adversarial relationship with some folks who didn't have a clue about the realities of life on a prison unit. At the time, I was a nineteen-year veteran of TDC who had worked for three previous directors, and I had a good understanding of how to do my job.

Now, I'm just an old country boy from Central Texas, and perhaps I took Gunn's words too personally, but it sounded like he was calling me a "stonewalling obstructionist" who likes to "kick their ass and whip 'em with the rubber hose." The more I read Gunn's remarks, the angrier I became and finally I took the article to Warden Terrell and advised him that I didn't appreciate the fact that some guy I had never even met was questioning our ethics and calling us names in the newspaper. At first Warden Terrell was at least as livid as I was, but then I noticed a slow smile and he said, "Glenn, we might be taking this too seriously. We need to consider the source. This guy is a politically appointed member of the Board of Corrections and obviously doesn't know what he is talking about."

I checked into it and found out that Warden Terrell was right. Gunn was a politically connected geologist from Wichita Falls who had probably never even seen a convict or been inside a prison until he was appointed to the board. Gunn obviously didn't realize or didn't care that the experienced employees of the TDC were busting their collective butts trying to keep the TDC afloat. It was even more obvious that someone had convinced this guy that he was an expert in penology, when in fact he hunts rocks for a living.

In hindsight, this may have been the highlight of Gunn's egotistical foray into the arena of criminal justice. Having reached the pinnacle of his politically appointed career as a self-appointed penal expert, he now felt qualified to call a press conference and give his opinion about events and people that were unknown to him. As a state employee, I couldn't publicly respond to his comments without giving up my career. I had to remind myself that I didn't work for this loudmouth political appointee, the lawyers, or the federal judge he was pandering to. I filed his comments away in my scrapbook journal of political drivel and hoped to someday have a chance to respond. In the meantime, like a duck, I'd have to let his words roll off my back.

Ramsey I Unit Hostages

Tuesday, April 2, 1985, was the nightmare that all correctional employees pray never comes true. As days in the penitentiary go, the first part was rather pleasant. It was a nice spring day, with the sun shining and a gentle breeze blowing through the tops of the pecan trees that lined the front of the unit. I spent part of the day out on the inmate-recreation yards talking to convicts. They didn't seem to have any unusually significant problems. There were a few complaints about the food in the inmate dining room and the quality of the sewing-machine operator's work in the laundry, but nothing "unconstitutional."

(After interviewing thousands of convicts over the years, I have learned that where the quality of the laundry service and the food are concerned, convicts are never going to be satisfied. It is kind of a threshold complaint area for them—if everything else is going well, then they complain about the quality of the food or their clothes.)

The day passed with no special significance. I pride myself on being able to read convicts, and most of the time I've been able to see trouble before it happens. I have to confess that this time I didn't see it coming. Some months earlier, I had warned Warden Terrell of the fact that I thought Elisio "Chino" Martinez would do something if he got the chance, but Chino had been so quiet that I had hoped he had settled into the routine.

The ad-seg wing had been uncharacteristically quiet. Of the

eighty cells full of certified convict killers, violent gang members, and various other uncivilized misfits, not one of them had even thrown a food tray. The ad-seg officers were enjoying a well-deserved rest from the constant name-calling, flooded commodes, and the usual barrage of items being thrown at them from the cells. Looking back, it reminds me of the old western movies, when just before the bad guys attack the sheriff usually says, "It's quiet out there boys—yeah, too quiet."

I think for a moment I got lulled into believing that our security officers and procedures were good enough to prevent anything serious from happening. I can't emphasize how critical a mistake that is for a security supervisor to make. That is not to say that I could have prevented what happened, but overconfidence in one's ability to prevent the unknown is a reflection of a state of mind that no security supervisor should engage in. There is no such thing as an ultimately safe, secure prison, and there won't be any in the future as long as there are people involved in the process.

The cell doors in ad-seg were the type that could only be opened individually with a key. Each door had a round cylinder plunger that depressed into the door jamb whenever the door was locked. Utilizing typical convict engineering, several of the Texas Syndicate members discovered a unique way to defeat this doorlock system. Each time they were taken out of their cells for shower, recreation, legal visits, medical appointments, et cetera, they would compress a small piece of wet toilet paper into the hole in the cell-lock door jamb. Over a period of days or weeks, as the paper dried, they added more paper, and finally the hole in the cell-door jamb would fill to the point where the cylinder would no longer depress. Once the hole was filled with paper, the key would still turn in the lock, giving the appearance that the cell door was secure, when in fact all the convict had to do was push to open the door.

At 8:40 P.M. on Tuesday, April 2, 1985, Elisio "Chino" Martinez, who was housed in ad-seg two-row, number-nine cell, asked officer Richard Gallegos to pass a fan from his cell to two-row, number-two cell, housing Jose Cordova and Louis Goureal. Officer Richard Nelson advised officer Gallegos that he would assist in the passing of the fan. At 8:45 P.M. Officer Gallegos unlocked Chino's cell door to receive the fan. As the door unlocked, Chino kicked his cell door open. At the same moment, Texas Syndicate members Daniel Lopez and Alberto "Bones" Martinez (no relation to Chino) housed in two-row, number-five cell, pushed their own cell door open and came out onto the run. No key was necessary to open their cell door, as the paper stuffed into the door jamb had rendered the door lock useless. As Officer Nelson retreated back down the run, convict Daniel Lopez put a prison-made knife to the throat of Officer Gallegos. All three convicts had similar weapons.

Perhaps the officers could have handled one inmate with a weapon, but not three. Officer Craig Ragland was trapped near the end of number-two row. The convicts used the officer's own handcuffs to restrain Gallegos and Ragland and placed them in the now-empty number-two row, number-nine cell. In the meantime, inmate Alberto Martinez was chasing Officer Nelson. Officer Nelson yelled at Sergeant Moises Villalobos, who was at the front of the wing talking to an inmate suicide risk who had been placed in the first "strip cell." Villalobos turned to see a very excited Officer Nelson running down the cellblock run toward him. A confrontation ensued as Martinez attempted to stab both Officer Nelson and Sergeant Villalobos. They tried in vain to subdue him. In their attempt to get away from the knife-wielding Martinez, Officer Nelson dropped his ring of security-door keys. As inmate Martinez stopped to pick up the keys, Officer Nelson and Sergeant Villalobos managed to get through the slam gates before the inmate could reach them.

I know those officers have second-guessed themselves a thousand times for going through that gate when they did, leaving their fellow officers behind. There is no question in my mind that they did not only the smart thing for themselves, but they did what was demanded of them from the standpoint of sound correctional practice. If they had not gotten through the slam gates when they did, the convicts would have had five hostages instead of three; they could have extended the time of discovery and would have had a much stronger bargaining position.

Officer Richard Anderson was over on the other side of the double-row cellblock, and didn't know that his fellow officers were in trouble. As Chino used the keys Nelson had dropped to let selected inmates out of their cells, several other masked inmates surrounded Anderson with knives drawn. They threatened Officer Anderson and restrained him with his own handcuffs. They quickly blindfolded him for the walk over to number-one row, where they placed him with the other two hostages.

Chino Martinez and a half-dozen TS members now had complete control of the Ramsey I Unit ad-seg building. Chino took command and started down the rows of cells deciding who would be allowed the opportunity to join his cause. Of course, the other TS members came first. They had a stash of several weapons, which were issued to those who professed loyalty to Chino's cause. Twelve Hispanics (not all of them were TS members) volunteered to come out of their cells and join in the takeover. Chino must have been feeling powerful by that time, because he did something that I have always thought was out of character. He let three Aryan Brotherhood members, who had their own knives, out of their cells. Two of the three ABT members were in segregation because they had recently murdered other inmates while serving their current sentences. They quickly went about the business of breaking all of the overhead lights on both sides of the ad-seg wing.

By now, Sergeant Villalobos was on the phone trying to explain to Warden Terrell that three of his staff members had been taken hostage by armed members of the TS. At 8:45 P.M. I received the first call about the incident at my unit residence. A usually calm and collected Assistant Warden Jim Shaw was on the other end of the phone. The serious nature of the situation evident in his voice, he said, "Lon, we need you at the building. They've taken some hostages in ad-seg."

Still in uniform from being at work that day, I met Warden Terrell and Jim Shaw at the unit armory in front of the main building. We had all arrived within five minutes of the first call. I'm sure Warden Terrell's guts were churning, but you couldn't tell it by looking at him. He calmly devised a tentative approach to the situation. He said that he was going into the building to try establishing contact with the convicts, either directly or indirectly. He said he would try and find out about the officers and the status of their physical condition. He told Jim Shaw and me to go into the compound through the back gate and see if there was any way to quickly gain access to the ad-seg area. We were to assemble assault squads, maintain radio contact, and stand by for instructions in case the situation changed.

I grabbed a couple of continuous-burn CS-gas grenades, stuffed them into the pockets of my jacket and headed for the back gate. I knew even before I arrived at the back of the ad-seg wing that there was no way to get inside that cellblock short of using a blowtorch on the doors. The steel security doors were locked with a metal padlock from the inside, and there were iron mesh expanded metal doors on the inside. Any attempt to enter the wing from the outside would give the convicts plenty of time to kill the hostages.

Warden Terrell reached the outer office of the ad-seg wing and was briefed by Sergeant Villalobos. His worst fears were confirmed. There were at least fifteen of the most dangerous convicts in all of the TDC in charge of the Ramsey I Segregation Unit. They had the keys to the inside doors and we were locked out. The only way in was with welding torches. The lights had all been knocked out. The convicts had three officers held hostage and were confirmed to have several prison-made shanks in their possession. The fact that the ABT was in on this was not a good sign. They were the most unpredictable group of killers in ad-seg. At least the TS usually had a reason for killing their enemies. That was not always true of the ABT.

After being briefed by Sergeant Villalobos, Warden Terrell stepped to the metal door on the inside of the segregation-wing row and through the small four-by-eight-inch window asked, "Who's in charge?"

Elisio "Chino" Martinez stepped to the door and said, "I am." It was immediately clear that Chino was still in control, and when asked he said he spoke for all of the inmates.

Chino's word was, "No one will be hurt if our demands are met, but if you use tear gas or try to take us by force, we will execute the officers."

The demands were as follows:

    1. Elisio "Chino" Martinez will be allowed to meet with the
    TDC Director, Raymond "The Pro" Procunier.
    2. All the hostage-takers will be allowed to meet with the

news media to voice complaints about general living conditions and grievances.

After a brief conversation with Chino about what he wanted, Warden Terrell asked to see the officers to verify their good health and safety. The officers were brought forward, and Terrell asked them questions to make sure they hadn't been abused or coached in any way. Although scared—with good reason—the officers appeared to be in good health. Once assured that the officers were temporarily okay, Warden Terrell returned to the ad-seg office.

Contacted by radio, I advised Warden Terrell that the security doors at the rear of the ad-seg wing were locked with padlocks on the inside and that any attempt to enter with an assault team would be significantly delayed. Warden Terrell made and received several phone calls from the TDC regional director, Internal Affairs, and local law-enforcement officers.

After walking around the outside of the ad-seg building for a few minutes, I finally convinced myself that there was absolutely no way to get in without getting the hostages killed. We couldn't even use gas in this situation, because it wasn't about regaining control; it was about keeping those officers alive. I thought about putting a couple of snipers on top of the building next to the segregation to shoot the hostage-takers, but there were too many inmates involved to try and take them all out at one time. Even if a marksman could have gotten into position, it would have been almost impossible to get a clear shot into that darkened cellblock. We wouldn't know if we were shooting convicts or hostage officers dressed up to look like convicts.

I used my flashlight to beat on the solid-steel back door of the cellblock. Chino pulled back the rag they had placed over the small window in the door. I said, "I want to see my officers, now!"

My security captain came running up and asked, "What are you doing?"

I said, "I want to see if my officers are all right, but I also want to look into Chino's eyes and hear what's on his mind."

Chino pulled the curtain back again, and I could see the officers with the flashlight. They were blindfolded, cuffed, but essentially okay. Chino said, "Major, have I ever lied to you?"

I truthfully answered, "Not that I know of."

He said, "Well, I'm not going to lie to you now. The officers will not be hurt if y'all don't try to break in here on us."

I advised him, "Chino, don't drag this out. You and I both know that this thing is going to go south quick if one of those officers gets hurt. If one of those officers goes down, we're not going to wait on the director, the governor, or anybody else. If you want to get out of this thing without getting your head torn up or getting killed, you need to release those officers, and the sooner the better!"

His voice was slow and weary-sounding as he said, "I've got to go now. I need time to think."

In my experience, the one thing convicts can always relate to, unless they're psychotic or suicidal, is self-preservation. Chino was a lot of things, but suicidal was not one of them. He was first and foremost a survivor, and I knew him well enough to know that he had no intention of going down with this ship.

I had been standing on the small back porch concentrating on the little window in the door while talking to Chino and had not paid much attention to what was going on around me. When I turned around, I saw all six-foot-four of Brazoria County Sheriff Joe King standing right behind me. There were four Texas Rangers and six or seven TDC wardens standing near the steps behind them. There was a crowd of at least two hundred assorted TDC, Department of Public Safety, and sheriff's-department officers standing inside the compound fence. Many of them were dressed in riot gear. It had only been about twenty minutes since the first call went out. I had never before seen or even heard about an emergency response with that kind of size and speed.

Chino came back to the door and pulled the curtain back and said, "Major, we've got one down."

I said, "Who?"

He said, "The AB's got one of them niggers."

"What about my officers?" I said, trying to keep from yelling at him.

"They're okay!" I could hear the strong fear in his voice. He was losing control.

The ABs were going after some of the black inmates who had been trading insults with them from behind the no-longer-safe sanctuary of their cell bars. The blacks had tied their cell doors with extension cords and sheets, but it was just a matter of time until the killers got the doors open.

This was the most dangerous time, and everyone knew it, especially Chino. He knew that if the violence spread, even if was inmate-on-inmate, we would have to stop it, hostages or no hostages, regardless of the consequences. As I talked to Chino, I could see the blindfolded hostages in the background. They were completely helpless, only a few feet away, and yet we could not take any direct action to help them.

I heard the Life Flight helicopter land in the open area by the backgate. As I stood there watching it land, I said a quiet prayer hoping we wouldn't have to use it, while knowing that, all things considered, we probably would.

Chino came back to the door. "If I put them all back in their cells and turn in the shanks, will you give me your word that when y'all come in here you won't mess over us?"

There was urgency in his voice and I answered quickly. "If my officers are all right, I give you my word that your people won't be hurt."

Chino said he was going to the other door to talk to Warden Terrell. For the first time, I was a little optimistic that we might get our officers back in good shape. Chino was no longer talking about the news media or the director; he was just trying to survive. The last thing I needed at that moment was some Huntsville politician showing up and trying to "negotiate" with Chino. It would have elevated Chino's status and given him the impression that he was truly powerful and in command. He could have dragged the situation out for weeks.

These academically trained administrators, like lawyers, always want to negotiate, which in the inmate mind equates with compromise. You cannot successfully compromise with a convict, because if you give him anything at all, he wins. He is always going to ask you for something else, which inspires other inmates to engage in similar quests.

Finally, Chino pulled the curtain back and said, "Warden Terrell is coming around to the back. When he gets here, I'll let y'all in."

I looked back into the crowd and found Larry Johns. I

motioned for him to come forward and said, "Chino says he is going to let us in after he puts them all back in their cells. I don't know if he will, but his word is all we have to go on. I have given Chino my word that neither he nor his people will be harmed in any way if my officers come out unhurt. I want you to help me ensure that my word is kept."

Larry, with firm resolve written on his face, said, "You got it."

Just then Warden Terrell made his way to the back door. I beat on the door with the flashlight. It was not only time to see if Chino's word was any good, it was time to see if he still had control of the psychotic group of killers under his command.

Chino pulled the curtain back and unlocked the outer door. He couldn't unlock the inner steel-mesh door without a key. Someone handed me a set of bolt cutters, and I reached through the bars and cut the padlock. Chino handed four knives to Warden Terrell as he walked through the door and then followed my instructions to lay facedown on the floor. As I placed handcuffs on him, I pointed at Larry Johns, saying, "He's all yours."

Larry came through the door and sat down beside Chino on the floor. "I got him, I got him," he said. We didn't try to talk to the three officer hostages, but they were free now and seemed to have only minor scratches and bruises. There would be plenty of time to debrief them later.

Warden Terrell and Jim Shaw walked down the darkened row, shining flashlights ahead of them as they went. I could see a body lying in front of the number-fifteen cell, about a third of the way down the row. Wardens Terrell and Shaw walked by the inmate's body, thinking he was already dead. It would have been easy for anyone to make that assumption. The mangled body was lying in a contorted position in a huge pool of blood. There were no easily recognizable features to identify. I didn't know it was a black inmate until I wiped some blood away from what had once been his face.

I took his pulse on his throat below his ear. It was very weak, but he was still alive. I yelled back up the row to Larry, who was still protecting Chino, to call in the medical team from the Life Flight chopper. The victim had been beaten, kicked, stabbed, and left for dead. At some point, he had quit fighting back and collapsed on the floor. It was the only reason he was still alive.

When he quit fighting back and fell to the floor, his attackers kicked him a few times to see if he would move, then broke off the assault thinking he was dead. The victim's cell door was open, and it hadn't occurred to me before to look into the cell. I shined my flashlight inside and found his cell partner sitting frozen in place on the back of the commode. Pointing to the body on the floor, I asked him, "Who is he?"

His mouth fell open, but no words followed. He was too frightened to move, talk, or even blink. I knew him by sight. His name was Clifton Long, and apparently, he'd had a ringside seat for the assault on his cell partner. He knew he had come closer to a very painful death than most folks ever would and that realization had rendered him catatonic.

One of the convicts in the next darkened cell spoke up and said, "That's Charles Young, man." Until that point, I had no idea as to the identity of the convict on the floor. I knew Young as being one of the more vocal black convicts in segregation. He was always trading insults with the white supremacist housed in the row of cells behind his. It seemed that the ABs had used this occasion to get even.

The Life Flight team managed to get Charles Young's mangled body on a gurney and down to the unit infirmary. They had to stabilize him before attempting the flight to a Houston hospital. Young very nearly bled to death. He had suffered at least fourteen deep stab wounds, numerous lacerations, and severe trauma from taking a terrible beating. One of the nurses told me that they used six pints of blood before putting him on the Life Flight chopper. As he left, his body looked like a pincushion, with IV tubes running down both arms and pressure bandages covering the rest of him. In all honesty, I did not expect to ever see Charles Young alive again.

When the ABs came, Charles Young and Clifton Long tried to put up a fight. As the killers cut through the electrical cords and sheets tied around the cell door, they told the two trapped convicts inside what they intended to do to them. When they finally got the door open, Young tried to use his small metal electric fan as a club to fight them off. He may have gotten in a couple of licks, but after dragging him out of the cell and stabbing him a few times, they took his makeshift weapon away and beat him with his own fan. I remember seeing what was left of the fan on the floor next to the body. It had no blades or fan guard left, and the base that had supported the upper part of the fan was covered with blood.

I walked the rows making sure that all the missing keys were accounted for and that all the cells were securely locked. We spent most of the night searching cells and shaking down inmates. We found a half-dozen knives, some handcuffs, and handcuff keys. I discovered that several of the trapped inmates had come up with a unique way to keep invaders out of their cell. Some of them spliced extension cords and tied the bare wires to the bars on their cell doors, then threw water from their commodes on the floor outside the cell to complete the electrical ground. If anyone attempted to enter the cell, they would plug in the extension cord, electrifying the cell door. This was not a long-term solution, but as a delaying tactic it was fairly successful. After what had happened to Charles Young, it was hard to convince some of the less-secure convicts that it was no longer necessary to tie their cell doors shut.

We spent some time debriefing the three officer hostages and began making the case for prosecution of the convicts involved. It would be months before a trial, but by the time a trial date did come around, we had a solid case for conviction. The star witness against the ABTs would have been Charles Young, who made a miraculous recovery from his injuries, but once the defendants found out that Charles was alive, most all of them were more than willing to accept plea bargains in exchange for additional time. The only convicts who insisted on a jury trial were Chino Martinez and Alberto Martinez. Convicted of aggravated kidnapping, each of them was sentenced to an additional thirty years, not to begin until they completed their current sentences. Chino was already serving twenty years and Alberto Martinez was serving thirty-three years. Even if they both decided to suddenly become model inmates, which was not likely, they would not be eligible for parole until far into the next century.

There was one positive thing that came out of this hostage incident. The fact that the incident had been handled without the "assistance" of any of the Huntsville politicians brought the

TDC's Southern Regional personnel and Brazoria County law enforcement closer together.

Chino was shipped off to one of the northern units and placed in "super segregation," a new custody category for modern-day "incorrigible" convicts. I saw him a few years later when he was placed in protection after turning state's evidence in a TS homicide. He was being transferred around to different units in an effort to keep his whereabouts unknown. When I heard he was on the unit, I went to his cell. He acted like it was old-home week, and he produced a very sincere apology for his part in the Ramsey I Unit hostage incident. He said it was "just business." I told him I wasn't interested in his lame excuses.

I've never been big on apologies. Generally, what people mean when they say they're sorry is that they're sorry for getting caught. If they were really sorry, they probably wouldn't have done it in the first place. That's just me, though. Most people like apologies, if for no other reason than to hear someone, somewhere acknowledge that they've been wronged. I would have had more respect for him if he had just told the truth and said, "I'm a coldblooded killer-gangster; that's what I do."

Chino had been living on one excuse or another for years, and he could rationalize almost any violent action he was involved in as necessary for his survival. He didn't understand the difference between a *reason* and an *excuse*. A reason is a persuasive basis for an action; an excuse is a basis that is not persuasive. Distiguishing between the two can be very subjective if you make decisions based on your emotions. To the hard-hearted, too many reasons are believed to be excuses; to the soft-hearted, too many excuses are believed to be reasons. The difference between a reason and an excuse becomes more clear only if you make objective decisions based not on your emotions, but on a factual frame of reference. It's not easy to learn to do this; emotional education isn't taught in school, and life's lessons often come too late.

A convict like Chino lives from moment to moment. If he has any awareness of a future, it is something fixed in place, beyond his control; things happen to him, he does not make them happen. Impulse governs his behavior, either because he cannot discipline himself to sacrifice a present for a future satisfaction or because he has no sense of the future. Since he is living in the moment, deterrence simply isn't a factor in his criminal activities. Getting caught or having to face punishment never enters a convict's mind. Being locked up causes no embarrassment, and it may even enhance his stature among his career-criminal peers.

I remember the Ramsey I Unit hostage situation as the worst single experience in my thirty-year TDC career. Not so much because of the violence or the threats that occurred, but because of the utter and absolute helplessness that I felt during the time that those three officers were held hostage. Two of the three officers resigned their employment with TDC. It wasn't that they had been injured. They just couldn't face going back into that environment again. The hazards of the job had all of a sudden become very real to them. Sergeant Villalobos remained with TDC, but took a voluntary demotion back to rank-and-file correctional officer. He had been an excellent supervisor and did all that could have been done during the hostage situation, but he no longer wanted the decision-making responsibility required of rank.

What stands out in my mind is the realization that it can happen again, at any time, at any prison in the state. Anyone who enters a prison unit is vulnerable, and the level of risk is steadily increasing. As a warden, I can tell you that the chance of successfully "negotiating" an outcome in these situations is not good and it's getting more difficult by the day.

Why? The percentage of inmates facing longer and longer sentences with little or no chance for parole is increasing dramatically. What do you offer a convicted killer who has nothing to lose?

There is usually no logic involved in an inmate's decision to take a hostage. It may start out as an attempt to escape through hostage exchange, but realistically and statistically, there is almost no chance of success. It may be that he is just tired of taking orders and doing time. Maybe he got a Dear John letter or his mother died. Perhaps his parole was denied; it could be that other convicts are threatening him, or that he has come to the realization that he is going to spend the rest of his life in prison. For any of those or a thousand other "reasons," which all seem perfectly legitimate to him at the time, a convict may lose control and decide to take some of his fellow convicts or possibly an employee with him down the road to oblivion.

The quietly acknowledged reality is that there are literally thousands of convicts in TDCJ whose only goal in life is to take someone with them when they go. It is just a question of when, where, and how many people will be hurt or killed.

Identifying which convicts will attempt this can be nearly impossible. On many units, upwards of a third of the inmate population is on a steady diet of behavioral-modification psychotropic medication. In most cases, the security officers don't even know which inmates are on these medications, because of medical-records confidentiality rules. Inmates who for whatever reason have not taken their prescribed medication precipitate many of the use-of-force situations that occur between staff and inmates. The convict refuses to take his medication, becomes delusional, and strikes out at other inmates or some officer who happens to be passing by.

Officers and inmates are not the only ones at risk. There is a sign on the entrance to most TDC units that says: "In the event any officers or employees have been seized as hostages, no officers or employees on duty shall disregard, alter, modify or change in any manner the prescribed duties, obligations, or responsibilities of their position on demand by the prisoners, or plea from the hostages, regardless of the consequences." The ominous warning to all entering into TDC units is a written-in-stone policy and means exactly what it says. There will be no exceptions granted. Inmates will not be released in exchange for hostages, not even if the hostages are the governor, the TDC director, the unit warden, visitors to the unit, or any group of male or female employees. Anyone who is contemplating entering a TDC unit for any reason, even to visit, should seriously consider the possible implications of the warning. Once inside a unit, it is too late.

THE RISE AND FALL AND RISE OF MARK FRONKIEWICZ

In 1982 Mark Fronkiewicz found himself at the Darrington Unit, two cells down from the leader of the Texas Mafia, Larry Sherrod. One day Fronkiewicz came back from chow and found a black inmate leaning against the bars of his cell attempting to sexually solicit a young boy who also lived in the cell. When the black inmate saw Fronkiewicz, he knew trouble was at hand. The black inmate informed Mark that whatever was going on was none of his business. Of course Fronkiewicz explained to him, "It's my cage, my wing, my cell partner, my prison, and that makes it my business." The inmate walked off, but Mark knew it wasn't over. He told the kid to open the back of his radio and hand him the shank inside.

While Fronkiewicz was wrapping the handle on the shank, he heard Larry Sherrod from two cells down ask, "Have you got someone to cover your back?" Mark told him he didn't, and the two of them set off to face the blacks. There were only ten or twelve whites on the 150-man cellblock. When the two armed convicts brazenly walked into the dayroom and confronted the blacks, they "craw-fished." Even though Mark and his backup were outnumbered 20 to 1, the fact that they were bold enough to be there and obviously willing enough to use their weapons earned them the appropriate amount of respect. The black inmate who had tried to hog Fronkiewicz's young cell partner went to the administration and requested protection.

Shortly after this encounter, Sherrod approached Fronkiewicz about joining his gang. The goal of the gang was simple: to survive at any cost. If you wanted power or status within the Texas Mafia, you had to earn it by being smarter or more vicious than the next guy.

Given the opportunity, Mark didn't hesitate to move up in the group. There were fifteen or twenty TM members at a meeting in the unit law library one day. Mark walked in and placed one knife on the table and held the other in his hand. He stated, "I will be captain of captains for all Texas Mafia. Any questions?" There were none, and so the matter was settled.

The twenty-fifth and final inmate homicide of 1984 occurred on December 16 at approximately 1:00 P.M. in an ad-seg dayroom at the Eastham Unit north of Huntsville. The body of inmate David Alan Robidoux, twenty-four, wasn't found until 2:30 P.M., an hour and a half after the killing occurred. Several Texas Mafia gang members who had been in the dayroom at the time of the killing had already been released back to their cells by the time the officers found the body. The only eyewitnesses to the homicide were inmates. At trial it was established that while one Texas Mafia member distracted guards, three others stabbed Robidoux and hid his body under some exercise mats. Robidoux, a white inmate serving an eight-year sentence for aggravated assault, burglary of a building, and retaliation in Dallas County, died of multiple wounds to the upper body. One of the murder weapons, a foot-long rod with a cloth-wrapped handle, was found near the body. The rod was originally part of the push-button toilet assembly that was becoming common in all TDC inmate-cell construction. It didn't take the convicts long to figure out that the push-button on the toilet could be removed and the rod that was attached to it could be pulled back into the cell. These foot-long brass rods make excellent weapons.

Robidoux was a former member of the Texas Mafia who was suspected by the gang of being an informer. With Robidoux's homicide, TDC began a new strategy of attempting to obtain the death sentence for gang-related inmate killings. Four inmates were indicted for capital murder. The prosecutor, David Weeks, said at the time, "This is murder for hire. It really has nothing to do with being in prison." The Houston County grand jury indicted Tony Rice, twenty-eight, who was serving fifteen years for a Polk County burglary; Mark Fronkiewicz, twenty-seven, serving ten years for a Jefferson County conviction of aggravated assault on a peace officer; Darrell Craig Adams, twenty-seven, serving fifteen years for a Fort Bend County escape; and Ricky Meadows, twenty-six, serving ten years for an Orange County burglary.

The prosecution said that the Texas Mafia had a standing practice of paying for the deaths of its enemies and presented the case as a contracted killing for hire. As an alleged murder for remuneration, the charge met the technical criteria for capital murder, punishable by the death sentence. The problem for the prosecution was that they could not demonstrate a payment or a promise to pay the alleged killers except through informant convict testimony, which would prove to be questionable at best. There is an old saying in the penitentiary business, "When a killing happens in Hell, there are no angels for witnesses." The Robidoux trial demonstrated that there is at least some truth to that.

By the time the convict accomplices and informants got through testifying and the state-sponsored immunity deals were over with, the jury gave TM members Tony Rice and "Captain of Captains" Mark Fronkiewicz the death sentence. They were the first TDC inmates in the history of TDC to be convicted of capital murder and subsequently receive a death sentence for killing another inmate. Prosecutor Weeks said after the verdict, "We hope these two verdicts will put an end to the Texas Mafia and to a chapter of violence in the Texas Department of Corrections."

Unfortunately for the prosecution, the capital-murder charge was based on less-than-credible inmate witnesses and would not be upheld. It took years for the case to reach the Texas Court of Criminal Appeals, but when it did in 1993, the death sentences were thrown out. The convictions were reversed with an order sent back to the trial court for acquittal. The Criminal Court of Appeals ruled that prosecutors failed to demonstrate that the convict killers would actually be paid for the killing, disqualifying the charge of capital murder.

After almost six years on death row, Tony Rice and Mark Fronkiewicz were released back into the TDC general-inmate population. They could not be retried. In hindsight, the prosecution should have gone for simple murder convictions and waited for a stronger case that didn't depend on convict testimony before attempting to obtain a death sentence for the capital murder of an inmate. To date, all capital-murder convictions and death sentences for convict-on-convict homicides have been reversed on appeal. Although several Texas convicts have received death sentences at trial, no inmate has yet been executed for the murder of another inmate.

The simple truth is that the Texas Mafia controlled its membership with pure fear, sometimes mistakenly called respect. The prosecution gave them credit for being much more sophisticated than they were. There were fewer than 125 known Texas Mafia members system-wide when David Robidoux was killed. There was only a handful of original members. The only alliance was with the Texas Syndicate. The Texas Mafia was one of the few gangs that allowed other races to participate as members. Membership was largely based on what a potential member could do for the group. Drugs, extortion, smuggling, protection, and murder were all avenues to membership and leadership positions. The Texas Mafia never had the large membership numbers of some of the other gangs, but on a percentage basis the TM was one of the deadliest gangs in the TDC.

Fast forward for a moment to the Ramsey III Unit in 1993, when Texas Mafia Captain of Captains Mark Fronkiewicz was being released from death row. I got a call from Salvador (Sammy) Buentello, the head of TDC Gang Intelligence. He didn't call very often, and when he did it was usually bad news. This call would be no exception. After the small talk he said, "Warden, I need you to do something for me."

"Yeah, what can I do for you, Sam?" I answered, feeling like a rented mule.

"I'm going to send Mark Fronkiewicz to you for general-population assignment. What do you think?"

I knew Fronkiewicz by reputation and I said, "I think it will be a toss-up as to whether he kills or gets killed first."

Sammy said, "Oh I think he will be fine if you just talk to him. He only has a couple of years left on his original sentence, and he knows he has a shot at getting back to the free world again. He doesn't want any trouble."

I skeptically asked Sammy, "Assuming you're right and he doesn't want any trouble, how do I keep these other thugs off of him?"

The silence on the other end of the phone told me he didn't have an answer. He ended the call by saying, "I know you can handle it, Glenn. Stay in touch."

Sammy was in charge of monitoring the disruptive threat groups and had been gradually turning some of the older gang members back out into the general-inmate population. After being locked in ad-seg for years, many of them agreed to "debrief," telling everything they knew about the gang and its members and promising to turn away from their past evil ways. Of course, it's not easy to quit an organization that requires the spilling of blood to get in or out. Most of these gangs don't have a retirement clause in their membership criteria. It may sound overdramatic, but violence is the main control mechanism used to keep the membership in line. One of the quickest ways to get killed in TDC is to snitch, roll over, inform, debrief, or rat out on a gang. When a gang member says he doesn't want to be in the gang anymore, his life expectancy generally decreases considerably.

I had several so-called ex–gang members in population, but none that had held Fronkiewicz's number-two position on the ABT's hit list. Most ex–gang members worked real hard at keeping a low profile, hoping no one would discover that they were even on the unit. I didn't view Fronkiewicz as so much of a threat as I did a potential victim. It was like turning the fastest gun in the West loose in Dodge City. Every two-bit punk out there who wanted to build himself a reputation could do it just by taking a shot at Fronkiewicz.

As the second-in-command, Mark Fronkiewicz had had a lot to do with setting the Texas Mafia's agenda. As much as its members may have admired the real mafia, as an imposing business enterprise, the Texas Mafia, like other prison gangs, is made up of a bunch of cons who boss one another around and physically assault each other in prison in puny power struggles. If they are lucky and live long enough to get back to the streets, they usually screw up in short order and end up back in prison. Most don't have the savvy to make even a basic living, much less run an organized criminal enterprise. That is not to say they're not dangerous. Prison gangs don't have a sophisticated political agenda that encompasses some far-reaching worldview. These guys are not going to take over the world, since most of them aren't going to spend that much time in the free world. They're not even going to take over TDC, but they are a continuing threat in terms of killing one another, killing staff, and perhaps taking over individual prison units.

It turned out, though, that Fronkiewicz was by far one of the more fascinating convicts I'd met. Fronkiewicz didn't really fit the gang profile. He was very intelligent, even scholarly, totally self-taught, an enormous reader. He had an immediately recognizable charisma. He smiled, he was helpful, and he was courteous when his surroundings were non-threatening. Although he was a multiple offender with a well-documented history of violence, he had one thing most gang members will never have. He had a desire to lead a straight life.

I've found myself thinking about that a lot. What was it that made Fronkiewicz different from the others? I had observed some of the same qualities years before in Herberto "Herbie" Huerta, before he became president of the Mexican Mafia in Texas. All this wasted talent, especially among the gang leaders, who are smart, agile, strong, and capable of learning.

Unfortunately, most of these outlaws are the way they are because they don't want to change. Feelings of guilt or conscience over the things they do could lead to change, but conscience seems absent. If the wrong kind of person gets killed, a child or a woman, it could be a problem, but no card-carrying gang member feels bad about killing dope dealers, child molesters, or snitches.

Prison gangs are built around loyalty issues, and each member theoretically lives by a code. That code takes precedence over individual guilt feelings. You're never supposed to snitch, although that is exactly what the majority of them end up doing. They want to be gunslingers, just like in the Old West. Unfortunately for them, this is no longer the frontier; law and order did come to the West. In the end, after it's too late and they're in prison serving an eternity, the realization finally hits them hard: They're all losers.

Looking back, I think that Mark Fronkiewicz was turned around by that kind of realization. Like most inmates on death row, Mark found religion, but along with that, he was just dog-tired of being a loser. All he had to do was look around at his fellow inmates to realize that he was capable of doing better. He found himself on death row with almost no hope of survival, and he was smart enough to realize that his own earlier decisions and actions had put him there. When his case was reversed, not because he didn't kill Robidoux, but because the prosecutor had filed the wrong charge, he got a second chance at life. I think he made a personal decision that he didn't want to be a loser anymore.

Fronkiewicz was in his thirties when he was released from TDC in 1996. He married an ex-officer he met while working in the inmate law library at the Ramsey III Unit. As of 1998, he was working as a paralegal for a Houston lawyer. I'm not going to comment on whether Mark Fronkiewicz is "rehabilitated," but by any standard of measure he has come back from the abyss.

Going straight is usually a one-day-at-a-time proposition, and the odds of any ex-con living a long, peaceful life are not very good. On the positive side, Fronkiewicz has already proven his mettle by surviving several prisons, prison gangs, and death row. All things considered, it must be a pleasure for him to wake up each morning knowing he is no longer a loser.

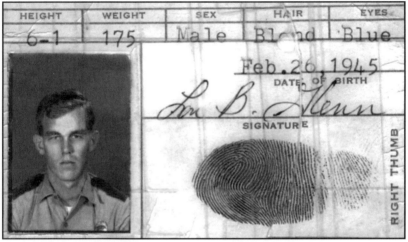

HEIGHT	WEIGHT	SEX	HAIR	EYES
6-1	175	Male	Blond	Blue

Feb. 26, 1945
DATE OF BIRTH

SIGNATURE

RIGHT THUMB

Author's TDC identification card, circa 1966.
Note signature of then-Director George Beto.

—Courtesy TDCJ archives

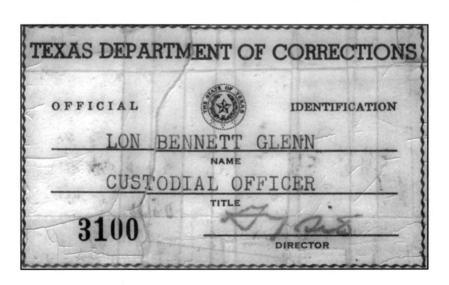

TEXAS DEPARTMENT OF CORRECTIONS

OFFICIAL   IDENTIFICATION

LON BENNETT GLENN
NAME

CUSTODIAL OFFICER
TITLE

3100

DIRECTOR

The Retrieve Unit Warden's House, circa 1931. Note the wooden buildings in background where prisoners were housed. The warden's house was the boyhood home of I. K. Kelley Jr. during his pre-teen years. His father, I. K. Kelley Sr., was the unit warden during prohibition. This photo was taken from the unit water tower across the road from the house. This is very likely the site of the original Retrieve Plantation, one of the first established during the early days of Stephen F. Austin's land grants. The area is rich in early Texas archeological artifacts, including a buried train engine from the old Columbia Tap Railroad. All buildings in this area were demolished during 1938, when the new Retrieve Unit was completed.
—Courtesy I. K. Kelly Jr. and family

The Retrieve Unit, circa 1969, as it looked when the author arrived as a twenty-three-year-old field lieutenant. Note the old twelve-cell "Heartbreak Hotel" solitary building located just outside the compound fence at rear. The white-roofed building inside the compound was the unit laundry.

—Courtesy TDCJ archives

From left to right: The "New Fireproof Retrieve Unit Building," circa 1938. In center of photo is the not-so-fireproof (made mostly of wood) Bachelor Officers' Quarters (BOQ). On the far right is one of the first unit warden's residences to be constructed of brick. Perhaps owing to the fact that the designer lived in Huntsville, Texas, the warden's house came equipped with a basement game room, which began to hold water almost immediately. The Retrieve Unit is only nine feet above sea level, and permanent water pumps had to be installed in order to prevent the basement from becoming an underground swimming pool.

—Courtesy TDCJ archives

Forty-two field officers assembled at the Ramsey Unit, circa early 1960s. Work was a priority and officers on horseback supervised inmate work squads, ensuring that the individual prison units were as self-sufficient as possible.

—From author's collection

A typical Texas-prison-unit solitary building, at Ramsey Unit, circa 1960s. Few if any photos of the Clemens or Retrieve solitary buildings exist; however, they were both similar in construction to this building. Unlike the Ramsey solitary, the Clemens building had an eight-inch steam pipe that ran through the back of the cells. The Retrieve Unit solitary had no commode fixtures; a simple drain-covered hole in the concrete floor served as bathroom facilities. Once in solitary for a while, few convicts wanted a return trip.

—From author's collection

A group of assistant wardens, also known as "little captains," circa 1946. Note the dress. At the time, prison employees had to buy their own uniforms. In the front row, far left, is E. Robinson ("Captain Red Dick"), who was until his retirement during the mid 1960s the little captain of the Retrieve Unit. To his left is O. O. Stewart, assistant warden of the Ramsey Unit. On the far right of front row is George Parker, and second from left on back row is Buddy Thompson.

—Courtesy the Dickie Stricklin family

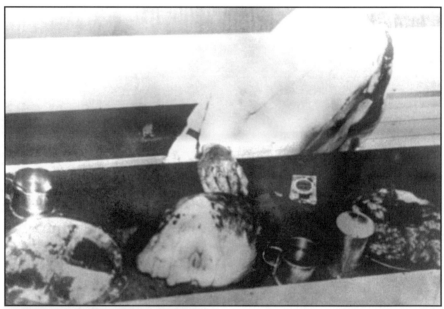

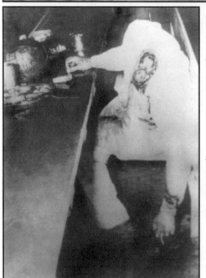

Crime-scene photo, December 15, 1948, Retrieve Unit. Inmate Clarence M. Redwine was decapitated while sitting at a table in the inmate dining room. According to witnesses, the assailant, Earnest "Cleave" Jones, accomplished this with only one blow with a "cane knife." Jones subsequently received an additional five-year sentence for the murder.

—From author's collection

A posed side-view photo of Clarence M. Redwine's body, which was alleged to have remained upright after decapitation. Note: Someone has placed a burning cigarette between the fingers of the left hand.

—From author's collection

Actual "cane knife" used by inmate Earnest Jones to decapitate Clarence M. Redwine. The knife has a six-inch wooden handle and a thirteen-inch tapered blade. The blade is approximately two and a half inches wide.

—Courtesy the City of Brazoria Community Museum

Warden I. K. Kelley and Officer Curtis Carlton. The men are standing in the front entrance of the Clemens Unit, located south on Highway 36, just outside Brazoria, Texas, circa July 1939.
—Courtesy I. K. Kelley Jr.

The building in background is the old "Retrieve Hunting Club," located on "Club Lake," also known by the locals as "Horseshoe Lake," on the present-day Retrieve Unit. The club building no longer exists, but was in continuous operation throughout the Prohibition era. Photo circa 1931.
—Courtesy I. K. Kelley Jr.

Retrieve Unit Warden (1951–67) Zan E. Harrelson ("Red Devil"). Prior to his promotion to senior warden, he served for several years as food-service steward and assistant warden. Harrelson, an old-school warden, exerted his influence over the Retrieve Unit like a feudal lord. He was instrumental in helping the Retrieve Unit earn the nickname "The Burning Hell." Photo circa 1968.
—Courtesy TDCJ archives

Assistant Warden G. H. "Dick" Stricklin (seated at left), circa mid-1960s. A man of high moral fiber and impeccable integrity, Stricklin began his career as a dog sergeant and worked his way up through the ranks to serve the State of Texas as warden of the Clemens, Central, and Retrieve units.

—Courtesy Dickie Stricklin family

Chain gangs arriving at the Huntsville Walls Unit, Huntsville, Texas, circa 1950s. At this time, convicts routinely wore neck chains during transport from unit to unit.

—Courtesy TDCJ archives

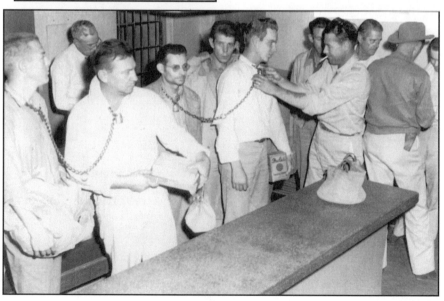

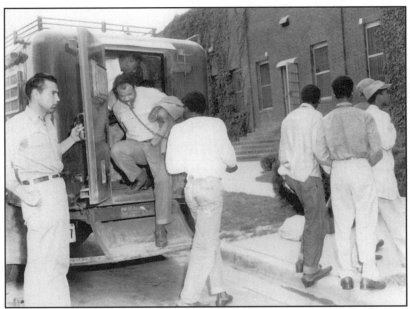

TDC transport van known as a "Black Betty," circa 1950s. Prior to the 1960s, inmates were transported between units by means of these small, armored vans. Inmates were individually handcuffed and chained at the neck to another convict for the duration of the trip.

—Courtesy TDCJ archives

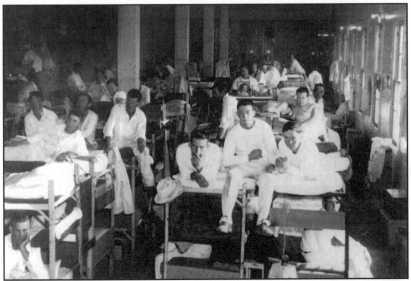

A typical double-bunk dormitory, or "tank," circa early 1960s. One hundred or more inmates were assigned to each tank. All inmate living areas were segregated, as were most of the work assignments.

—Courtesy TDCJ archives

Weighing cotton, circa early 1960s. There was a time in Texas prisons when convicts were required to work to produce the cotton mattresses, sheets, and pillows they slept on. They also had to work to grow the food that went on the table—that is, if they wanted to eat. In today's Texas prisons, if cotton is grown at all, it's harvested with machines instead of by convicts.The new enlightened Texas criminal-justice system is much too civilized to require convicts to "stoop to labor."

—From author's collection

Rodeo Hands at Retrieve Unit, circa mid-1960s. Fourth from left is Henry Pettis, fifth from left is Walter Henderson.On far right is Willie Jones (aka "Black Betty"). Jones was an inmate horse trainer for more than twenty years.

—From author's collection

Retrieve Unit wardens, 1970. From left to right: Warden Hal H. "Hookin' Bull" Husbands and Assistant Warden Bobby D. Morgan. They were both respected by their peers and by convicts as firm, but also fair.

—From author's collection

Retrieve Unit Field Boss: Lieutenant Lon B. Glenn and "Calvin," circa 1971. Calvin was the second-best horse I ever threw a boot over.

—From author's collection

Retrieve Unit cotton pickers, circa 1969.

—From author's collection

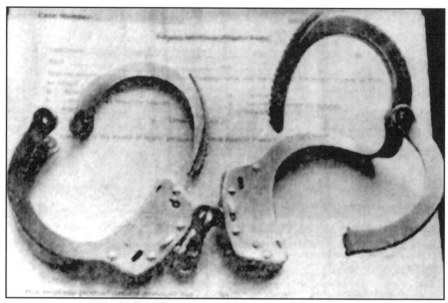

*Handcuffs—after muscle-bound convict Douglas Collins
decided he didn't want to wear them.*

—From author's collection

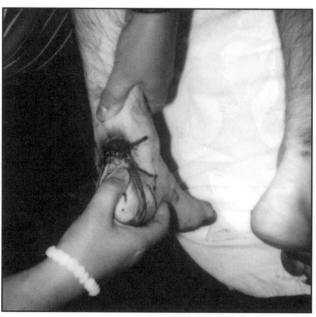

*Self-mutilation known as
"heel-stringing," circa mid-
1970s. Although common
in pre-1975 Texas prisons,
heel-stringing, or the cutting of one or both heel ten-
dons in an attempt to get
out of work, is almost
unheard-of today.*

—From author's collection

Angleton, Texas, manhunt, circa 1982. Left to right: Captain Lon B. Glenn; unknown Brazoria County Sheriff's Dept. Deputy; Retrieve Unit Dog Sergeant Johnny Mansker.

—From author's collection

Retrieve Unit Field Major Bobby Crawford, sitting on his favorite horse, "Payday," circa 1982. Although he later became one of the last "real" senior wardens in TDCJ, Crawford was never as comfortable behind a desk as he was in the saddle.

—From author's collection

The Retrieve Unit inmate drill team, "The High Rollers," circa early 1980s. Originated by Warden Hal H. Husbands in 1970, the precision marching drill team performed at the annual prison rodeo, in parades, county fairs, and numerous other public events for more than thirteen years. They even made appearances at the Houston Astrodome. Although the total sentence-time assessed to the inmates on the drill team amounted to over a thousand years, there were never any attempts to escape during their travels.

—From author's collection

From left to right: Dr. George Beto ("Walking George"), director of TDC 1962–72, and W. J. Estelle ("Big Jim"), director of TDC 1972–83. They were both men of high moral fiber and singleminded purpose. They served with the safety of prison staff, the welfare of the citizens of Texas, and the security of the inmate population foremost in mind. Circa 1982.

—Courtesy TDCJ archives

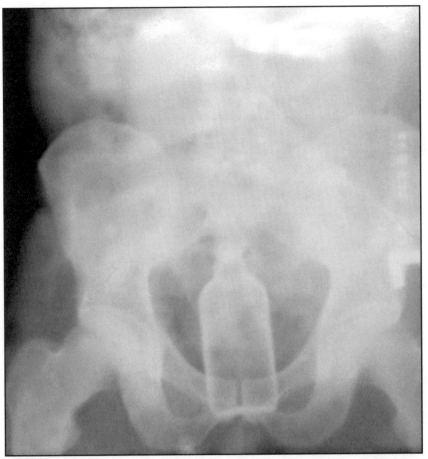

Retrieve Unit drug search, circa 1982. How far will a convict go to smuggle drugs? An inmate returning from furlough aroused suspicion by walking with a limp and complaining of abdominal pain. Security insisted that he be checked by medical personnel. When a preliminary examination didn't reveal the source of pain, the nurse began preparation for an x-ray. The convict resisted, but the x-ray revealed a bottle, approximately eight inches tall and four inches wide, inside his rectum. The bottle had three balloons full of heroin inside. The convict was advised, "Either you remove it, or we will." With the aid of petroleum jelly, he was successful in removing the bottle.

—From author's collection

Ramsey I Unit segregation, circa 1985. During one weekend, the convicts in ad-seg tore twenty-two metal bunks from the walls of their cells. They burned everything that would burn, then threw the one-inch metal bolts and other remnants of their destroyed cell fixtures at the officers. A favorite pastime for ad-seg inmates is to save their urine and feces and throw it at passing staff members.

—From author's collection

Ramsey I Unit drug search, circa 1985. Officer Clyde Hargrove discovered these eighteen grams of cocaine hidden in a pair of inmate work boots he found sitting out on a common-area window ledge in an inmate cellblock.

—From author's collection

Retrieve Unit drug search, circa 1988. Half-gallon of Crown Royal whiskey; three balloons, one containing heroin; two grams of cocaine; four syringes; one well-used "roach clip;" six knives.

—From author's collection

Retrieve Unit drug search, circa 1989. One two-bladed free-world folding knife. One two-ounce bag of marijuana. Two gram bags of crystal methamphetamine. One eighteen-inch bread knife. Fifty-two toothpick-sized hand-rolled marijuana cigarettes. One ladle cup missing sixteen-inch handle.

—From author's collection

Ramsey I Unit weapons search, circa 1985. TDC was averaging a homicide a week during this extremely danger-ous time. Inmate gang mem-bers and wannabe gang mem-bers were stabbing and killing each other in record numbers. Unit wardens were frustrated, because we couldn't even get the Huntsville administration to admit that there was a gang problem.

Ramsey I Unit, Circa 1986. From left to right: Heavyweight Champ George Foreman, inmate Ricky Murphy, Chaplain Hulen, and Assistant Warden Lon Glenn. Foreman, a guest preacher one Sunday, gave an inspirational sermon that had a calming affect on the inmate population lasting for several days. Inmate Murphy and Foreman had been childhood friends while growing up in Houston, Texas.

—From author's collection

Retrieve Unit first-shift security staff, circa 1988. The solidarity of this group of officers was demonstrated on a daily basis and contributed immensely to the overall success of the Retrieve Unit. As these officers arrived for work each day, they left whatever individual differences they may have had outside the fence. They were fiercely loyal toward each other and worked as a team. There is nothing convicts hate more than a dedicated group of officers who work as a team.

—From author's collection

Retrieve Unit work squad, circa 1989. Convicts working, raising the food they will eat. The philosophy of the modern-day TDCJ Board of Criminal Justice is to shun the agriculturally based "plantation mentality" that has kept past taxpayer-cost low and provided productive work for generations of inmates. In today's Texas prisons, it is no longer politically correct to compel a convict to work for his keep.

—From author's collection

The Last "Real" Warden, Bobby Crawford, retires, circa 1989. Some of the older Retrieve inmates gathered to say goodbye. Front row, left to right: Larry "Dog" Keagle, Raymond Williams, Warden Bobby R. Crawford, Billy Wayne "Speedy" Hopper, Warden II Lon B. Glenn, Gus "Old Folks" Bright.

Second Row, left to right: Ray Blandsett, Billy "Dirty Red" Henson, George "Gorillon" Hermesillo, Machado, Robert "Cornbread" Lockhart, Charles Mask, Ben "Preacher" Williams, Johnny Pete, Johnny "Nigger Please" Gilstrap.

From left to right, third row: Billy "Sidewinder" Duncan, Griffin, Sam "Flap-Jack" Eaglin (waving), Robert "Bug-eye" Jones, Scott, and "Big-head" Williams.

—From author's collection

Ramsey III Unit, circa 1995. From left to right: Warden II Lon B. Glenn and Dog Sergeant Joel Anderson. The only way to start an otherwise stressful day is with an early morning horseback ride. I spent the last month of my TDCJ career in the saddle. The only way the bean counters could find me was by horse.

—From author's collection

The Retrieve Unit, circa 1998. First owned by Jared A. Groce, who obtained a five-league land grant as one of Stephen F. Austin's first colonists. The first plantation owner to actually develop the land was Major Abner Jackson in 1839. From that time on, the farm has been in continuous operation as either a plantation or as prison unit. Texas inmates were first brought to the plantation under the lease program in 1871. The State of Texas finally purchased the Retrieve Plantation from T. Martin and his wife Alleen for $320,879.60, with $20,679.60 paid in cash, and the remainder in notes bearing 5 percent interest. Once known as "The Burning Hell" or the "Devil's Island of Texas," Retrieve is now known more as a retirement home for older, worn-out convicts.

—CHAPTER ELEVEN—
WHY TEXANS ALWAYS
SUPPORT THE DEATH PENALTY

"Any person will kill if the desire and
opportunity hit at the same time."
—MARK TWAIN

In early 1924, Texas politicians approved electrocution as a more humane method of executing the worst in Texas society. On January 1, 1924, Captain R. F. Coleman, warden of the Walls Unit in Huntsville, and also the legislatively designated executioner, submitted his letter of resignation. The first scheduled electrocutions were supposed to take place later in the month. When asked for his reasons, he said, "It just couldn't be done, boys. A warden can't be a warden and a killer, too. The penitentiary is a place to reform a man, not to kill him."

On February 4, 1924, Walter Monroe Miller, the former sheriff of Johnson County, near Fort Worth, replaced Warden Coleman as the warden of the Walls Unit. Miller had none of the former warden's qualms about being an executioner. He said, "It's a case of duty to me. I have hanged several men while I was sheriff, and to touch the button or pull the switch on an electric chair means no more to me than pulling the lever of the gallows. . ."

On February 8, 1924, just after midnight, Charles Reynolds walked through the entrance to the room housing the new electric chair. He was strapped by TDC officers into the chair and after three surges of electricity was pronounced dead at 12:16 A.M. In quick succession, Reynolds' death was followed by the execu-

203

tions of Ewell Morris, George Washington, and Mack Matthews. A fifth man, Melvin Johnson, also scheduled to die, obtained a last-minute stay of execution from Acting Governor T. W. Davidson. Johnson's stay lasted only an hour, however, and when no additional reprieves were granted, he was electrocuted and pronounced dead shortly after 2:00 A.M.

Thus began the use of the electric chair in Texas. The five condemned killers, all black and from East Texas, were electrocuted on the same night, and the electric chair immediately gained a nickname—"Old Sparky." In the years that followed, the chair became more famous than many of those who died in it. Between February 1924 and July 1964, 361 condemned men (and no women) were executed.

The main reason Texas began holding executions in Huntsville was to gain some consistency and control over the execution process. Prior to 1924, executions had always been held in the county of conviction and more often than not took place just ahead of a lynch mob. These "legal hangings" were, by design, public shows. Public executions were attended by not only the local riff-raff, but also all manner of polite society, who considered the executions a high-toned form of entertainment.

THE ELOQUENT JUDGE

Texans have always supported the death penalty, even from the days of the early settlers. The first Texas Rangers, appointed by Stephen F. Austin, had the authority to dispense justice on sight, to include the informal imposition of the death penalty. When the Civil War broke out, Texans were paying taxes on more than 200,000 slaves, who constituted a third of the state's total population. When the war ended and federal troops were sent in to enforce Reconstruction efforts, lynching became extremely popular in Texas. In 1868 General Reynolds, commander of the Texas Fifth Military District, reported, "The murder of Negroes is so common as to render it impossible to keep an accurate count of them."

In those days, Texas was not a nation of laws, but rather a semi-lawless state ruled by men with guns. The Texas Rangers and various groups of vigilantes enforced the "Code of the West," an often unwritten standard of decency that evolved at least partly from the old pre–Civil War South. In the Old West, whatever passed for justice often occurred swiftly. More often than not, the sentences were carried out summarily and without fanfare. The judges were often men of modest education, and the language of sentencing was usually blunt and without legal niceties.

In the 1881 case *United States of America v. Gonzales,* the eloquent oratory of Judge Franklin Pierce Benedict demonstrates not only his clear acceptance of the death penalty, but also an unusual blend of lyricism and frontier crudity. The judge's sentencing is quoted as follows:

> Jose Manuel Xavier Gonzales, in a few short weeks, it will be spring. The snows of winter will flee away. The ice will vanish, and the air will become soft and balmy. In short, Jose Manuel Miguel Xavier Gonzales, the annual miracle of the years will awaken and come to pass, but you won't be there.
>
> The rivulet will run its soaring course to the sea, the timid desert flowers will put forth their tender shoots, the glorious valleys of this imperial domain will blossom as the rose. Still, you won't be here to see.
>
> From every tree top some wild woods songster will carol his mating song, butterflies will sport in the sunshine, the busy bee will hum happily as it pursues its accustomed vocation. The gentle breeze will tease the tassels of the wild grasses, and all nature, Jose Manuel Miguel Xavier Gonzales, will be glad but you. You won't be here to enjoy it because I command the sheriff or some other officer of this country to lead you out to some remote spot, swing you by the neck from a knotting bough of a sturdy oak, and let you hang until you are dead.
>
> And then, Jose Manuel Miguel Xavier Gonzales, I further command that such officer or officers retire quickly from your dangling corpse, that vultures may descend from the heavens upon your filthy body until nothing shall remain but bare, bleached bones of a coldblooded, copper-colored, blood-thirsty, throat-cutting, chili-eating, sheep-herding, murdering son-of-a-bitch.

There are no recorded details of Gonzales' crime and very little is known about the judicial career of Judge Benedict. Only this gem of eloquence remains as a testimony of his oratory prowess.

There are many penologists even today who will argue that

if we really want the death penalty to have a deterrent effect on crime, then the sentence should be carried out as soon after the original crime as possible. In the late 1800s and early 1900s there were many people who believed that an occasional lynching was not necessarily a bad thing. This point of view is graphically demonstrated by noting the number of lynching incidents that occurred during this time. On those rare occasions when a particularly heinous crime had occurred and the law didn't deliver the appropriate amount of justice in a timely manner, a group of civic-minded citizens might intervene.

THE LAW OF THE ROPE

Before the advent of the death penalty in Texas, vigilante action was common. And unlike modern court-findings, what passed for justice was often just revenge. Between 1889 and 1918, Texas ranked third in the country in number of lynchings (335), behind Georgia and Mississippi. On October 3, 1901, five blacks were lynched in Harrison County, Texas. During 1908 twenty-one blacks were lynched in Texas, nine on a single day in June of that year in the small town of Hemphill, Texas. The following year, some sixty miles north of Hemphill, four more lynchings were carried out in the space of four days.

In 1911 a race riot erupted in Palestine, Texas, claiming the lives of eighteen blacks. Some five years later, in 1916, a particularly gruesome lynching/burning occurred in Waco, Texas. The incident would later be referred to as the "Waco Horror" due to the widely circulated and graphically detailed report of a seventeen-year-old black boy's death. He was accused of killing a white woman, removed from the jail, dragged through town, mutilated, hanged, and eventually burned.

The apparent popularity of swift "justice" was demonstrated once again on May 6, 1922, when citizens of Fairfield, in Freestone County, seventy miles east of Waco, burned three blacks near the town square. When black members of the community threatened revenge for the brutal burnings, Governor Neff sent Texas Rangers to ensure the peace. Two days later, another black was lynched. Tensions intensified, and over the next two weeks a total of nine blacks lost their lives to lynch mobs. This series of lynchings, coupled with the massive publicity generated by the "Waco Horror" was a strong catalyst leading to the introduction of legislation requiring all executions be conducted using the electric chair in the central location of Huntsville, Texas.

Once Texas began using the electric chair in 1924, the number of lynching incidents subsided. Since then, Texans have mostly been content to let the courts dispense justice. If the death penalty were abolished, it seems logical to conclude that mob lynchings might become prevalent again. The last known mob lynching occurred five years after Texas began using the electric chair.

THE LAST MOB LYNCHING IN TEXAS

The last known mob lynching in Texas occurred on November 19, 1929. The chain of events leading up to the lynching was somewhat unusual, even for the time. In Cisco, a Central Texas boomtown 100 miles west of Fort Worth, on December 23, 1927, Marshall Ratliff, dressed as Santa Claus, and three accomplices strolled into the First National Bank. The bank robbers pulled guns and announced loudly, "This is a stick-up." The bank robbers shot a teller in the jaw, stuffed $12,000 in cash and $150,000 worth of securities into a potato sack and took two girls hostage. During the getaway, they killed the police chief G. E. "Bit" Bedford and another police officer. Several bystanders were wounded in the ensuing gun battle. The hostages—made to stand in the getaway car as human shields—escaped unharmed. The loot was later found in one of the stolen getaway cars. One of the robbers, Louis Davis, was shot and wounded badly at the bank.

In the disastrous six-day manhunt that followed, the Palo Pinto County sheriff shot himself in the leg and died from the loss of blood. When one of the getaway cars had a flat, the robbers abandoned Louis Davis and left him to be captured by the pursuing posse. Before the robbers left town, an attempt to hijack a car driven by a fourteen-year-old boy was foiled when the youth pocketed the keys and fled. Law officers initially placed the wounded Davis in the Cisco jail, but when a mob began to gather, the officers hid him and secretly transported him inside a grocery truck to Fort Worth, where he was placed in the Tarrant County Jail. Davis died from his wounds the next day.

Four days later, Ratliff was stunned by a bullet at a police barricade and captured; his two remaining accomplices, Henry Helms and Robert Hill, were arrested two days later without resistance near the town of Graham. Helms later died in the electric chair. After spending the next sixteen years in prison, Robert Hill was released on parole, changed his name, and became a model citizen in the Midland, Texas, area.

Marshall Ratliff was sentenced to ninety-nine years in prison in one trial and received the death sentence in another, according to court records and newspaper accounts. He was on death row in Huntsville when his mother, Rilla Carter of Cisco, filed an affidavit on October 24, 1928, contending that her son was insane. Ratliff began acting peculiarly on death row. Eastland County officials, fearing that Ratliff would escape execution by feigning insanity, had him returned to stand trial on the bank-robbery charge. Collapsing intermittently and letting his head loll about, he convinced guards that he was so mentally impaired that they left his cell door open. Ratliff, thinking he was running out of chances, attempted a daring but unsuccessful jailbreak. Ratliff grabbed a jailer's gun and shot a guard, Thomas "Uncle Tom" Jones.

Reports at the time said hundreds, perhaps thousands, gathered outside the Eastland County Jail. It was a cold November day, and the north wind whipped through the crowd. Some witnesses said Ratliff was naked when they brought him out, with one man holding each limb. Still other witnesses say he was crying and praying. The rope was thrown over a guy wire between two poles across the street from the jail, but it broke under Ratliff's weight. Someone ran to the lumberyard and got a coil of heavier rope. This time the rope held.

Most witnesses say they hanged him naked and then afterward somebody slipped a pair of pants on his dangling body as it slowly turned and twisted at the end of the rope. Some witnesses said Ratliff was wearing khaki pants held up by a rope belt when he went to his death. One thing not in dispute is that after he died, several in the crowd cut off parts of the rope belt for souvenirs. Nowadays, folks say that rope must have been fifty miles long, because as the years have passed by, pieces of it have turned up in hundreds of homes around the county.

A few hours after the lynching, Ratliff was cut down and taken to the Hamner Funeral Home, where his body was embalmed and placed in a $50.00 coffin. The body was then taken to a downtown Eastland furniture store and put on public view. Finally it was turned over to Ratliff's mother, who took her son's body to Fort Worth, where he was buried by Shannon's Funeral Chapel. The funeral home's records list the cause of death as "hanging by mob."

The beloved old jailer, whom Ratliff shot, died shortly after learning that his assailant had been lynched. Of the hundreds, if not thousands, of citizens who witnessed this lynching, no one could be found to testify against the mob's direct participants. No one was ever arrested or brought to trial.

Today in Eastland County, there is a granite slab at the corner of North Mulberry and White streets, across the street and just north of the Eastland County Jail. The granite slab discreetly marks the location of the last mob lynching in Texas. At first glance, it looks more like a marker for a grave than a monument to civic outrage that led to violence.

OLD SPARKY

In the forty-nine years that passed between 1923 and 1972, 510 men were sentenced to die in Old Sparky. Of the 510 sentenced to die, 361 were actually executed. Electrocution was not free. Initially, the county of conviction had to pay the prison system twenty-five dollars for services rendered. The cost included the feeding, housing, and executing of the convict. The county also had to pay $8.47 for burial clothes. Later, in 1943, the fee was increased to $19.92, along with a dollar for a headstone if one was needed. If a convict's family chose not to claim the body, the condemned was buried in the prison cemetery, named the Captain Joe Byrd Prison Cemetery after the death of an assistant warden and longtime executioner. Byrd began working for the prison system in 1936 and died on the job in 1964.

Convicts on death row face death in different ways. There have been numerous eleventh-hour suicide attempts, beginning in August 1925, when Clem C. Gray, a former sheriff convicted of murder in Titus County, slashed his throat and wrist with a razor blade on the day of the scheduled execution. The suicide attempt was unsuccessful, however, and Gray's wounds were quickly patched up. Unfortunately for Gray and those in the death chamber with him, once in the chair, his stitches didn't hold. The result was a grisly display of blood shooting from his wounds when the voltage from Old Sparky hit him.

Some convicts have written confessions, some have plotted endless plans of escape, some fight for survival, and others are fatalistic, quietly resigned to their deaths. Most of them have religious conversions, either real or imaginary. On death row, it's hard to tell fact from fiction. The observation has been made with some justification that God must live on death row since so many find Him there.

The sound of an electrocution has been described as a "loud crunch," a noise that swells into a whine, mounts higher, subsides, mounts, subsides, then fades away. In the late evenings preceding an execution, the *crunch* sound could be heard as Captain Byrd tested his equipment. The streetlights in downtown Huntsville would dim and flicker as the voltage behind the walls was turned on.

Finally, at midnight the condemned was brought into the death chamber. The warden would address the convict by name and in a kindly voice ask, "Do you have anything to say?" Some spoke, others declined to make a final statement, but the next instruction from the warden was always the same: "Have a seat, please."

The convict would move to the chair, and the three guards would move in quickly, efficiently, to strap him in. He would cringe when a guard stuffed cotton into his nostrils to trap blood that might gush from ruptured veins in his brain. A mask would be pulled down across his face. The guards would step back and the warden would turn and nod in the direction of the one-way mirror where Captain Joe Byrd stood waiting.

You knew it was coming, but the *crunch* always came suddenly. The mounting whine and the snarl of the generator were the only sounds. Under the hood, the convict's lips peeled back. The throat strained for a last desperate cry, the body would arch against the restraining straps as the generator whined and snarled again. The features purple, steam and smoke rose from the bald spots on the head and leg while the sickly sweet smell of burning flesh permeated the little room.

The whine finally subsided as the generator purred to a halt. The physician stepped forward, placed his stethoscope against the still-smoking chest, and listened intently. He turned to the warden and said, "I pronounce this man dead." The deadly ritual ended. Afterward, the men on death row were usually silent. In the dim light, quiet reigned, and what passed for normalcy returned until the next execution. This gave the death-row guard at the end row a chance to sit quietly and sip his cup of coffee.

OLD SPARKY TRIVIA

The youngest convict electrocuted was Henderson Young, death row #196, a convicted rapist of African-American heritage from Harrison County. Born on May 15, 1921, Young was executed on May 6, 1938, less than nine days short of his seventeenth birthday.

The oldest convict electrocuted was Clemens Matura, who was sixty-seven years old when executed for murder on July 2, 1937.

The most executions to occur in one night were five on February 8, 1924, the first time Old Sparky was used.

Three executions in one night occurred on three occasions— December 29, 1933, February 9, 1934, and July 10, 1936.

Two executions in the same night have occurred on twenty-two occasions.

The first convicts executed for killing a Texas prison guard (during the infamous Bonnie and Clyde–assisted escape from the Eastham Unit) were Joe Palmer, death row number #146, and Raymond Hamilton, death row #147. The two were executed consecutively on the same night, May 10, 1935. Luke Trammell, death row #187, from Brazoria County, was the third on August 20, 1937.

Ironically, in 1933, Retrieve Unit prison guard Jim Sneed was killed during a late-night attempted prison break from the old wooden Retrieve building. At about 11:00 one night, as Sneed sat in his chair at his inside picket post, two prisoners shot him with guns smuggled in to them by the sister of one of the convicts. Warden I. K. Kelly stopped the escape attempt, and the killers were tried for the murder of the guard. Although eligible for the death sentence, the laws at the time would not allow the jury to hear information about parole or goodtime laws. One of the killers was already doing a life sentence and the other fifty years. The jury solemnly awarded the two convicts life sentences on top of their previous sentences. In reality, since the sentences were to run concurrently, the two convicts walked out of the courtroom with no additional time.

The first convict executed for killing another Texas convict was Sam Phillips, death row #33, from Fort Bend County, on May 14, 1926.

Four sets of brothers were electrocuted, Frank and Lorenzo Noel, executed July 3, 1925; S. A. and Forest Robins, executed April 6, 1929; Oscar and Mack Brown, executed July 10, 1936; and Roscoe and Henderson Young, executed May 6, 1938.

Between 1924 and 1972, only three women, Emma Oliver, death row #340; Maggie Morgan, death row #427; and Carolyn Lima, #443, were sentenced to death. All had their sentences commuted to life. Emma Oliver began her criminal career in May 1934, repeatedly charged with vagrancy and prostitution; she was arrested four times for murder, seven times for aggravated assault, and once for attempted murder. She was convicted of one murder in 1947, but only served a year and a half before being released. Within a year after her release, she was arrested three times for aggravated assault.

In February 1949, she was charged with murder with malice and sentenced to death for killing a forty-year-old black male acquaintance in San Antonio in a dispute over three dollars. After her trial, Emma became the first woman in Texas to be sentenced to death by electrocution. This was twenty-five years after the death by electrocution statute was passed. Governor Allan Shivers commuted Emma Oliver's death sentence to life imprisonment on June 29, 1951. Emma died in prison of cancer, twelve years later, in February 1963.

Maggie Morgan was sentenced to death in May 1961 for the murder of a forty-eight-year-old white female in Houston. Evidence at trial indicated that she had killed the victim for a promised payment of $1,600 from the woman's husband, who was a client of Maggie's massage parlor. The victim's husband received a life sentence. Governor Price Daniel commuted Maggie

Morgan's death sentence to life imprisonment on July 25, 1961. She died in prison on September 12, 1970.

Carolyn Lima was sentenced to death in January 1963, along with codefendant Leslie Ashley, for the 1961 slaying of a forty-five-year-old male in Houston. Evidence at trial revealed that Lima, a prostitute, had a lengthy sexual relationship with the victim. In February 1961, Lima and Ashley went to the victim's office, where an altercation occurred over sex and/or money. At some point, Ashley shot the victim once. The victim allegedly brandished a bayonet at Lima, who then grabbed the pistol and shot the victim five more times. Ashley and Lima took the body to a field, soaked it in gasoline, and set it on fire. The couple then fled Texas and were later captured in New York City.

After receiving six reprieves while on death row, Lima's death sentence was finally commuted to five years' imprisonment in April 1965. She was released from prison on the same day of her commutation. The rationale used for her release was that the offense was precipitated by the victim and thus a matter of self-defense. Her codefendant's sentence was commuted to a fifteen-year sentence on January 14, 1966.

THE LAST MAN EXECUTED IN THE ELECTRIC CHAIR IN TEXAS

The last man executed in Old Sparky was Joseph Johnson Jr. of Houston, Texas. On July 30, 1964, Johnson, a thirty-year-old laborer, sang a spiritual and carried a Bible on his walk to the death chamber. Once inside the chamber, Johnson asked for permission to pray. With permission granted, he fell on his knees and prayed. He then sat in the chair, his Bible in his lap, and held his head high as the officers strapped him down. Just before the mask was pulled down over his face he said, "I'm going to meet my maker, the Lord Jesus Christ." Johnson's Bible fell from his lap when the first jolt of electricity hit him at 12:04 A.M. The prison physician pronounced him dead at 12:08.

To the end, Johnson had maintained his innocence in the death of a grocery storeowner during a robbery and subsequent shootout on February 1, 1962. Joseph Ying, thirty-six, proprietor of the J.C. Food Market at 3235 Holman, was killed and his wife wounded in an exchange of gunfire that netted $77.00.

Furman v. Georgia

After July 1964, a moratorium suspended all executions in Texas. On June 29, 1972, in a 5-to-4 split opinion, the Supreme Court in *Furman v. Georgia* ruled that capital punishment was "cruel and unusual punishment and therefore in violation of the Eighth Amendment" and a violation of the equal protection clause of the Fourteenth Amendment. The remedy imposed by the court was total abolition.

This decision temporarily but effectively ended a 150-year-old Texas tradition. Between July 1972 and January of 1973, Governor Price Daniel commuted all of the forty-seven inmates physically present on death row at the time *Furman* was announced. Seven other convicts, who had been sentenced to death but had not arrived on death row, also had their sentences commuted. The death sentences were commuted to either life or ninety-nine years. The fifty-four ex–death row convicts were processed like new inmates and spread throughout the prison system to join the general-inmate population. Texas has never had life sentences without parole; therefore, the entire group of once-condemned men could now look forward to parole eligibility.

On January 1, 1974, a new Texas Penal Code with a revised capital punishment statute went into effect. Although the new death penalty hadn't passed muster in the federal courts, there were several district attorneys ready and willing to test the new law. A month later, a man named John DeVries, death row #507, was the first to be assessed the death penalty under the new death-penalty statute. He was convicted in Jefferson County of murder/burglary, sentenced to death, and assigned a cell on death row in February of 1974. He committed suicide six months later by hanging himself in his cell.

Lethal Injection

It didn't take long for the post-*Furman* death row to begin to fill up as the newly condemned inmates filed appeals challenging the new death penalty law and obtained stays of execution. TDC realized that the small death row, as it then existed in Huntsville, was not going to be large enough to meet the needs of the growing condemned population. With legislative approval, a new death row was created at the Ellis Unit, about thirteen miles outside of Huntsville.

In 1976 the Supreme Court approved the newly passed Texas Penal Code and reinstated the death penalty. The following year, Texas ceased to use the electric chair and adopted lethal injection as the official means to carry out the death penalty. The new method called for the intravenous injection "of a substance or substances in a lethal quantity sufficient to cause death." It was hoped that the injection of massive amounts of chemicals would permit the victim to drift painlessly into death. One of the motives for Texas moving away from the electric chair to lethal injection was a Dallas federal judge's ruling that would have allowed the televising of an electrocution.

One of the first of many legal challenges to the lethal-injection method of execution came from inmates who argued unsuccessfully that the federal Food and Drug Administration had not approved the drugs for the express purpose and use during executions.

The first post-*Furman* execution in Texas and the first in U.S. history by lethal injection took place on December 7, 1982, when Charlie Brooks, Texas death row #592, was executed shortly after midnight. As the drugs entered his veins, Brooks lay still, looking up at the ceiling. In a moment he took a couple of deep, rasping breaths. His stomach heaved, and there was some trembling in the fingers. Brooks' head turned slightly to the right, and he lay quietly. A few short seconds went by, and there was a brief second gasp. All movement ceased, and Charlie Brooks was pronounced dead.

Earlier in the evening, Brooks had dined on a last meal of T-bone steak, French fries, hot rolls, iced tea, and peach cobbler. In reflecting about the execution and Brooks' final thoughts, one reporter observed, "When taking irreversible actions, we all develop qualms about our actions."

Brooks had been convicted four years earlier in Dallas of kidnapping/robbery and murder. Evidence at the trial revealed that Brooks had abducted a mechanic from a used-car lot and forced him to go for a test drive in one of the cars. The victim was bound and gagged with adhesive tape and a clothes hanger wire.

The helpless mechanic was taken to a motel, where Brooks killed him by shooting him once in the head.

While Brooks' execution was proceeding inside the walls, a media circus was underway on the street outside. Several hundred students from nearby Sam Houston State University, curious citizens of Huntsville, and the news media were all out in force. Some spectators carried signs that read, "Kill him in the vein," "Bring back Old Sparky," and "Goodbye Charlie." In contrast, there were a few protesting capital punishment, standing quietly in a candlelight vigil. In the following years, this process was repeated numerous times, but over time the public mostly lost interest in performing in these demonstrations.

It would be two years before three more convicts were executed in 1984, followed by six in 1985, ten in 1986, six in 1987, three in 1988, four in both 1989 and 1990, and five in 1991.

At least eight of the post-*Furman* inmates have died on death row, including three suicides and one murder. More than eighty death sentences have been commuted, either through judicial review or intervention by the governor's office.

The majority of inmates awaiting execution on death row are not disruptive to staff or threatening to other inmates. Some of the inmates have on a case by case basis been approved as "work capable" and allowed to work in a special garment factory, set aside for death row inmates. While examples of death row violence are rare, there have been some significant exceptions.

BAD TO THE BONE

I visited the old Ellis I Unit's death row on several occasions during my career. The convicts always impressed me as an odd assortment of stupid, inept losers who for whatever reason had committed subhuman acts. A far cry from the public perception of cunning, exotic, and glamorously wild desperadoes, most were just simple-minded predators who took advantage of the weak and helpless.

On one occasion, during the mid-eighties, I was introduced to James "Doom" Demouchette, death row #572, dubbed "the meanest man on death row." As I observed him during a daily recreation period in one of the death-row dayrooms, he casually puffed on a cigar, paced the floor, and stared back through the bars at me. I wasn't sure at the time whether his blank stare reflected idle curiosity or was perhaps a feeble attempt at intimidation.

Raised as one of fourteen children, by the time he reached junior high school James had failed five times, including the first grade. He wet the bed until he was thirteen and had expressed a joyful pleasure in the indiscriminant killing of dogs and cats from an early age. James dropped out of junior high school and graduated to the Gateville State School for Boys for, as he calmly said, "killing a boy." Released in 1972 at seventeen, James quickly demonstrated a continued willingness to kill for little or no reason. Although he was not prosecuted for the crimes, authorities attribute at least two other attempted homicides, committed during burglaries, to Demouchette. The two victims luckily survived, even though one had been shot three times. Demouchette's next victims would not be so fortunate.

On October 16, 1976, a twenty-one-year-old James Demouchette, with his younger brother, Chris, entered a Pizza Hut on Antoine Road in Northwest Houston. By now James was a loose cannon with heroin flowing through his veins. He needed money for drugs, and he had a .38 caliber revolver that he fully intended to use.

It was closing time at the pizza parlor, and the three young employees were the only ones left besides James and his brother. James proudly displayed his .38 revolver and passed it around for the others to see. After a brief discussion with the three young men about the gun, it was passed back to James. Once the gun returned to his hands, Demouchette opened fire, shooting all three of the pizza-parlor employees at point-blank range. Leaving the three victims for dead, James and his brother Chris stole the change from the register and a piece of used music equipment and went looking for drugs. James would soon find out that he had made a mistake that would ultimately cost him his life. One of the victims, Geof Hambrick, was still alive. The bullet from Demouchette's gun had only grazed Hambrick's head, and he had lain in his own blood, playing dead in order to survive.

On July 20, 1977, a jury took less than two hours to find James Demouchette guilty of the capital murder of nineteen-year-old Scott Sorrell and twenty-year-old Robert White during the pizza-parlor robbery. It only took the jury another thirty-nine minutes to give him the death penalty. James' younger brother Chris, who killed no one and probably had no idea what was going to happen when they entered the pizza parlor, received a life sentence. After Hambrick's testimony sealed his fate, James Demouchette made a remark to a courtroom bailiff, referring to the survival of the witness as "the onliest mistake I ever made."

There were many in law enforcement that hoped they had heard the last of James Demouchette. They had not.

During the sixteen years between his arrest and execution, Demouchette:

1. Raped and stabbed a Harris County Jail inmate.
2. Killed one other convict on death row at the Ellis I Unit.
3. Beat and stabbed two other convicts.
4. Stabbed at least four TDC officers.
5. Threw lye in the face of another TDC officer.
6. Set fire to his cell twice.
7. Destroyed a TV and a commode with his hands.

In May of 1982 the Texas Court of Criminal Appeals overturned Demouchette's conviction and death sentence. The court's abstract reasoning centered on the fact that the court-appointed psychologist, prior to a competency hearing, had not warned Demouchette that he had a right to remain silent. On April 13, 1983, after an expensive second trial, another jury took only thirty minutes to sentence James Demouchette to death for the second time.

On August 2, 1983, Demouchette walked into the dayroom at the Ellis I Unit where he found fellow convict and self-appointed writ-writer Johnny E. Swift talking to one of his potential convict clients. Swift was a forty-two-year-old convict serving 101 years for murder with malice. He professed to be a communist of the Marxist-Leninist variety and routinely attempted to recruit other convicts to his cause. Seeing Demouchette as potential muscle for his Marxist clique, Swift attempted to get James to join. Demouchette, not having the slightest clue what a Marxist was, declined Swift's offer.

Swift took Demouchette's refusal as a personal insult and

retaliated against James by putting out the rumor that he was a snitch and had even, according to Demouchette, threatened him. Finding Swift in the dayroom was a blessing for James, as it would give him a long-awaited chance to settle the matter his way. Demouchette walked up to Swift, and after a short exchange of name-calling, James began stabbing Swift with a fourteen-inch sharpened ladle handle from the prison's kitchen. There was one officer near the dayroom, but he was unarmed and could do little to stop the assault.

As Swift fell to the dayroom floor, Demouchette continued the assault. Witnesses said Demouchette was stabbing Swift in the chest with such force that the blade was hitting the concrete floor on the other side of the victim's body, causing sparks to fly. Finally a TDC sergeant opened the dayroom door and ordered Demouchette to drop the weapon. Demouchette, however, was in no mood to drop the weapon and told the officer, "Nah, I ain't through killin' this nigger yet!" After stabbing the lifeless Swift a few more times, Demouchette ceased his assault, stood up, and said, "Now I'm through; the son of a bitch is dead." James then surrendered the weapon and after wiping some of the blood from his hands, calmly lit a cigar.

Autopsy revealed that Swift had been stabbed more than sixteen times; any one of the wounds would have been fatal. Demouchette was subsequently charged with murder, tried, and convicted, and received a life sentence for killing Johnny E. Swift. I've often thought that as a writ-writer, Swift would have appreciated the fact that the courts gave a life sentence to his killer, who already had a death sentence.

As a side note to this incident, there were more than a few TDC employees who breathed a sigh of relief when Johnny E. Swift died. Not that anyone truly wanted Swift to die, but he was a prolific writ-writer, and his many pending lawsuits against TDC security officers and other employees died with him. Demouchette didn't realize it, but he probably saved Texas tax-payers several million dollars in court costs when the attorney general's office didn't have to defend against Johnny E. Swift's lawsuits.

In 1992, as his final appeals ran out and his court-appointed lawyers informed him that they no longer represented him,

Demouchette asked the Texas Court of Criminal Appeals for a reprieve. Only three days from execution, Robert L. McGlasson of the University of Texas Law School, acting as Demouchette's lawyer on an emergency basis, presented the court with "mitigating facts about his childhood that were never placed before jury." The U.S. Supreme Court denied all subsequent appeals.

When the day of execution finally came, James was unusually reserved and quiet. In the early evening, he received his last meal of steak and baked potato. After eating, he calmly sat back and puffed on cigars as he awaited the executioner. On September 22, 1992, the "meanest man on death row," who had once vowed to kill a guard on the way to the death chamber, calmly walked down the hall to his death. He climbed onto the lethal injection table without assistance and was strapped down and executed in a rather routine manner.

A Civilized Way to Die

During the late 1970s, while on a visit to the Ellis Unit, I met a particularly loathsome death-row convict named Ronald Clark O'Bryan, death row #529 (*aka* the Candyman). Like James Demouchette, O'Bryan had to be isolated from other inmates much of the time, but for vastly different reasons. O'Bryan was a child killer who had poisoned his own eight-year-old son, Timothy, on Halloween night in 1976. The motive was life insurance money, and O'Bryan hoped the poison would be blamed on trick-or-treat candy.

On the night in question, O'Bryan visited some of the houses in the neighborhood and returned home, passing out some Pixy Stix candy to his son and some friends who were trick-or-treating. Later in the evening his son, Timothy, ate some of the poisoned candy and died an extremely slow, painful death. Evidence presented at trial demonstrated that O'Bryan had recently increased his son's life-insurance coverage. He had pretended to get the Pixy Styx candies from the neighbor's house, when in fact he had made and given them to the children himself. This crime earned him the nickname "the Candyman."

Generally speaking, baby rapists and child killers represent the lowest form of life in prison and if they are not extremely careful around their fellow inmates, unfortunate accidents can occur. O'Bryan was considered a potential victim by the TDC administration, and precautions were taken to ensure that some convict didn't prematurely exterminate him before the State of Texas could get around to a formal execution.

In perhaps one of the most absurd legal briefs filed in the twentieth century, O'Bryan's lawyers, in an attempt to delay his execution, argued that to have massive doses of drugs pumped through one's veins as a form of execution constituted an inhumane way to die. This, on behalf of a man convicted of feeding his eight-year-old son cyanide-laced candy, seemed hypocritical even to the U.S. Supreme Court.

Ironically, in a unique display of true Texas justice, O'Bryan was sentenced to die by lethal injection on Halloween night, October 31, 1982. Although he appealed and obtained stays delaying the inevitable, he was eventually executed on Halloween night in 1984. History doesn't reveal whether the technician-executioner said "trick or treat" to the convict before he started the deadly drugs flowing through O'Bryan's veins at 12:38 A.M., but we do know that ten minutes later he was pronounced dead.

In sharp contrast to his son's gruesome death, O'Bryan's death went smoothly. He was rendered unconscious quickly and exhibited no apparent signs that he was in any pain. Comparing the excruciating nature of his young son's death with O'Bryan's subsequent painless execution, lethal injection seems entirely too civilized.

SEVENTEEN WASTED YEARS

By May of 1991, most Texans were tired of hearing about Ignacio Cuevas. As ex–TDC Director W. J. Estelle said at the time, "Seventeen years is too long for justice to be done." Cuevas, a forty-two-year-old Mexican national, was serving a forty-five-year sentence for murder in Pecos County when fellow convict and ex–drug kingpin Fred Gomez Carrasco, thirty-four, recruited him and Rudolfo Dominguez, twenty-seven, to join in what later became known as the longest prison siege in U.S. history.

At the end, the desperate convicts murdered their helpless

women hostages by shooting them at point-blank range. Ignacio Cuevas didn't hesitate to shoot his hostage, the prison chaplain, Roman Catholic priest Joseph O'Brien, once in the chest, also at point-blank range. Thinking he had killed the priest, Cuevas fired a few random shots at no one in particular. Then, like the coward he was, Cuevas fainted, or as some have contended, "played possum," rather than fight it out. He played dead until the gun battle ended, hiding under the pile of debris and bodies until someone noticed he was still alive.

Carrasco and Dominguez both received swift and appropriate levels of justice on the second-floor ramp below the library. Unfortunately for Texas taxpayers, Ignacio Cuevas survived.

Cuevas was charged with capital murder, based on the Texas Penal Code that makes murder a capital offense when committed during arson, kidnapping, burglary, or escape from prison. This meant that Cuevas would be eligible for the death penalty even though the priest had survived the bullet in his chest that came from Cuevas' gun.

Over the next seventeen years, Cuevas had three trials, at an estimated cost of $600,000. His first two convictions were overturned because of errors in jury selection. Attorneys for the Austin based Texas Resource Center, a federally funded organization that recruits lawyers for condemned convicts, said Cuevas was mentally retarded and should not be executed because he was less to blame than Carrasco or Dominguez. Some of the victims' families said in a joint statement that "Justice delayed is justice denied."

Even though no evidence was introduced into any of the trials to indicate that Cuevas had killed anyone during the siege, and despite numerous delays in the trials, three separate juries gave Cuevas the death penalty.

When asked what he thought about Cuevas' long, tedious march through the legal system, ex–TDC Director W. J. Estelle said, "I've got a lot of scars about it. I think somebody needs to be reminded that there are sons of bitches still like that out there in the population." As the execution date neared, Estelle was even more specific, saying that there was only one way he wished Cuevas could have met his end on that ramp back in 1974: "Only if I could have fired the bullet."

Finally, on May 23, 1991, at age fifty-nine, Ignacio Cuevas

was executed by lethal injection inside the Walls Unit death chamber, only a few yards from where the infamous escape attempt had ended seventeen years earlier. When the long ordeal was finally over, I couldn't help thinking about what W. J. Estelle had said about wishing he could have fired that last bullet. I know in my heart that those Texas Rangers and the other officers on that library ramp that night did their duty as the law requires, and I don't fault any of them for their actions. Still, I believe that if there were some magical parallel universe in which the people of Texas could have voted on the issue, most of us would have granted W. J. Estelle's wish.

POSTER BOY FOR THE DEATH PENALTY

Kenneth Alan McDuff—TDC#227123—death row #485.

McDuff was, without a doubt, the most pitiful excuse for a human being I've ever had the misfortune to personally come in contact with in thirty years of working around Texas convicts. To refer to McDuff as a convict is an insult to real convicts. The chronology of his story goes like this:

1965: Kenneth McDuff is a small-town bully who dropped out of school in the eighth grade and has since spent most of his time drinking, fighting, and trying to outrun the law. His mother, Addie McDuff, has always fought his battles for him, but after he turns eighteen and is charged with committing a string of fourteen burglaries in Bell, Milam, and Falls counties, she can no longer protect him. McDuff is convicted and begins serving his first TDC sentence on March 10, 1965, eleven days short of his nineteenth birthday. As a "non-violent first offender," McDuff makes outside trusty within three months and is released on parole on December 29, 1965, only nine months after entering prison.

1966: Six months after his release, McDuff and his follower, Roy Dale Green, are now armed predators and full-fledged dope fiends, riding around Fort Worth in McDuff's new Dodge Charger looking for trouble. On the night of August 6, 1966, after selecting the victims purely by chance, McDuff and Green kidnap sixteen-year-old Edna Sullivan, seventeen-year-old Robert Brand, and fifteen-year-old Mark Dunnam. After robbing the boys at gunpoint, McDuff forces all three into the trunk of their own Ford.

With Roy Dale Green driving the Dodge and McDuff driving the victims' car, they drive to a vacant field outside of town. McDuff forces Edna to get out of the trunk of the Ford and into the trunk of the Dodge, then turns the gun on the boys. Still on their knees in the trunk of the Ford, McDuff executes both the boys by shooting them in the face with the .38 at point-blank range. Just to make sure they are dead, he shoots Brand twice and Dunnam four times. With sixteen-year-old Edna in the trunk of the Dodge, McDuff and Green leave the dead boys in the trunk of their car and drive south into Johnson County.

Once over the county line, McDuff stops along a desolate country road and forces Edna out of the trunk. He makes her undress, throws her into the back seat, and begins raping her. After thoroughly brutalizing her, McDuff turns her over to Green. When Green finishes raping the girl, McDuff brutalizes her again. Temporarily satisfied, they drive to another remote area, where McDuff decides to get rid of the last witness. McDuff drags the helpless, nude girl out of the car, and with Green helping to hold her down, he presses a broomstick to Edna's throat until she strangles to death. They hide the body in some weeds, try to destroy any potential evidence, and drive back to Falls County.

Within a day or two, Roy Dale Green knows that he can't live with what they have done and turns state's evidence against Kenneth McDuff. Eventually, McDuff is convicted and sentenced to die in the electric chair for causing the death of Edna Sullivan. Roy Dale Green will serve five years and be released.

October 9, 1968: Kenneth McDuff is received at TDC under sentence of death from Tarrant County for capital murder with malice. He is assigned death row #485. Between 1968 and 1972, McDuff comes within a few days of being executed several times. On each occasion he is granted a stay.

1972: In a monumental miscarriage of justice, the Supreme Court hands down its landmark *Furman v. Georgia* ruling proclaiming that the death penalty amounts to cruel and unusual punishment and is thus unconstitutional. All inmates on death row, including McDuff, have their sentences commuted to life.

August 23, 1973: Kenneth McDuff, his death sentence commuted, leaves death row and is sent to the Ramsey I Unit in Brazoria County. As Texas has never had "life without parole,"

McDuff will eventually be considered for parole. Upon arrival at the Ramsey I Unit, he is assigned to the field, loses several fights with other inmates, and becomes a minor disciplinary problem. He solicits employees to violate the rules and is found to be in possession of contraband. Due to intimidation by other convicts, he is temporarily placed in protection status. Eventually returned to the general population, McDuff continues to pick up minor disciplinary cases, mostly for possession of contraband or "chock," homemade alcohol.

August 15, 1977: Kenneth McDuff is transferred to the Retrieve Unit in Brazoria County. I meet him for the first time during his initial interview, when new inmates are given a housing and job assignment. McDuff is a thirty-one-year-old, six-foot-four, 235-pound mental midget with an IQ of 92. A perpetually underdeveloped teenager, his intellectual development ceased sometime before he dropped out of school in the eighth grade.

Although he is clearly no intellectual giant, McDuff knows right from wrong. The problem is, he is morally corrupt beyond any hope of redemption, with absolutely no evidence of adult guidance or social development. He has no fundamental understanding or appreciation that there is a need for him to make morally acceptable choices. He claims he is religious, a member of the Assembly of God church in his hometown of Rosebud. Like most child killers and rapists, he denies guilt of his present offense. His demeanor is withdrawn, timid, and his voice is low. He answers questions with a "Yes, sir" or "No, sir" without elaboration. There is a slight sneer on his face and there is something about his eyes, a silent message that says, "You've got me now and I'm helpless, but if the tables are ever turned, you'll get no mercy from me."

McDuff was initially assigned to number-one hoe squad, where the meanest, biggest inmates who pose discipline problems and security risks were generally assigned. He was in three fights within the first two weeks. He lost them all. It didn't take the older multirecidivists at Retrieve long to figure out that McDuff was a tall bigmouth who couldn't fight and who tried to bluff his way through life. The older convicts at Retrieve didn't bluff.

I was fortunate enough to witness one of McDuff's particularly embarrassing altercations. One hot morning shortly after McDuff arrived at Retrieve, I was observing the line squads shoestring the grass and weeds off the end of a set of rows when the water wagon pulled up. Bubba Carter, a tall, skinny three-time loser was reining in the two horses pulling the water wagon. The number-one hoe boss, John Bennett, yelled for his squad to "Get a drink if you want it." As the squad put their hoes down and gathered around the water wagon, McDuff slapped one of the horses on the butt, causing the wagon to jump a few feet. Bubba saw what McDuff had done and looked over at me for guidance. He said, "Can I have 'im, Boss?" Bubba meant he wanted to have a "come to Jesus meeting" with McDuff over his rude treatment of the animals.

Since McDuff was physically larger and heavier than Bubba, I answered, "Sure, Bubba, tell him that's no way to treat a horse."

Bubba walked around the wagon and got right up in McDuff's face, saying, "Man, don't you be fucking with my hosses."

McDuff laughed, rolled his eyes in mock fear and said, "Fuck you, nigger."

The next part happened so fast it was just a blur. Bubba hit him three or four times in the face before McDuff hit the ground. He tried to get up, but as he kneeled forward a gaseous noise emanated from his rear end—he defecated on himself. The whole squad of convicts, even Bubba, started laughing. They thought this was hilarious.

McDuff, only semi-conscious, was looking up at me through blood-covered eyelids as he tried to talk while spitting up more blood. I asked him, "Do you think you can leave those horses alone now?" He nodded in the affirmative as number-one hoe broke into laughter again. McDuff was going to need some minor medical attention, so I used the handheld radio to call for transportation. When one of the farm pickups arrived, I instructed Bubba and a couple of other convicts to help him onto the back of the truck. They hesitated, and after looking back and forth at one another, one of them finally asked, "Do we have to, Boss? He stinks awful bad."

I ordered McDuff, "Get on the truck." He reached for the

bumper and pulled himself up and into the back of the pickup. His white-cotton inmate pants were an oily brown from the waist down now.

Major Lanham rode over to see what all the commotion was about. He got a whiff of McDuff as I was telling him about the horses. He said, "Damn, get him out of here, and wash out that truck when you get him to the building." I rode in the cab with the plow-squad boss on the way in, and we had to roll the windows all the way up in order to breathe.

When Buddy Walden, the back-gate boss, saw what was in the back of the truck, he told McDuff, "Get naked—you ain't going in my building like that." Buddy turned on the water hose and gave him a bath right there on the sidewalk. As we drove off, I could see him limping across the yard butt naked.

Much has been written about what a dangerous man Kenneth McDuff was, mostly by people who dealt with him in the free world. I am here to tell you that during the ten years I knew Kenneth McDuff while he was assigned to the Retrieve Unit, he wasn't a threat to anyone. He was scared to death of the other convicts, and after a couple of "come to Jesus meetings" with the building tenders, he was embarrassingly polite to the staff.

On another occasion, when there was a disagreement over TV channel selection, I actually heard a short black convict nicknamed "Sugar-ray," who clearly wasn't afraid of McDuff, get right up in his face. Pointing a threatening finger at him in front of about seventy convicts, he said, "McDuff, there ain't no young girls or kids in this tank, so I guess you ain't runnin' nothing, huh?" McDuff didn't argue or say anything; he just dropped his head, turned around and walked off. By that time he'd lost so many fights that the simple shame of an uncontested verbal challenge no longer meant anything to him. McDuff took orders; he didn't give them. The thought of any convict taking instructions from McDuff was out of the realm of reality.

McDuff was a shameless informant who volunteered "snitch" information on other convicts, and he didn't care who knew it. He attempted to trade information to the prison staff in exchange for favorable jobs and housing assignments. For the most part, his information was useless, because as he was a known snitch, other convicts wouldn't have anything to do with him. Due to his size, some in the unit administration kept trying to use him as a building tender; one had to have a certain physical prowess in order to survive in the job. McDuff received so little respect from the other convicts, including the other building tenders, that he rarely did more than sweep or mop the floor. He was clearly intimidated by the other convicts, too weak, both in mind and stature, for the job. He was eventually assigned to the unit laundry, where he spent six days a week sorting and folding inmate clothing. In the ten years that I knew him, I never saw or heard of him winning a fight.

September 7, 1977: McDuff passes a polygraph on the subject of the crimes for which he received the death penalty. The polygraph examiner determines that "No deceptive criteria is indicated to the relevant questions. It is our conclusive opinion that the subject has been truthful."

An accomplished liar, in McDuff's feeble mind a falsehood was the same as the truth—he made no distinction between the two. Polygraphs are only useful on people with a moral code, or at least some basic concept of human decency. McDuff didn't qualify in either area.

1980: McDuff receives his first vote of approval, from Parole Commissioner Edward Johnson. At the time, there is a three-member parole team, and only two favorable votes are necessary for release.

1981: McDuff again receives one vote of approval for parole, from Commissioner Helen Copitka.

1982: Kenneth McDuff offers Parole Commissioner Glen Heckmann a $10,000 bribe for his vote. Heckmann, an ex–TDC security field major and a man of irreproachable integrity, immediately files a charge of bribery against McDuff. The jury finds McDuff guilty of bribery, but only sentences him to two years. Due to the embarrassment of the bribery conviction, McDuff's parole reviews are all unanimously denied from 1982 through 1984.

1985: Parole Commissioner Sue Cunningham gives McDuff her favorable vote, only three years after his attempt to bribe Commissioner Heckmann. Cunningham also votes to release

McDuff in 1986 and 1987. On January 7, 1985, Addie McDuff calls the Retrieve Unit with a death message. In a monitored phone call she tells Kenneth that his older brother, Lonnie McDuff (*aka* "Rough Tough"), has been killed, shot to death in a squabble over a woman or drugs, by ex-convict Larry Don Carrol. Kenneth's immediate reaction is an expressed disappointment to several other convicts that he has lost his most reliable source of drugs.

1986: Kenneth McDuff begins receiving letters and photos from an attractive young woman named Teresa, who claims to be his daughter as the result of a rape McDuff had committed as a teenager. She begins visiting McDuff. Although McDuff had not known of the woman until that first letter, he never questions the fact that she is his daughter.

I monitored the correspondence and visits between the two, as I suspected but couldn't prove that McDuff was using his new-found relative as a replacement "mule" for his now-deceased brother, who had always been ready to smuggle drugs, cash, and other contraband into the unit. Some of the letters to Teresa sounded more like a courtship ritual rather than any father-daughter relationship. After a few visits, Teresa changed the visitation relationship from daughter to "friend." I never did determine the reason for this; however, it may have been that she had become uneasy about sitting across the table from McDuff during contact visits. Later, when McDuff was released, Teresa became even less enchanted with him, broke off all contact, and moved out of state.

1987: Governor Bill Clements begins his second term in office by ordering the release of as many inmates as possible.

The state parole laws were seen as an impediment to reaching a settlement with the federal courts regarding the overcrowding issue. The problem was that all the hot-check writers, white-collar thieves, and other petty criminals had already been released. So, with Judge William Wayne Justice breathing down their necks, threatening to close the prison or fine the taxpayers for not meeting his limited inmate-population capacity numbers, the parole board reached into the slimy bottom of the barrel and began to release certifiably dangerous convicts onto the streets of Texas.

1989: By this time, old time convicts like McDuff have become just numbers. They are rarely ever seen at actual physical parole interviews. A "paper-review," which is a review of a convict's file, is all parole has time to do. TDC is so overcrowded they are paroling 750 convicts a week, or 8 out of 10 inmates reviewed, in order to ensure that cell space is available for incoming inmates.

The criteria for an "acceptable risk" to be considered for release now included almost all convicts. Keeping the streets of Texas safe was no longer a priority. The parole board's goal was to pacify a federal judge and a few Austin politicians and to keep the plaintiffs' lawyers at bay, thereby holding onto their politically appointed jobs.

On October 11, 1989, twenty-three years and two months after being sentenced to death for murder with malice aforethought, Kenneth McDuff is set free. On his fifteenth petition for parole, in spite of letters of protest from law enforcement, Falls County District Attorney Tom Sehon, and District Judge Byron Matthews, McDuff is released on parole.

The administrative parole panel was made up of board members Chris Mealy, Henry Keene, and Doctor James Granberry, an orthodontist who was the politically connected chairman of the Texas Parole Board at the time. Mealy and Granberry voted to parole McDuff, and Keene cast the dissenting vote.

In 1993 ex–Parole Board Chairman Dr. Granberry would plead guilty to perjury after he lied to a federal court regarding the nature and extent of his parole-consulting business. He was placed on five years' probation and sentenced to stay in a halfway house and perform 150 hours of community service. Granberry, at that time, was the highest ranking State of Texas official ever convicted of a federal crime. After his release, McDuff often bragged about paying a large amount of money in exchange for being released from prison, and his daughter Teresa alleged that $25,000 had been paid, but the evidence on that point was never sufficient to bring formal charges. Later, during the 1992 investigation into the disappearance of one of McDuff's victims, a business card from ex–parole commissioner, now private parole "consultant," Helen Copitka is found in McDuff's billfold in his abandoned car. In a subsequent interview with investigators, McDuff's parents denied allegations of bribery, but insisted they paid an attorney named Bill Habern to represent their son. McDuff's mother, Addie McDuff, readily acknowledged that Helen Copitka worked for Bill Habern.

As Andy Kahan, the crime victims' director for the City of Houston, would later say, "The ghost of McDuff will haunt this state forever." Kahan also noted that McDuff was only one of sixty-eight former death-row inmates to be subsequently paroled.

Three days after McDuff was released, the body of Sarafia Parker, a twenty-nine-year-old suspected prostitute, was found dead, beaten and strangled in Temple, Texas, the Central Texas town to which McDuff had been paroled.

October 11, 1990: McDuff is returned to prison for admittedly making a terrorist threat to a black teenager while holding a knife, in his hometown of Rosebud, Texas. Shortly after McDuff is returned to TDC, his attorney lobbies the chairman of the Texas Parole Board, Dr. Granberry, for a reinstatement of his parole. The terrorist-threat charges are dropped because witnesses and the victim are too terrified of McDuff to testify. Less than three months after reentering TDC, McDuff is released again. Without a formal hearing, on December 18, 1990, parole staff counsel Betty Wells makes the bureaucratic decision to release Kenneth McDuff on parole to his parents' Falls County home.

1991: Moving frequently, McDuff stays in Temple, Rockdale, Cameron, Bellmead, Tyler, and Dallas. By spring, several Waco-area prostitutes are reported missing. One of the first victims traced back to McDuff is Regenia Moore, who had been seen kicking and screaming in the cab of his red pickup truck shortly before her disappearance. McDuff is suspected of the crime, but due to the absence of a body and/or evidence, he is not charged.

February 24, 1992: Valencia Kay Joshua is last seen alive looking for McDuff's dormitory room at the technical school he sometimes attends. Her body is later found in a shallow grave in the field behind the school.

On the evening of March 1, 1992, McDuff kidnaps twenty-three-year-old Melissa Ann Northrup and steals $252.04 from the register of the convenience store where she works. Her body is found several weeks later, bound and floating in a gravel pit in Dallas County.

In October 1992, Brenda Thompson disappears from the "Waco Cut," an area known for its available prostitutes. Her body would not be found for several years.

On December 29, 1992, McDuff and his new ex-convict follower, Alva Hank Worley, abduct twenty-eight-year-old Colleen Reed from an Austin car wash. McDuff rapes and tortures his helpless victim, then turns her over to Worley. After Worley rapes her, McDuff forces Reed into the trunk. As McDuff lets his accomplice out of the car later that evening, Worley asks what McDuff intends to do with the girl. McDuff answers coldly, "I'm going to use her up." That is the last time Colleen Reed was seen alive.

1993: Finally, some hardworking, dedicated lawmen put together enough physical evidence to convince Hank Worley to turn state's evidence against McDuff. Realizing his days are numbered, McDuff flees the state and becomes the most wanted man in the country. On May 1, Colleen Reed's sister, Lori Bible, makes an appearance on the nationally televised show *America's Most Wanted*. Two days after the show, a tip is received that allows Texas lawmen to capture McDuff in Kansas City, Missouri. McDuff is captured as he works on his trash-pickup job under the name of Richard Dale Fowler. The five-man team of officers does not give him a chance to offer any resistance

Although still protesting his innocence, it only takes a Travis County jury of eight men and four women an hour to convict McDuff of the murder of Colleen Reed. It takes less than an hour for them to decide on a death sentence. In yet another strange twist of fate, McDuff's conviction is overturned because the foreman of the Travis County Grand Jury had been indicted years before for passing a bad check. The case would have to be retried.

McDuff is subsequently tried in Harris County for the kidnap/murder of Melissa Ann Northrup, for which he receives yet another death penalty. The Northrup case is upheld as being on solid legal ground and is the one that ultimately succeeds in getting McDuff executed.

While on death row, McDuff is diagnosed with Hepatitis C,

and there is fear in some circles that McDuff will die from the disease before he can be executed. The victim's relatives from McDuff's original death sentence waited thirty-two years to see justice prevail. Although McDuff never admits guilt to any of the murders, in the last weeks of his life he allows himself to be taken by van, in chains and under heavy guard, from death row to the banks of the Brazos River in Central Texas. Director Wayne Scott approves this rare departure from procedure in a last-ditch effort to find McDuff's remaining victims. Upon arrival, McDuff gives detailed directions to the locations of the shallow graves where he had buried the bodies of Brenda Thompson, Regenia Moore, and Colleen Reed.

The regular death-penalty protesters were noticeably absent on the evening of McDuff's execution. Typically, a few dozen anti-death penalty advocates attend all executions, but even the most steadfast opponents of capital punishment were not wholly opposed to seeing McDuff die. When one veteran of more than a hundred death-row protests was asked about her absence, she said, "If anybody needed to die, he did. I really hate the death penalty, but I would've done it for the state if they'd asked."

On November 17, 1998, in midafternoon, McDuff showered and changed into clean inmate clothing. He had requested a last meal of two T-bone steaks, but his request was denied. He received a last meal of ground beef and vegetables. As 6:00 approached, McDuff was escorted into the death chamber, where he cooperated fully with the execution team. When the time came, Warden Jim Willett asked McDuff if he had any final statement. McDuff responded, "Release me." Those were the last words he would ever say. He gasped several times before slipping into unconsciousness. Eight minutes later, at 6:26 P.M., he was pronounced dead. By all accounts, McDuff died a much easier death than any of his victims did.

The McDuff case is a textbook example of what can happen when society fails to execute a verified predator. No one knows exactly how many people McDuff killed in his lifetime, though various law-enforcement professionals have speculated that the number is between twelve and fifteen women and children. There is one irrefutable fact that emerged from the McDuff saga.

Without any doubt, if McDuff had been executed after the first jury of his peers justly awarded him the death penalty, at a minimum, nine of his future victims would not have had to suffer torture and eventual death at his hands. Kenneth McDuff stands as a monument to the accuracy of the argument that the death penalty is in fact a very specific and 100-percent effective deterrent to those predators, who will, if left alive, commit future capital crimes.

Texas juries did their job of finding McDuff guilty and sentencing him to death not once, but three times. How absurd is it when society has to wait thirty-two years to receive justice?

McDuff is on record as the only capital murderer in Texas to ever receive a death sentence, have it commuted, be paroled, and subsequently be returned to death row convicted of not one, but two additional capital murders. He was also the first and only convict in Texas to ever receive two death-row execution numbers, #485 in 1968 and #161 in 1993.

Who was to blame for the Kenneth McDuff fiasco? We can start with the 1970s-era liberal Supreme Court that chose to release McDuff in the first place. Add weak, uninformed politicians and a host of politically appointed self-serving parole board members who succumbed to federal court–ordered threats by District Judge William Wayne Justice to relieve overcrowding in Texas prisons, or else. In addition, we can add the lawyers who defended McDuff, the ones who pled for his release and lobbied the parole board even in the face of overwhelming evidence of his guilt.

Changes have been made in parole-board procedures, and now the full eighteen-member panel is required to vote on the release of capital offenders, but the citizens of Texas are well-advised to remember Kenneth McDuff. There are always going to be weak politicians, liberal federal court judges, and predatory convicts. I submit that it is incumbent upon a civilized society to protect the weak and helpless among us. We must punish predatory behavior with the death penalty in order to ensure that our citizens are not preyed upon. It is not too great a sacrifice to ask our society and our system of justice to rise to the occasion.

TEXAS CHIVALRY

Of the 1,300-plus people known to have been executed in Texas prior to 1998, only three have been women. This is largely due to a unique brand of southern chivalry that is still alive in Texas today. Texas history clearly demonstrates that juries just don't like the idea of executing women. The first recorded execution of a woman in Texas was a slave named Jane (possibly Jane Elkins), who was hanged on May 27, 1853, in Dallas. Her crime was killing a white man, possibly her owner, by splitting his head with an ax. Five years later, in 1858, another slave, known only as "Lucy," was hanged after being found guilty of clubbing to death her owner, Marie Dougherty, who ran the Columbia Hotel in Galveston.

The last woman executed in Texas, prior to Karla Faye Tucker in 1998, was Josefa "Chipita" Rodriguez, who was hanged on Friday, November 13, 1863. Chipita was described as being "very old," but was probably in her sixties. On August 25, 1863, the body of horsetrader John Savage was found downstream from Chipita's inn. He had been killed with an ax, presumably for the $600 in gold he was carrying. Chipita and a second defendant, Juan Silvera, were taken into custody at San Patricio. On October 7, they were indicted. Two days later, a trial was held.

Legend has it that Silvera was either Chipita's son or lover, but there is no evidence to support either alleged relationship. Some say the murder charge was intended to scare Chipita into naming the real killer, but the only words she ever said were "Not guilty," or in Spanish, *"No soy culpable."*

The trial lasted only one day. The jury said, "On account of her old age and the circumstantial evidence against her, we do recommend her to the mercy of the court." Judge Benjamin Neal, not being the chivalrous type, sentenced her to death. Silvera was given five years in prison "at hard labor."

There were clearly some legal improprieties during Chipita's trial. Sheriff William Means, who investigated Savage's murder and brought charges against Chipita, served as foreman of the grand jury that indicted her. At least three members of the grand jury also served on the trial jury. The initial motive for the slaying was thought to have been some gold coins that Savage was known to have earned from his horsetrading; however, shortly after the trial, Savage's saddlebags were found downriver still holding $600 in gold coins.

There would be no appeal for Chipita. After thwarting a couple of lynch mobs, approximately one month after the verdict, Chipita was hanged. Legend says that it was a dark and stormy day, and that as the hangman tightened the rope around Chipita's neck, lightning struck the tree. Some say Chipita was still alive when they buried her. Twenty-five years after her death, a man confessed on his deathbed that he killed John Savage and that Chipita was innocent.

It would be 135 years before Texas executed another woman. I never personally met Karla Faye Tucker, but I included her in this chapter because her place in history is secure in the annals of Texas prison lore.

KARLA FAYE "PICK AXE" TUCKER

On June 13, 1983, Daniel Ryan Garret and his wild-eyed, twenty-three-year-old prostitute lover, Karla Faye Tucker, went to the Northwest Houston apartment of Jerry Lynn Dean. This was just the next irrational step in Karla Faye's criminal career, which began when she started using marijuana at the age of eight. She went on to heroin at ten, was a groupie at thirteen, and married at seventeen; then she turned to prostitution to support her drug habit.

After a weekend orgy of heroin, Dilaudid, Valium, Placidyls, Somas, Percodan, Mandrax, marijuana, rum, and tequila, Karla Faye was running like an oil-burning racehorse. Jerry Lynn Dean had met his thirty-two-year-old companion, Deborah Thornton, earlier in the evening at a party. She had fought with her husband and stormed off, choosing to return to the apartment with Dean.

Karla was irritated with Dean, because on a prior occasion he had parked his leaking motorcycle in her living room; he had also destroyed her wedding pictures and the only pictures she had of herself with her mother. Neither Garret nor Karla Faye had ever met Deborah Thornton. In her drug-crazed brain, Karla Faye thought this seemed like a good time to settle the score. It was just Deborah Thornton's bad luck to get caught in the path of two drugged out psychopaths.

Dean and Thornton were lying in bed asleep when Garret and Karla Faye entered the room and attacked. Daniel Garret approached Jerry Dean and struck him several times in the head with a hammer. Karla Faye, watching, smiling maniacally, raised her three-foot pickax and swung her first blow at the semi-conscious Dean. Flesh was ripped; blood spewed and bones cracked as Karla Faye repeatedly sank the weapon into Dean. After several blows, she stopped and surveyed the damage. Dean's throat made a gurgling sound, and Karla Faye swung the pickax again and again, until her victim was quiet. While Dean was being assaulted, Deborah Thornton was lying, shaking under a bed sheet. Thornton was already covered in Dean's blood when Karla Faye finally turned the pickax on her. After hitting Thornton more than twenty times, Karla Faye left the pickax embedded in her chest. Karla Faye, a twenty-three-year-old divorcee, later bragged to her sister that she achieved sexual gratification each time the pickax sank into the victims.

This was no doubt one of the grisliest murders in Houston history; even veteran homicide detectives were stunned at the level of violence. Texas juries appropriately decided that both Garret and Karla Faye deserved the death penalty. Garret, thirty-seven, died of liver failure while awaiting retrial in connection with Dean's death. Karla Faye testified against Garret at trial, and after she did so, the Harris County District Attorney's Office dropped the second murder charge against her in connection with Thornton's murder. Although Karla Faye pleaded not guilty at trial, once she was convicted, she never again denied the murders. She said, "I was advised by my attorneys to plead not guilty and I was trusting their legal expertise. They knew I murdered Jerry and Deborah. I did not lie to them about it . . . I am, in fact, guilty. Very guilty."

Like many a convict before her, once in jail Karla Faye allegedly had what some have referred to as a call to Christ, or a religious conversion. Portrayed by some as the prodigal daughter who finally found peace and redemption in a Harris County jail cell, Tucker and her lawyers waged a massive legal and international public relations appeal for clemency.

All of a sudden, after Karla Faye had spent fourteen years on death row, an international debate erupted over whether Texas should execute its first woman since 1863. People argued that she was a born-again Christian and should not be put to death. They said that since she was a woman she should not have to die. Of course, the politically correct position is that men and women are equal in everything that bears on civil, or indeed military, life. What this appears to tell us is that no quarter or consideration of any kind should have been given to the fact that Karla Faye Tucker was a woman. To her everlasting credit, Karla Faye said, "Gender is not the issue . . . if you believe in the death penalty for one, you believe in it for all." As for the religion question, true separation of church and state means that no governor should be inclined toward clemency for anyone merely because that person has embraced religion. Amen.

Most Texans who listened to Karla Faye's pleas for mercy, based mainly on her newfound status as a rehabilitated, born-again Christian, had a hard time buying into it. After all, a jury of her taxpaying Texas peers had listened to the evidence, found her guilty, and sentenced her to death. When, as in Karla Faye's case, the public has to listen to an orchestrated outpouring of sympathy from a bunch of out-of-town celebrities, religious icons, and publicity-seeking politicians, all on behalf of a coldblooded killer, it seems, at best, insincere. After all, in 1983, when the two pickax murders occurred, the news media barely noticed Karla Faye—there were 556 homicides in Houston that year. When Texans think of all the innocent people who suffer extreme pain and die every day at the hands of these predators, pleas for mercy, even from a woman, ring a little hollow.

In a serious capital punishment state like Texas, the death-penalty opponents have to pick their fights carefully. Karla Faye, an attractive, youngish woman and an alleged born-again Christian who professed regret for her crime, became their ideal "poster child." There was, however, one important obstacle to mercy in the mind of the public—the overwhelming horror of her crime. There was no getting around the fact that this angelic-looking female hacked two people to death with a pickax. No one on the death-penalty opposition's side of the issue could figure out how to remove that pickax from the poster-child image.

On the day of execution, there was a surreal atmosphere outside the Walls Unit in Huntsville. Some prayed, some cried, and some jeered as the moment of execution came closer. Some of the signs reflected the college students in attendance: "Hi Mom! Send Money!" "Don't Use a Needle—Use a Pickax!" and "Bye Bye, Karla Faye."

News helicopters buzzed overhead. All the TV stations were represented—CNN, ABC, NBC, CBS, even KTMD and KXLN Channel 45, two Spanish-language stations, had crews there. The print media were there from all over the world. Religious representatives from several faith groups were in attendance. Appeals for her life came from conservative Christian Pat Robertson and Pope John Paul II, the National Council of Churches, and numerous other religious groups.

It was like most high-profile death penalty cases—the closer to execution you get the less voice the victims have. In some morbid way, by the time of execution, all of the attention had turned Karla Faye Tucker from killer to victim. Justice For All, a victims' rights group, collected donations to finance Deborah Thornton's family's trip to Huntsville; otherwise they could not have afforded to attend. Richard Thornton, Deborah's surviving husband, had some pretty strong opinions, "I came to see Karla Faye Tucker die . . . As soon as she was apprehended, the cross popped out on her chest. If her religious conversion has any basis, then I'm very happy for her. She's going to need it when she meets her maker." His words were a solemn reminder that somewhere in all the media hype surrounding the efforts to save Tucker's life, two other voices went unheard. They spoke only silently from their graves, for justice.

Inside the Walls, Karla Faye had requested a last meal of banana and a peach with a tossed salad and ranch dressing, but had only eaten some crackers and a soft drink since arriving at the Walls on Monday. "She said she was starting to feel a little weak," TDCJ spokesman David Nunnelee said. "But she's been calm and quiet." She visited with her husband, father, and sister.

When she entered the death chamber, she was very cooperative, and as she lay on the table, she said she was sorry and apologized to the families of Jerry Lynn Dean and Deborah Thornton. She said goodbye to her family, Warden Baggett, and the TDCJ employees in the room. Her last remarks were, "I'm going to be face to face with Jesus now. I will see you all when you get there. I will wait for you." She then closed her eyes, licked her lips, and appeared to say a silent prayer. She coughed twice, groaned softly, and went silent as the drugs took effect. Some of those in attendance said it looked too peaceful. There was no blood and no pickax now, just a quiet, harmless killer who can never hurt anyone again.

A mere six days after Karla Faye was told to stop sniveling and take it like a woman, and while the death penalty apologists were still debating whether she was a victim, vixen, or cold-blooded killer, TDCJ executed its next condemned man. After the spectacle of the Tucker execution, forty-year-old Steven Renfro's death was an uneventful affair. There had been well over 1,200 spectators and at least 200 news media personnel in attendance for Karla Faye's execution. Only about 20 lonely death-penalty protesters, who came as a group and arrived at the last minute outside the Walls, were present when Steven Renfro was executed. The irony was, Renfro's crime was not all that different from Karla Faye's. He had gone on a killing spree, fueled by drugs and alcohol. Wearing camouflage clothing and dark shoe polish on his face, he armed himself with an AR-15 semiautomatic rifle, .45- and .50-caliber handgun and 500 rounds of ammo. He shot his girlfriend, Rena Fuller, and his aunt, Rose Rutledge. Then he went to the nearby trailer home of an acquaintance, forty-year-old George Counts, against whom he had a grudge. Renfro fatally shot Counts by standing outside his trailer and firing more than 150 rounds through the mobile home. When police arrived, Renfro opened fire on them, wounding Officer Dominic Pondant. Despite his wound, Pondant was able to shoot Renfro during the ensuing gun battle. As the officers approached the wounded Renfro lying on the ground, he said, "I killed them all."

Renfro, like Karla Faye, professed to be a born-again Christian, but on execution day there were no news media, no evangelists, no celebrities, and no worldwide condemnation of his impending death. In sharp contrast to Karla Faye's execution, when Renfro went to his uneventful demise, the appearance—and perhaps even the reality—was that nobody really cared.

In looking back on the whole bizarre chain of events, there was one aspect of the Karla Faye Tucker hoopla that I still don't understand. During the demonstrations at her execution, I looked for feminists in the crowd, but didn't see any. I thought they would surely be out in force. Now that Karla Faye had broken the glass ceiling, the path was cleared for all women to finally take their rightful place alongside men and be treated like responsible adults, whether they wanted to be or not. As I look back on it, this was, or could have been, a truly momentous occasion for the women's-rights movement in Texas. This was a Texas woman who had clearly paid her dues, stood on her own two feet, and accepted responsibility for her actions. I still believe the National Organization for Women missed a great opportunity to demonstrate and perhaps strike a blow for true equality. Well, no matter, there are currently seven more women on death row. Perhaps they will get another chance.

TEXAS OWES NO APLOLGY FOR DEATH PENALTY

The real base of support for capital punishment is granted by society, in which murder is rampant. Texas polls have consistently demonstrated overwhelming public support for the death penalty, in some surveys as high as 82 percent. When surveyed, even a majority of the convicts in TDCJ support the death penalty, although they would add "baby rape" to the list of crimes eligible for execution. Actually, I agree with the convicts on that point, and I would like to see the Legislature vote to change the law. I suspect there is considerable support among their constituencies.

As a prison administrator and a lifelong supporter of capital punishment, I've often found myself defending my position against those who say that executing criminals is a violation of human rights. These are the arguments most often used by critics:

1. They say capital punishment does not deter crime.
2. They say innocent people could be executed.
3. They say that the state does not have the moral right to kill.

General Deterrence: This is the idea that when the state executes a convicted murderer, it sends a message to others thinking about murder and discourages them from killing. There is no empirical evidence suggesting that mass numbers of the criminal population are deterred from committing future capital crimes because an execution occurs on death row. A major problem with the "general deterrence" argument is that violent criminals do not engage in cost-benefit analysis. Crackheads don't think about the potential consequences of their actions as they are robbing and killing someone to get drugs. Deadly robberies still occur every day although Texas leads the nation in the number of executions.

There is, however, a segment of the population that common sense will tell you *is* deterred by the execution of capital offenders. They are the taxpaying, law-abiding citizens of our state who go about their daily lives while obeying the rest of our laws. The death penalty is a clear deterrent to those citizens who might otherwise seek vengeance on their own when a friend or family member is brutalized. The liberal elitists should be careful. It is a dangerous thing to deny people justice. Historically, vigilantism has always been the result of a failure of the state to perform one of its most basic functions: providing justice. People can endure poverty, hardship, and grief, but injustice burns at the soul like a red-hot branding iron. Injustice has fathered more violence and revolutions than anything else, with the possible exception of religion.

The death penalty gives victims hope for a just, although lengthy, resolution to a potentially catastrophic situation. This is no small matter to the citizens of Texas. Without a penalty sufficient to fit the brutality of a crime, citizens may well succumb to the urge to take the law into their own hands. Rather than engage in vigilantism, as was common in Texas before competent law enforcement became widespread, today's citizens, for the most part, rely on the law. There are significantly more law-abiding citizens in our state than there are capital criminals. Just as the sight of a police vehicle encourages our citizens to refrain from speeding, so does the death penalty encourage law-abiding citizens to not take the law into their own hands. I submit that the death penalty serves as a clear deterrent in preventing some of our otherwise law-respecting citizens from breaking the law and becoming vigilantes.

Specific Deterrence: This is the idea that executions do send a message to a particular murderer, i.e., the one that is executed. That murderer, at least, will never kill again. No one has ever successfully argued with the compelling statistical evidence that is provided by the specific-deterrence rationale. It is true, as a factual matter, that 100 percent of executed murderers never murder again.

When faced with the successful argument of specific deterrence, well-read opponents of the death penalty will almost immediately say, "What about a life sentence without parole?" Never mind that Texas does not now, nor has it ever had, life without parole. State law specifically prohibits Texas juries from considering parole laws during sentencing deliberations. A good realistic test for anyone who truly believes in the idea of life without parole is for him or her to put on a correctional-officer's uniform, go into a close-custody prison unit, and work for a while around some convicts who truly have nothing to lose.

Law-enforcement professionals, district attorneys, and prison officials are all opposed to life without parole. Wayne Scott, executive director of the Texas Department of Criminal Justice, said on the subject, "From our standpoint, we are very concerned about the management of long-term offenders who have no hope of getting out of prison." He has good reason to be concerned. Life without parole takes away all incentive an inmate has for appropriate behavior, because they have no hope of ever being released. Scott added, "We have seen an upswing in management problems with those long-term inmates, ever since lawmakers started enacting longer minimum sentences for violent offenders."

Allan Polunsky, chairman of the Texas Board of Criminal Justice, was even more outspoken. He said, "There are certain crimes committed that are so brutal and heinous that the death penalty is the only appropriate punishment that should be handed out."

Harris County District Attorney Johnny Holmes, whose prosecutors have sent more people to death row than almost all other Texas counties combined, said, "As a practical matter, it would be real, real, hard to get twelve people to say, 'This person should die,' when as an alternative you could lock them up forever. That's going to be a cold jury." Holmes continued, "Personally, I think there are some cases that, even if we had that rule, that we ought not support these slugs for the rest of their lives at $25,000 a year. Is that cold? That's realistic."

My own personal experience from working around convicts for thirty years tells me that life without parole is simply a bad idea. The concept is shortsighted, does not qualify as sound management or correctional practice, and will be a long-term economic disaster if enacted. Some of the questions I have not found satisfactory answers for are:

1. Who is going to work around these convicts?
2. What is the public willing to pay TDCJ employees to risk their lives every day by working around convicts who have absolutely nothing to lose? It seems to me that the salary would have to be significant to justify the risk.
3. If a convict serving a life sentence without parole kills an officer or another convict, what additional penalty could a jury give him? Is another sentence of life without parole meaningful? How many people does a convict have to kill before the death sentence is considered?
4. What mitigating circumstances would allow life without parole for one defendant and a death sentence for another?
5. Do we as taxpayers really want to pay $25,000 (minimum) per year, per convict for fifty, sixty, seventy, or eighty years while we wait for him/her to die of natural causes? Note that the $25,000-per-year figure does not include medical expenses incurred by the state of Texas for the convict's long-term care.

The 1991 homicide of a Tyler, Texas, youth, Chad Choice, illustrates some of the potential problems associated with life without parole. One Patrick Horn, twenty-five, was already serving a life sentence in federal prison without parole when he was implicated in the death of eight-year-old Chad Choice. Horn, a convicted bank robber and carjacker, was a high-school senior when he kidnapped his best friend's younger brother, shot him, and buried him in the backyard of his home. He killed the boy because the victim's uncle had outstanding drug debts. After killing the boy, Horn terrorized the victim's family with ransom notes for four years, finally ordering his younger brother to dig up the boy's skull and place it on the family's front porch. The jury in this case took four hours to decide to give Horn the death sentence. Thankfully, the jury did not have life without parole as an option. If such an option had been available, the taxpayers of Texas could well have been forced to support this child killer for the rest of his life.

The issue regarding the fear of executing innocent people: There have been several high-profile cases of death-row inmates being released due to the presentation of new evidence, trial errors, successful appeals, and the presentation of DNA evidence. The fact that some death-row inmates are released is a clear demonstration that although the system's review process is exorbitantly lengthy, it is meticulous and it works. That is not to imply that all those released from death row are innocent. In most cases, inmates are released because of technical trial errors, lost, forgotten, or destroyed evidence, the death of witnesses, or the absence of resources and budgetary constraints of district attorneys to retry expensive murder cases. These cases are scrutinized and re-scrutinized. How many trials are enough? It is not unusual for a death-row case to be reviewed by ten or twelve separate trial judges before going to the Supreme Court. The system is mired in frivolous appeals, most often funded at taxpayer expense.

Death-row convicts and their attorneys covet delay. Our criminal-justice system is no doubt imperfect, but one must realize that even the constitution of the United States doesn't promise perfection. It does promise a hearing by a jury of our peers. The killers get their day in court—actually, several courts. They get almost endless appeals that can easily drag the process out for twenty years or more. The entire appeals process is designed to protect the rights of a convicted killer. Now if we could only find a way to extend those same rights to the deceased, voiceless victims, then the process would truly be fair.

Contrary to popular belief, there is no direct evidence that any Texas inmate has ever been wrongfully executed, with the possible exception of Josefa "Chipita" Rodriguez in 1863. Death-penalty opponents have attempted to retry this case, but alas, the deathbed confession of the alleged killer cannot be verified, none of the evidence from the trial survived, and there is no DNA to match nor a video-enhanced crime scene to inspect. In all likelihood, history will continue to record that whether guilty or not, Chipita had an extraordinary run of bad luck.

The final argument: Is capital punishment immoral? Does the State have a right to kill? The ability to make moral decisions is a characteristic that distinguishes human beings from animals. An animal does not consciously choose evil over good. An animal that kills is not "bad" in the sense that a human who chooses to kill is "bad." If we treat a murderer as though he is not responsible for his/her act, then aren't we treating him like an irresponsible animal?

We impose the death penalty because criminals can and should be held responsible for their actions. To fail to hold people responsible for their choices would be to treat them inhumanely. Indeed, failing to impose capital punishment on convicted murderers could be considered a human-rights violation, particularly if we take into account the human rights that murderers violate when they are left alive to kill again (i.e. Kenneth Allen McDuff).

Just as an individual may legally kill in order to protect himself or his family under the self-defense statute, so does society have the right, indeed the duty, to kill in order to protect its most vulnerable citizens from vicious predators. Society has every right to set the standard of answering the most heinous of crimes with the most serious punishment.

THE RECKONING

There is at least one other reason to require the predators in our society to pay with the ultimate price, and I personally find it to be the most compelling. Almost every day now, we are barraged with the latest smiling death-row killer who has achieved celebrity status.

Liberal death-penalty apologists hope that the criminal-justice system is not only blind, but deaf and star-struck, as well. They think that bringing in a few out-of-town celebrities will sway those involved in the process into forgetting that the victim was murdered in cold blood. It is painfully easy to see that their detached philosophical views and skillful verbiage are on an abstract plane, not at all connected to the victims, who due to their deceased status are not able to express their views. The weak-minded apologists have not been in the shoes of the police officer who has to look into the eyes of a victim's family while delivering death-message news and see firsthand the void that will be permanently filled with sorrow.

The death penalty doesn't need defending; it is legal, Texans are not ashamed of it, and we don't need Amnesty International or anybody else giving us any lectures on human rights. After hearing all the gory details from crimes committed by killers Ronald Clark O'Bryan, Kenneth Allen McDuff, and Karla Faye Tucker, most Texans have heard enough. Thankfully, true justice did prevail in these infamous cases and those killers forfeited the right to breathe the same air as law-abiding Texans.

It has always been a constant source of amazement to me that these dangerous desperadoes can talk the talk, but when it comes down to it, they don't want to walk the walk. Very few ever take responsibility for their actions. They try to hide behind their lawyers or their psychiatrists, they become choirboys and choirgirls, and they blame their families for giving them deprived childhoods.

In the final analysis, it's not about feeling hate, anger, or outrage over these events, although the victims' families and friends are certainly entitled to those emotions. What is even more important is "The Reckoning," the knowledge that at some point, however delayed, the simple execution of justice will prevail. Supreme Court Justice Anthony M. Kennedy said it best: "Perpetual disrespect for the finality of convictions disparages the entire criminal justice system." The final reality of our resolve is the execution of sentence. Understanding the importance of finality is easier to comprehend if one can imagine being in that place.

In the late afternoon hours in a cell on death row in Huntsville, Texas, you eat your last meal, take your last shower, change clothes, and see the priest. Just before 6:00, you're shackled and escorted down the hallway to the death chamber. You're strapped down onto the gurney. They stick a needle in each arm and start the IV drip. You mumble some meaningless last words and then you see the deadly fluid start to flow down the tube. Panic sets in, and you know you're going to die. At that moment your mind is racing with a thousand thoughts as suddenly a blinding flash of reality overtakes you, a moment of clarity, if you will. In that brief moment, you realize that in a civilized society there are real consequences to pay for animalistic behavior. Deep down in your soul, you know that you will never again kill anyone . . .

And if that's not justice, my friends, it will have to do.

CHAPTER TWELVE

THE WAR ON DRUGS

"Given the invincible ignorance on the part of the public and most legislators in criminal justice matters, we will continue to incarcerate the poor, the stupid and the inept in our penal institutions."

—DR. GEORGE BETO, 1989

The first time I can remember hearing the term "war on drugs" was in 1971—like most other things in a state bureaucracy, it took a few years for the idea to trickle down. If there was a war on drugs going on in the free world, TDCJ was only receiving the casualties. TDCJ had always maintained a zero-tolerance policy on any illegal substance, so the newly declared war did not change the way in which prison units conducted business, at least not right away. The general attitude among my peers was, if more dope fiends are going to be locked up for longer periods of time, that is a good thing, because it translates into more job security for TDCJ employees. The humanist will say that outlook doesn't reflect a caring attitude toward our fellow members of mankind, but it was, nevertheless, accurate.

In an uncharacteristic public statement in 1978, President Jimmy Carter said, "Penalties against possession of a drug should not be more damaging to the individual than the use of the drug itself."

The number of Americans who tried illegal drugs during the mid-1960s was estimated at around 4 million. By 1985 that number had risen to 23.3 million and a person of no less stature than the president of the United States had firmly committed the country to a "War on Drugs."

By virtue of having a longer stretch of international border with Mexico than any other state, Texas was thrust onto the front line of this war. Our governors and other politicians were now routinely using the "war on drugs" phrase to sound like they were tough on crime. It was easy to get caught up in the righteous hoopla of the moment, and besides, it seemed like a noble cause, so we in law enforcement all joined up.

Like the fellow said after jumping into a bed of cactus, it seemed like the right (read politically correct) thing to do at the time. We succeeded in obtaining massive arrests, convictions, and incarcerations. We may not have won any decisive victories, but we sure took our fair share of prisoners of war. In Texas, the prison population grew from 14,000 to 35,000 in less than ten years. By 1988 James "Andy" Collins, who was the latest up-and-coming deputy director of TDCJ, said, referring to the convicts in TDCJ, "I've never met anybody down here that wasn't a drinker or wasn't a drug user. About 80 percent of them admit it; the other 20 percent are lying."

In 1980 President Ronald Reagan said, "Government exists to protect us from each other. Where government has gone beyond its limits is in deciding to protect us from ourselves." First Lady Nancy Reagan made her own pronouncement as to what one should do about drugs. She said to "Just say no." But by the mid-1980s, there were clearly a lot of people who were not just saying no.

In 1981, when Judge Justice forced TDC to finally get rid of the building tenders, we lost the ability to control the flow of narcotics into the institutions. The informational links to the inmate population that the wardens had always relied on were broken. The power base within the inmate population shifted from the staff-controlled building tenders to the organized convict cliques. The gang leaders realized that whoever controlled the drug trade also controlled the other convict rackets. Inmate gangs took over the institutional drug trade from the few independent dealers who had previously only operated on a small scale under the watchful eyes of the building tenders.

In the power vacuum left when the courts dismantled the building-tender system, the gangs flourished. The gang wars began, and for the next three years convicts were beaten, stabbed, and killed by their fellow inmates on almost a daily basis. Finally, TDC built enough cells and hired enough staff to effectively lock up the known gang members in administrative segregation. This action by TDCJ did eventually stop the gang killing, but the influx of narcotics into the units was here to stay.

DIRTY EMPLOYEES

Are correctional officers corrupted by the war on drugs? Well, is a snake's belly close to the ground? The corruption of correctional staff and law enforcement in general is a byproduct of the war on drugs. Nationally, according to the General Accounting Office, half of the police officers convicted as a result of FBI-led corruption investigations between 1993 and 1997 were found guilty of drug-related offenses. Prohibition had a similar effect in the late 1920s. By 1929, 25 percent of all federal agents had been fired for charges ranging from bribery to extortion, conspiracy, embezzlement, and the submission of false reports.

TDCJ doesn't release statistics on the number of employees who are allowed to resign or are terminated, arrested, or prosecuted for smuggling money or narcotics to convicts, but if I had a dime for every one I saw during my career, I could have retired five years earlier.

It doesn't take long for weak, criminally minded employees to figure out that they can make more money smuggling drugs to convicts than by being loyal, by-the-book correctional officers who serve the taxpayers of Texas. These crooked officers soon find out that as long as you don't mind being a criminal, there is not much of a downside, at least in terms of formal legal consequences. Even on those few occasions when a smuggler is caught, they are rarely prosecuted. As much as a unit warden may want to prosecute crooked employees, TDCJ is so fearful of retaliatory lawsuits that the powers that be are usually more than satisfied to simply get rid of them.

By 1983 the level of corruption within Texas prisons was pervasive enough that an inmate with resources could obtain almost any item. For $3.00 or $4.00 you could buy a toothpick-sized marijuana cigarette, or a half-ounce of marijuana, a three-finger bag, for $75.00. A used syringe sold for $5.00, unused $10.00. You could pay $75.00 for half a gram of heroin or cocaine, and a pint of cheap liquor went for $10.00. The cost of a crude homemade prison shank would start at $5.00 or more; a real, free-world knife might cost as much as $25.00. The prices of amphetamines, barbiturates, street-processed speed, and crank were negotiable.

Occasionally, a visitor made a drug drop and then eventually it was smuggled into the unit by convicts, but most contraband, especially narcotics, were and still are smuggled in by employees. I don't mean to imply that all or even most TDCJ employees are involved in smuggling. My experience tells me that only a very small percentage, perhaps 5 to 10 percent, of a unit's total staff engage in it, but that is enough to undermine the security and safety of all employees and inmates.

I have spent many a dark, mosquito-ridden night on stake-out, up in some tree or lying in the grass with binoculars, trying to catch drug smugglers dropping off drugs around my unit. On rare occasions we even caught a few of them, but most of the drugs are hand carried into the units by employees. From the smuggler's standpoint, drugs are too valuable to leave on the side of the road or buried somewhere. Smugglers want guaranteed hand delivery done in a timely manner. They also know we can't search every employee every time they enter the unit.

MEN AND WOMEN OF LOW MORAL FIBER

These self-important, interpersonally exploitative smugglers have no regard for the safety of officers or inmates. It is deplorable enough when a man decides to make his living by standing on a street corner in Houston, Texas, selling drugs. It is beyond all arrogance for a man (or woman) to put on the uniform of a Texas Department of Criminal Justice correctional officer, walk into a state prison, and while pretending to be a representative of law enforcement, proceed to sell smuggled drugs to convicts. In some cases they don't sell the drugs, they give them to the convicts in exchange for participation in sexual activity.

Unfortunately, sexual affairs between staff and convicts are all too common, both homosexual and heterosexual. On more occasions than I care to count, male employees have been caught giving oral sex to convicts, sometimes several convicts. On one occasion, two homosexual employees got into a jealousy-inspired physical altercation over a convict "punk" who was "playing" both of them. Another officer, who was caught giving oral sex to an inmate, had only been on the job for six days. During questioning, he admitted to having initiated sexual relations with five other inmates, two of whom were HIV positive. He said he "just couldn't help himself." Although TDCJ quickly terminated these officers from employment, none of them were ever charged with a crime.

These inmate-employee relationships are extremely dangerous and undermine the safety of all those who enter the units. These incidents are a constant embarrassment to the agency and the many fine officers who have worked hard to instill a high level of personal pride in the wearing of the uniform.

In some cases, services are more valuable than cash or drugs. This is especially true at the women's units, where the inmates use sex, or the promise of sex, to obtain money, favors, drugs, or whatever from staff, other inmates, or their pen pal sweethearts. Unfortunately, since women began working contact positions in male institutions in 1984, this has also become a major problem on all of the male units.

THE TRAP

In contrast to the sex-based, service-oriented corruption methods utilized by female inmates, the male inmates are more likely to use a direct offer of cash or drugs in their initial attempts to corrupt staff. However, if the cash is not readily accepted, the next step is often a threat of physical violence directed either at the staff member or his/her family. The latter method is often very effective when used on young, naive, and idealistic new employees. On the male units, there is even an acceptable price for which some female employees will stand and pose for a convict. Unfortunately, this has become an all-too-common practice. Once a price is agreed upon, she will voluntarily place herself in a strategic position in full view of the front of a convict's cell or dormitory cubicle and allow the inmate to masturbate while using use her for inspiration. As strange as it may seem, some female employees will allow this activity to occur for no fee at all. I used to try and figure out why any woman would volunteer to do this, but I've never gotten a straight answer on the subject from any of these delicate flowers. They usually feign embarrassment and decline to discuss the sordid details of their involvement, preferring instead to discreetly resign employment. I've concluded that it has something to do with the perception of power and who controls it.

If a convict desires, and can actually afford, a contact relationship with one of the female employees, he must carefully choose a potentially willing target. There are two common, basic avenues toward achieving success. The first is blackmail, which can involve months of daily conversations, setup preparation, and negotiation with the intended target; the second is strictly a direct offer of something of value—cash, jewelry, craft items, bodyguard or protection services, drugs or drug connections, or any other item. Most often it is money and is a direct services-for-cash transaction. These liaisons require planning and can cost between $200.00 and $400.00 depending on the woman in question and the perceived value of her virtue.

Lest one think that the uniformed female correctional officers are the only ones who participate in such activities, nothing could be further from the truth. Numerous other female employees, and a few homosexual males, of all manner of job description have been caught in the act in various locations around the unit, some on videotape. Why would one need to videotape? Because if you don't have actual physical, iron-clad evidence of voluntary sexual activity, the employee in question is going to accuse the administration and particularly her staff accusers of entrapment, sexual harassment, unfair treatment, discrimination, being singled out, and various other civil-rights violations.

In addition to the numerous female correctional officers verified to be sexually active with inmates, successful investigations have conclusively implicated nurses, both RNs and LVNs; school-teachers, both academic and vocational; religious volunteers; sociologists; secretarial clerks; food-service staff; and substance-abuse counselors. Although employee involvement in these sexual escapades may represent only a small percentage of a unit's total employee staff, in my opinion, these relationships represent the single greatest threat to the security of any prison.

So what is the big deal if an employee chooses to get up close and personal with a convict? Aside from the obvious absence of professionalism and dishonor brought into the workplace, these relationships create a very real physical danger to both employees and inmates. Every warden knows he has mules working inside the unit, and thinking about the potential catastrophes that can arise from their actions scares unit administrators to death. The threat lies in the fact that once an employee is sexually involved with an inmate, the inmate owns that employee, who is now too compromised to do his or her job.

Employees involved with an inmate no longer work for TDCJ; they work for a convict. The convict has a hammer to hold over the employee's head. The inmate can always threaten to end the employee's career by going to the warden or internal affairs if he or she attempts to refuse any of the inmate's requests. Since it is a felony criminal offense to have even consensual sex with a convict, TDCJ workers could not only lose their jobs; they could conceivably go to jail. The only way to avoid this, apart from resigning, is to become the convict's "mule" and do whatever they want. Thus, employees will find themselves smuggling drugs, money, liquor, weapons, or anything else the convict and his friends may want.

These sexual relationships compromise employees completely; once involved, the employee is at the convict's mercy. If a female employee doesn't volunteer them, she will be required to give the convict graphically depicted nude photographs of herself. Since there are no secrets among convicts, she will at some point be pressured into having sex with some of her new lover's friends, in order to ensure their silence. There is nothing more jealous than a convict who suspects a female employee is sharing intimate stolen moments with one of his peers. If the jealousy is not quickly resolved through sex, drugs, or other methods of payoff, the left-out convict will of course have to snitch to the administration.

All information in a prison has value, particularly that which relates to employees. Once an employee-inmate relationship becomes common knowledge in the inmate population, all those who know about it will certainly try to obtain payment in exchange for their silence. If the lovers don't want to cooperate, the snitch can usually figure out a way to profit from the situation by trading or selling what he knows to other convicts. The snitch also has the option of trading his information to the administration in exchange for a favorable job assignment, new housing assignment, or possibly even a transfer to another unit.

Far too many of these female employees are young, modestly educated, single, and new to the workforce. TDCJ pays them a salary that they cannot easily replace in the free-world marketplace. I have seen several instances during my career where a female employee, after getting caught up in some convict blackmail scheme and fearing the loss of her job, was passed around from inmate to inmate.

FEDS GET TOUGH

In 1988 the federal government passed the "drug-kingpin law," allowing the imposition of the death penalty for murder resulting from large-scale illegal drug dealing. Shortly after the law was passed, Juan Raul Garza, a Brownsville, Texas, man, was convicted in a U.S. Federal District Court for the murders of four men in Mexico. In an effort to demonstrate to the public that the U.S. was going to get tough on drug dealers, Garza was given a federal death sentence.

Garza has been on federal death row for eleven years, and if he is executed, will be the first federal inmate to be put to death in thirty-six years. (The last federal inmate to actually be executed was Victor Feguer, who was hanged in 1963 for the kidnapping and murder of an Iowa physician.) Garza will also be the first federal inmate to die by lethal injection. The status of his execution probably depends more on whether we have a Republican or Democrat in the White House when his appeals finally run out. A Democrat will be hard-pressed by his constituents to commute Garza's sentence to life without parole.

At his trial, federal prosecutors portrayed Garza as a vicious drug boss who controlled underlings by killing those—even a son-in-law—who got out of line. The case caused a sensation in the Texas border town of Brownsville, a city so popular with smugglers that it's called "Marijuana Boulevard." The prosecution produced sixty-six witnesses to testify against Garza, including one of his own nephews. U.S. Attorney Jose Moreno called Garza a drug-lord who "thought he was so far above the law that killing was just a matter of business."

Garza said he was no "drug baron." He lived in a mobile home on two acres of land, which the government dug up with backhoes looking for buried money. "They were under the impression I had money, but they never found a red cent," Garza said. It remains to be seen whether Garza will be executed, but when one looks at the numerous drug cartels that continue to operate with impunity on both sides of our borders, his conviction does not stand out as a defining moment of success.

ARE WE WINNING THE WAR ON DRUGS?

In 1987 the federal government spent $4.7 billion on the war on drugs. By 1998, the same war cost $16 billion. More than 50 percent of the convicts confined in federal prisons in 1999 were first-time, non-violent drug offenders. The total number of Americans arrested for all drug offenses in 1997: 1.5 million. Of this number, 79 percent were arrested for simple possession. The number of Americans arrested for all marijuana offenses in 1997: 695,200. Of this number, 87 percent were arrested for possession.

Are we winning the war on drugs? The number of people in federal and state prisons in 1980 for violating drug laws: 23,900. The number of people in federal and state prisons in 1996 for violating drug laws: 292,794. That represents an increase of 268,894 drug prisoners within a sixteen-year period, or a 340-percent rise in the rate of incarceration. Based on the constantly increasing number of drug war casualties in state and federal prisons, one might think that the war is being won, but other questions must be asked.

Is the number of users decreasing? There were roughly 4 million drug users in 1962, as opposed to 23.3 million in 1985. The minimum number of adults estimated to be using drugs in 1997: 13.9 million. In 1999 Texas had the country's largest criminal-justice system, with 545,000 people in prison, in jail, or on probation or parole. Texas prisons hold 724 inmates for every

100,000 residents. This is a point of pride for many Texans, but a day is coming when that may no longer be the case. At the current rate of incarceration, no state or federal prison system will be able to afford to build cells fast enough to hold all the drug offenders.

Is the Drug War Racist?

Our most reliable estimates tell us that 80 percent of drug users are white, yet prisons are overflowing with black men and women convicted on drug charges. Blacks, on average, do almost 50 percent more time than do whites for drug offenses.

Where are the Winners in the War on Driugs?

Has the drug war become a growth industry? I think the federal government's own budget figures for the year 1998 go a long way toward answering that question:

$2.02 billion: Federal Bureau of Prisons
$1.33 billion: Substance Abuse and Mental Health Services Administration
$1.15 billion: Drug Enforcement Agency
$865 million: Federal Bureau of Investigation
$641 million: Customs Service
$621 million: Federal Judiciary
$549 million: National Institute on Drug Abuse
$389 million: U.S. Coast Guard
$361 million: Office of National Drug Control Policy
$295 million: Interagency Crime and Drug Enforcement
$281 million: Federal Prisoner Detention
$269 million: U.S. Attorneys
$ 61 million: Federal Law Enforcement Training Center
$ 28 million: Department of Justice Criminal Division
$ 13 million: Financial Crimes Enforcement Network

In Texas, taxpayers paid $4.6 billion for the TDCJ 1995–96 biennium budget. In 1999 TDCJ had four new units currently under construction. In addition to the 144,000 currently incarcerated inmates in the TDCJ, there are at present, thirty-seven private prison companies doing business in Texas. A one-day jury trial at the county level is estimated to cost a minimum of $10,000. As one looks for winners in the war on drugs, the obvious standout recipients in terms of monetary blessings are the criminal-justice infrastructure agencies. Also, there are two groups at the top of this taxpayer-supported food chain who are receiving a particularly lucrative windfall. They are the judges and court-appointed lawyers who, without the war on drugs, would otherwise have to work for a living, instead of spending their time negotiating plea bargains.

Are the state and federal courts effectively handling the ever-increasing number of drug cases being dumped on their doorstep? One result of the war on drugs has been to backlog federal courts to the point of gridlock. When asked to address the American Bar Association in 1992, Chief Justice William Rehnquist said that the war on drugs has "created havoc in the federal courts so acute that the explosive rise in federal drug prosecutions is making it next to impossible for many judges to give timely and adequate attention to their civil dockets."

Is the War on Drugs Lost?

In the summer of 1987, at the Retrieve Unit, we busted five male officers as a result of a long drug-smuggling investigation. These uniformed correctional officers had been bringing in drugs to several convicts over a period of months. In an effort to avoid detection or the chance of possibly being paid in marked money, they were receiving payment through American Express money orders.

The plan was simple: The convicts pooled their resources and had their relatives and friends send money to the wife or mother of one of the inmates. Without using prison-inspected correspondence, the free-world participants received their instructions from the convicts during contact visitation. In some cases, the free-world relative did not know that anything illegal was occurring. The convict would convince the naive visitor that he was in debt to an officer who had provided some favor or legal service for him. As payment for the officer's kindness and to ensure his or her continued favor, the inmate would instruct the visitor to send an

American Express money order in the officer's name to a specific address. The officer never had to disclose his or her identity to anyone, but the inmate, but he did have to sign the receipt at the American Express office when he picked up the money order.

As I sat in my office looking at the money-order receipts totaling several thousand dollars with the officers' signatures on them, I knew they were guilty. A convict's mother had saved some of the receipts, and she consented to forward them to me after her inmate son was caught with drugs. I had made a deal with the convict: "Give me the evidence on the officers and I will not prosecute you." My strategy or priority in these matters was always to catch the dirty officer, no matter how many convicts I had to deal with. My rationalization was that at least the convicts were already in prison and weren't pretending to be something they're not.

Convicts, by definition, are convicted felons. One should not be too surprised when it is discovered that a verified criminal has yet again broken the law; after all, breaking the law is his chosen profession, it's what he does. When convicts violate the law, it is a prison employee's job to try and catch them, just as it is the convicts' "job" to try and not get caught. Correctional employees, on the other hand, are supposed to be representatives of law enforcement. When they step across the line and voluntarily commit criminal acts that place their fellow officers in jeopardy, the punishment should be swift and severe.

As soon as I received those money-order receipts, I knew my case against the officers was complete. The next day, as the five officers came in to work, they were arrested and charged with accepting bribes from convicts.

As I watched those five officers being handcuffed, put in white convict clothing and escorted out to a waiting Brazoria County Sheriff's Department patrol car, a feeling of helplessness came over me. I should have been in a good mood after the successful conclusion of the lengthy drug investigation, but I wasn't.

If I had to trace my way back to a single moment in time when I realized that the war on drugs could not be won, it was then. It dawned on me that the war was over and we had lost. I had an overwhelming feeling that no matter how many resources were devoted to this "war," drugs would never be defeated. I was

never going to be able to keep drugs out of the prison unit. And if
I, as a prison warden, with hundreds of officers at my disposal and
double-chain-link fences topped with razor ribbon, couldn't keep
the drugs out, how could law-enforcement officers, school principals, or any small town in America be expected to keep them out?

Does the Nation Have the Will to Win a War on Drugs?

It would take a substantial shift in our priorities and our laws for
America to win a war on drugs. As a prison warden in the mid-
1990s, I couldn't even require a convict to submit to a drug screen
without first being able to demonstrate "probable cause." TDCJ,
with some justification, was afraid of a civil-rights lawsuit;
prison administrators were required to have "other substantial
evidence of drug use" prior to requesting the drug screening of
inmates or employees.

Beginning in 1999, TDCJ began drug-screening some
inmates as a result of federal mandate. The testing process is
largely ineffective and costs more than $400,000 per year. TDCJ
did not want to drug-screen convicts, because of the "prohibitive
cost," but agreed to do it when the government said they would
withdraw federal grant money if Texas didn't comply. The names
of those to be drug-screened are chosen in Austin by some
bureaucrat who doesn't know one inmate from another. The unit
wardens still have no input into the testing process. New TDCJ-
ID employees are drug-screened during their initial training, but
after arriving at a unit assignment, probable cause and regional-
director approval are required prior to "asking" employees to submit to a search and/or drug-screen. Even if prior approval is
granted, the employee has the right to refuse the search and
drug-screen. Cars and employee living areas on state property can
be searched, but this is rarely done because the unit administration always runs the risk of harassment lawsuits claiming violation of civil rights.

The hard truth is, this country doesn't have the will to fight
a drug war, much less win one. How much money is enough, and
to what extremes would the citizens of this country be willing to
go to win the war on drugs? It is a question every American will

have to answer in the not-too-distant future. The Drug Enforcement Agency has been trying for years and has spent billions upon billions of dollars, but is no closer to controlling or stopping drug traffic than when it began the effort. In order to actually win a war on drugs, this country would have to make some serious fundamental sacrifices that U.S. citizens are not going to be willing to make:

1. The Bill of Rights would have to be suspended.
2. All U.S. international borders would have to be closed and controlled by the military.
3. All employers, school principals, law enforcement, and prison administrators would have to have the right to require drug testing on demand.
4. The public would have to be willing to pay for the cost of tripling the size of the present criminal-justice infrastructure in order to handle the incoming drug-war casualties. In Texas, that would mean, at a minimum, tripling inmate cell-space capacity and incarcerating an additional 288,000 of its citizens.
5. The government would have to have the unrestricted right to monitor *all* communications and financial transactions.

I don't pretend to be a politician, but my gut and thirty years of experience in dealing with government bureaucracies tell me that the liberals, the ACLU, the American Bar Association, et cetera, would turn this country over to the dopers before any of those reforms were allowed to occur.

If, in fact, the above-described reforms would protect future generations of Americans from being exposed to the ravages of drug addiction, I, for one, could accept them. I am not trying to present pro-drugs arguments from the intellectual or moral high ground. The fundamental question is, or should be, how is America going to survive this real and most serious threat to our society? The United States of America simply cannot win the war on drugs. More importantly, if we continue on our present course to wage this war without taking note of the serious, irreversible harm being caused, it is going to destroy the very fabric of our nation.

Texas has a thousand miles of coastline and another thousand miles of international border with Mexico. There are several million illegal immigrants pouring into Texas every year with no end in sight. With all that in mind, what would make anyone think we could effectively keep illegal drugs out? Even with the astronomical numbers of people being sent to prison on drug charges today, the supply of forbidden drugs remains a reality of American life. There is a lesson to be learned here. We need to acknowledge what Americans came to understand about alcohol after fourteen years of that noble experiment called Prohibition. That is, drugs are here to stay, and we have no choice but to learn to live with them so that they cause the least amount of harm. It is time to end our second noble experiment.

NAME YOUR OWN POISON

Most proponents of harm reduction or "decriminalization" do not favor legalization of drugs, but they do recognize that prohibition has failed to curtail drug abuse that is responsible for much of the crime, corruption, disease, and death associated with drugs. Those against legalization must also understand that the cost associated with the present system of uncontrolled drug abuse will continue to rise every year for the foreseeable future.

Drugs are a bad choice for anyone to make—especially the young. They're a handicap, but our society should stop short of putting people in prison at taxpayer expense, sometimes for years, for using them. If the government controlled and regulated drugs, the price could be kept low enough that there would be no need for people to kill each other in order to obtain them. State and federal government could tax the drugs and control the point of sale through prescriptions or license, much like liquor and cigarettes are sold today. Each drug package sold could carry a message like this:

> "This product will kill you. Anyone who uses this product does so at his or her own risk. The American taxpayers cannot be held responsible for any medical costs incurred as a result of using this drug or in the event of the user's death."

While we would probably have to get used to seeing a few more drug-related deaths reported on the evening news, I suspect that would be a short-term phenomenon, limited to the initial break-in period. The end result of having access to cheap, high-potency drugs on a massive scale would no doubt send a lethal message to those fortunate survivors of the first wave of legalization that perhaps a little restraint is in order.

As the initial euphoria of legalization wore off, I suspect stark realities involving the consequences of drug use would soon settle into the national psyche, that it would become clear that drugs are a poor career choice. Just as alcoholics are not in fashion today, drug users would not be in fashion tomorrow. After all, when the risk and the glamour is removed from a drug, all that's left is the potential for harm.

I have come to believe that we are not giving the citizens of this nation enough credit for having the common sense to choose the correct path for themselves. It is only right that individual Americans over the age of twenty-one should have the right to harm themselves with whatever substance they choose to use. Some will no doubt choose the wrong path and in so doing provide a deadly object lesson that will serve as deterrent to current drug users and future generations of our youth.

The process of legalization would only add more governmental control to an obviously out-of-control situation. If the government required the licensing and control of all drug sales, while mandating that they be sold legally for no more than a 2-percent profit, plus cost and tax, it would put the drug cartels out of business overnight. If the criminal element can be removed from the equation and tax dollars generated from drug sales to accomplish worthwhile goals, then our society will be well-served. The bottom line is that with legalization we could restore sanity where there is none and work toward that kinder, gentler, safer society we all want.

I've never completely understood the rationale behind allowing a physician to prescribe Valium, Percodan, or Dilaudid, but not marijuana, cocaine, or heroin. In my mind, the only appreciable difference is the public perception that one drug is "legal" and the other is "illegal." It's not that there aren't plenty of substances around with which our citizens could choose to kill themselves, should they choose to do so. The problem in the minds of so many American drug users is the fact that they just don't like being told that this or that drug is "forbidden." In simpler terms, they just want the right to choose their own poison. As America is advertised as the freest country on earth, I don't have any qualms about giving them that right as long as it doesn't infringe on the rights of other Americans.

Our society could no doubt use the additional revenue gained from the tax and sale of government-controlled drugs. Perhaps we could feed the homeless, improve the availability of healthcare for all Americans, or even lower the federal income tax for non–drug users. Whatever we did with the money would be an improvement on the system in place today. The money saved in the cost of future incarcerations alone makes trying some form of drug legalization worthwhile. One additional plus to drug legalization is that there almost certainly wouldn't be a need for so many court-appointed attorneys. In my view, fewer attorneys equals less litigation, which is clearly a positive thing for all of us.

When Prohibition ended in 1933, did the United States suddenly go to Hell, with all its citizens becoming alcoholic? No. If we ended the war on drugs, legalized these drugs, and allowed people to buy them by prescription or from carefully licensed and regulated dealers, would the United States go to Hell and all its citizens become addicts? I don't think so. For evidence of that, we have pre–drug-ban history, during which life went on pretty much as normal. How, then, can we justify continuing this failed effort that has caused more damage to the Constitution than it has to the drug dealers—all of whom, of course, are replaceable? Personally, I don't think people should take drugs, not even most of the ones their doctors prescribe. I do, however, believe that in a free society, adults should be free to choose and free to suffer the consequences of their choices.

The drug war is a racket masquerading as prudent law-enforcement. Everybody except the taxpayer is making money on it, and, even after thirty-five years of concentrated eradication efforts, illicit drugs are flowing as freely as, or even more freely than, before. In the meantime, the government uses the drug war as an excuse to whittle away the traditional rights and liberties of every American citizen. A drug is just a drug. If people become addicted to them—and thousands of people become addicted to doctor-prescribed drugs already—then that is a health problem, not a law-enforcement problem. There is nothing inherently evil in morphine, heroin, marijuana or cocaine. They each produce certain effects, just as other drugs do, but those effects don't cause people to commit crimes. What does cause people to commit crime is drug prohibition. It limits supply to illegal dealers and therefore drives up prices. Addicts will sometimes resort to crime in order to obtain drugs to support their addiction or sell drugs to make money, but it is important to understand that those actions are motivated by the legality of drug prohibition, not the drug.

Prior to the war on drugs, criminal cases by and large were brought before grand juries on the basis of law-enforcement investigations supported by documented objective evidence, surveillance, observation, or forensic evidence. It was only in our zeal to make more and more criminal cases in the war on drugs that we began to cultivate informants. TDCJ breeds informants and has probably relied and used them more effectively than any other state, dating back to the philosophy behind the use of building tenders. Prosecutors will tell you that sometimes the use of an informant is the only way to obtain the information necessary to make a case, and they're right. There is no question that the use of informants is an effective device from a law-enforcement point of view. There is nothing illegal about it, but it is particularly worrisome in a drug case, because it just doesn't pass the smell test.

In most cases, the informant has engaged in criminal conduct him- or herself. How much validity can one reasonably give to the testimony of a criminal? Sending someone to prison for simple possession of a drug based on no more than the word of a convicted felon is troublesome. There is always an inherent risk of dishonesty on the part of the person who is plea-bargaining with information that is obtainable for a price. If it were a crime of violence, a terrorist threat, or a matter of national security, one might be justified in using an informant, but the mere possession of a drug just doesn't seem to rise to the required threat level. Juries have to make decisions on whom to believe every day. Logic tells us that since we have not discovered a foolproof way of getting inside the human mind, at least some of the time those juries are led astray.

After thirty years of observing the casualties of the war on drugs, I have come to believe that criminal penalties are not the way to deal with the drug problem. The whole concept behind the government-driven policy that supports the war on drugs is flawed. It does not work. Furthermore, I am satisfied that it will not work in the future. I have come to believe that drug use in a legal setting would cause no significant problems other than to the user, which is the case with alcohol consumption. We would still have laws against working in sensitive areas or operating a vehicle while under the influence of drugs, just as we do in the case of alcohol.

A good many Americans, including police chiefs, doctors, and prison wardens, believe that it's time for a change in our failed drug policy. It is our political leaders who are afraid to change. I wonder how much longer the American people are going to tolerate our politicians making fools out of us—because that is exactly what is happening. While these self-righteous politicians feed the public drug-war propaganda, they are, at the same time, extracting billions of dollars from the pockets of taxpayers only to waste it on chasing people who are simply supplying a product for which there is a demand.

Thanks to the media's insatiable appetite for reporting the seamy side of life and the supply of government-sponsored publicity surrounding drug seizures, arrests, and convictions, many Americans are of the opinion that these punitive measures are effective, which in fact, they are not. Sooner rather than later, every American will have to make a choice on this issue. One can only hope that sanity prevails, because otherwise we will have failed on a grand scale. It will take someone with courage and broad-based public support to stand up and admit that it is time to end our second costly, ineffective, well-fought, but hopelessly lost noble experiment.

In 1992 Bill Clinton said, "Insanity is doing the same old thing over and over again and expecting a different result." This may be the only issue on which I have ever agreed with Bill Clinton.

A short list of prominent Americans who have publicly advocated the decrimalization or outright legalization of drugs:

June Osborne—Physician Leadership on National Drug Policy

Gary Johnson—Governor of New Mexico (1999)
Kirt Schmoke—Mayor of Baltimore
Milton Friedman—Nobel Laureate economist
Robert Sweet—U.S. District Judge, former federal prosecutor
Joycelyn Elders—Surgeon General, U.S.A.
Scott Ehlers—Drug Policy Foundation
George P. Shultz—Former U.S. Secretary of State
Ann Landers—Syndicated columnist
Raul Craig Roberts—Washington, D.C., syndicated columnist
William F. Buckley Jr.—syndicated columnist

As of the publication of this book, voters in Alaska, Arizona, California, Nevada, Oregon, Maine, and Washington have approved measures in support of medical marijuana. However, marijuana remains banned in all states by federal law. The Institute of Medicine has said that because the chemicals in marijuana ease pain and reduce nausea and vomiting, they can be helpful for people undergoing chemotherapy and/or people with AIDS.

The U.S. Coast Guard recently stopped the Panamanian-flagged freighter *China Breeze*. After it was towed into the port of Galveston, four tons of cocaine was found inside some inoperable sewage tanks aboard the ship. The cocaine had an estimated street value of $347 million. It was the second large vessel to have been seized and taken to the port of Galveston that year. In January 1999, law-enforcement officials seized 9,500 pounds of cocaine from the Greek-owned *M/V Cannes*. The cocaine was found under 26 metric tons of iron ore.

Lieutenant J. G. Brian Hollis, a Coast Guard officer in Galveston, was interviewed regarding the drug seizure. He said, "Drug interdiction is a top priority for the Coast Guard. In an average day, the Coast Guard seizes 209 pounds of marijuana and 170 pounds of cocaine worth $9.2 million." The sad and utterly disheartening thing about Hollis' observation is that he still thinks he's winning the war on drugs.

WAR CLOUDS IN COLOMBIA

As the year 2000 approached, the debate in Washington was over whether we should give Colombia $1.7 billion in the latest round of the drug war. President Clinton's "Drug Czar," General Barry McCaffrey, also wants to send them thirty advanced Black-hawk helicopters at $13 million a copy, and other "counterinsurgency equipment as an emergency priority."

Coincidentally, Laurie Hiett, the wife of the former commander of the U.S. Army's anti-drug operation in Colombia, pled guilty in January 2000 to smuggling heroin into the United States while her husband was stationed at the U.S. Embassy in Bogotá. After months of stonewalling, Col. James C. Hiett dropped earlier denials and admitted storing in his apartment and embassy office safe as much as $45,000 given to him by his wife. At the time of his wife's smuggling, Hiett was in charge of 200 U.S. troops who were supposed to be training Colombian forces for counter–drug operations. What's wrong with this picture? Does anybody really think sinking $1.7 billion into this "war" is really going to change anything?

Underlying the U.S.-sponsored Colombian drug war is a real forty-year-old social struggle between Marxist guerrillas and right-wing vigilantes. The reality is, there were 32,000 "drug war"–related killings in Colombia in 1999 and more than 3,000 kidnappings. Does anybody remember how Vietnam started? I do, and the similarities are scary.

CHAPTER THIRTEEN

CONVICT PSYCHOLOGY 101

"A neurotic is someone who builds castles in the sky.
A psychotic is someone who lives in those castles.
A psychiatrist is one who collects the rent on the castles."
—UNKNOWN

Insanity is a legal concept—not a medical one. It refers to society's reluctance to punish a person, even if guilty of a crime, who did not know his conduct to be wrong. There is a difference between "incompetence" and "insanity," and neither is equivalent to "mental illness." Incompetence has to do with whether or not the party in question has the rational and factual knowledge of any proceedings against him and can reasonably assist his attorney in his own defense. Mental illness is a separate concept, medical rather than legal in nature, and mentally ill persons are most often found "competent" to stand trial.

In Texas, if a defendant were found to be "insane" at the time of offense and was determined not to have been aware that his conduct was wrong, he could be found not guilty by reason of insanity. If, however, the defendant is determined to have known that society would view his acts as wrongful, but still carefully planned and carried out an illegal act, then, despite behavior arising from bizarre or delusional beliefs, the defendant is considered legally sane.

A couple of decades ago, many states, including Texas, had laws that allowed people to commit mentally ill family members to institutions without their consent. A family could petition a judge; the person would be picked up, held in custody, and examined by two or more psychiatrists, who would then report to the judge. It was then up to the judge to weigh the needs of the patient against the safety of the community and determine whether or not inpatient facility care was appropriate. In some cases, the process was no doubt abused. The civil libertarians rallied successfully to dismantle most of those laws. They said it infringed on the rights of the mentally ill.

The result: It is very difficult for family, or anyone else, to have anyone involuntarily committed. In Texas, it is almost impossible unless the person "does something"—as in kills a police officer or molests a child. Too many district attorneys hide behind the cowardly statement, "Sorry, we can't really do anything until this person breaks the law." By then, of course, it is too late to avoid what could have been an avoidable tragedy. Civil-rights laws and entitlements have given individuals immunity from necessary care and confinement, thereby denying families, communities, and states the right to public protection from and responsibility for the severely mentally impaired.

The majority of people who need an ongoing regimen of anti-psychotic drugs are literally not available for those medications because they are not in a controlled, managed environment. One of the difficulties in the treatment of mental illness is that so often the person does not, of course, believe he is ill. The civil libertarians have pushed the concept of "freedom from coercion" so far that we now have a population of some 10 million severely mentally impaired individuals who desperately need someone to take control of their tragically out-of-control lives. Many of these individuals don't even accept the fact that their illness is out of control.

Finally, broken, desperate, and unable to function in "normal society," these sick individuals begin breaking the law. Once in the criminal-justice system, they are caught in a never-ending revolving door of various levels of incarceration. Through its numerous empowering civil-rights rulings, the federal courts have gradually mandated the growing jurisdiction of our criminal-justice system over the mental health of our citizens. We have returned to the medieval practice of imprisoning our crazy neighbors and "street people," who are too sick to respond to outpa-

tient clinics for medication or hold a steady job. The best estimates indicate that a full 40 percent of inmates in the United
States should be in mental institutions that were legislated away
long ago. A layman might logically ask, where is the sanity in
that?

MENTAL CASE

Over the past fifteen years, Texas has moved toward the concept
of "guilty but mentally ill," and where there are grounds to protect the public, the offender is incarcerated, even if he is mentally
ill and was at the time of the offense.

As a non-lawyer observer, it appears to me that the old legal
standard of the prudent and reasonable man has been lost. If I
had to put my finger on the exact moment in time when the prudent and reasonable man concept disappeared in Texas, it would
have been sometime during 1981, when Federal District Judge
William Wayne Justice dropped his hammer on the TDCJ. Judge
Justice mandated that the taxpayers of Texas begin hiring psychiatrists at a cost of $800 a day (in 1981 dollars) to ensure that all
TDCJ inmates with questionable command of their mental facul-
ties receive appropriate care.

As the news of this ruling swept through the prison system,
you could almost feel the convict IQ-level dropping. All of a sudden, convicts who had never before entertained the thought of seeing a psychiatrist developed self-diagnosed mental problems.
Convicts can always be counted on to take advantage of any perceived flaw in the system. If they can use a psychiatric appointment to obtain drugs, get a lay-in from work, or just to provide a
change in their routine, they will do so. Of course, every time one
of these convicts has an appointment it costs the taxpayers of
Texas $95.00 per hour.

Prior to this landmark stance by the old judge from Tyler,
TDCJ had pretty much relied on a few underpaid but highly motivated psychologists. The most commonly prescribed drug at the
time was Thorazine. It was common practice for a third of a
unit's inmate population to be walking around under the influence of Thorazine or some equally powerful psychotropic drug.
Although an inmate's medical record and his prescribed medica-

272 — The Largest Hotel Chain in Texas

tion is strictly a confidential matter, it was not too difficult to tell which inmates were on Thorazine. After taking the drug for a while, convicts tended to get a yellow, jaundiced look about them. The blank stare and the short, stuttering steps referred to as "the Thorazine shuffle," made them look like zombies as they slowly marched down the hallway. Their speech became slurred and their mental reactions slowed; a previously loud, disruptive convict would adopt a meek and mild manner. Later, other drugs were put into use that, although effective, did not create the easily identifiable symptoms of Thorazine.

A SERIOUS DILEMMA

In a perfect world, all inmates with mental impairments would be inpatients in facilities specifically designed to meet their needs. Prior to 1984, Texas prisons only had one small inpatient facility, located in Rusk, Texas. In the present system, there are a few units that were designed with the mentally impaired in mind. Unfortunately, these units are capable of holding only a fraction of the mentally impaired inmate population. Only the most acute-care cases are sent to the regional "treatment centers."

A mentally impaired convict presents a serious dilemma for unit correctional officers. Because the inmate's medical status is "private," a correctional officer is not going to know by sight which inmates are mentally impaired, on the psychiatric caseload, in counseling, or on psychotropic medication. Although most mentally impaired convicts are not particularly violent, the control and the monitored compliance of psychotropic medication are extremely important to the safety of both the convict and staff. A mentally impaired inmate is most dangerous when coming off of prescribed psychotropic drugs, and there is no way for a correctional officer to know when that is. Since by law the convict's medical record must remain private, the correctional officers are not going to know if or when the convict is or is not taking his medication. Neither the doctor nor any other health-care provider is required to advise prison-unit security personnel as to the state of an inmate's medication compliance, mental status, or even if the convict is on the psychiatric caseload. Consequently, a large number of "use of force" incidents occur because of con-

frontational situations that occur as a result of an inmate's failure to comply with instructions or the officer's failure to recognize the convict's mental impairment. Convicts who act out without warning or apparent reason routinely injure inmates and
staff as a result of these unavoidable confrontational situations.

As a security administrator, I tried for years to find a way to
resolve this impasse between medical and security, but was not
successful in doing so. The TDCJ administration was not willing
to address the issue, and the medical hierarchy, bent on building
a medical empire within TDCJ, always circled their wagons and
hid behind the arcane laws of medical confidentiality.

Amazingly enough, I've had a psychiatrist, psychologist,
and sociologist advise me that even if they knew that a convict
with a documented history of violence was not compliant with
his medication, they would still refuse to advise security administrators that a convict had made threats directed at a staff member. When confronted with this weird standard of logic, I usually
tried to impress upon them the seriousness of the situation. I
would ask, "What if the convict threatens to harm a member of
the medical staff?"

The answer was always, "Oh, well—I would have to ensure
that medical staff were protected."

I would then ask, "Isn't that a violation of medical confidentiality?" The response usually began with "Yeah, but . . ."
Somehow in their elitist, academically arrogant thinking, they
could never ascribe the same value to the life of a correctional
officer that they did to a medical-staff member.

PHYSICIAN, HEAL THYSELF

Some of the most delusional people I've come into contact with
during my thirty years with the TDCJ worked in the psychiatric
departments of prison units. Some noted examples of strange
behavior by psychiatric staff:

1. In 1984 a unit psychologist whose main function was to counsel with sex offenders was charged and found guilty of the sexual assault of a fifteen-year-old girl. His wife was found guilty
   of urging the teen to have sex with her husband. The fifteen-

year-old testified that she met the psychologist and his wife through a friend who took her to his apartment to play a fantasy game. The girl testified that she was shown nude pictures, frequently consumed alcohol, and had sex with the psychologist with his wife's permission at their apartment. This psychologist's private life clearly seemed to be at odds with his professional calling.

2. On one occasion, a unit psychiatrist attempted to order me to assemble an assorted group of maximum-security, segregation-status gang members into a room so that he could conduct a group counseling session. He actually wanted me to remove the restraints and place opposing members of the Mexican Mafia, Texas Syndicate, Aryan Brotherhood, and various other sworn enemies into a room "for a talk." In hindsight, I've often thought I should have allowed the psychiatrist to do this. It might have been worth watching.

3. One young female sociologist, whose job entailed counseling a group of inmates with various stages of AIDS, became romantically involved with several of the convicts. When she was away from the unit, she would write them love letters. When she finally left her job and moved to Houston, she continued to write to several members of the inmate-counseling group. Although she knew the medical histories of the inmates, she nevertheless allowed one of the HIV-positive convicts to move into her apartment with her and her twelve-year-old daughter after he made parole. Unfortunately, the convict sexually assaulted her twelve-year-old daughter. The ex-convict was subsequently convicted and sentenced to life in prison for the crime. As parents, we all make mistakes, but on a professional level this sociologist demonstrated an utter absence of logic and a blanket disregard for the safety of both herself and her daughter.

During psychoanalysis, both the analyst and the convict can and often do demonstrate delusional personalities. The psychologist is persuaded by the dependent convict that he alone has the answers to his problems. The convict is persuaded through praise and "empowerment" over his personality flaws by the therapist, who bestows unearned self-esteem upon him, when in reality the convict cannot cope. As an observer of this ritualistic dance between the overeducated elite and the mentally challenged, I have noticed that environment often plays a significant role. In some cases, the convict has the advantage simply because he is more at home in his world than the analyst is in his. Those unfamiliar with the dynamics of prison life are often unaware that psychotic and sociopathic personalities are the norm in a convict society.

A local college professor who once taught inmate classes in abnormal psychology at my unit made an interesting observation. He said, "I don't have to look far to find examples of deviant behavior for the class—they're all sitting right in front of me." He was right. The schizophrenics, the bipolar disorders, the major depressions, and the occasional psychopath are all there.

Although not necessarily considered mentally ill, sexual predators are prominently represented on most units' psychiatric caseloads. There is limited expertise for treating sexual predators, and such treatment is expensive and rarely successful. When resources have been diverted to attempt treatment of sex offenders, these efforts have not met with success. Even at $95 an hour, it seems psychiatrists don't have all the answers. Sexual predators have the highest return rate of any offender group. There is no known way, short of execution or life without parole, to successfully keep sex offenders from re-offending.

SUICIDE: THE FINE ART OF KILLING ONESELF

Nationally, in the general population, a suicide occurs every seventeen minutes. More than 30,000 people killed themselves in 1998. Suicide is the number-two killer of college students. Texas ranks thirty-third nationally in the rate of suicide. Most persons who die by suicide are facing a crisis that seems impossible for them to solve. Suicidal persons can be despondent, frightened, demoralized, and profoundly discouraged. In society at large, persons contemplating suicide seem to lack the capacity to understand that their situation is only temporary. The good news, at least for those in the free world, is that if intervention occurs in the early stages, there is a very good chance that suicide can be avoided.

In prison, suicide is not always an irrational decision. Unlike in the free world, a convict's situation may not only be miserable, but it is rarely temporary. The one thing that most convicts can count on is the undeniable fact that their lives are going to get much worse before they ever have a chance to get better. The growing popularity of long-term sentences is in conflict with the idea espoused by many liberals that our institutions should provide a purely sanctified environment and promote a healthy state of mental bliss for those confined. To the contrary, there are many factors that may lead one to consider suicide:

1. As many as 30 to 40 percent of all inmates are HIV-positive. Exact numbers are unavailable, because TDCJ only began testing incoming inmates in March 1998. There is no current plan to test those untested inmates already confined.
2. Forty percent of all inmates are on the psychiatric caseload.
3. As many as 40 percent of all inmates may have either hepatitis A, B, or C. Exact numbers are unavailable because all inmates have not been tested.
4. There is an ever-present fear of airborne viruses, such as an untreatable strain of tuberculosis that occurs eight times more often in prisons than in the general population.
5. There is an ever-present threat of violence and gang activity.
6. Drug usage, both medical and illegal, and drug smuggling create an environment that can turn deadly at any moment.
7. Homosexuality is rampant and often forced upon weaker inmates and those who cannot or will not pay their debts.
8. Increasingly, inmates are sentenced to longer terms with average parole dates that are thirty to forty years away.
9. The absence or loss of family, friends, and significant others contributes to an already isolated existence.

These are understandable reasons for becoming suicidal. Even so, not every convict who threatens suicide is on the level.

In thirty years of working around inmates, I've literally seen thousands of convicts who were labeled suicidal. The vast majority of them were not. For every inmate in TDCJ who actually commits suicide, there are at least fifty who make frivolous attention-getting attempts. Of all the games that convicts play in prison, the threat of suicide is perhaps one of the most common and most costly. The threat of suicide is the one sure way a convict knows he can get attention, a transfer, psychotropic medication, or perhaps even get his girlfriend to come and visit him. In many cases, it is an attempt to get a transfer to one of the regional treatment centers. These facilities are air-conditioned, have special indoor-recreation areas, private cells, a treatment specialist who will sit and talk with you, and softly painted "non-threatening" walls. The primary purpose of treatment centers is to house the most serious, long-term mentally impaired inmates, not provide a revolving door for abusers of short-term "crisis management."

If Texas tries to build treatment centers for every convict claiming to be in crisis, the taxpayers can get ready to spend another five or six billion dollars. It's not hard to see why some convict living in a hot, two-man cell, with a cell partner he doesn't like, might want a pleasant break from his otherwise drab routine. The bottom line is, convicts can and do manipulate the psychiatrist into transferring them to treatment centers by feigning suicide attempts. They know the unit psychiatrist will ship him, because the last thing a medical professional wants is the responsibility for an inmate death, especially if the convict has gone on record as stating that he intends to kill himself.

The problem with this form of "ambulance therapy" is that it costs thousands of taxpayer dollars every time the psychiatrist decides to transfer one of these allegedly suicidal convicts. The situation begs for these psychiatric specialists to take more responsibility for treating these alleged suicide candidates on their current units of assignment. It doesn't seem reasonable or prudent for a psychiatrist to earn $95 an hour to phone in a transfer order just to get rid of a convict who may or may not be "in crisis." Even if TDCJ had to build a small twelve-cell psychiatric ward on each unit, it would be preferable to these nightly ambulance runs up and down the highway with these manipulating, semi-sane convicts.

Admittedly, the suicide rate might go up for a while, until the frivolous actors discover they aren't going to get transferred every time they yell suicide. In the final analysis, a convict can kill himself at a treatment center just as easily as he can on a unit. In the case of a convict who truly intends to commit suicide, I'm not sure what purpose is served by ordering a transfer to a treatment center, other than placating a very expensive psychiatrist.

WHERE THERE'S A WILL, THERE'S A WAY

There is truth in the old "Where there's a will, there's a way" cliché. I've seen convicts die from drinking hair tonic containing 15 percent-by-volume alcohol while trying to get drunk. I've seen deaths that resulted from inmates drinking mimeograph fluid and alcohol-based leather dye. I've seen convicts make homemade chock out of tomato puree that smelled bad enough to gag a buzzard off a gut wagon, but they drank it anyway. One convict died after drinking sour starch from the unit laundry, thinking it was chock.

Convicts will hang themselves with anything from a wire unraveled from a spiral notebook to socks tied together, to sheets, towels, or underwear. They will cut themselves with mirrors, plastic, the side of a metal bunk, a razorblade melted into the side of a toothbrush handle, or any other object sharp enough to get the job done. An inmate has died from stuffing a rag down his throat. There was at least one inmate who managed to kill himself by scratching and cutting at his neck with his fingernails until he exposed the carotid artery. Once exposed, he dug his finger into his neck, found the artery, pulled it in two, and bled to death in a matter of seconds. Suffice to say, if a convict wants to die bad enough, he/she will find a way to get the job done.

In the early 1980s there was an inmate on death row named Richard Vargas. He had once been a member of the notorious "Brady Bunch" that committed a series of robberies and killings, primarily in Hispanic communities around Houston. He was finally sentenced to death, execution #535, for a 1974 robbery/murder in Harris County.

In prison, Vargas became increasingly intent on dying by his own hand before the State of Texas had a chance to execute him. TDCJ took all necessary precautions to preclude Vargus from causing himself any harm. When Vargas first cut himself, he was stitched up. When he intentionally ripped out the stitches, he was tied to his bunk. When he tried to starve himself, he was fed through a tube. When Vargas beat his head against his metal bed and cell wall, he was outfitted with a straitjacket and a motorcycle helmet. Despite TDC's best efforts to keep him alive, Vargas continuously strained against his bonds until he finally succumbed to heart failure on May 31, 1981.

The convicts know that no matter how frivolous it may appear, each suicide threat must be taken seriously. It can be a serious, career-ending mistake for any correctional employee to do otherwise. As policy currently stands, only those with the appropriate medical expertise can determine the seriousness, or lack thereof, of a convict's intent to harm himself.

I knew an assistant warden who was called to an inmate's cell after he had been reported to have a knife. This particular convict was confined to segregation and had a history of threatening suicide on a regular basis. There was no psychologist available, so the warden went to the inmate's cell. He found the convict standing back from the door with a foot-long homemade shank in his hand.

At first the warden tried to calmly talk the convict into giving up the shank, but to no avail. After a few minutes, the convict began repeating that he was going to stab himself, but would not express a reason as to why he intended to do so. The warden continued to listen and cajole the convict, telling him that he would get him some help as soon as he could. The convict gradually became more and more agitated, repeatedly stating that he was going to stab himself. After about ten minutes of this, the warden finally lost his patience, and the next time the convict said he was going to stab himself, the warden abruptly told him, "Go ahead."

Immediately upon hearing the warden's words, the convict sank the shank eight inches deep into his abdomen. As the blood spattered out between the cell bars, the startled, panic-stricken warden yelled, "God damn! Get the ambulance ready!"

After some hasty needlework by a rattled LVN and a swift trip to a local emergency room, the convict survived. The moral to this little story, if there is one, is to never call a potentially suicidal convict's bluff, particularly if he is showing you the weapon with which he intends to carry out his threat. Unfortunately, as sentences get longer, the inmate population grows and disruptive convicts are by necessity forced to spend more and more time in solitude, these situations are going to occur more frequently.

A young convict just starting on a life sentence knows he

has to do forty years day-for-day before anyone is even going to talk to him about a parole. Even then there is no guarantee that he is going to be set free. Without taking away from the basic fact that a convict is, or at least should be, held accountable for his actions and no doubt deserves every day of his sentence, imagine yourself in a similar situation, and you can quickly begin to feel the hopelessness. If one adds to that a catastrophic disease like AIDS or hepatitis, the prospects of living the rest of one's existence behind bars can become a most unbearable situation.

NNING SCARED

Prison employees, unlike convicts, get to choose whether or not they want to be inside a prison every day of their working lives. Why would anyone make a conscious choice to do that? None of the prison employees I've ever talked to have said that they consider their job the fulfillment of a childhood dream. Prison work is not the kind of dream job that most people aspire to.

Most prison employees put up a front, acting like they are strong, silent types, but underneath that facade, there is a lot of fear. Some of that fear is well-justified. There is the constant concern of working with dangerous convicts, of course, but that's not the source of most employee fear. It's the potential for the exposure to disease that worries most of them—that is, those who are even vaguely familiar with the unseen hazards in their surroundings.

The TDCJ medical personnel don't tell correctional staff which inmates have AIDS or other deadly infectious disease. Of course, the medical staff are all well aware which inmates are HIV-positive and carry other potentially deadly diseases. There is even a policy that states that these inmates will not be allowed to work in the medical department. The medical staff says this rule is intended solely to "prevent the spread of disease," but some non-biased observers have found the rule self-serving. The reasoning that allows an infected inmate to work in the food-service department, where hundreds of inmates are fed daily, or work in the inmate barbershop, where inmates use the same chairs and barber tools, yet forbids assignment as a janitor in the medical department is not only self-serving, it's asinine.

General policy states that employees are supposed to protect themselves by treating all inmates as if they have an infectious disease. Of course, that's not entirely practical when you're defending yourself or a fellow officer from an inmate assault or attempting to keep one inmate from killing another. You may not have time to wait for a protective mask, rubber gloves, or a one-way breathing device.

A TDCJ official spokesman said, "With the proper training, testing and tools, the TDCJ can prevent most employees from being exposed to AIDS." Somehow, I don't think that statement comforts most rank-and-file employees. Other than thin rubber gloves and spill kits intended for the clean-up of body fluids, TDCJ provides no special equipment for the protection from the spread of disease for its employees. TDCJ does pay for the testing of an employee *after* exposure to the body fluids of an inmate, but that is primarily an attempt by TDCJ's Legal Affairs Office to head off lawsuits by employees.

Rather than rubber gloves, what employees really need is information. TDCJ has repeatedly said it is "too costly and ineffective to test all inmates" for HIV. (TDCJ has begun testing incoming inmates.) There are no known statistics to demonstrate how many employees have contracted deadly disease by direct exposure from convicts. In many cases, employees may be entirely unaware that they have been exposed, but then, unless employees are tested, how would anyone know? There is another question TDCJ employees may want to ponder. Is TDCJ like the military insofar as AIDS is concerned? Is it a don't ask, don't tell situation? How many of your fellow employees are HIV-positive? In the event of an emergency, employee assault, stabbing, and so forth, how does HIV affect your personal safety and the safety of your family?

THE OLD, THE GRAY, AND THE INVALID

In January of 1998, the TDCJ contracted for sixty beds at the Restful Acres Nursing Home in Karnes County to handle terminally ill prisoners. This contract guarantees that there will be available space for the placement of ex-cons in nursing homes, which typically are hesitant to accept them. A lot of nursing homes and their clients don't want convicts placed into a bed next to someone's grandmother.

A sixty-bed nursing home obviously is not the long-term solution. In 1992 there were 639 inmates age sixty or older in the TDCJ-ID. In 1998 there were 1,849. Current state law requires all aggravated-case offenders to serve at least half of their sentence day for day, regardless of their age. Actually, most of the elderly inmates I met are quite content to be in prison, especially the ones with significant medical problems. The problem with this trend now is that TDCJ is running the most expensive nursing homes in Texas. I mean, how much of a threat is a seventy-five-year old convict who can't breathe without an oxygen bottle strapped to his back?

The rising incidence of AIDS will no doubt exacerbate the problem. While the disease primarily afflicts younger inmates, newer and more expensive drug therapies have increased survival rates, meaning a larger percentage of older inmates will be affected years from now.

The parole rate in Texas in 1998 was 17 percent, down from a high of 79 percent in 1992, when convicts were paroled out the back door as new inmates came in the front, in an effort to relieve overcrowding. Texas voters approved the largest prison expansion in the history of the world. Now the beds are almost full again. When one looks at the wisdom that requires invalids to be kept locked up behind bricks and steel as opposed to the younger, more violent convicts coming into the system, I think it may be time for a reality check. Just as a matter of common sense, it is not very smart policy. It may sound tough on crime to those unfamiliar with the realities of the system, but it sure isn't smart. In 1997, 114 emergency releases were granted. Those are inmates released on a "special needs" basis after a determination that they have less than six months to live. Also in 1997, 196 inmates died in prison of natural causes, 84 of those deaths attributed to AIDS.

Prisons are designed, for the most part, for vigorous young predators, but now decreasingly dangerous individuals are occupying increasingly valuable cells. These elderly convicts are taxing the capacity of prison medical systems, which are already buckling under the burden of the AIDS epidemic. Even if one accepts that prison medical care is not optimal, the courts have held that denial of adequate care violates the Eighth Amendment prohibition of cruel and unusual punishment. As the tax burden on the Texas taxpayer rises to support an ever-more-costly "department of corrections," one might ask, what is it about these elderly convicts that is being corrected?

CHAPTER FOURTEEN

BOW TIES AND
RED SUSPENDERS

"You can get by on charm for about 15 minutes.
After that, you better know something."
—H. JACKSON BROWN

THE LAST REAL WARDEN

When Retrieve Unit Warden Bobby R. Crawford retired in 1990, it was the end of an era—the last of the real wardens was gone. Oh, there were a couple of wannabe wardens who went through the motions of acting like they were in charge, but it was a pitiful display to those few of us left who remembered what a real warden looked like.

Bobby Crawford was one of the last wardens who spent more time around convicts than in his office. A modern-day Texas prison warden envisions him- or herself as the equivalent of the CEO of some major corporation. They spend most of the time in their offices on the phone or answering e-mails. Wardens today are way too busy going to seminars, doing lunch, and networking to worry about unit operations. In the not-too-distant past they called them "good ol' boys"; nowadays it's "networking." The end result is the same.

In fairness to the new breed, it's not all their fault. It's hard for a warden to act like he's in charge when you have to get permission from some secretary or a bean counter in the regional office every time you have to make a decision that affects your unit.

THE ULTIMATE HUNT

In late April of 1989, right in the middle of a heated governor's race, the vice-chairman of the Texas Board of Criminal Justice, Jerry Hodge, forty-seven, made one of the dumbest decisions in the history of TDCJ. Hodge, a businessman and ex-mayor of Amarillo, decided to take two of his friends on what he termed "The Ultimate Hunt." James Lynaugh and soon-to-be director James "Andy" Collins accompanied them, as did the Ellis I Unit dog sergeant. Hodge, who was at the time on Republican gubernatorial candidate Clayton Williams' campaign staff, invited Glenn McMennamy, a Texas Department of Human Services board member, and retired Indianapolis businessman Bob Wiles on a horseback hunt exercise designed to train tracking dogs to find escaped inmates.

Mr. Hodge obviously viewed the training of tracking dogs as a recreational opportunity and passed out souvenir jackets embroidered, "The Ultimate Hunt," to his friends. If it hadn't been for the embroidered jackets, Hodge and company might have gotten by without being burned by the media, but guys walking around in jackets labeled "The Ultimate Hunt" naturally drew a crowd. The legal counsel for the Texas Civil Liberties Union, Jim Harrington, said, "That's not a sport. It's outrageous for a state official . . . and then you take along friends . . . and then you boast about it. That's just unconscionable that you have people like that in leadership." He called for Hodge and McMennamy to resign.

State Rep. Ron Wilson, D-Houston, said he was outraged by the men's participation in the exercise. "There's no doubt their actions are inappropriate for officials serving in their capacity," Wilson said. He added that such exercises were reminiscent of the Wild West days. "Their kind of slave sport should be outlawed in Texas," he said.

The media sharks descended on TDCJ like starved bloodhounds attacking raw meat. Hodge lost the opportunity to become the next chairman of the Board of Criminal Justice. Dog-training exercises were temporarily banned, because all of a sudden every media source in Texas wanted to ride along on an "Ultimate Hunt." The director put out a directive banning all media from the units, but had to retract the order when reporters yelled cover-up. The chairman of the Board of Criminal Justice called for an "outside expert" to come in and review the political correctness of using live inmates for dog bait.

Meanwhile, Jerry Hodge further upset some members of the governor's staff when he ignored their advice and appeared on Oprah Winfrey's television show to answer questions about the Ultimate Hunt. Hodge apologized at least twice on the show, admitting he had shown poor taste by having the jackets made.

Somewhere in all the political backbiting, the fact that the dogs are an integral part of the job of catching escaped convicts got lost in the shuffle. At first the dog sergeants were told not to run the dogs at all. Then they were told to run exercise tracks, but not to allow the dogs to have any contact with the dogboys.

It is in the nature of tracking dogs to hunt, but if you don't allow them to catch what they're chasing once in a while, the dogs will lose interest. When the board said the dogs could no longer have any contact with the dogboys, it took all the incentive out of the chase. The entire dog-training program suffered. It took months before the heat died down enough for the board to finally allow the dogboys to go back to fighting the dogs. By then, many of the dogs had lost interest, and some of them never recovered from the absence of training. The overall effectiveness of a tried and truly tested tool utilized to apprehend dangerous escaped convicts was almost lost, all because a politician wanted to show off for his friends.

SMOKE AND MIRRORS

In January of 1990, James A. "Andy" Collins was named director of the institutional division. He had been the deputy director for operation since 1987, responsible for the day-to-day operations of all state correctional facilities. Even then Collins had been the real power behind the throne, because the former institutional director, James Lynaugh, was by profession an accountant and showed little interest in individual unit matters. In Lynaugh's new job as executive director over Parole, State Jails and the Institutional Division of TDC, he would in effect be the figurehead for three of the largest criminal-justice agencies in Texas. I did not see his departure from the institutional director's job as significant. In the four years Lynaugh was director, I only saw him once outside of a formal meeting, when he spent less than an hour touring the Retrieve Unit. The difference between Lynaugh and Collins was that at least Lynaugh admitted he didn't know much about unit administration and therefore confined himself primarily to budgetary matters and interaction with the Legislature and the board. Collins, on the other hand, had worked as liaison to the Texas Board of Criminal Justice, liked to hang out with politicians, and felt that he had the capacity for strong central leadership, including the ability to micromanage the units.

Shortly after Collins was appointed to the directorship, the wardens were all summoned to Mount Olympus for a meeting at the old Goree Unit Clubhouse. Wayne Scott had been appointed to the director-of-operations job and he brought the meeting to order. After a couple of short announcements, he introduced Mr. Collins.

A large, mildly obese man, Collins appeared to be in his early forties. He had begun his criminal-justice career as a summer intern while earning his degree from Sam Houston State University. Collins advanced through the custodial ranks without attracting much notice. Eventually, through attrition and political posturing, he was promoted to warden of the Beto I Unit, where even his friends admit he was a failure. Collins represented the new wave of prison administrators, more at home in a room full of lobbyists and legislators than convicts. In hindsight, his strength seems to have been in his ability to rattle off volumes of esoteric data to uninformed politicians who mostly didn't have a clue as to what he was talking about. His weakness was that he sometimes forgot who his audience was.

Collins arose from his chair, took off his suit coat, and wowed us all with a bright red bow tie and matching suspenders. His public persona was somewhere between a carnival barker and a Southern Baptist preacher on a revival crusade. As Collins preached his sermon, déjà vu began to set in. I wasn't the only one in the room who realized we had heard the speech before. This was just a showcase opportunity for James "Andy" Collins to make a stage appearance, and he seemed to revel in the moment.

As he spoke, he paced side to side, giving his once-fellow wardens an economics lesson. It was the same tired old mantra we had been hearing ever since Judge Justice took over the department in 1981. Texas was scratching a broke ass and we were "going to have to do more with less." The unit wardens were being told to cut their operations to the bone while the Collins administration hired more assistant directors and upper-level roadrunners. Even the assistants had assistants. The rampant hiring of less-qualified individuals, often recommended by influential politicians or so-called "prison consultants," profoundly demoralized rank-and-file TDCJ employees.

Andy was a chameleonic charmer who cajoled, beguiled, and manipulated anybody who could help him achieve what he wanted. He was standing in front of his wardens now, trying desperately to persuade us that *his* purpose, *his* goals, *his* needs were more important than ours and that *his* ends justified *his* means. Andy had perfected the art of convincing himself—and usually others—that black was white and rich was poor, all because it furthered his quest to stand on the top of the mountain.

At some point in Collins' presentation, Larry Johns leaned over and made an observation. "Man, anybody who talks that fast has got to be lying some of the time."

I answered, "Yeah, well, he's wasting rhetoric on these folks. He must think he's talking to the governor or some of those silk-stocking street politicians, 'cause these people know better."

Retrieve Unit Hostages

On October 3, 1990, at approximately 9:50 A.M., inmate Winslow Beaver, #512971, walked into the Retrieve Unit building captain's office. Beaver, who was assigned to work in the Retrieve Unit food-service department, had stolen a sixteen-inch butcher knife from his work site and hidden it underneath his shirt.

When Beaver first entered the office, Captain Stan Kinney, Food Service Manager Michael Davenport, and inmate Aaron Powell, #274166, were having a meeting. Upon seeing Beaver enter, Captain Kinney ordered Mr. Davenport and inmate Powell to leave and waved to First-Shift Lt. Rene Munoz to step inside the office. As Lieutenant Munoz entered the office, Beaver pulled the sixteen-inch butcher knife from under his shirt and took Captain Kinney and Lieutenant Munoz hostage at knifepoint.

This was the second time within a five-year period that I would be faced with a situation in which a convict was holding some of my staff at knifepoint. I had known Captain Kinney since 1984, when he'd worked as an administrative segregation sergeant at Ramsey. Lt. Rene Munoz began his career at Retrieve as a correctional officer, and we had been friends for several years.

I was in a meeting in the administrative offices when the warden's secretary, Brenda Goolsby, came running in saying, "An inmate in the building has a knife and he is holding the captain hostage." The call came from an excited Lt. Enrique Franco, who was just outside the building captain's office at the center-hall searcher's desk phone. Captain Bravo and I ran from my office, through the three electronically controlled gates that led into the main hall.

Capt. Genero Rodriguez and Lieutenant Franco had already isolated the situation, cleared the hallway of inmates and locked down the building. They were both solid staff officers who stood ready to do whatever was necessary to save the hostages. Captain Rodriguez advised that the convict was armed with a large butcher knife and that he and Lieutenant Franco had tried to open the door to the Captain Kinney's office, but the convict had threatened "to stick anyone who tried to come in." I would later discover that inmate Beaver told his hostages, "Y'all been fucking with me—I'm tired of it. I got a lot of time and I don't care about dying."

I walked up to the windows outside the office in which the hostages were being held. I could see the inmate, the knife, and the hostages, who were standing behind a desk about six feet from the convict. Beaver was standing next to the solid metal office door. When Captain Rodriguez and Lieutenant Franco initially tried to push the door open, the convict had succeeded in keeping them out by placing his foot against the door and threatening to use the knife if they came in. At that point, they made the wise decision of backing off and further assessing the situation.

For·one fleeting moment, I entertained thoughts of sending Captain Rodriguez out to one of the pickets for a .357-magnum pistol. I could easily have killed Beaver by calling him to the door or just shooting him through the glass. I would have been technically accurate and on legally sound ground if I had shot Beaver, but it would also have been seen as politically insensitive. I would've been second-guessed by all those Monday-morning quarterbacks who promote using only the least amount of physical force necessary. To be honest, my first priority was to get those officers out of there unharmed. Every other consideration was secondary. In my mind, if that meant inmate Beaver's health or well-being had to be sacrificed, then so be it.

While we stood outside the office trying to find the best way to proceed, Beaver was telling Captain Kinney and Lieutenant Munoz, "If they come in here, I'm going to come across that desk and get one of you. I know they'll get me, but I'll get some of you first." Captain Kinney continued to talk to Beaver in his steady, calm voice, attempting to explain the futility of his action. Neither officer had any chance of getting past the sixteen-inch knife at the door. Lieutenant Munoz, known to be a man with opinions on almost every subject, was being uncharacteristically silent. I remember thinking that I didn't want this to drag out any longer than necessary, because as it stood, it was a no-win situation for the officers.

I asked Captain Rodriguez for his riot baton and knocked on the steel door. I stood with my head close to the small window in the door where the inmate could see me. It must have looked to the convict like an overture to talk things over. Actually, I had no intention of negotiating with the convict, and I knew I couldn't afford to further compromise the safety of those officers. This was not the time to roll the dice. The last thing I needed was to get someone injured or killed trying to enter the office or allow Beaver to get another hostage. When the convict briefly leaned away from the door to look through the window at me, I pushed the door open just a crack. The opening was just wide enough for my arm to squeeze through with a riot baton. I pitched the baton across the room to Captain Kinney, who made a major-league catch.

At first, the convict was visibly upset, especially when he realized that Captain Kinney now had a twenty-four-inch metal riot baton in his hands.

Beaver turned his wrath on me, saying, "What did he do that for? I once trusted him, but that was stupid. I let him in and he did that!" The bottom line was that the balance of power had shifted. A metal riot baton is a formidable weapon. One blow can easily break an arm or leg or cause a skull fracture.

Beaver was a little slow in grasping the realities of the situation but finally realized it was a standoff, Captain Kinney's twenty-four-inch metal riot baton against a sixteen-inch butcher knife. The officers' odds were perhaps not the best in the world, but at least they were no longer defenseless. As a predator used to taking advantage of the unarmed and helpless, Beaver showed his true colors: In the end, he was a coward. In the face of a real possibility of personal injury if he chose to use the knife, Beaver laid the weapon down. He offered no further resistance and was handcuffed and escorted to the medical department for evaluation and eventual lockup.

Admittedly, the tactics I chose to use in resolving this hostage incident are not in the hostage-situation manual. Others would no doubt have chosen to negotiate. In hostage situations, there is undeniably a place for some degree of negotiation, but my personal view is that the concept is vastly overrated. I never liked the idea of ordering correctional staff or other employees to do things that I personally would not do, and I've always maintained that in the event I was being held hostage, I wouldn't want anyone to spend a lot of time negotiating with some convict over my freedom. I want someone, with some brains and firepower, to forcefully intervene on my behalf, either killing or capturing the convict and freeing me. And if I should have been injured or killed during such intervention, I would accept that as part of the calculated risk that all employees take when they choose to set foot inside of a prison.

I would not want the negotiation process to drag out for hours or days. In fact, if some benevolent negotiator ever had allowed me to be at a convict's mercy for hours or days in a hostage situation, the negotiator would have been better off if the convict did kill me. If I were fortunate enough to survive such an ordeal, the first person I would want to seek revenge on would be the hostage negotiator.

A MAN OF HIGH MORAL FIBER

Beginning in late 1990, all unit personnel were ordered to attend special classes on the subject of ethics. It was a showcase, system-wide attempt to stem the tide of employee involvement in graft and corruption. The problem was that the vast majority of the ethics problems originated at the highest levels of administrative power. After all, unit staff didn't control the agency budget, have legislative input, control hiring practices, or have any real power. Unit wardens had long ago lost the authority to hire or fire their own employees. However, the following incident demonstrates just how far some TDCJ administrators were willing to go in order to protect their own.

In July 1991, Warden Terry Terrell, my old mentor from the Ramsey I Unit, was fired from his job as senior warden of the 3,500-man Beto I Unit. His firing was the culmination of a long-standing dispute between Terrell and his regional director. Executive Director James Lynaugh finally called Terrell to his office in a last attempt at getting Terrell to bend to his will. Lynaugh offered Terrell a transfer to another unit, but at a $12,000-per-year pay cut. Terrell declined the pay cut, was fired immediately, and subsequently began a three-year fight to clear his name.

The dispute began when Terrell attempted to discipline one of his security majors and his regional director intervened. I knew Terry Terrell to be a man of impeccable honesty and integrity, and it just wasn't his style to allow any employee, no matter how well-connected, to violate rules with impunity. Terrell had taken umbrage over the fact that this employee was allegedly attempting to use a personal friendship with the regional director to avoid being disciplined for failing to stop a prisoner who had plotted to stab another inmate.

When the regional director intervened and would not allow Terrell to discipline his own employee, Terrell filed an internal grievance. When that was denied, he appealed to Executive Director James Lynaugh. Terrell wrote letters to Governor Ann Richards and to Board of Criminal Justice members. Finally, when called to Austin by Selden Hale, chairman of the Texas Board of Criminal Justice, Terrell accused Institutional Director

James "Andy" Collins of being a "pathological liar" who couldn't be trusted.

As far as I can determine, this was the first time in the history of the prison system that a unit warden used TDCJ's own procedures to openly challenge the authority of the administration. By any measure, it was a bold move, because TDCJ is an "employer at will," which means, theoretically at least, that any employee can be fired at any time for any reason, or no reason. Terry Terrell was not a physically imposing presence, but as one astute observer accurately put it at the time, "He's got nuts like a water buffalo."

One had to admire Terrell's forthright ability to call a spade a spade. What the administration saw as rebellion, most rank-and-filers saw as a courageous attempt by one man to stand up to a bureaucratic machine and try to achieve some level of justice.

Terrell patiently pursued his lawsuit over the next three years as it gradually wound its way through the legal system. Finally, he got his day in court. In June of 1993, an Anderson County jury awarded Terrell more than $700,000 and agreed that he had been maliciously fired for reporting "extensive administrative corruption" among prison officials. The jury also awarded Terrell $7,000 for mental anguish, $51,000 in attorney fees, and $6,000 for court costs. Terry Terrell eventually went to work for a private prison company and is currently a regional administrator.

Those in state government would never admit it, but in losing Terry Terrell, Texas lost an honest, capable man who possessed a higher level of integrity than the employees TDCJ wasted vast sums of tax dollars attempting to protect. Unfortunately, men like Terrell don't come along very often, and the TDCJ hierarchy still does not realize that there should be a premium placed on retaining such men and women. Personal integrity, high ethical standards, and a strong moral code are the most essential qualities any prospective employee must possess if one hopes to survive a long-term career in criminal justice.

POLITICALLY INCORRECT

Shortly after the new regional director arrived, an assistant warden at the Darrington Unit made an unbelievably inept public-relations mistake. He announced to his shift employees that

Director Wayne Scott and some of the plaintiff's attorneys were going to tour the southern units on a *Ruiz*-compliance inspection. The announcement would have been all right, except that during his speech he referred to one of the plaintiff's female attorneys as a "bull dyke."

On inspection day, several Darrington employees who obviously did not have the assistant warden's best interests at heart told the female attorney what he had called her. Without delay, the attorney let Wayne Scott know that she was absolutely livid at being referred to in such a derogatory manner by this good ol' boy from Texas. As Wayne Scott was representing TDCJ on the tour, he was hard-pressed to do something about it.

Having met the attorney in question, I can see where her less-than-feminine demeanor may have led the assistant warden to his assumption; however, since he had no direct evidence of her sexual orientation, he immediately found himself in hot water. The assistant warden was advised that speculation about the sexual orientation of visiting attorneys was not an appropriate subject for an employee shift meeting. After some behind-closed-door negotiations, the assistant warden was made to suffer disciplinary consequences, but luckily managed to keep his job.

Glenn's Law: Be careful what you ask for, because you just might get it. Large bureaucracies don't like it when you don't actively and cheerfully support whatever little plan they have for you. The TDCJ views itself as a paramilitary entity and enjoys moving its troops around the state "at will," regardless of any personal or family concerns that employees may have. That attitude, especially prevalent among post-1981 upper-level TDCJ management, is part of the reason why, nationally, career correctional officers have triple the divorce rate of people in other professions and a life expectancy of less than fifty-nine years.

Those who do not bend to the will of the administration are not promoted to senior-warden positions or any other silk-stocking street jobs. Those who sit on Mount Olympus look down upon such malcontents as abject failures who are disloyal and obviously don't have the interests of the department at heart.

Effective December 1, 1992, I was reassigned to the Ramsey III Unit, near Rosharon, Texas, in Brazoria County. This would be the first time in my career that I would have the opportunity to work on a minimum-security unit. To be more accurate, Ramsey III is, for the most part, a geriatric unit. Well over 50 percent of the assigned convicts were designated "fourth-class medical." The next stop for most of them was either a nursing home or the cemetery.

On my first tour of the Ramsey III unit, I stood in center hall and watched the call-out for the noon meal. It looked like the march of the walking wounded. Almost every convict had a cane, a walker, a wheelchair, or a neck brace. The eye patches, amputees, and colostomy bags were common.

Ramsey III was basically a large tin barn, with no general-population cellblocks, divided into twenty separate dormitories, each with fifty-man cubicles on each side of a long main hallway. Security was laughable in light of the prefabricated, bolted-together metal buildings and a single compound fence. If the convicts wanted out of the building, all they had to do was kick a hole in the wall between the rusted metal panels and walk out onto the yard.

Unfortunately, ever since TDCJ began hiring every warm body they could find in order to try to meet the staffing demands required by Judge Justice, employee discipline had become an all-consuming nightmare for unit administrators. In the absence of employee discipline, anarchy reigns and that is especially true inside a prison unit. Discipline is an unpleasant but integral part of the job. Ramsey III, in 1992, needed employee discipline more than any unit I have ever worked on.

Employee complaints at the Ramsey III Unit reminded me of the whining of children. For instance, a young female correctional officer came in crying, "Warden, he called me a homosexual."

As I handed her a Kleenex, I just had to ask, "Ahaaaa, could that be because you announced at the shift meeting that you had to have time off to play ball in your lesbian softball league?" I didn't want to appear insensitive, or for anyone to think that I was opposed to lesbian softball, but I thought the point should be well-taken. If one announces participation in such an activity to the world, then I think it is entirely reasonable for one's peers to speculate that they might be homosexual.

Romance, or something akin to it, between employees and convicts was in full bloom at Ramsey III. One female food-service sergeant had delivered two children by the same convict over a period of three years before she finally got caught. She was a bold young woman; even with thirty other convicts on duty at 3:00 A.M. in the food-service department, she would take her lover into a locked food pantry for romantic trysts. She had other inmates act as lookouts while they were having sex. We probably wouldn't have caught her, except some of the other convicts got jealous and wanted in on the action. When she either couldn't or wouldn't accommodate all of them, convicts being convicts, they snitched. In a subsequent search of her convict lover's property, security found pictures of her children and graphic nude photos of the soon-to-be ex-food-service manager.

In an equally deplorable situation, we started getting complaints from several convicts that an officer was soliciting them for homosexual activity. After a lengthy internal-affairs investigation using several convicts and a hidden recording device, an eight-year male veteran officer who usually worked in the recreation area was caught soliciting inmates for sex.

FOURTEENTH WARDEN

It had been twenty-seven long years since I began my career under Warden Scott Valentine on the old Clemens Unit, and I'd now worked for thirteen different wardens. I'd seen every management style that exists and several others that probably don't exist anymore. That said, I really didn't quite know what to think of Warden David Doughty when he arrived at Ramsey III, fresh from the West Texas T. L. Roach Unit, in Childress.

On paper, Doughty fit the mold of the modern warden, with the standard Sam Houston State University criminal-justice degree, but he also had an up-through-the-ranks security-boss background. He chain-smoked, his language was less than cultured, and he had an easygoing, what-you-see-is-what-you-get persona that was refreshing. I liked him at first sight. His laid-back East Texas personality belied the fact that he was smart, compassionate, and goal-oriented. If the times would have allowed, Doughty would have made a first-rate "real warden," but under present circumstances, I was afraid that he had been born about twenty-five years too late.

TDCJ decided to build a 350-bed, low-security, two-story

expansion facility across the street from the Ramsey III Unit. When I say low-security, I mean this was basically a tin barn with a fence around it. Of course, the first thing TDCJ did when the facility opened was fill it up with medium-custody convicts. After a few minor fights, assaults, and verbal altercations, one of the convicts wrote Warden Doughty a note threatening to burn the new expansion facility to the ground.

Threatening notes, especially anonymous ones, are fairly common in prisons, but for some reason, perhaps because he was still fairly new to the unit, this note motivated Doughty to take some action. He called the ranking security supervisors in for a meeting to plan an assault on the facility, to include the use of gas and riot teams. He kept reading the threatening note and saying to no one in particular, "They just don't know me." His inclination was to show them who was boss and to leave no doubt in their minds as to who was in charge. I sat through the meeting without offering any advice, until everyone except us two had left the office. As we sat there sipping on coffee, I casually observed, "You know, Warden, they really haven't done anything yet."

His adrenaline was still pumping. "I'm not going to let these punks tear that new building up."

"If we gas them," I pointed out, "they can still tear up your new building, and some people are probably going to get hurt."

"They just don't know who they're threatening," Doughty insisted.

"Most of them are line-ones and sat-fours," I pointed out. "These guys have lots of good-time to lose if they decide to get radical. If they were to become involved in a riot, it would significantly change their discharge dates, and I think 99% of them already know that."

"So, you don't think we should gas them, huh?"

"Well, Warden, it's your call and it's your unit, but I don't think we ought to be the ones making the first move. You can always gas them, but then what? They haven't done enough yet to justify transfer, and we're going to have the same problems tomorrow."

After a moment of silence, Doughty asked, "What do you think our next step should be?"

"There is a time to fight, I just don't think we're there yet.

How about if I take Major Mohr and one of the captains over there and do some interviews? Maybe we can identify a dozen or so of the agitators and move them back into the main building. That should defuse things for a while."

"Let's do it," said Doughty. As I got up to leave the office, he added, "Thanks, Glenn, I appreciate it."

All he had needed was time to cool off. I didn't tell him anything he hadn't already known. He just didn't want to see it through the anger. I had noticed the same trait in other wardens over the years; most of them had later regretted making quick decisions in the heat of the moment.

After a day or two of talking to convicts, we pulled a few hardheads back to the main building, and peace and quiet was restored at the Ramsey III Unit.

ANOTHER FEMALE OFFICER RAPED

As new units were gradually completed and filled with convicts doing longer and longer sentences, the level of violence began to escalate. The administration stuck to its policy of working female officers in hazardous areas, and some of them paid the price. Assaults on staff, especially the female officers, were becoming a daily, on some units hourly, occurrence throughout the system.

On the morning of February 28, 1993, at the Michael Unit, just outside Palestine, Texas, an inmate inside the clothing-issue area took hostage three female officers. Although it was clearly not sound correctional practice, these three female officers had been allowed to work supervising convicts in an isolated area of the building; the only keys available were locked inside the clothing-issue area, which was controlled by the hostage-taker. Help would be slow in coming.

After severely beating all three of the officers, he locked one of them in a closet while he took his time raping and fondling the other two. Initially, and for some time after the convict took charge, no other employees even knew that there was a hostage situation going on. Approximately an hour and a half later, security staff finally realized that the officers were in trouble and attempted to gain access to the area. The entry took several minutes, because two steel security doors had to be cut from their hinges with a welding torch and removed. As the security team finally succeeded in entering the barricaded area, the convict made a half-hearted attempt to hang himself, but was unsuccessful.

Although severely traumatized, these officers were lucky, at least in the sense that they escaped with their lives. Unfortunately, these incidents are becoming all too common. In today's Texas prison units, female employees are assaulted with increasing frequency, yet in the name of diversity and political correctness they are still being placed in harm's way every day.

$2 LAWSUIT

In late 1993, after a nine-day civil trial under the watchful eye of Judge William Wayne Justice, convict and writ-writer David Ruiz won a cash award from two TDCJ correctional officer defendants. Ruiz, now back in prison for the fourth time, had accused eighteen TDCJ employees of retaliating against him for his role in the 1972 *Ruiz v. Estelle* lawsuit. The jury deliberated for about eight hours before returning the verdict. The jury decided that two of the eighteen accused officers had in fact "abused their duties as prison employees."

The federal jury, in a moment of supreme clarity, awarded David Ruiz $2.00 in damages for his suffering, one dollar from each officer. Judge Justice, accustomed to issuing decrees without the tempering influence of a jury, was no doubt disappointed in the two-dollar decision.

In hindsight and in the interest of justice, the taxpayers of Texas may wonder just how much of their money could have been saved if only a jury could have heard the entire *Ruiz* litigation.

A BUREAUCRATIC BLACK MARKET

In a decision that had the effect of immediately doubling the size of an already huge black market within the prison system, the Board of Criminal Justice voted unanimously to prohibit tobacco products from all Texas prisons effective March 1, 1995. The ban applied to all properties owned or leased by the department. TDCJ employees would henceforth be allowed to possess, but not use, tobacco products while on state property.

It was readily apparent that the folks making up these rules had no concept of life on a Texas prison unit. At the time this rule went into effect, roughly 60 percent of TDCJ employees smoked, as did 65 to 70 percent of the inmates. The year before the ban went into effect, TDCJ commissaries took in more than $5.4 million in sales from tobacco products. The tobacco rules were almost impossible to enforce.

According to the Board of Criminal Justice, this monumental decision was being made "for the good of the inmate population, as well as the taxpayers that must pay for prison medical care." As laudable as this may sound at first hearing, I submit there was an even stronger and more practical reason for the tobacco ban. The unspoken motivation behind the ban was the liability. A few judges in other states had handed down some scary rulings holding prisons responsible for the health and safety of the institutional environment. It doesn't take much insight to figure out that sooner, rather than later, Judge Justice or some equally despotic judicial icon would use a cancer-motivated non-smoker lawsuit to take another couple of billion out of the pockets of Texas taxpayers. The tobacco ban was a preemptive strike to avoid litigation, motivated first and foremost by the TDCJ's absolute terror of a class-action lawsuit.

Regardless of the reasons for the ban, the overall benefit to the inmate population was real. Units became cleaner, instantly. The air and clothing no longer reeked of cigarette smoke. No more cigarette butts on the floor, no yellow film on the walls, no more harassment from the indigent bums who used to irritate everyone by begging for a cigarette twenty times a day.

However, the fact that tobacco was still a legal substance that every other adult citizen in the country could buy and indulge in should they choose to do so was a point deemed unimportant. The compromise option of a designated smoking area was not even considered. Forget the rights of the smokers, employee or inmate. My question was, in an environment where at least seven out of ten people smoked regularly and were essentially being told to quit cold turkey, was the prison really going to be a better place at the end of the day?

This question was answered two weeks after the ban went into effect. A food-service manager got caught on his way into work with fifty-two packs of Bugler rolling tobacco taped to his body. During the interview after this first tobacco bust, the guy admitted that he had made two previous tobacco-smuggling trips into the unit. He said he could buy the packs of Bugler tobacco cheaply enough to turn an 85-percent profit. He was turning a 90-percent profit on packs of "readyrolls," meaning name-brand packs of cigarettes. He said he could make more money and take less risk smuggling tobacco than people made peddling dope. I put a pencil to it and figured out that if half of what he was telling me was true, the guy was also making more money smuggling tobacco than he was on his state-employee paycheck.

The food-service manager chose to resign rather than face formal disciplinary charges, but just before he left he said, "You know, Warden, I'm not the only one doing this. The money is just too good for most of these bosses to turn down." After he left, I sat there hoping he was wrong, but his assessment of the situation showed more insight than the board had when they wrote the rule. Smuggling tobacco was highly profitable, and the consequences if caught were minimal. Possession of tobacco was only an institutional-rules infraction, not a violation of law like the smuggling of illegal drugs.

The Board of Criminal Justice created a bureaucratic black market of immense size. Literally hundreds of TDCJ employees have been fired for smuggling tobacco products to convicts. Clearly, a majority of officers don't smuggle tobacco, but enough of them do to make me question whether having designated smoking areas may not have been a preferable policy. (TDCJ later backed off of restricting employees from using tobacco on state property and granted designated smoking areas for them, but not for inmates.) I fought the tobacco smugglers right along with the dopers, right up until the day I retired, and it remains a major problem in Texas prisons.

CURTIS WEEKS

In thirty years of dealing with some fairly ornery convicts, I don't think I ever met one quite as ill-tempered as Curtis "Hard Time" Weeks. He had arrived straight from a Houston, Texas, courtroom after being found guilty of the 1988 attempted murder of correctional officer Ron Alford, whom Weeks had spat on. Weeks, who had previously been serving a two-year sentence for aggravated robbery, had AIDS.

As Weeks was led from the courtroom after being sentenced to life, he spat in the face of another correctional officer. He was not tried on the second incident, but from that day forward all possible precautions were taken in order to avoid additional employee exposure. The basis of Weeks' conviction was the scientific contention that AIDS could be passed through saliva. Scientific speculation aside, Curtis evidently thought he could infect others that way, because he was constantly threatening to kill people by spitting or throwing other bodily fluids on them. A special Plexiglas shield was designed to fit over the outer bars of his cell to shield staff and inmates who passed by his cell. Curtis even tried to bite and spit at the medical staff when they attempted to treat him, which as his disease progressed was sometimes several times a day.

At the same time he was attempting to bite and spit on my staff, he was steadily writing everybody he knew and telling them that we were violating his constitutional rights and mistreating him.

Over a five-year period, he was married and divorced twice from various pen pals. Those relationships usually turned sour after Curtis persisted in requesting that they send him more money. He gradually grew more and more irrational. One day he would be content to sit in his cell and not say a word. The next day he would be begging every officer who passed by for forgiveness and promising he would never even attempt to hurt anyone again. Then, in the next five minutes, he would be spitting at the chaplain, one of the nurses, or someone else who was only trying to help him.

I had known Curtis' father, Winifred Weeks (*aka* Wimpy) who had served time years before on the Ramsey I Unit. He had escaped while on an approved furlough trip to his grandmother's funeral and had hid out in Mexico for several years. The convict grapevine said that Wimpy, in an extreme effort to avoid capture, had married the daughter of the mayor of Guadalajara while he was on the run. In any case, he was finally captured and brought back to finish his sentence.

Curtis' mother, Panda, had once been an exotic dancer and

part-time drug dealer in Houston. Houston vice detectives referred to her as "an oil-burning racehorse," but they mostly left her alone. They knew that Panda had to have drugs to get up and face each new day, and besides, it wasn't like she was hard to find. She knew every thug and criminal in Houston and was scared to death of a jail cell. Occasionally, they would pick her up just for the conversation. She always managed to tell them just enough to stay out of jail. On rare occasions, Wimpy and Panda came to visit Curtis, and I tried to see if I could get them to exert some positive influence over his actions, but to no avail. They had long since lost the ability to motivate Curtis to do anything.

Finally, after Curtis tormented staff for seven years, the disease caught up with him. He was defiant to the last, cursing the officers who put him on the ambulance en route to the TDCJ Hospital at Galveston. After numerous use-of-force incidents and his almost constant attempts to assault staff, Curtis "Hard Time" Weeks died at the young age of thirty-four on July 24, 1995.

THE GREAT VITAPRO CAPER

As an old horseshoe-nailing convict from Retrieve, Billy "Dirty-Red" Henson, was fond of saying, "You know, Boss, y'all ain't got all the cons locked up." He was right, of course, but when I first hired on to this outfit, I was pretty confident that at least the folks at the top of the food chain were righteous, law-abiding citizens, folks who were supposed to be serving as role models for the rest of us. I don't know if that was ever really 100-percent true, but it was certainly more accurate in the early days of my career than toward the end.

In April 1994, James A. "Andy" Collins was promoted to the executive director's job, with authority over parole, adult probation, and the institutional divisions of the Texas Department of Criminal Justice. Andy was forty-three years old and a twenty-two-year veteran of the agency. His salary was now up to $120,000 per year, plus the perk of living in a large, state-owned mansion, with convict servants, all at state expense. Andy must have been feeling like he was nine feet tall, bullet-proof, and invisible. Who could blame him? But most folks with all that would have been satisfied.

Not Andy. The more he got away with, the more he believed he was exempt from the rules. He was the undisputed head of the largest prison system ever conceived by a free society. Naturally, every con artist in the country was trying to figure out how to get rich off Texas taxpayers. Just as Texas prison expansion became a feeding frenzy, there Andy was, right in the catbird seat. The fast-buck artists, prison-board members, lawyers, and politicians all wanted a piece.

If only he had attended a few more of those ethics classes, or perhaps if he'd been mentored by someone with integrity—but unfortunately, Andy just couldn't hold out against the greed. He was only motivated by what was good for Andy. He was not concerned about the consequences to others. He shaved the truth, he let others make excuses for his behavior, and he manipulated his friends in order to achieve his personal goals.

Andy had been involved in several questionable deals by the time he announced his intention to feed VitaPro, a new soy-based meat substitute made in Canada, to the TDCJ inmate population. He also stated that not only would TDCJ inmates be eating the new beef substitute, but that TDCJ would become the Texas marketer and distributor for the soy product.

To hear Collins talk, VitaPro was the best thing since sliced bread. Unlike beef, it didn't need refrigeration, wouldn't shrink when cooked, required less cooking time, had a long shelf-life, could be shipped easily, and converted into an edible product four times its dry weight. In other words, VitaPro could be used in place of instant hamburger without the fat or cholesterol—or any taste.

Setting aside the question of flavor, where is the beef with VitaPro? I mean, after all, the stuff was cheap and healthful. The problem was, nobody was asking the hard questions. Was the VitaPro deal moral, ethical, and legal? What was Andy Collins getting out of this? Most of the Huntsville bureaucrats who were close enough to the situation to know what was going on were too afraid of Collins to challenge the process. There was one exception. Janie Thomas, food-service manager for the department, tried to stand up to Collins and fought aggressively to avoid using the massive amounts of VitaPro Collins was insisting upon. When Collins found out about her resistance, she was unceremoniously called in and told to "be a team player," with the underlying implication that if she didn't, she could look for employment elsewhere.

My first indication of a problem came when the unit food-service manager came into my office complaining that he was being forced to serve VitaPro almost daily in place of meat on the unit's master menu. He said, "It doesn't matter what seasoning I use or how I fix it, I can't get anybody to eat the stuff, and I don't blame them. I wouldn't eat it either." When VitaPro was served, less than 40 percent of the convicts would even go to the dining room. Convicts generally don't like to be served cold food, but 99 percent of them preferred bologna and cheese sandwiches to VitaPro.

The more VitaPro Huntsville sent to the units, the more it backed up in kitchens and warehouses, and the maintenance staff grew concerned that we would face wastewater-treatment fines because so much of the uneaten product was being flushed down the drains. The convict complaints grew louder, until VitaPro was a hot topic for inmate grievances by the end of 1994. When I called the Huntsville Food Service Office, Janie Thomas said that she understood the problem and regretted that she couldn't help, but her hands were tied by the top administration.

By early 1995, some of the details of the VitaPro deal were beginning to be made public. Yank Barry, the president of VitaPro Foods Inc. of Quebec, Canada, was an ex-convict who had been convicted of extortion and served a six-year sentence under his real name, Gerald Barry Falovitch. He had subsequently been indicted on two counts of bribery, two counts of money launder-ing, and one count of fraud. Although all TDCJ employees are forbidden to associate with ex-convicts, Collins allegedly assisted Yank Barry in obtaining an employee-identification card by giv-ing a phony social security card number, which gave the ex-con-vict access to all TDCJ prison units.

In November of 1994, William McCray, the top financial offi-cer for TDCJ; David McNutt, the number-two financial officer; Caldwell Prejean, assistant director for purchasing and utilities; and Larry Kyle, director of prison industries, had signed a "deci-sion memorandum" to bypass formal bidding processes and pur-chase VitaPro.

In December 1995, McCray received a $9,200 bonus authorized by Andy Collins. McCray was subsequently promoted to a newly created position, director of administrative services, and received a $14,581 annual raise. In October 1995, Kyle received the new job title of deputy director, and a $14,481 annual pay raise, a 24-percent increase that brought his base pay to $75,748. (He was suspended with pay during the VitaPro investigation.) McNutt was also promoted to a newly created deputy-director position, receiving a 31-percent raise amounting to $18,733 annually. Prejean was the only one of the individuals who did not receive a pay raise. All of this money changing hands was in sharp contrast to correctional-staff salaries; they hadn't even received a minimal pay raise since 1991.

Finally, in December of 1995, Andy Collins "retired" under the weight of pressure and scrutiny over VitaPro and other purchasing scandals. It was subsequently discovered that Collins had received at least $20,000 from VitaPro Foods Inc. while still on the payroll of TDCJ. Although a trial shipment of VitaPro had initially been purchased through General Services under the bid process, the specifications were written to ensure that VitaPro got the contract. Only one other company submitted bids. The original bid for $62,000 worth of the food product was then amended four times to purchase more than $33 million worth of VitaPro over five years.

Under the VitaPro contract agreements approved by Collins, TDCJ would now have to pay $33 million over five years in a deal that was not submitted, as required by law, through the competitive-bidding process. After paying VitaPro $3.3 million, TDCJ sued to get the remaining contract thrown out, on grounds that it was not approved through competitive bidding. A federal grand jury in Houston indicted Collins on six counts of conspiracy, which carries up to five years in prison and a $250,000 fine; bribery, which carries a ten-year prison sentence and a $350,000 fine; money laundering, which carries a twenty-year prison sentence and a $5 million fine; and false representation of a social security card, which carries a five-year prison sentence and a $250,000 fine. Collins has since filed for bankruptcy twice and is currently waiting on his court date.

In the end, Collins lost the ability to admit the truth, even to himself. The agency eventually reached a low point when even the media found out that the director of the largest prison system in the free world was doing business in the name of the State of Texas with an ex-convict. It became clear that someone should have questioned Collins long before. We all have to accept part of the blame for the VitaPro scandal, because as a system, we didn't hold Collins accountable earlier in his career, when he was only telling small lies.

The larger problem is that many of the people around Collins are just like him. They single-mindedly pursue their own ambitious agendas. They are self-serving under the guise of sanctimonious rhetoric. Many have skeletons in the closet waiting to be exposed, either against their will or by their own confession at the eleventh hour just before the media puts it all on the front page. It is not so much the system that is flawed, it's the narcissistic, amoral, and arrogant attitude of individuals who seek, achieve, and then abuse the public trust.

It is patently ridiculous to pretend that a politically appointed civilian Board of Criminal Justice is ever going to protect the citizens of Texas from such abuse. These self-important, politically appointed figureheads are forever going to fall prey to the Andy Collinses of this world, because they don't have a clue as to what the prison system is about. They're so willing to allow guys like Collins to perform for them that they fail to see the real people who make up the agency. If Texas is to avoid future VitaPro-like scandals, we have to go back to the fundamentals of the leadership-selection process. It's not typically the yes men, the polite political animals, or the silver-tongued devils who make the best leaders. We need more men of character, people with high moral fiber. As examples, the names of Bobby R. Crawford, Terry Terrell, Dr. George Beto, James Estelle, and my first warden, Grady H. Stricklin, come to mind. They fulfilled their mandate to the people of Texas, and right or wrong, we always knew where they stood.

Sometimes we need to look past the smoke, mirrors, and polished résumés to see the honest, ethical, sincere, hard-working folks who actually have our best interests at heart.

AN OFFER I COULDN'T REFUSE

As the ugly facts of the great VitaPro fiasco and numerous other scandals gradually unfolded, I became less enchanted with the TDCJ administration with each passing day. It had been a long thirty years, and I was tired. I looked around at the young, helpless faces of the officers, most just out of high school, and thought, *This is insane. This is worse than leading lambs to the slaughter; this is just plain suicide. No one has even told them they're sitting on a keg of dynamite with a lit fuse and it's burning shorter every day.*

Just to satisfy my own mind, I dressed a convict up in an officer's uniform and had him walk back and forth through the control picket and the front-compound security gates as a test of security. The convict was using his inmate picture I.D. card as identification to get by the officers. They didn't even notice. Beyond that, they didn't care. This little exercise scared me, but it didn't seem to upset any of the staff. They were just there to get a paycheck; there was no pride or professionalism left in them.

A couple of days later, Ilse Moore, the personnel lieutenant, came into my office with a smile on her face. She said, "I got some good news for you."

I said, "Good, I can use some."

She said, "The Employees Retirement System has just announced an incentive of 2.4 percent for all those who retire before August 31, 1995." I was on the phone to ERS within the next few minutes, and it didn't take long to figure out that the State of Texas would actually pay me more retired than if I continued to work. Who was I to argue with such magnificent logic? The next day, I applied for full retirement, effective August 31, 1995.

In mid-July, before my retirement took effect, I advised the building major, Gary Mohr, that this would be a good time for him to practice his assistant-warden skills, as I was not going to be in the office for the foreseeable future. He hadn't been practicing long when we got an e-mail advising that Major Gary Mohr had been promoted to the position of assistant warden . . . in Colorado City. Gary had been a major for a long time, and nobody deserved a promotion more. I called him into the office to give him the news. When he entered the office I asked, "Do you know where Colorado City is?"

He said, "No—?"

"Well, you might want to find a map and check it out, because you have been promoted to be their next assistant warden," I said.

The look on his face was somewhere between happiness and utter confusion. When I pointed out that Colorado City was in the desert on the other side of Texas, about a tumbleweed roll from New Mexico, he just sat in silence absorbing the information. Although the new job meant an increase in salary for Gary, his wife would have to give up a good job in order to go with him. When the dust settled, he would have a new job title, more responsibility, and less money. Gary was still young enough, loyal enough, and motivated enough to make it work, but he certainly didn't relish the thought of moving his family into deep West Texas.

I called the dog sergeant, Joel Anderson, and asked that he have a horse saddled and tied to the front gate each morning. I spent the last six weeks of my TDCJ career in the saddle and hanging out at the dog pens, following the tracking dogs and generally enjoying the 17,000 acres of the Ramsey Unit's great outdoors. It felt good to be away from the phones, the bean counters and the whining employees.

Many people have asked if I ever regretted retiring. The unqualified answer is, no. The amazing thing to me is the fact that I stayed for thirty years. There is one thing I miss, though: Ever since I was promoted to lieutenant in 1969, on whatever unit I was assigned to, I always had this small button installed underneath my desk. When I pushed that button, a convict porter would bring coffee. I do miss that.

CHAPTER FIFTEEN

REVELATIONS
FOR A NEW MILLENNIUM

"First thing we do, let's kill all the lawyers."
—WILLIAM SHAKESPEARE

I am confident that when future historians write about the decline and fall of the criminal-justice system in Texas, the failure of those who were in a position to do something to prevent it will be listed as the principle cause.

LAWYERS AND JUDGES

If this country is ruined, it will be lawyers, the elitist federal judges, and the legal aristocracy who are responsible. There has been much talk of late about "equal rights." The reality of the situation is that there haven't been equal rights for anyone on this planet since only two people existed on earth, and neither one of them were lawyers. If you want to know what your individual rights are, divide yourself into the total global population. In the interest of fairness, I'll say that there are still a few local, elected judges and underbudgeted district attorneys who work hard to put some measure of parity into the judicial process. Unfortunately, few in our society want to accept responsibility for their actions anymore; they just don't think there ought to be consequences. It is getting harder with each passing day for the average American to really believe in the presumption of innocence.

The federal courts, however, have lost touch with the people.

Once in federal court, your rights are protected by and dependent upon a judge who is politically appointed for life and answerable to no one. Plaintiffs and defendants are at the mercy of a system of justice that is too often dependent on a combination of which side can afford the highest-priced lawyers and the whims of twelve uninformed citizens who are not smart enough to get out of jury duty.

EDUCATING CONVICTS

If we are to ever restore any sanity to the Texas prison system, we must first get rid of the century-old, politically motivated notion that educating criminals somehow equates to rehabilitation. It doesn't, it never has, and it never will. The most blatant fraud being perpetrated on Texas taxpayers today is the publicly stated policy claiming that we rehabilitate convicts through education. I submit that as we go forward into a new century, we ought to at least be honest enough to admit that this "education-cures-all-evils" philosophy has failed.

Our society has provided a free public education, through the twelfth-grade level, for well over a hundred years now. That is money well spent, but I submit that there should be a limit to how much taxpayers are forced to pay for a convict's education. The funding limit should begin with all those violent, predatory multiple offenders who have failed to take advantage of any prior educational opportunities and repeatedly insist on preying upon our citizens. Institutionalization invariably breeds standardization, but humans don't come in a standard model. The variations in IQ, health, family background, energy levels, motivation, and talents are practically infinite.

The TDCJ Windham School District, established in 1969, is one of the largest school districts in Texas, currently serving 150,000 incarcerated inmate "students." With its average annual budget of $59 million, Windham focuses most of its money on getting convicts to perform the basic educational skills they lack. As a partial response to criticism from Judge Justice during the *Ruiz* lawsuit, Texas law now mandates that every inmate who fails to demonstrate educational skills at the sixth-grade level or higher is required to attend school.

The stated mission of the Windham School District is "to provide appropriate educational programming and services to meet the needs of the offender population in TDCJ and reduce recidivism by assisting offenders in becoming responsible, productive members of their communities."

The stated goals of the Windham School District are:

1. To reduce recidivism.
2. To reduce the cost of confinement or imprisonment.
3. To increase the success of former offenders in obtaining and maintaining employment.
4. To provide an incentive to offenders to behave in positive ways during confinement or imprisonment.

According to TDCJ statistics, the typical convict student:

Dropped out of school in the sixth or seventh grade.
Functions at the fifth-grade level.
Has an IQ of 89.
Has an average age of thirty-three.
Has a history of academic failure.
Has a defensive and/or negative attitude.
Has low self-esteem.
Has little or no confidence in self to be productively employed.
Has little or no vision for the future to lead a normal, productive life.
Often has difficulty with family and other relationships.
Has difficulty in controlling anger and other emotions.
Often seeks escape from self or reality by drug/alcohol abuse or other compulsive behavior.

The Sunbelt Institute, a nonprofit, bipartisan research organization, found through its Texas literacy survey that more than 33.3 percent of all adult Texans have less than an eighth-grade education. This statistical study has led some observers to believe that those sending grammar-school-age children to institutions (private, regimented schools) at the first sign of academic failure are on the right course. The reasoning is that if in fact forced learning can be achieved at a young age, then perhaps an individual can avoid a lifetime of criminal activity. There is plenty of room for government intervention, as national recidivism rates for adults are running at 60 percent and nearly 80 percent for juveniles.

Using Windham's own mission statement as a criterion, the district has failed miserably. It has not "met the needs of the eligible offender population," because the need is so overwhelmingly unachievable. They have not "reduced recidivism," nor will they ever, because education in and of itself doesn't change criminal behavior, nor does it have any significant impact on turning a thirty-three-year-old convict into a "responsible, productive member of their community." The bottom line is, in spite of all Windham's scholarly efforts, there currently exists no empirical data verifying any positive impact on recidivism rates in Texas. If the Texas Legislature really based Windham School District's budget on whether the forced education of convicts reduces recidivism, the school district would have to close up shop immediately.

The prison system has gone so far as to provide free job-skills classes to convicts, thus giving convicted felons an advantage over other Texans, who must pay for such training. Texas businesses can even get a tax break for hiring ex-convicts. Furthermore, these programs are largely ineffective. The plain hard fact is that the vast majority of convicts who actually complete vocational courses in which they theoretically learn a job skill rarely utilize that skill once released from prison.

Spending $60 million a year on trying to educate thirty-three-year-old convicts is supreme idiocy, a monumental waste of resources, and a dismal failure. Texas taxpayers are not getting what they are paying for. If we are ever going to break the cycle of crime, we must do it on the front end of the equation. It costs more to send a convict to TDCJ than it does to send a student through the University of Texas, and it's going to get even more expensive as we go forward.

The only answer is to break the ever-escalating cycle of incarceration. Our society will be much safer if we write off the current prison population as the failures they are and use that $60 million annual Windham School District budget to make sure that every child in Texas, from nursery school, through preschool, to high school and beyond has an education and/or a marketable job skill. If we are going to force education on people, then let it begin in the first few years of life, when all the available evidence says that most learning occurs. If we can begin early enough and maintain continuity throughout adolescence, we at least have a fighting chance to prevent the mindset that creates criminals in the first place.

It is not as easy as some would have you believe to get into prison. By the time most convicts arrive for the first time, their parents, their churches, the juvenile programs, probation, and schools have already given up on them. It is an undisputed fact that Texas convicts now have better schools, recreation equipment, and gymnasiums than many public schools. While many in the general taxpaying public work two jobs trying to afford a standard of living that will allow them to buy health insurance or dental insurance or to pay back the loans they had to take out in order to educate their children, the convicts receive all of these things for free. If a convict decides to sue the state of Texas, we, the taxpayers, even pay for his postage so that he can mail his lawsuit directly to Judge Justice. If the benevolent citizens of Texas want to continue to provide educational opportunities for young first offenders who may have "fallen through the cracks," then so be it, but let's at least be honest and quit pretending that we're rehabilitating convicts through education.

WORK

As a criminal-justice professional, I've always been amazed at how fast the clank of prison bars suddenly stirs the emotion of "human rights" in the criminal element. When on the streets, they rob, steal, rape, and kill and generally have no regard for the rights of others, but once incarcerated, they suddenly have fits of righteous indignation. I've had more than one convict try to convince me that having to work in prison is both "unjust and demeaning."

A few years ago, when TDCJ actually had convicts doing some real manual labor in the farm fields around Brazoria County, I found an odd irony. Occasionally, some honest, hardworking, and well-meaning citizen would make a remark about those "poor convicts who have to pick cotton," or some equally distasteful form of agricultural endeavor. I found it odd that the same citizen could drive down the same road and see a guy building a house or working in his garden and not feel the same sympathy for his fellow taxpaying citizens as he had for the convict. I had to ask, *What is it about a convicted felon that makes him seem less capable of work than taxpaying citizens?* I never got a definitive answer to the question, but I think is has something to do with the perception that the convict is somehow being mistreated.

There is no doubt about it, convicts do get insulted when you tell them they have to go to work; I should know—I've insulted thousands of them during my career. I always thought about the thousands and thousands of taxpaying Texans who have to work in order to feed and provide for their families. When the temperature reaches 100 degrees, the taxpaying citizens of Texas don't have the luxury of sitting around, watching TV, and waiting for cooler weather—they have bills and taxes to pay. These are the same working people who have to pay for the food, clothing, shelter, medical care, law libraries, gymnasiums, and recreational equipment for the convicts. I mean really, who is it that's really being mistreated here?

Convicts by nature are takers; they want to be fed, showered, and recreated and to watch a little TV. Then they want to be released, so that they can once again take from you and me and the rest of society. They demand everything and refuse to work for any of it. Historically, the federal courts and the U.S. Department of Justice have been the convicts' best friends.

According to the *Corrections Yearbook,* the average workday for convicts was slightly shorter than 6.9 hours, or 34.5 hours per week, based on a five-day work week. The statistics are misleading, because they only refer to a convict's job schedule—not the actual number of hours worked. The TDCJ will tell you that, with the exception of total invalids, "all inmates have a job assignment," and that is true, but it doesn't mean that all inmates, or even most, participate in work. In fact, when an inmate refuses to work, he can no longer be physically compelled to do so. So for the thousands of inmates serving aggravated sentences, there is no incentive to work and no real penalty for refusing. Convicts receiving disciplinary reports for refusing to work routinely refuse to even attend disciplinary hearings. The once-feared solitary confinement has been diluted to the point that it is now actually a preferred private cell, a vacation-status assignment, where officers (gray slaves) stand ready to ensure that showers are on time, that the food is hot, and that legal materials are available.

Most states have given up even trying to get convicts to work to defray the cost of running the prisons that hold them. Many states, in a trend I find particularly nauseating, pay convicts to work. Texas prisons, in an effort to be as self-sufficient as possible, used to make every effort, including the use of occasional physical force, to ensure that convicts worked in farm fields and in producing such items as mattresses, sheets, uniforms, and shoes. The federal courts and the politicians said these were "outdated, labor-intensive, low-technology processes." They said, "Although inmates learn fundamental work ethics, the resulting job skills lead to few job opportunities for released felons."

The ex-chairman of the Board of Criminal Justice, Allan B. Polunsky, a staunch disciple of rehabilitation, jumped on board the no-work bandwagon when he accused top TDCJ officials of having a "plantation mentality." He threatened mass firings if the TDCJ management didn't see things his way. On November 21, 1997, Polunsky was reported in the *Houston Chronicle* saying, "This situation is going to change and change quickly, or we will find other people who will be willing to do it." At the time, TDCJ was operating forty-four inmate-staffed factories that employed approximately 8,000 felons at prison units across Texas.

So, nowadays, more and more convicts spend their time in an air-conditioned Windham School classroom taking a computer course or learning their ABCs. The rest sit around in segregation cells cursing officers, or too afraid to come out of protection status. General-population convicts spend most of their time on the recreation yards, pumping iron, and playing volleyball or basketball. In the dormitories you can find the building-service hands, the kitchen and laundry workers, and a few others who actually work. Even these convicts don't work because they have to. Most are volunteers, tired of watching endless soap operas or just terminally bored.

The saddest thing is that it's only going to get worse. Texas must somehow figure out a way to get the federal courts out of its business. One option, of course, is to step aside and let the federal courts have the prisons, but then they would build swimming pools, golf courses, and tennis courts, and the judge would still send the bill to the taxpayers of Texas.

Most wardens will tell you that if the Legislature took the

TVs and barbells away from the convicts, it would cause "inmate unrest and add to the unsafe working environment for prison staff." The TDCJ administration likes to think of the TVs and weights as "control tools" that management can use to decrease the tension levels and decrease the potential for life-threatening violence against both inmates and staff. I think that's a bunch of heifer dust that at some point is going to cause some officers to get hurt. Lifting weights only makes convicts stronger—and for what purpose? And TV may serve as an adult pacifier, but there is no evidence that it serves as a deterrent to violence or as a positive influence on an incarcerated population. The satellite-dish programming available to most Texas prisons is not the least bit "rehabilitative" in nature.

I still like the idea of hard physical work for convicts. As long as the public has to work for a living, I think convicts ought to be required to work to support the taxpayers who are forced to support the prison system. Whatever one may say about pre-*Ruiz* Texas prisons, at least the convicts worked. The work was hard, dirty, and steady, but many of those convicts learned to take pride in their work. The convicts who grew up under the old system are older now, and even they regret seeing this new wave of lazy, bloodsucking leeches taking advantage of the system.

The well of sympathy is dry. The public is tired of wasting huge resources on human garbage whose response is not gratitude, but more demands and more excuse-making and more barbaric acts. It is time for these dregs of society to grow up, shut up, quit sniveling, and go to work. Who knows? If we could only get a day's work out of the convicts, perhaps we wouldn't need all those barbells and gymnasiums. If introducing convicts to hot, hard work will create an environment to which they don't want to return, then so much the better. If Texas has to hurt a few of their delicate feelings or downright insult some of them to get it done, then so be it.

REHABILITATION

To *rehabilitate* is defined as, "to restore a good condition: regenerate, or make over in improved form. To reestablish in good repute or accepted respectfully, as a person of character. To restore formally to a former capacity or standing, or to rank." In thirty years of working in prisons, I have never met a "rehabilitated" convict, at least not as defined by *The American College Dictionary*. How does one who was never in a "good condition" to begin with be restored to a good condition? How does one return to "good repute" someone whose reputation was never good? Should we be restoring criminals to "a former capacity" if their only capacity was for crime?

In point of fact, the official standard to qualify as rehabilitated is somewhat low in Texas. I was a warden for the last ten years of my career, and I read my job description very carefully. There was nothing in there that required me to make any convicts repent of their sins, see that they attended church, or make them earn a master's degree. The only thing the citizens of Texas insist upon is that when they leave prison, they don't violate the law. Even if an ex-convict gets shot down in the street on his first day out of prison, we consider him rehabilitated. Why? Because he didn't return to prison. For all practical purposes, he is "rehabilitated." Anyone released from prison who doesn't come back is a success story. If an ex-convict leaves Texas and ends up in some other prison system, Texas still considers him rehabilitated, because he didn't return to a Texas prison. If an ex-convict dies of natural causes while on the way to rob a bank, TDCJ puts a check by his name as another case of successful rehabilitation.

Get used to it, folks—Elvis is dead, there are no UFOs, and there is no effective way to rehabilitate anyone. There is, however, a phenomenon that takes place in most adult criminals, generally sometime between the ages of forty and fifty. Although this phenomenon doesn't meet the pure definition of "rehabilitation," it does qualify an ex-offender as a "statistical success story," because it has prevented some from returning to prison. It is known as old age. When ex-convicts begin to get old and tired, they are inclined to commit fewer crimes. I realize that this revelation is not rocket science, but keeping violent offenders in prison long enough for the old-age phenomenon to take effect is the one workable thing that Texans can do to slow down repeat offenders.

As a society, we may have to admit that keeping violent offenders in prison longer is as close as one can reasonably hope to get to actual rehabilitation. The first priority of any prison system should be keeping the convicts secure and the public safe.

Sensitivity to the rights of criminals should be replaced by a concern for the rights of victims and society. Retaliation rather than rehabilitation should be the focus of the criminal-justice system. Prison should be intended to inflict pain, primarily psychological and social pain, but also the physical pain of work. Let me be absolutely clear on this point. By "pain" I do not mean physical torture, physical abuse, or mental abuse; I mean, rather, the pain of legitimate punishment.

Thanks largely to the federal courts, step by step, serving a sentence in Texas prisons has become an essentially painless process. The paradox is that, particularly with respect to not having to work and the expanded access to leisure-time activities, punishment no longer punishes the criminal. The prison experience ought to be sufficiently painful to the extent that an ex-convict should absolutely hate the thought of returning to prison. It should also serve as an example to deter others from traveling the same path. Admittedly, deterrence does not qualify as meeting that elusive, unattainable, and in my opinion, mythical goal of rehabilitation, but it is probably the best we can do. Almost 50 percent of all released convicts return to Texas prisons within three years. With the 1997–98 Texas-offender recidivism rate running at a steady 48 percent I, like most law-abiding taxpayers, am more concerned with public safety than with convict rehabilitation.

I've heard the argument that "getting caught never enters the mind of a crackhead," so, therefore, tough prisons are not a deterrent to crime. That, friends, is a load of academic horsefeathers. That logic only applies to those first offenders who haven't experienced the joys of prison life. It's true that a crackhead, or any other first offender, might actually enhance his status among his peers by going to the penitentiary, but I've never met any convict who actually enjoyed prison so much that he looked forward to a second prison experience. It is true that there are many fifty- and sixty-year-old convicts who have become institutionalized to the point that they are afraid of life outside prison, but that shouldn't be confused with the notion that they are where they want to be. I have had some of these older convicts tell me that they committed crimes because they couldn't function on the streets, needed medical care, or were in other desperate circumstances. As they get older and less able to care for themselves, some actually prefer prison life. After all, sleeping in a dry, warm prison where someone feeds you three times a day, where there is a TV to watch, and your medical needs are met is preferable to sleeping under a bridge, but I wouldn't call it a calculated career choice.

It is time to admit that rehabilitation not only doesn't work, it doesn't exist. The concept of rehabilitation is a warm, fuzzy, bureaucratic bedtime story for those who can't or won't accept the facts. Since Texas taxpayers pay the bill for the criminal-justice growth industry, I think it only fair that the politicians and bureaucrats who run it make more of an effort to at least be a little more honest with the public. We should call prisons, prisons—not correctional facilities—because they don't correct a damn thing. We should forget about all the phony, politically correct, self-esteem building niceties that have crept into our vocabulary, like calling convicts "clients" or "offenders," and addressing them as "sir."

After thirty years in the criminal-justice arena, my conscience no longer bothers me, because I have come to terms with the reality of the situation. First, I realize that although I have the ability to empathize with criminals, this serves no useful purpose except to make me feel good about myself. Second, I do not want to see convicts go free simply because life has been difficult for them—the safety of my family and community is too important. Third, history has demonstrated, and my own experiences lead me to believe, that the criminal-justice system cannot successfully rehabilitate the adult criminal element in our society.

THE MEDIA

My best advice for criminal-justice employees regarding media relations comes from a quote by John F. Kennedy. When asked how he felt about harsh editorial attacks by a newspaper critic, JFK thought for a moment, smiled, and said, "My daddy told me a long time ago never to pick a fight with a man who buys his ink by the barrel."

If you know nothing else about media, understand its power—convicts and their attorneys certainly do. Some inmate advocates spend all their time promoting TV and print coverage in an attempt to generate sympathy for and political pressure regarding various convict causes. Some may just want to generate publicity to increase sales of craft-shop items or their artifacts on the murder-memorabilia market, or to enhance their status among their peers. The media is usually more than willing to accommodate them.

The one minority that is almost always left out of these media inquiries is the victim. Victims get upset—at least, the live ones do—when convicts receive celebrity treatment from the media. The victims are right to be upset, but the power of the press being what it is, there is very little a correctional administrator can do to prevent media access. Under the Supreme Court ruling *Pell v. Procunier,* the court identified only four reasons to deny access: rehabilitation of offenders; protection of the public; deterrence of crime; and security of the institution. Unless a prison can demonstrate that media access will adversely affect one of these criteria, access must be granted. It is increasingly more and more difficult for prison administrators to prevent the media exposure that allows criminals to enjoy notoriety at the expense of others.

In the past thirty years, I have seen my share of self-serving, arrogant, pseudointellectual drive-by reporters and wannabe journalists stomp into my office spouting their First Amendment rights and trying to lay claim to the moral high ground. Of course, their true religion is not "freedom of the press"; it actually has more to do with capitalism. When you get right down to where the rubber meets the road, those journalists are just selling newspapers or TV shows. They always come in with an attitude of outrage and moral indignation—but never lose sight of the fact that they are there because of money. And make no mistake, they will do whatever is necessary to get it.

A year-end survey by the Pew Research Center on People and Press found that half of the top ten stories Americans said they followed "very closely" concerned either a fatal accident involving multiple deaths, murder, multiple murder, or mass murder. This is a fairly strong indication that the longtime axiom of the local news editor really is "If it bleeds, it leads." Despite high-toned claims to the contrary, the media can't overcome its penchant for sensationalism. Sensationalism equals sales; sales equal money; and therein lies the problem.

About 90 percent of everything wrong with the media has to do with money. Reporters are basically crusaders who believe if everyone knew everything, the world would be a better place, but then the business people step in—the accounting department, the owners, and the stockholders. It's no longer about "free speech," it's about "plausible deniability" and money. When it comes down to a battle between maintaining journalistic integrity, honor, and credibility or receiving a paycheck, guess who wins? This money-before-integrity phenomenon leads to media hypocrisy of a magnitude that staggers the imagination.

CONVICTS AND RELIGION

Based on the number of convicts who claim to find Jesus in prison, I'm almost tempted to suggest that more folks look for him there. Unfortunately, these jailhouse conversions are rarely sincere or longlasting.

It is true that organized religion is responsible for a moral code. In our never-ending search for understanding of the forces that control human behavior, we must not ignore religion, for there is no denying that belief in, and therefore fear of, a Supreme Being is a strong motivating force. In a perfect world, a wise, omnipotent being would watch over us all and our lives would be less infringed upon by those two familiar twins, fear and hate. Unfortunately, within the prison environment, competing religious dogmas create at least as much dissension as unity. The 300-plus versions of Christianity, Islam, Catholicism, Buddhism, Moorish Science Temple, Hinduism, Judaism, various Indian tribes, a few assorted Satanists, et cetera, are all constantly competing for space and followers.

The prison environment is corrupting, especially to those professing to be of strong religious persuasion. Over the past thirty years, I've seen two TDCJ priests and several lay ministers terminated for smuggling various items to convicts. I've lost count of the number of "religious volunteers" who have been banned from the prisons for smuggling or being romantically involved with convicts.

To many, dare I say most, convicts, religion is just another game that has become a part of everyday prison life. With the exception of special guest appearances by evangelical ministers or celebrities, the average attendance at church services runs below 5 percent.

Convicts will turn anything into a game if they can. They make decks of cards out of the prayer cards passed out by the chaplains. They claim to be Indians so that they can carry a medicine pouch, grow longer hair, and go to the sweat lodge. They claim to be Islamic in order to get a half-day off for prayers on Fridays. The Catholics all want a crucifix or rosary beads, preferably made from some precious metal and encrusted with diamonds. The Jehovah's Witnesses all want a day of rest on Saturdays. Convicts who haven't ever been inside a synagogue claim to be Jewish in order to get kosher food.

Other convicts claim to be members of the Aryan Nation's "Church" in order to be allowed to meet with their fellow white supremacists. There are those claiming to believe in animism, a term meaning belief in spirits of nature or other ancient tribal religions. There is even a Church of the Divine Filet Mignon, whose followers only believe in eating steaks as often as possible. The list goes on and on, but suffice to say, it is no small undertaking to accommodate all of these diverse groups given security concerns and the limited meeting places.

The federal courts have been most accommodating to the inmate population. With respect to religion, the First Amendment to the U.S. Constitution says: "Congress shall pass no law respecting an establishment of religion, or prohibiting the free exercise thereof." The federal courts have basically interpreted this to mean that if a convict decides he wants to worship a goat, TDCJ has to provide a place for him to do it. Under the federal religious reformation act, prisons must allow convicts to worship at whatever "religious" altar they choose. TDCJ must allow this even if a convict professes to be a Satanist one week, a Catholic the next, and a Muslim the week after that.

Laymen religious volunteers, of all persuasions and levels of motivation, are allowed into the units to witness to the spiritually deprived. Most of these volunteers don't have a clue as to the danger they are placing themselves or TDCJ staff in just by being there. Some of these benevolent volunteers have the best of intentions; some don't. Many of these volunteers are female, which provides an additional attendance incentive for convicts who normally don't participate in such programs. The one thing all of them grossly underestimate is convicts' ability to connive and manipulate and use their fellow human beings.

What these noble, compassionate volunteers never seem to grasp is that the real physical power lies in the hands of their convict congregation, and if the convicts ever choose to turn volunteers into victims, they can do so in a heartbeat. For every convict who is temporarily "redeemed" through these programs, there are thirty more who will cut your throat and watch you bleed to death. Having witnessed more of these gatherings than I care to remember, I can tell you, the assemblage more closely resembles some kind of weird preternatural courtship than a worship service. I am loathe to predict that in the coming years, serious injury and death will occur as a direct result of these volunteer programs. With each passing day, the TDCJ gets closer and closer to its own Armageddon.

SAVING MONEY AND IMPROVING SECURITY

The single greatest cost-saving measure the TDCJ can make going in the new millennium is in the area of perimeter security. It costs $75,000 to $100,000 to build a perimeter picket tower. It costs between $100,000 to $125,000, minimum, to place an officer, plus relief staff, in a perimeter tower during three shifts, 365 days per year. Many TDC units, especially the older ones, have as many as five or six towers on their perimeter fences.

Texas should join California, Indiana, and Massachusetts in building electric fences around all TDCJ units. An electric fence can be built for the cost of manning one picket tower. It carries 4,000 volts and 500 amperes, enough to electrocute anyone instantly. The electric fence should be located in a no-man's land between two non-electrified, twelve-foot fences. Warning signs posted in English and Spanish and bearing the international skull-and-crossbones warning should be posted on both sides of the non-electrified fences.

TDCJ would still have to man at least two picket towers per

unit in order to guard gates and sally-port exits, but the savings derived from reducing the number of staff required to man perimeter towers would amount to $40 to $60 million over a biennial budget period. This savings alone would allow TDCJ-ID to raise the salaries of its correctional officers up to the national average.

The installation of an electric-fence system would also prevent desperate attempts such as the Friday, November 27, 1998, death-row escape. If electric fences had been in place, death-row convict Martin Gurule would not have been able to successfully climb two fences under the not-so-watchful eye of a picket officer. There were six other death-row convicts who almost reached the same fence Gurule went over. Although the escapee's body was eventually found in Harmon Creek, only 2.8 miles from the Ellis Unit, the ensuing search for him lasted for seven days. These convict chases can cost hundreds of thousands of tax dollars per day. For the cost of one extended manhunt, electric fences can prevent future fiascos of this kind.

On Saturday, July 21, 1934, three prisoners under sentence of death escaped from the Huntsville, Walls Unit death-row cellblock. The three men, Raymond Hamilton, Joe "Cowboy" Palmer, and Blackie Thompson, with the aid of a pistol smuggled in by an officer, successfully escaped from the cellblock and made their way to the outer wall. Involved with them were four others serving life terms, Charlie Frazier, Whitey Walker, Roy Johnson, and Hub Standley. During the shootout, one prison officer was shot to death when he refused to open a gate. Picket Officer Roberts shot Whitey Walker to death as he tried to follow the other escapees over a ladder that had been placed against the outer wall. Charlie Frazier and Hub Standley were both severely wounded by officer gunfire.

Could it happen again? Could today's TDCJ officers smuggle guns in to death-row convicts? Of course it can happen again, and yes, officers could very easily smuggle guns to convicts. In fact, the odds are that as higher numbers of more desperate convicts are sent to death row and other "maximum security" units, it *will* happen again. Prisons are designed to keep people on the inside, not to keep people out. Prisons are notoriously easy to enter. Two or three determined guys with guns could easily enter, and take over a prison or facilitate the escape of large numbers of Texas convicts, should they choose to do so. An electric fence is one economical way to lessen the chances of a successful escape and to control a unit's perimeter from both inside and out.

Violence

The TDCJ has so far been able to outbuild the overcrowding monster that hovers just over the horizon. The system is reaching the breaking point in terms of available tax dollars versus the constant need for the construction of prisons. Texas inmates are assaulting guards at an alarming rate, using increasingly violent methods from homemade shanks to throwing hot liquids. A continuation of the war on drugs is going to more than double the size of TDCJ over the next decade. Texas cannot build high-security prisons fast enough to meet the demand, and lower security prisons will not serve to protect the public.

During the mid- to late 1980s, when the TDCJ was last in a serious overcrowding mode, the convicts killed each other in record numbers. Since that time, the system has gotten bigger and has lost much of its experienced staff and replaced them with young employees right out of high school. In addition, more than half of the unit-warden and security-administration positions are held by people who have never worn a correctional officer's uniform. The average rank-and-file officer is under twenty-six years of age and has been with TDCJ less than five years, and over a third of the new officers are female. The really cruel part is, the TDCJ management allows these inexperienced, helpless employees, who really have no frame of reference to draw upon, to suffer under a delusion that they're actually in control.

In 1994 convicts assaulted 311 prison guards and other employees. By 1996 the number of attacks had tripled to 918. The Connally Unit, Beeville, Texas, reported the most assaults—340— against staff between 1995 and June 1997. According to the *Corrections Yearbook,* in the 1997–98 period, 1,442 TDCJ staff members were assaulted by inmates system-wide. There is obviously little deterrent to staff assault.

In 1992 a Texas inmate typically served only 17 percent of his or her sentence. By 1996 they about 36 percent was served.

Increased prison time is due to a 1993 law that requires violent offenders to serve half of their sentence before becoming eligible for parole. As judges sentence more and more young, violent convicts to serve a minimum of half of their sentence day-for-day, the level of violence both among inmates and directed toward employees will escalate. Violent felons don't quit being violent just because they are incarcerated; to the contrary, prison just gives them one more reason to be violent.

In 1997–98, according to the *Corrections Yearbook*, 41,860 inmates were doing sentences of twenty years to life—that's 32 percent of the total population. As the aggravated-offender percentage rises to 50 percent and higher, as it will within the next five years, assaults on employees will most assuredly rise with it. The fact is, most new convicts arrive at TDCJ with no chance of getting out in less than thirty to forty years. They feel they have little to lose. The new convicts coming to prison today are younger, and more violent than in the past, and they don't have any respect for anybody. The larger problem is that violent prisons are not unique to Texas—it's a nationwide problem.

In 1997–98, TDCJ lost 6,134 employees who resigned, were fired for cause, or retired. The employee-turnover rate had risen to a steady 20-percent rate. At the end of 1999, the TDCJ was understaffed by 2,700 employees. Several hundred frustrated, underpaid, and overworked officers marched up the steps of the Austin statehouse to demand a pay raise. The governor told them they were too late and that they would have to wait another two years before their request could be considered. This, at a time when the department has been losing experienced employees out the back door faster than they can hire green replacements through the front. The agency is losing an average of 400 officers per month. That means TDCJ has to hire and train at least that many just to break even. And the personnel department advises that it takes six employment applications just to fill one position.

Though many are too proud to admit it, most TDCJ-ID officers are scared. In point of fact, they would be fools not to be afraid. It's going to get worse before it gets better. In the not-so-distant past, being a correctional officer was statistically one of the safer forms of law-enforcement employment. Unfortunately, ever since the federal courts tilted the prison comfort level to favor the incarcerated, that's not true anymore. For the first time in over a half-century, Texas prisons are more dangerous for employees than for convicts.

On April 16, 1996, a forty-five-year-old female officer at the Telford Unit, near New Boston, Texas, was pulled into a restroom by two convicts and raped. The woman was the only officer overseeing the kitchen area at 4:00 A.M. when inmate Robert Earl Horton told her he had found a $20 bill in a nearby restroom. When the guard went to investigate, Horton slammed the door and overpowered her, striking her numerous times. A second inmate, Dekenya Nelson, entered the restroom a short time later. Both convicts raped the guard, but she was fortunate enough to have survived the attack. Horton, serving a seventy-seven-year sentence for attempted capital murder, had already had two years added to his sentence for assaulting another guard in 1986.

On December 13, 1998, a young female officer at the Robertson Unit, near Abilene, Texas, was pulled into a cell and raped repeatedly at knifepoint. The female officer was counting convicts at 2:40 A.M. on a Sunday morning when convicted rapist Jesse Trevino Cortez grabbed her and dragged her into his cell, holding an eight-inch piece of sharpened metal to her throat. It is not known whether the cell lock malfunctioned or if the convict manipulated the cell-door lock to get it open.

Inmate Cortez and his cellmate, Shane Arnold Hooks, were alone with the young officer for approximately two and a half hours while Warden Tim Morgan, Assistant Wardens Robert Eason and James Mayfield, and a chaplain stood just outside the cell door and "negotiated" for her release. Cortez, already serving two life terms for aggravated sexual assault and aggravated robbery in Lubbock County, covered the small window of his cell with a towel to keep negotiators from seeing what was going on inside. Finally, the convict tired of his young captive, released the officer, and gave up his weapon. At least she was alive.

Cortez was already serving two life terms, and the most the law allowed in this case was an additional 99-year sentence. I wonder if the judge thinks his new 99-year term will keep Cortez from sexually assaulting other prison guards?

On Friday, December 17, 1999, Officer Danny Nagle, thirty-seven, was found in a pool of blood after being stabbed repeatedly with a sharp metal rod. Nagle had been a prison guard since June 1, 1996, and left a wife and three small children, one of whom was a newborn. Nagle was supervising inmates in a minimum-security housing area sometime after 3:15 P.M. when he was stabbed. Nagle's body was found at approximately 3:45 P.M. lying in the fetal position near an entrance to a multipurpose room within a minimum-security housing area. There were no employee witnesses; however, there were several convicts in a recreation area across the hall from where the officer was found. This employee homicide occurred at the maximum-security McConnell Unit located in Beeville, Texas.

Danny Nagle was the first TDCJ officer killed at the hands of a convict in fourteen years. The level of violence toward officers had been gradually building, as evidenced by daily assaults upon staff, but not since convict Raymond Mata stabbed TDCJ officer Minnie R. Houston to death at the Ellis I Unit on June 3, 1985, had another employee been murdered. At the time of his death, officer Nagle was the president of the Beeville chapter of the American Federation of State, County and Municipal Employees, which represents corrections officers. In an interview with the *Dallas Morning News* a month before his death, Nagle said, "The reason we're underpaid is people don't understand what's going on," he said. "You have police officers on the street to arrest these people—they have the most dangerous jobs in the world, supposedly. But once they arrest them and they go through the system, they're done with them. We, on the other hand, put up with them for the rest of their lives." His statement was prophetic. Two weeks prior to his death, Nagle made an even more prophetic statement when speaking at an employee rally in Austin: "Someone will have to be killed before TDCJ does anything about the shortage of staff in Texas prisons."

Unfortunately, but inevitably, I see the death of Danny Nagle as the beginning of another violent trend in the TDCJ. There will be a difference this time, however. Instead of violent gang members killing each other, this time the convicts are going to go after the staff. As the system gradually gets more overcrowded and cellblocks become more valuable, TDCJ will be forced into once again bastardizing the court-approved classification plan. As a higher and higher premium is placed on the need for individual cells in order to meet the ever-rising tide of close-custody convicts, the agency will do the only thing it can do. The TDCJ will use the older, less secure facilities to house hardcore, close-custody and medium-custody convicts. Placing these hardcore convicts in these overcrowded and less secure facilities will begin an era more dangerous than any TDCJ has yet had to face. When you take everything away from a convict, even if he deserves it, then he has nothing left to lose. He becomes extremely dangerous. When you place many of these dangerous convicts in facilities that are not equipped with experienced staff or the physical barriers to contain them, you have written a prescription for disaster. Add to that an employee turnover currently reaching an all-time high, with more leaving every day, and the situation becomes even more critical. It serves no useful purpose to hire officers in record numbers if they're going out the back door faster than you can send them to units. Even if TDCJ could retain staff, the sheer number of hardcore convicts serving longer terms is going to be overwhelming.

WAKE-UP CALL

On April 25, 2000, at the Preston E. Smith Unit in the small West Texas town of Lamesa, a riot began in the unit mess hall when a black convict fondled himself in front of a female correctional officer. A Hispanic convict took exception to what the black convict was doing, and a fight ensued. Although staff removed the two fighters from the mess hall, news of the dispute spread to other areas of the medium-security prison, and a full-blown riot erupted twenty minutes later. For the next five hours, Hell was in session at the Smith Unit.

The rioters went after correctional officers stationed in a cellblock picket. Within the first few minutes, the officers ran out of CS gas and called for additional help. Help would be slow in coming. Meanwhile, the rioting convicts broke into utility and equipment closets to grab weapons and set fires. An inner security fence was breached when two hundred or so rioters overran it in order to gain access to the inside-yard-squad tool building. Once inside the tool building, the convicts obtained pickaxes, field hoes, and shovels, and they made several weapons from mops and brooms. The inmate dining room and food-preparation area were gutted by fire, and substantial property damage was sustained in numerous other areas of the unit; inmate housing, the inside-yard building, the property and supply area, turn-out areas, and recreation yards. The convicts used pickaxes, hoes, shovels, broken broomsticks, glass shards, and metal pieces from the fence to attack one other. Several convicts suffered severe cuts when they climbed perimeter fences attempting to escape and got tangled in razor wire.

Finally, five hours after it began, after more than 300 correctional officers responded to the call for assistance, the rioters were brought under control. One inmate, twenty-year-old Fernando Trejo, was dead, and thirty-one additional inmates were hospitalized; four were placed in intensive care. Miraculously, only three officers were injured during the riot. One was hit over the head with a shovel, another was burned when a gas grenade exploded in his hand, and the last officer was hit in the arm by an inmate wielding a hoe. Several other officers were hit by flying projectiles, but none sustained serious injuries as a result. The official spokesman for the TDCJ, Larry Fitzgerald, said, "It got very bad. I talked to some of the officers, and they were scared. The inmates were on a rampage."

The Smith Unit is a medium-security unit. It was thirty officers short of full staff when the riot occurred. As the year 2000 began, some of the larger, maximum-security units were a hundred or more officers understaffed. According to TDCJ statistics, between 1988 and 1999 there were 53 inmate-on-inmate homicides, with the highest in any one year being ten in 1997. During the same time frame, inmate-on-staff assaults went from a low of 127 in 1989 to a high of 2,044 in 1999. In 2000, there were at least six major violent events; twice that year officers were taken hostage. In December, an officer was stabbed to death and a major riot followed. How many warnings do the higher-ups need? How many staff members and convicts have to die? How much clearer can it be that the mother of all prison riots is on its way?

Texas has the potential for prison riots that will make Attica, New York, and New Mexico pale by comparison. Unfortunately, it is probably already too late to stop the violence. TDCJ is grossly understaffed by inexperienced, underpaid people, and is also mismanaged. I use the word mismanaged, although I have the utmost respect for TDCJ Executive Director Wayne Scott and Institutional Director Gary Johnson. They both came up through the security ranks, and I am sure they would do all that they could to avoid an outbreak of violence, if it were within their power to do so. They, like James Estelle, are at the mercy of the Legislative budget board. Unfortunately, the Board of Corrections and the Legislature, which relies on their guidance, are out of touch with the state of corrections in Texas. These political appointees are not correctional professionals, and they always make assumptions about correctional work that are not true. The first assumption they make is that working in a prison is easy. They believe this because most of them have never been in a prison and don't know any better. The second assumption they make is that, since it is easy, we can hire anybody to do this job. This idiotic idea stems from the fallacy that all prison guards do is stand around and watch convicts. Wrong, wrong, wrong! Nothing could be further from the truth.

BEFORE THE STORM

Decades from now, I'm afraid we're going to refer to this period as the time before the storm. One would hope our elected representatives could see the storm clouds forming, but in our hearts, we all know it's not in the nature of such men to be proactive. They always have to wait until the rain, or blood in this case, is filling up their boots before they see a need to act. The real truth is that Texas prisons and the people who work in them just aren't high enough on the priority list to matter.

It should be a prerequisite for all criminal-justice board members and state politicians who want to pretend to have any criminal-justice credibility to first work in a prison. They need to put on correctional uniforms and work on a close-custody cellblock for a while. They need to understand how the rising percentage of close-custody convicts is creating an ever-more-hazardous environment for our correctional staff. Any politician who has a vote on Texas prison issues should get out of his or her ivy-covered Austin office and meet some convicts up close and personal. There is nothing like working in a war zone, a close-custody cellblock at chow time, to help one truly appreciate the challenge of being a Texas correctional officer working in a maximum-security prison. Then, having obtained enlightenment from the experience, perhaps a politician could more easily understand how ridiculous it is for a nine-member civilian board with no correctional expertise to write and enforce policy for rank-and-file correctional staff. These politicians, who claim to care about their constituencies, need to feel the fear and smell the violence that is surely coming, if it's not already too late.

Worst of all, TDCJ is still suffering under a longstanding federal-court order that critically undermines security staff's ability to even protect itself. I defy any politician to effectively restrain a violent convict without violating the court-mandated "use of force plan." Must we continue to allow our officers to be beaten, stabbed, killed, and raped before we take action?

I am loathe to say that in the absence of massive intervention, there are going to be some prison-unit takeovers, more hostage situations, rapes, and employee homicides. As the violence against staff becomes more prevalent, hiring competent officers at any price is going to be difficult, if not impossible. When the violence comes, it won't really be a surprise. The few older hands who are still working know it's coming; so do the older convicts.

On January 14, 2000, TDCJ Director of Training Charles Godwin wrote an editorial in the *Corpus Christi Caller-Times* calling for the resignations of Wayne Scott, his executive administration, and the Texas Board of Criminal Justice. Godwin broke ranks with the administration and wrote a public letter directly to Governor George Bush claiming that the assault and subsequent death of Officer Daniel Nagle was not an isolated incident. Bush didn't respond, as he was busy in New Hampshire running for president of the United States. In his letter, Godwin outlined thirty-two staff assaults that occurred after November 1998 that could have resulted in employee deaths. One of the incidents involved an assault in which an officer was stabbed with a twenty-six-inch steel rod and another in which a prisoner tried to throw an officer off of a second-tier cellblock run onto a concrete floor.

The newly appointed Criminal Justice Board chairman, Alfred "Mac" Stringfellow of San Antonio, was quick to respond.

He wrote a public letter to Godwin saying that his serious accusations required investigation, but he also warned that if Godwin's accusations are wrong, "they are defamatory, irresponsible and at a minimum inconsistent with your current position as director of training." Godwin was subsequently transferred from his job as director of training into a less high-profile position.

Godwin was not the Messiah; he was only a director of training with a well-earned reputation as a whistleblower; as such, he may not have been the right messenger to attempt to speak on behalf of masses of correctional officers. Godwin was, however, right about the serious nature of the increasing number of assaults on correctional staff. He wasn't really telling TDCJ Executive Director Wayne Scott anything he didn't already know. The larger problem is, how do you compel politically appointed civilian board members to put their butts on the line and motivate them into doing something about the problem? How do you get them to go to their boss, the governor, and ask for a 25-percent pay raise for all correctional staff and a career ladder to help retain experience?

The new board chairman, Alfred Stringfellow, is the owner and president of Stringfellow Investments, an oil, gas, real estate, and ranching investment firm. In addition to being TDCJ Board chairman, Stringfellow is also listed a member of the Board of the Cancer Therapy and Research Center and the Board of Trustees of Southwestern University, and is past director of the Santa Rosa Children's Hospital Foundation. I've never met Mr. Stringfellow, but they say he's a nice guy. I don't doubt for a moment that he is. Of course, like the board chairman before him and the other eight board members, he has absolutely no experience or qualified expertise in running a 150,000-man maximum-security prison.

BLOOD ON OUR HANDS

When the blame game starts, as it always does, the failure to pay and retain experienced security staff will be near the top of the list of things we should have done. People will bemoan the fact that we didn't do more to professionalize the overall security-team response capability. They will point out that somewhere along the line, the powers that be forgot that in a prison, security is always the number-one priority. Some other less well-known TDCJ practices will also be faulted, like the agency's failure to promote unit wardens from within security ranks and the rampant promotion of politicians and pencil-pushing bean counters into security-administration positions. Those who have never worn a security uniform have no business in a position of unit administration.

When, not if, it comes time to place blame, let's not forget past governors with blood on their hands, beginning with Mark White. As attorney general, he signed the ridiculously restrictive administrative-segregation plan. As governors, White, Bill Clements, and Ann Richards stood by and watched a group of California lawyers redesign and effectively castrate what once had been the best and safest prison system in the country. Last but not least, let's not forget Judge William Wayne Justice, whose judicial robe was first drenched in blood during the 1984–85 gang wars, when fifty-two convicts died as a direct result of his outlawing the building tenders. His legacy continues, as with each passing day more and more TDCJ officers are assaulted, raped, killed, and taken hostage. Even with the security of Texas hanging in the balance, the judge's sympathies are still with the predators in our society.

Of course, the public will have to share some of the blame. After all, we continue to elect these uninformed political representatives, who in turn appoint their even more uninformed political cronies to positions on the Texas Board of Criminal Justice. It is certain, in any case, that ignorance allied with power is the most savage enemy justice can have. My gut feeling is that history will not be kind to these mindless bureaucrats who sit on the sidelines while a real life-and-death struggle is being played out. You see, in the final analysis there are only two kinds of people in Texas prisons: the gray and the white. Just in case there's any doubt left in anyone's mind, the guys in gray, with the state of Texas patch on their arm, are the good guys. The ones in white are the convicted felons. Sometimes that simple fact tends to get lost in all the rhetoric.

On June 7, 2000, Irene Fonseca, thirty-five, a female officer just trying to do her job at the Connally Unit, was beaten unconscious after finding contraband in a convict's cell. She was flown to University Hospital in San Antonio with multiple facial fractures, swelling around her brain, and most of her teeth missing. Doctors hoped to prevent permanent brain damage. As we wait for the next correctional officer to fall, I have to wonder which unit, which officer, will be next, and really, just how important is the security of Texas prisons? The answer to that question will say a lot about who we are as a state and as a society.

Sleep well, my fellow Texans.

The original manuscript for this work was completed during the late summer of 2000. Since that time, conditions within the Texas Department of Criminal Justice have continued to deteriorate.

In late June of 2000, an extremely embarrassing event for the agency occurred when French Robertson Unit Senior Warden Doyle McElvaney was nabbed during a Saturday-night undercover prostitution sting in Abilene, Texas. Known for his attention to detail, McElvaney had a reputation as a consummate professional who held his employees to the highest standards. After being charged with soliciting prostitution, he resigned/retired from service.

On Monday, July 3, 2000, convict Ricky Newman, serving a life sentence, attempted to sexually assault a twenty-eight-year-old correctional officer, Shelly Culp, at the Huntsville (Walls) Unit. He threatened Culp with a single-edged razorblade and forced her into a utility closet. Although injured, the officer survived the attack, largely due to assistance from another convict, who intervened when he heard Culp struggling with inmate Newman.

On Monday, August 14, 2000, at the French Robertson Unit, convict Michael Wayne Roy, forty-five, serving a life sentence for aggravated rape, sexually assaulted a female officer in the office area of the prison gymnasium. Although severely beaten, raped, and traumatized, the officer survived the attack. Shortly after the attack, the inmate committed suicide by hanging himself in the room where the assault occurred.

On December 13, 2000, the single largest mass escape in modern-day Texas prison history occurred at the maximum-security Connally Unit, near Kenedy, Texas. Seven convicts, all serving long sentences for violent offenses, successfully escaped in one of the prison unit's own vehicles. The meticulously planned and flawlessly executed mass escape demonstrated clearly that security is not being taken seriously in Texas prison units.

The largest multi-state manhunt in Texas history followed after the seven escapees were implicated in the brutal killing of Dallas Police officer Aubrey Hawkins during the robbery of an Oshman's Sporting Goods store. As the reward money for the seven escapees reached $500,000 and the mother of the slain officer called for those responsible to be held accountable, even the state's usually stonewalling Legislature had to conduct hearings on the status of Texas prisons.

Six of the seven escapees were finally captured in Colorado after forty days on the run. One committed suicide rather than surrender. All seven could face the death penalty.

On January 1, 2001, convict Dekenya Nelson, twenty-five, assigned to the Smith Unit in Lamesa, Texas, was diagnosed with possible internal bleeding after swallowing a can opener. Nelson was serving a 140-year sentence for sexual assault, burglary, and car theft, including the rape of a female civilian prison employee in 1996.

A Smith Unit physician ordered Nelson to be transferred for further treatment to the University Medical Center in Lubbock, Texas. Two armed officers, one male, one female,were assigned to provide security for the transport. Shortly after arrival, Nelson produced what appeared to be a handgun. In point of fact it was a handgun facsimile fashioned from a hairbrush, a deodorant bottle, soap, and pages from a Bible. It was dyed black and had all the appearance of a real gun. Nelson used the fake gun to bluff the two armed officers out of the room and took two of his nurses hostage. He removed his restraints with his own hidden handcuff key, placed them on his hostages, and then proceeded to sexually assault the two nurses. After holding the two nurses for about ninety minutes, Nelson surrendered.

The hospital subsequently gave the required ninety-day notice and canceled its $72 million annual contract with the TDCJ, declining to treat any more inmates at the facility. A spokesman for the hospital said, "The risk is too high. We think it's in the best interest of the hospital."

Two months into its session, the 2001 Texas Legislature has not found it necessary to act. The political platitudes continue. None of the unenlightened Texas politicians convened in Austin have so far found it necessary to adequately address the pitifully low pay of correctional staff, currently thirty-eighth in the nation, or the security crisis that grows more serious with each passing day.

GLENN'S LAW

RULES AND OBSERVATIONS
FOR THE ENHANCEMENT OF PRISON-EMPLOYEE SURVIVAL

1. Do not assume that the Texas Department of Criminal Justice-ID uniform is bulletproof, knife-proof, or bomb-proof. The uniform does not allow officers to stop bullets, leap tall buildings, bend steel bars, or stop speeding cars or trains.

2. On those occasions when you have the right to remain silent, shut the f—up. Blessed are those who have nothing to say and cannot be persuaded to say it.

3. There is law, and there is justice. One doesn't necessarily have anything to do with the other. Seek to obey the law—let justice take care of itself.

4. Keep both feet in the stirrups. For as any field officer knows, without a horse, a man is afoot.

5. Forget about romance in the workplace. Good women, like good parking places, are all gone.

6. Be cautious of those who are loud. It is true that intelligence is like a river: The deeper it is, the less noise it makes.

7. Listen to gossip, but don't repeat it. We live in a world where rumor becomes fact and innuendo is a headline.

8. Payday is always sweeter when you know you have earned it.

9. You can believe in faith, hope, and charity, but in the prison

environment, none of these are possible without first achieving and then maintaining good security.

10. Always maintain a reverent and respectful appreciation for the tenacity of ignorance.

11. When a crime is committed in Hell, don't expect angels to come forward as witnesses.

12. Females in general love outlaws like little girls love a stray dog. Given the opportunity, they will generally take one home just as quickly.

13. You're never as tired as you think you are, especially when someone is threatening your life.

14. Beware of emancipated women; they don't know how to lose.

15. Your own self-preservation and that of your fellow employees is your first priority.

16. Don't put your faith in lawyers or politicians. The only thing worse is a child-molesting dope peddler.

17. Don't expect the prison business to ever make sense. It's a crapshoot played with loaded dice.

18. When your job becomes the last thing you think of before you go to sleep and the first thing you think of when you wake up, you're working too hard.

19. Beware the convict who has an exceptionally bad institutional record. Convicts become dangerous when they start believing their own rap sheets.

20. Don't count on a good reputation to save you in delicate circumstances. The media and the public feed on our short-comings, not our virtues.

21. The absence of honor among criminals is real. There is no code of honor in prison. Perhaps thirty years ago a few of the old-timers had a code. It no longer exists. Greed is the name of the game. Bad things can and will come from any direction, without warning.

22. Beware the person who tells you he is not scared, for he is either a liar or a fool.

23. Prison-employment success defined: If you have survived to live another day above ground, you have achieved success.

24. Never give convicts choices you don't want them to take.

25. If you are really hungry, even lousy food is delicious, and if you have to, you can eat a meal in ten minutes or less.

26. It's not courage that makes ordinary people perform extraordinary deeds. It's the shame of letting down people who are counting on you.

27. Having someone you trust watching your back makes all things seem possible.

CONVICT SLANG GLOSSARY

AB—Aryan Brotherhood. A white-supremacist prison gang.

AC—Aryan Circle. A white-supremacist prison gang.

ace—best friend or close friend.

ace boon coon—best friend.

ad-seg—administrative segregation. A non-punitive status in a controlled cellblock environment away from the general population. Ad-seg is usually reserved for gang members, protection-status inmates, or extremely violent inmates.

Aggie—a long-handled hoe, used in agricultural fieldwork.

amp joint—a marijuana joint laced with some other form of drug.

amping—accelerated heartbeat.

attitude adjustment—the need for physical intervention, as in, "A good ass-kicking would sure adjust his attitude."

B.G.—Baby Gangster. A young gang member, new to the group; also implies that he has yet to commit any serious crimes.

babydoll—**Texas Syndicate** slang for Mexican Mafia members.

bag—a bag of coffee.

banging—to fight, as in "gang banging," or to have sex.

basing—short for freebasing (smoking cocaine through a pipe).

BGF—the Black Gorilla Family, an African-American prison gang.

big bitch—convicted under a Habitual Criminal statute, which carries a mandatory life sentence. See also **little bitch.**

big jab—lethal injection, or "the stainless steel ride," "the needle," or "gonna get his doctorate in applied chemistry."

345

bitch up—to cry, give in, or act like a whining woman.

blanket party—when a victim has a blanket thrown over him, so he or she can't identify an attacker.

blind—an area where officers cannot see, as in "Let's go to the blind."

blood in–blood out—Some prison gangs require that new members "shed blood" in order to be accepted. Therefore, prospective members know that they must commit an assault (possibly murder) to get into a gang. More importantly, a prospective gang member learns that he will be assaulted (or possibly murdered) if he tries to get out of the gang. Most gangs don't have a retirement plan.

blue slip—refers to a form required to make a "special purchase," i.e., television sets, radios, leather, or other craft supplies.

boned out—got scared, chickened out.

boneroo—a convict's best set of clothes, usually saved for visiting day.

boneyard—the contact or family-visitation area.

bong—a cylindrical pipe used to smoke marijuana.

boo-coo (or **beaucoup**)—a lot of one thing, i.e. "We're having a boo-coo spread."

boof—contraband concealed in the rectum.

books—an inmate's trust fund account, i.e., "How much money do you have on the books?"

boost—to shoplift or steal.

boss—an inmate term for officers or other TDCJ employees. Also "sorry son of a bitch" spelled backwards.

boy—a street name for heroin.

bread—money, or some other item of value.

breakdown—a shotgun that one has to "break" open in the middle to load.

brew—homemade alcohol, "rasinjack" "pruno," "hooch," "chock."

brogans—high-top work boots. Also referred to as "bros."

brownie queen—a male homosexual who takes the female role.

buck—to refuse to perform a required activity, usually work or school. Also slow buck, which is to intentionally work at an extremely slow pace.

building tender—an outlawed form of Texas inmate control through the use of convict turnkeys, row tenders, hallboys, lead rows, and tail rows. Prior to 1981, the Texas Legislature would not authorize funding for enough staff to safely operate TDCJ prisons without some utilization of convict enforcers.

bull dagging—homosexual activities between women; taking a homosexual lover. A *bull dagger* is a macho-acting lesbian.

bum rap—an allegedly false charge.

burnout—a habitual drug user who is constantly in a state of apathy.

bus therapy—repetitiously transferring prisoners from one unit to another on short notice. This can have the effect of keeping inmates away from their property and interfering with visits, mail, and other contacts. This is particularly popular in the federal prison system. Also known as "diesel therapy," or "grey goose therapy."

bush pass—to escape from the field.

busted a cap—shot at someone.

buzz—slang term for being high on drugs or drug-induced euphoria, as in, "He buzzing."

cadillac—coffee with cream and sugar, or a cushy job on the inside. The best.

camel-toe—a term referring to the crease formation between a woman's legs. In prison it is most often created when a female officer wears her uniform pants so tight that the outline of her genitalia/labia can be seen.

cantones—prisons. Also prison camps.

carnal—a fellow gang member, brother, homeboy, or close associate.

case—an institutional-rules violation. A written offense report charging an inmate with a violation of a rule.

catch the square—"Let's fight," as in, "I'll meet you on the square, bitch." Derives from the corners of a boxing ring.

catcher—sexually passive or submissive homosexual; takes the female role and is often victimized.

cathead—yeast roll or large biscuit.

CC—two or more sentences served as one. Also referred to as consecutive sentencing.

cell pass—an official form allowing an inmate to stay in his cell.

cell warrior—a convict who talks loudly and threateningly from behind the safety of their cell bars. When the door is opened they become meek and mild. They are usually cowards or mentally unstable.

chain—the transfer bus or a group of inmates arriving or leaving on the transfer bus.

chase—the unofficial name for searching for an escaped convict.

chock—homemade alcoholic beverage. Also see "Hooch," "Rasin-Jack," "Pruno."

check in (or **catch out**)—to voluntarily go to protective custody. Also **ketch out.**

checking—fighting, usually just fistfights that are generally approved of by others. These fights often happen when new convicts are being tested to see if they are homosexuals or if they will "ride" or not. As in, "I checked that ho."

cheese-eater—an informant.

Chester—child molester, baby-raper and general all-around pervert. Also, diaper sniper.

chingasos—fighting. Spanish for "Hard hits."

chipping—when someone uses narcotics every now and then. Also when a married person has sexual relations with others, as in "I have been chippin' on my ol' lady."

chiva—heroin (Spanish). Also scam, gow, girl, hop.

cho-cho—an ice cream bar bought from the commissary.

chota—police or guard.

clavo—a stash or collection. "He has a clavo of shanks."

clica—gang (Spanish). Also "ganga." To **click up** is to join a gang.

click—when two or more convicts attack one inmate.

clipper pass—a special shaving pass that allows prisoners with medical conditions to shave only certain parts of their beards. This is widely abused in Texas prisons as most of the TDCJ physicians are afraid to refuse an inmate a clipper shave pass.

code 20—from TDCJ inmate offense code—masturbation. This is one of the more common offense reports written by staff, especially since women officers now work in inmate living areas.

cojones—a Mexican slang term for bravery (slang reference to "balls"). Also "juavos," "nuts." As in, "He's got *cojones* like a water buffalo."

cold shot—perceived unfair treatment.

con sofos—anything that is said goes back twice as bad.

convict—as opposed to "an inmate." A convict is one who has traditional values. One who, even though he is in prison, has respect and integrity.

convict boss—an officer who does his job without creating unnecessary aggravation, hassles or instigating trouble.

count board—a large board located in the count room that reflects all official inmate housing. Much of what used to be maintained on the count board is now in computers.

crab—a derogatory term used by the Bloods gang members for Crips gang members.

crack—also "pebbles/rock," cocaine in ready-to-smoke rock form.

cross-haul—archaic field-workforce term meaning to assign two inmates with hoes to a row. Each inmate would then be required to reach across the row and pull dirt from the other side back toward the row. This procedure is usually used when covering freshly planted potatoes.

crumb snatchers—children; also "rugrats."

cuernos—what Texas Syndicate members call one other. Spanish for "horns."

cutting up—an attempt to commit suicide by cutting oneself.

daddy—usually used in women's prison, term for an aggressive female homosexual taking a male role.

dagging—two convicts trading out anal sodomy.

dead—aside from the conventional meaning, it also means to be deprived of something, as in, "Naw man, that's dead, he wouldn't let me go to rec."

debrief—A convict wanting to establish that he is no longer associated with a gang, usually with hopes of getting out of segregation, must provide information regarding all gang activities. The convict must give names of other gang members and identify any and all criminal information that he has. This is a very dangerous contract for any convict. From that point on, the inmate will have to rely on the prison system to protect him.

deck—a pack of cigarettes. Also known as "squares."

deuce it up—walking in pairs.

dime—the quantity of drugs that can be sold on the street for $10. Also represents the 10-percent street tax that some gangs (Mexican Mafia) charge for dealing drugs in their area of control. Also, to inform, as in, "I dropped a dime on that dude."

diaper sniper—a child molester

dis—to show disrespect.

dog—a friend or homeboy; a road-dog or close associate to "ride" with.

dogboy—an inmate who works for the dog sergeant, feeding, training, and laying practice tracks for the dogs. Formally known as "kennel-men."

donkey dick—link pork sausage, served often in TDCJ inmate dining rooms. At the women's units, link sausage is sometimes cut into small pieces prior to serving in order to discourage inmates from using it as a sexual aid.

doo rag—any piece of cloth utilized as a hair or head cover, more often used by black inmates.

drive up—a new officer or inmate, as in, "He just drove up."

driver—a "hard driver" is a hard worker.

drop a dime—archaic term for informing on someone. Derived from when a pay-phone call cost a dime.

drop salt—spreading negative information (true or untrue) about someone.

drove—a term meaning tired of working, as in, "Man, I'm drove."

duccat (or ducats)—money, commissary items, other items of value, or a pass of admittance that allows movement from one area to another in a prison.

eight-ball—one-eighth ounce of cocaine. Also "Eight-Ball Posse," a small prison gang.

eme—Spanish for the letter "M." Name for the Mexican Mafia, currently the largest prison gang in the Texas prison system.

ese—Spanish slang for homeboy or guy.

estact—a methamphetamine-based control substance.

fade the heat—to take the blame. "He took responsibility for his own actions; he faded his own heat." Also expressed as, "carry your own water."

fall—received a conviction, as in, "I fell out of Bell County."

fall partner—two or more convicts sentenced for committing the same crime.

featherwood—a slang term for a peckerwood's woman.

field force—an almost archaic term used to describe an inmate workforce that is assigned to do "field" or agricultural work while being supervised by officers on horseback.

firma—Spanish for *firm;* used to mean extremely committed, or "down."

fishing line—a string used to pull items from cell to cell, floor to floor, room to room, or building to building.

flat time—to serve a sentence day-for-day, or straight time. No time off for good behavior, no parole, et cetera.

flat weeding—term for cutting weeds off at the ground using a long-handled hoe.

forty-five—a .45-caliber handgun. Also, slang term for the *Hermanos Pistoleros Latinos,* a prison gang that began in Texas prisons in the mid-1980s. The group split several years ago into the "Forty-fives" and the "16/12s." Some of the members use the .45-caliber pistol tattoo as an identifying symbol.

free world—the world outside of prison.

front in—to talk negatively about someone or to embarrass another person.

fudge packer—slang term for a male homosexual.

G.I.—gang investigator.

gang jacket—identified as a gang member; also snitch jacket, identified as an informant.

ganja—a strong form of marijuana.

gavacho—Hispanic slang for white convicts.

get a job—an archaic term that used to mean any job assignment other
than fieldwork. Fieldwork is all but gone in today's system, and this
term now generally refers to a job with perceived power or special status, like teacher's aide, law-library clerk, head kitchen cook, et cetera.

get your heart right—improve your attitude; get with the program; be
a team player.

girl—homosexual reference when used by a member of the same sex,
as in "He's my girl," or "She's my girl."

gladiator fight—a show fight or fight for status. Also a fight between
two known convict enemies staged by officers for entertainment purposes.

gladiator schools—prison units that are classified as first-offender
units. These prisons are filled with ex–youth offenders and wannabe
tough guys trying to prove themselves. These young, mostly illiterate,
baby gangsters spend the majority of their time trying to build reputations as "bad-actors." For this reason, these units have ten times
the number of fights as the older prisons.

good time—time credits awarded toward one's sentence in return for
good behavior, completing school programs, et cetera.

goon squad—slang term used by convicts to describe a Special
Operations Response Team (SORT.)

gray slaves—convict terminology for officers required by policy and job
description to wait on convicts who are confined in cells. TDCJ
employees must deliver food, legal material, medical attention and
medications, religious material, educational material, mail, and more
to the convicts.

green light—a slang term meaning that someone has been targeted for
death, as when one gang member says to another, "You have a green
light on, Carlos."

hard time—an inmate who fails to follow the rules and thereby intentionally causes his time to be more difficult than it would ordinarily be.

hash (short for hashish)—a form of refined marijuana made from the cannabis sativa plant.

head running—unnecessary or excessive talking.

heart—to have strong beliefs or convictions, as in, "He has a lot of heart."

high roller—a hard worker or exceptionally fast worker. Also a convict with an unrealistic view of his or her importance. Reference to the now-defunct Retrieve Unit Drill Team, a traveling team of inmates renowned for their ability to perform precision marching drills during the years 1972–82.

hit—a term meaning to kill or murder. Also a term for smoking crack, marijuana, et cetera.

ho—slang abbreviation for whore, as in, "I checked that ho."

ho check—a fight or beating by one or more inmates on another inmate. This is usually a way of determining whether a new inmate will stand up for himself. "Ho" is a slang abbreviation of "whore."

hog law—a convict who hasn't picked enough cotton or done enough work to avoid a disciplinary report has been caught by the "hog law."

hole—as in "The Hole," an archaic term for solitary confinement or disciplinary detention cells. In today's Texas prisons, solitary confinement is often a preferred assignment, because of the privacy and the fact that officers deliver everything to the convict's cell door. (See **gray slaves.**)

hot lips—oral sodomy.

hogged—forced to submit, physically or sexually, or forced to give up property or some other item of value. Also, to be "sold a hog" is to be lied to or bluffed into submitting without physical resistance.

holding—to have possession of something; in prison this usually means to hide some item that is illegal.

homes—a general greeting between inmates, not necessarily "homeboys," but associates.

homie—an inmate from the same town or area.

honky—a derogatory term for white people. Primarily used by black racists and/or minority gang members to describe anyone who is Caucasian in appearance. Other terms include "white bread" and "milktoast."

honor squad—archaic term for a hardworking hoe squad. As a reward for good work, some of the older wardens used to allow some of the better inmate workers to work without squad-officer supervision. This was a special squad that was allowed to eat, shower, and recreate before others. They also attained other privileges as an incentive for their hard work. Since work is no longer recognized as a valued asset in TDCJ, honor squads have ceased to exist.

house—a reference to a convict's cell or dormitory living area, as in, "Man, during shakedown that boss sure tore up my house."

ice—a form of high-grade cocaine. Also, to be placed in segregation, as in, "I was put on ice."

idiot stick—a hoe or weed cutter.

in the car—to join a clique or gang. Also, to have a tight circle of friends.

jacked up—to be robbed, beaten up, or assaulted.

jailin'—a laid-back form of doing time. When a convict accepts that he is going to be locked up for the foreseeable future, he forgets the streets and starts "jailin'." He accepts prison as the only reality, doesn't fight the system, and tries to do easy time.

jefa—Spanish for "the boss" or the woman in charge.

jefe—Spanish for "the boss" or the man in charge. Also, field officer.

jigger—an inmate who watches for security while some illegal activity is going on.

Jody—any alleged lover who may be taking a convict's place while in prison, as in, "Jody's got your girl an' gone." (Also Sancho.)

John Henry—a sack lunch, usually a couple of sandwiches, a piece of fruit, and something to drink. Many inmates actually prefer eating "Johnnies" on the job to going into the inmate dining room.

Johnny ground—a predetermined place near the field-work sight where the noon meal is eaten on those occasions when the workforce does not go to the main unit dining room to eat.

joint—a hand-rolled marijuana cigarette.

jonesing—the onset of narcotics withdrawal. A very strong desire for narcotics, as in, "Man, my jones is sure coming down on me."

joto—Spanish for a male homosexual or "punk."

jugging—to provoke someone to the point of anger, as in, "If he keeps on jugging at me, I'm gonna have to do something to his ass."

jura—police.

keester—to use one's rectum as a hiding place. Inmates have been known to hide several ounces of drugs, a revolver, a knife, or money in their rectums. Women inmates have been known to use their body cavities in similar fashion. (beaver bank.)

ketch-out—an inmate who refuses to be around other inmates. They usually request protection from one or more inmates, gangs, or sexual predators. Sometimes these inmates are informers who are afraid they have been found out.

kibbles & bits—street name for small amounts (rocks) of crack cocaine.

kill—aside from the literal meaning, it means to masturbate, as in, "I kill to my jack books every night."

kite—any written form of communication between convicts.

knock boots—to have sex, as in, "Man, I'd like to knock boots with that."

kop—"keep on person" medication. Inmates who are required to take medication often are sometimes allowed to possess advanced doses in order to avoid having to go to the pill window four times a day.

lame—derogatory term for an inmate who isn't liked, doesn't "fit in," or isn't trusted. Also "chump."

lay-in—an authorized pass that allows an inmate a legal excuse for missing work, school, or some other programmatic activity, as in "I don't have to work today, 'cause I have a parole lay-in."

laying a track—in order to train tracking dogs, an inmate dogboy (or the more politically correct term, "kennelman") will lay a practice track for training purposes.

lead row—archaic term for the first man in a hoe squad. He is always assigned to the first place in line or the first row and is responsible for setting a steady pace of work.

line—the mainline refers to all inmates in general population. The line force refers to an inmate work group, as in the cannery line, field line, or factory line. Shortline refers to an early meal or the first one in line to eat. The term is derived from earlier days when convicts were allowed to catch rabbits, armadillos, possums, fish, or most anything else that walks, crawls, or swims and cook it as a meal supplement.

lit up—to be shot at or chased while being under attack.

little bitch—an archaic term meaning a sentence of more than fifty years. The term was primarily used before aggravated-sentencing laws were passed in Texas. It is sometimes used in today's system to reflect any aggravated sentence that is less than a life sentence.

lockdown—to lock a part of the unit or the entire unit. All inmates are placed in their cells or living areas, or held in their work areas. None of the convicts are allowed to move during a lockdown. Everyone remains in place until the reason for the lockdown has passed.

long-distance call—an archaic term used in the early days of Texas prisons. Some prisoners were punished by having live electric wires hooked up to their testicles and/or other body parts. One method involved the use of an old windup telephone crank. The more one cranked, the more electricity the phone discharged. This was done in order to extract information and as punishment. Inmates who suffered through this ordeal were said to have received a "long-distance call."

L.W.O.P.—life without possibility of parole. Although Texas does enforce the death penalty, life without parole doesn't currently exist in the state. Currently, forty years is the maximum sentence an inmate is required to serve before being "considered" for parole.

mafias—dark sunglasses.

make it—to get by with something, as in "Hey man, I know I'm wrong, but let me make it."

man—the guy in charge, as in, "The Man."

merecidos—Spanish for "deserved ones." Various Hispanic gang members sometimes use the term to refer to one another.

Moe—a prison homosexual who has a wife in the free world and a "wife" in prison.

monster—an inmate with AIDS, or one who is suspected of being HIV-positive, as in, "He's got that monster."

mota—Spanish slang for marijuana. Also called "bo" or *"greefa."*

mud—coffee. Also called "mummy dust," "amp fuel" and "grounds."

narcing—a suspected informant, someone talking to the police.

nester—a member of Nuestra Familia (NF), a prison gang that originated in Northern California.

new boot—a new employee, usually a new correctional officer.

nut up—to resist authority, act crazy, or throw a tantrum.

O.G.—original gangster. Usually an older multiple offender, a convict who has been in a gang for a long time.

old school—an inmate who did time in the pre-1981, pre–*Ruiz v. Estelle* TDCJ. A convict who knows what it was to really have to work in prison and who did time during the building-tender era.

on pipe—a male homosexual or "punk," as in "Yeah, man, he's steady on that pipe." Also, one who uses a crack pipe.

on the bumper—a prospective gang member who wants in and is trying to get **"in the car."** These are some of the most dangerous convicts in prison, because the older gang members take advantage of their naivete. Knowing they have to prove themselves, these young wannabe gang members will do almost anything, to include stealing, maiming, and killing, to be allowed into the gang.

packin'—an armed convict. Also, a convict who has drugs for sale.

P.C.—protective custody. Usually reserved for informants, potential victims, weak convicts, sexual targets, ex–gang members, or offenders such as child molesters, who are targeted by other inmates.

PHD—pre-hearing detention. A temporary administrative segregation cell where an inmate is held for investigation or pending the outcome of a disciplinary hearing.

phone off the hook—someone is listening to this call.

PIA—parole in absentia, the practice allowing a convict to parole from a county jail after serving time there.

pica—shank or knife.

picket—a centralized area controlled by security. A secure room with reinforced glass or bars with door control within a tier or wing of a prison unit. Also a perimeter tower designed to prevent escapes.

pillow biter—a homosexual rape victim.

pill line—the line that forms in front of the pill window, where convicts receive prescribed medication.

pill window—window where medication is given out/sick call. Also see **pill line.**

pitcher—an aggressively dominant homosexual.

plantation—Many of the older units were actually plantations prior to becoming prison units. In the early days of the Texas prison system, the older units were operated on the plantation model. Convicts replaced slave labor on some of the old plantations, such as the Retrieve, Clemens, Darrington, and Ramsey units. This fact was not lost on today's convicts who still refer to them as plantations.

play crazy—to fake an attempted suicide in order gain attention or a transfer. Also, when a convict acts ignorant or violent and then blames his actions on "being crazy" or some medication he may be taking. This is a favorite convict game.

playing on ass—when a convict is gambling without commissary, money, or other items of value to back up his bet. If he loses, "it's his ass."

politician—an inmate who is always trying to con someone, usually staff. Also inmates who work in preferred prison jobs.

potty watch—when a convict is suspected of swallowing or smuggling drugs or money. The inmate is placed in a dry cell, with the water to his toilet cut off. The inmate is observed until the contraband shows up in his or her stool.

pouring it down—archaic phrase used by inmates to obtain permission from a field officer to urinate. "Port-a-cans" are the norm in TDCJ now, and the need for the term has ceased to exist.

pruno—homemade alcohol, a fermented juice, the original prison drink.

pull-dos—older convicts with physical disabilities. These inmates are often thought to be incapable of working with younger inmates. In my experience, they often work better than younger inmates when separated from them.

punk—a passive homosexual. Also, "punking out" is to perform sexual acts, either by force or voluntarily. An inmate known to be doing this is said to be "riding."

put in a cross—when one inmate gets another inmate in trouble, he is "putting him in a cross."

put your pen to the wind—usually an inmate's way of telling an officer that he is not afraid of a written offence report. Sometimes an officer will say this to an inmate who is threatening to file a grievance.

rabbit—inmate who has escaped or tried to escape and is considered a high escape risk.

rack-up—locking inmates into their cells.

Rev.—any inmate who appears outwardly as being religious.

ride—"to ride" is for an inmate to be turned out, prostituted, pimped out, or turned into an inmate whore. Sometimes inmates pay "protection" to other convicts as bodyguards in an effort to avoid these confrontations. The payoff is never enough.

riding leg—To be friendly toward staff in order to obtain a favor or status. Also called **sucking ass.**

road dogs—inmates who hang out together, eat together, and recreate together. They allegedly "watch each other's back."

ruca—an inmate's wife, girlfriend, main squeeze. Also used as derogatory term for staff, as in, "That boss is *mi ruca.*"

rugs—derogatory term for black inmates, primarily used by white racist gang members. Also "toads," "bugle-mouth."

sell a hog—to bluff or lie and be believed. Also selling "wolf tickets," as in, "I sold him a hog and he bought a bunch of wolf tickets, thinks I'm gonna do something to his ass."

serve all—parole recommendation denied; inmate must serve all of his sentence.

set—a gang or a part of a gang, as in, "The C-Wing set of the Bloods."

set tripping—to switch from one gang to another.

shoe-stringing—an archaic field-force term describing when hoe-squad inmates were required to line up and work in the same direction as the **lead row**. As the line moved, each man did his part to accomplish the task, such as scraping grass off of the end of a set of rows or cleaning under a fence line.

short—a cigarette butt. Also refers to an inmate who doesn't have much time left on his sentence, as in, "He's doing short time."

sidelineing—archaic field-force term for two inmates working on one row. Each inmate was required to clean the grass and weeds off half of the row while dragging his hoe blade in a backward motion. His row partner was required to do the same thing on the other side of the row.

slinging rock—a crack cocaine dealer or seller. Usually a small-time, street-level rock seller.

snitch—inmate informant. Also stoolie, cheese-eater, rat.

stacked—two or more sentences run consecutively.

stinger—an immersion heater, generally sold in unit commissaries and used for heating liquid such as coffee or soup.

stuck out—being late for something, as in, "He's stuck out for chow."

swole—angry, pouting, or unhappy about something, as in, "He's swole at me."

tack up—to put on a tattoo.

tail row—an archaic field-force term referring to the last man in a hoe squad. He was responsible for counting the rows for the other inmates and working with the lead row in setting a steady work pace for the squad.

tecate—heroin or morphine base.

tecato—a heroin addict.

thirty-eight—a .38-caliber pistol.

tight—close friends; trusted allies; to be in good favor. Also "heavy."

tight laces—store-bought cigarettes.

tip—prison gang or street gang, as in, "He's tipped up."

T-jones—reference to an inmate's mother, aunt, grandmother, or any female relative who is viewed as a parent figure.

toads—a derogatory term for black inmates, primarily used by white racist gang members. Also rugs, spear-chunkers.

toss-up—a woman who performs sexual acts for drugs. Also "crack ho"—convicts sometimes use this term to refer to female prison employees who are suspected of using drugs.

tree jumper—a rapist, sexual predator—especially a child molester.

trick—the bastard child of a prostitute. Also one who is an easy source of money or favors. Both prostitutes and dope dealers refer to their customers as "tricks." A convict will refer to anyone who sends him or her money as a "trick."

TS—the Texas Syndicate, a Hispanic gang that began in California prisons in the early 1970s. The TS is still a significant force within Texas prisons.

turd-hustler—an aggressive male homosexual. Also booty bandit, rump ranger, butt pirate.

turn out—to report for work, school, or any other group activity. Also to "pimp out," to rape or force into prostitution. In prison, to force someone into sexual slavery.

tush-hog—an ill-tempered, quick-to-rile, always-wants-to-fight convict. Also pronounced "touch hog"—usually by rookie employees.

tweaking—to be in a drug-induced state of paranoia. Usually refers to "speed freaks" or cocaine addicts.

verrio—neighborhood, same as *"barrio."*

veterano—a veteran gang member.

Viking—a lifestyle admired by the Aryan Brotherhood. To rape and plunder; to embrace the code of the "Norsemen."

Walls—the oldest established prison unit in Texas. Established in 1848 and located in downtown Huntsville, Texas.

wariche—coffee (Spanish).

wave cap—same as a "doo-rag"; a cloth worn on the head of an inmate.

weezo—an informant. Also cheese-eater, rat.

white ain't right—aside from the obvious racial meaning, also refers to the fact that Texas convicts wear white uniforms. The term implies that a convict wearing white is never believed over an officer wearing gray.

wigging—odd behavior, usually caused by excessive drug use, but sometimes a symptom caused by the failure of an inmate to take psychotropic drugs as prescribed.

wire—to receive a message. Also to be high on drugs—as in "He's wired." Also refers to someone who is carrying a recording device, as in, "Be careful—he's wired."

wolf—in prison, a wolf is a two-legged predator.

wood—a white convict, derived from "peckerwood."

world—the outside world; the free world, as in, "When I get back to the world . . ."

writ-writer—someone who files lawsuits, prison grievances—also a jailhouse lawyer.

yank his jacket—to confront another convict about some alleged transgression.

yard—recreation yard.

yo-yo—a weed cutter.

zig—rolling papers for marijuana cigarettes, as in the brand name "Zig-Zag."

TDCJ-ID
Senior Wardens, 1849–1995

Huntsville Unit
Established 1848

Morris M. Jones 1993–98

Hal H. Husbands 1973–78

Bobby D. Morgan 1971–72

Emmett Moore 1948–67

H. Emmett Moore 1944–46

Walter Waid 1930–42

W. A. McDaniel 1928

W. L. Miller 1924

R. F. Coleman 1921–24

John T. Luther 1919

J. P. Millar 1914–15

John T. Luther 1911–13

T. H. Brown 1903–7

Ben E. McCulloch 1883–88

D. M. Short 1879

All Inmates Leased

N.A.M. Dudley 1869–70

Thaddeus O. Bell 1867–69

James H. Murray 1858–59

Abner H. Cook 1848–50

Jack B. Pursley 1978–93

Lawrence D. Harvey 1972–73

Sidney Lanier 1967–71

A. C. Turner 1946–48

A. C. Turner 1942–44

E. F. Harrell 1928–30

Norman L. Speer 1924–28

Norman L. Speer 1924

Gus Harris 1919–21

D. E. Teague 1915–19

R. M. Warden 1913–14

R. H. Underwood 1907–11

James G. Smither 1888–1903

J. W. Middlebrook 1879–83

W. W. Lang 1879

A. J. Bennett 1870–77

C. E. Morse 1869

Thomas Carothers 1859–66

James Gillespie 1850–58

J. M. Wynne Unit
Established 1884

Michael W. Countz 1994–

Lester H. Beaird 1965–91

Don H. Costilow 1976–84

Carl L. McAdams 1969–73

Truman T. Easley 1951–56

Ewing Stanley 1946–48

D. V. Wright 1930–35

Dr. J. S. Christian 1928–28

Nolan T. Thornton 1919–25

John T. Luther 1919

William Oglesby 1911–14

H. B. Montgomery 1893–1902

J. L. Branch 1884–89

Jerry R. Peterson 1991–94

Randy D. McLeod 1985

Joseph Y. Walker 1973–76

Howard L. Sublett 1956–69

Ed L. Seay 1948–51

R. H. Baughn 1935–46

Claude O. Williams 1928–30

B. F. Ross 1925–28

W. S. Stevens 1919

Thomas G. Walker 1914–19

Thomas G. Walker 1902–11

James B. Abercrombie 1889–

Harlem Unit Camps I, II, and III
Established 1887
(Purchased 1886; Merged with Central Unit in 1940; Split from
Central in 1941; Renamed Jester I, II in 1967)

Lepher M. Jenkins 1993–96

David Myers 1979–83

Howard L. Sublett 1969–72

Virgle D. Starnes 1962–64

Joe Hines 1949–57

W. W. Hall 1942–43

A. N. Owen 1930–40

B. B. Monzingo 1927–30

J. M. Morgan 1922–25

Howell Mayes 1919

E. G. Douglas 1899–07

R. J. Ransom 1887–89

Morris M. Jones 1983–93

Paul F. Jacka 1972–83

T. C. Sanders 1964–69

Mat A. McGill 1957

H. G. Rambo 1943

R. J. Flanagan 1940–41

D. R. Vaughan 1930

R. E. Mcadams 1925–27

Woody Townsend 1919–22

T. C. Blakely 1907–19

Jacob A. Herring 1899

WILLIAM CLEMENS UNIT, EST. 1893
(Leased 1893; Bought 1899; Four Camps; Camp IV closed 1914)

Terry Foster 1996–	James H. Byrd 1994–96
Timothy E. West 1992–94	Gary L. Johnson 1990–92
David M. Moya 1983–90	Jack M. Garner 1981–83
Lester H. Beaird 1973–81	James V. Anderson 1972–73
Scott Valentine 1965–72	Leeford G. Bounds 1952–65
I. K. Kelley 1950–52	Ernest E. Moss 1936–50
W. M. Hickman 1928–36	J. L. Gentry 1915–28
E. B. Mills 1912–15	W. M. Brooks 1907–12
E. B. Mills 1902–7	J. E. Campbell 1893–1902

T. J. GOREE UNIT
Established 1900
(Matron system was used from 1911–54;
Husband was warden and wife was matron)

Dessie F. Cherry 1994–	Lanny A. Steel 1990–94
Richard H. Fortenberry 1985–90	Randy D. McLeod 1985
George R. Waldron 1983–85	Paul F. Jacka 1979–83
David Myers 1973–79	Clifford T. Olson 1973
Velda Q. Dobbs 1954–73	Frank Dobbs 1951–54
Ben P. Dillard 1951	B. C. Stricklin 1948–51
Marcus V. Heath 1930–48	G. W. Reed 1928–30
J. D. Black 1925–28	R. T. Burns 1921–25
G. R. Allphin 1919–21	John F. Standley 1915–19
R. H. Cabiness 1911–15	B. H. Tarver 1909–11
J. G. Bowden 1907–9	

IMPERIAL STATE FARM
Established 1908, Camps I, II, III, IV

(Camp IV built in 1911, closed 1916; Camp II changed to Neff Honor Camp 1924–25; New unit built at Camp II in 1934; Camp III closed in 1934; Harlem merged under Central Unit 1940; Blue Ridge unit renamed Central IV, 1957–59; Central consolidated into a single unit in 1969)

T. J. Medart 1999–	Margo K. Green 1993–99
Lepher M. Jenkins 1986–93	Howard W. Mitchell 1981–86
Bobby D. Morgan 1976–81	Scott Valentine 1972–76
Lloyd D. Hunt 1971–72	T. C. Sanders 1969–71
Hal H. Husbands 1952–69	L. J. Christian 1951–52
Roland R. Miller 1950–51	Ray Owens 1950
E. L. Slaughter 1949–50	R. J. Flanagan 1919–49
Ben Sira 1918–19	Dan Crow 1917–18
A. D. Addison 1911–17	Gus Harris 1910–11
F. G. Pryor 1908–10	

RAMSEY STATE FARM (UNITS I AND II)
Established 1908

(Leased 1908, bought 1913; Unit III built 1911; Unit IV built 1915; Units I and IV merged into one unit, 1941; Units II and III merged into one unit, 1943; Ramsey I and II switched in name only when the "new" Ramsey I building was completed in 1951; Both units separated into independent units in 1982)

Thomas D. Durbin 1978–82	Joseph Y. Walker 1976–78
James V. Anderson 1973–76	Sidney Lanier 1971–73
Carl L. McAdams 1951–61	L. J. Christian 1950–51
Otis O. Stewart 1948–50	H. Emmett Moore 1946–48
Otis O. Stewart 1944–46	Howard W. Miller 1942–44
Matt A. McGill 1941–42	D. R. Vaughan 1932–41
H. J. Jackson 1927–32	R. E. Smith 1925–27
F. C. Whatley 1921–25	J. H. Veale 1921
H. L. Gentry 1919–21	Gus Harris 1919
R. J. Worrell 1918–19	W. P. Whitworth 1917–18
K. F. Cunningham 1916–17	J. N. South 1911–16
T. J. Driscoll 1907–11	R. J. Worell 1907

RAMSEY I UNIT
Established as single unit 1982

David Doughty 1995–

Richard C. Thaler 1994–95

Herbert L. Scott 1991–94

James A. Shaw 1985–91

Terry L. Terrell 1984–85

Thomas D. Durbin 1982–84

RAMSEY II UNIT
Established as single unit 1982

Arthur H. Velasquez 1993–97

Fredrick E. Becker 1989–93

Michael A. Wilson 1986–89

Michael W. Moore 1984–85

Norman Kent Ramsey 1983–84

Jimmie G. Gremon 1982–83

Lepher M. Jenkins 1985–86

RETRIEVE UNIT
Established 1914
(Bought 1918; The Retrieve, Clemens, Ramsey, and Darrington units were all heavily worked by plantation owners using convict labor from 1871 until the lease periord expired on January 1, 1914)

Margo K. Green 1999–

Doyle B. McElvaney 1995–99

Dayton J. Poppell 1990–95

Bobby R. Crawford 1985–90

J. Keith Price 1984–85

Lloyd D. Hunt 1980–84

David Christian 1977–80

Edward H. Turner 1975–77

Oscar S. Savage 1973–75

Bobby L. Taylor 1973

Hal H. Husbands 1969–73

Eli F. Rushing 1967–69

Zan E. Harrelson 1951–67

Carl L. McAdams 1950–51

I. K. Kelly 1948–50

Joe Hines 1944–48

J. P. Lockwood 1942–44

H. W. Miller 1936–42

Rube W. Connor 1935–36

I. K. Kelly 1929–35

S. H. McLeod 1925–29

J. E. Barnes 1924–25

J. E. Ferguson 1921–24

Rube W. Connor 1921

W. V. Martin 1920–21

J. S. Murphy 1919–20

J. H. Weems 1914–19

Plantation Owners 1871–1914

DELLA EASTHAM UNIT
Established 1915

(Leased 1915, bought 1918; Camps I, II, 1940; Camp II closed 1942; Ferguson Unit placed under Eastham control, 1936–41; Ferguson closed due to fire, 1957–59)

Jimmie E. Alfred 1995–

George R. Waldron 1985–89

William A. Maples 1983–84

Oscar S. Savage 1975–79

Billy G. McMillan 1972–73

Eli F. Rushing 1956–67

Truman T. Easley 1948–51

Joe J. Oliver 1938–41

B. B. Monzingo 1930–37

D. C. Burks 1927–28

S. G. Granberry 1925–26

Rube W. Connor 1922–23

W. H. Rand 1921

John G. McKay 1918–20

Charles R. Martin 1989–95

David Myers 1984–85

Edward H. Turner 1979–83

Sidney Lanier 1973–75

Zan E. Harrelson 1967–72

Matt A. McGill 1951–56

Roland R. Miller 1941–48

James P Hamilton 1937–38

Ben H. Morgan 1928–30

Frank A. Harris 1926–27

H. J. Jackson 1923–25

John P. Barfield 1921–22

G. M. Rader 1920–21

S. G. Granberry 1915–18

JIM FERGUSON UNIT
Established 1916

(Under Eastham control, 1936–41; Honor camp, 1952–57; Fire closed unit, 1957-59.)

Charles R. Martin 1995–

Wesley C. Warner 1987–92

Jerry L. Gunnels 1984

Oscar S. Savage 1980–81

Scott Valentine 1976–77

Kenneth Coleman 1965–72

Unit Closed Due To Fire 1957–59

Richard C. Hopkins 1942–52

Unit Closed 1937–39

W. R. Crane 1927–30

R. E. McAdams 1921–25

Gary L. Johnson 1992–95

Charles A. Blanchette 1984–87

James A. Williamson 1981–84

Frank O. McCarty 1977–80

Bobby D. Morgan 1972–76

Jack D. Kyle 1959–65

Ben P. Dillard 1952–57

W. D. Sloane 1939–42

L. A. Martin 1930–37

H. J. Jackson 1925–27

Gus Harris 1921

Norman Speer 1921–21
E. T. Herring 1918–20
W. L. Bourn 1916–17

John P. Barfield 1920–21
John G. McKay 1917–18

DARRINGTON UNIT
Established 1917
(Bought 1918; Closed during World War II; Reopened 1946)

David Stacks 1995–
Gary J. Gomez 1993–94
Keith Price 1985–93
Timothy E. West 1984–85
David Christian 1980–84
Lester H. Beaird 1971–73
Robert M. Cousins 1962–69
Roland R. Miller 1951–53
Roland R. Miller 1948
John Easton 1947
Otis O. Stewart 1941–44
Ed L. Seay 1937–40
J. S. Murphy 1921–32
C. L. Jones 1920–21

Robert R. Treon 1994–95
Fredrick E. Becker 1993–94
Michael W. Moore 1985
Willis M. Gilliam 1984
Lloyd D. Hunt 1973–80
Charles A. Wilson 1969–71
Bobbie B. Bullard 1953–62
Joe A. Batson 1948–51
David Coers 1947–48
Howard W. Miller 1944
J. H. Midkiff 1940–41
H. J. Jackson 1932–37
J. R. Blocker 1921
J. H. Veale 1917–20

SMITHER FARM
Established 1960
(Bought 1959; Renamed O. B. Ellis Unit, 1961)

M. Bruce Thaler 1992–98
Jerry R. Peterson 1984–91
Oscar S. Savage 1981–83
Wallace Pack 1981
Oscar S. Savage 1979–79
Carl L. McAdams 1961–69

Lester H. Beaird 1991–92
Marshall D. Herklotz 1983–84
James A. Williamson 1981
Billy G. McMillan 1979–81
Robert M. Cousins 1969–79

Diagnostic Unit
Established 1964
(Renamed James H. Byrd Unit in 1997)

James W. Willett 1994–

Billy R. Ware 1980–90

Billy G. McMillan 1973–80

Dan V. McKaskle 1970–72

Lanny A. Steele 1990–94

Oscar S. Savage 1980

Lloyd D. Hunt 1972–73

Leon Hughes 1964–70

H. H. Coffield Unit
Established 1965

J. Keith Price 1995–

Jimmy E. Alford 1987–91

Robert M. Cousins 1979–83

James V. Anderson 1976–77

Leeford G. Bounds 1965–72

James A. Shaw 1991–95

Jack M. Garner 1983–87

Edward H. Turner 1977–79

Don H. Costilow 1972–76

Mountain View Unit
Established 1975

Linda S. Ament 1994–

Catherine M. Craig 1985–93

Jerry L. Gunnels 1985

Linda M. Moten 1993–94

Lucille G. Plane 1975–85

John Sealy Hospital
Established 1977
(Renamed Hospital at Galveston 1987)

Robert L. Ott 1994–

Margo K. Green 1992–93

Gary L. Johnson 1989–90

Wesley C. Warner 1985–87

Dan Lunsford 1982–84

Pamela E. Williams 1993–94

Edward G. Owens 1990–92

Fredrick E. Becker 1987–89

Richard H. Fortenberry 1984–85

BETO UNIT
Established 1980
(Name changed to Beto I, 1982; Renamed Beto Unit, 1995)

Herbert L. Scott 1994–

Terry L. Terrell 1985–91

Joseph Y. Walker 1978–84

Janie M. Cockrell 1991–94

James A. Collins 1984–85

GATESVILLE UNIT
Established 1980

Linda M. Moten 1994–

Linda Woodman 1979–85

Susan C. Cranford 1985–94

HILLTOP UNIT
Established 1981

Pamela S. Baggett 1994–

Linda M. Moten 1992–93

Mark W. Michael 1984–85

Linda S. Ament 1993–94

Jerry L. Gunnels 1985–92

Jerry L. Gunnels 1981–84

BETO II UNIT
Established 1982
(Renamed Louis G. Powledge Unit, 1995)

Fernando E. Figueroa 1993–

Janie M. Cockrell 1990–91

Elmer E. Alfred 1985–86

Wesley C. Warner 1984–85

Virgil E. Jordan 1982–83

Mitchell (Mickey) J. Liles 1991–93

Michael W. Countz 1986–90

Richard H. Fortenberry 1985

Marshall D. Herklotz 1983

JESTER III UNIT
Established 1982

Fredrick E. Becker 1995–

Morris M. Jones 1983–93

Lepher M. Jenkins 1993–95

David Myers 1982–83

WALLACE PACK I UNIT
Established 1982
(Renamed Wallace Pack Unit in 1995)

Douglas J. Dretke 1993–

Bobby D. Morgan 1981–90

David M. Moya 1990–93

WALLACE PACK UNIT II
Established 1982
(Renamed O. L. Luther Unit in 1995)

Neva J. Yarbourgh 1993–

Ronald D. Drewry 1988–92

George R. Waldron 1985

Richard H. Fortenberry 1982–84

Edward G. Owens 1992–93

Kenneth E. Hughes 1985–88

Bobby T. Maggard 1984–85

RAMSEY III UNIT
Established 1983

Jackie Edwards 1995–

Arthur H. Velasquez 1985–93

Terry L. Terrell 1983–84

David A. Doughty 1993–95

Michael W. Moore 1984–85

ELLIS II UNIT
Established 1984
(Renamed James Estelle Unit, 1995)

Fredrick E. Becker 1994–95

Randy D. McLeod 1985–90

Mickey Hubert 1984

Michael W. Countz 1990–94

D. Wayne Scott 1984–85

David Myers 1983–84

MARK W. MICHAEL UNIT
Established 1987

Larry A. Johns 1997–2000
Jimmy E. Alford 1991–95
Jack M. Garner 1987–90

Michael A. Wilson 1995–97
George R. Waldron 1990–91

SKYVIEW UNIT
Established 1988

Sharron J. Dishongh 1993–

Joe F. Collins 1988–93

DANIEL UNIT
Established 1989

Thomas J. Medart 1994–96
Leslie W. Woods 1989–93

Robert D. White 1993–94

WILLIAM HOBBY UNIT
Established 1989

Pamela E. Williams 1994–
Michael A. Wilson 1989–93

James J. Byrd 1993–94

WILLIAM CLEMENTS UNIT
Established 1990

Darwin D. Sanders 1995–
Randy D. McLeod 1990–93

Edward G. Owens 1993–95

L. V. HIGHTOWER UNIT
Established 1990

Timothy B. Keith 1995–
Gary J. Gomez 1992–94

Orlando Perez 1994–95
M. Bruce Thaler 1989–92

ALFRED HUGHES UNIT
Established 1990

David M. Moya 1995–98   Jack M. Garner 1990–95

GIB LEWIS UNIT
Established 1990

Larry A. Johns 1994–97   Wesley C. Warner 1993–94
W. Bruce Strickland 1990–93

T. L. ROACH UNIT
Established 1991

George Pierson 1994–   Robert R. Treon 1993–94
David A. Doughty 1991–93

WILLIAM R. BOYD UNIT
Established 1992

Jay T. Morgan 1994–   Jerry L. Gunnels 1992–94

DOLPH BRISCOE UNIT
Established 1992

Joe G. Gonzales 1991–

McCONNELL UNIT
Established 1992

Orlando Perez 1995–   Leslie W. Woods 1993–95
Wesley C. Warner 1992–93

FRENCH ROBERTSON UNIT
Established 1992

Ronald D. Drewry 1992–

PRESTON E. SMITH UNIT
Established 1992

James H. Black 1994–   Richard Thaler 1992–94

TORRES UNIT
Established 1992

Brian Hartnett 1995–   David Stacks 1992–95

SAN SABA UNIT
Established 1992

Bruce A. August 1993–   Pamela E. Williams 1992–93

TULIA UNIT
Established 1992

John Adams 1995–   Wilburn E. Gore 1994–95
Thomas J. Medart 1992–94

FORT STOCKTON UNIT
Established 1992

Thomas J. Prasifka 1994–   Terry Foster 1992–94

COTULLIA UNIT
Established 1992

Fernando M. Delarosa 1995–98   Lupe Lozano 1993–95

Robert R. Treon 1992–93

DIBOLL UNIT
Established 1992

Susan Perryman 1995–   Timothy J. New 1994–95

James H. Black 1994   Robert D. White 1992–95

JESTER IV UNIT
Established 1993

Kenneth O. Negbenebor 1994–   Lepher M. Jenkins 1993–94

RUFE JORDAN UNIT
Established 1993

Robert D. White 1995–   Darwin D. Sanders 1993–95

MARK STYLES UNIT
Established 1993

Timothy E. West 1994–96   Randy D. McLeod 1993–94

CHARLES TERRELL UNIT
Established 1993

Robert R. Treon 1996–   James A. Shaw 1995–96

J. Kieth Price 1993–95

GARZA EAST/WEST TRANSFER FACILITY
Established 1994

James R. Zeller

GURNEY TRANSFER FACILITY
Established 1994

Charles T. O'Reilly 1995–   Michael A. Wilson 1993–95

HOLLIDAY TRANSFER FACILITY
Established 1994

Mitchell J. Liles

JOHN MIDDLETON TRANSFER FACILITY
Established 1994

Richard G. Belanger 1995–   David M. Moya 1993–95

JAMES LYNAUGH UNIT
Established 1994

Terry Foster 1994–

NATHANIEL J. NEAL UNIT
Established 1994

Wilhelmenia S. Adams 1994–

DALHART UNIT
Established 1994

Randy D. McLeod 1994–

THOMAS HAVINS UNIT
Established 1994

Richard A. Trinci 1994–95

SAYLE UNIT
Established 1994

Fredia Richie 1995–   Charles C. Keeton 1994–95

STEVENSON UNIT
Established 1994

Roy A. Garcia 1994–

WALLACE UNIT
Established 1994

Rodney L. Cooper

BIBLIOGRAPHY

Martin, Steve, J. *Texas Prisons: The Walls Came Tumbling Down*. Austin, Texas: Texas Monthly Press, 1987.

Press, Aric, with Daniel Pederson, Daniel Shapiro, and Ann McDaniel. "Inside America's Toughest Prison." *Newsweek*, October 6, 1996.

Strobel, Abner J. *The Old Plantations and Their Owners of Brazoria County*. Houston, 1926; rev. ed., Houston: Bowman and Ross, 1930; rpt., Austin.

TDC and State of Texas Archive materials: The author's collection of these materials spans several decades. Any inquiries regarding these materials may be made to the author via the publisher.

324-326; drug traffic in, 151-153, 167, 248, 249-255, 258-260, 276; drug screening in, 260; educational programs of, 30-33, 35-38, 43-44, 50, 56-57, 60-61, 63-64, 84-86, 103-104, 106-108, 109-112, 113-117, 223, 286, 325, 337-338; employees of, vii-xi, xiii-xiv, 7-8, 17-18, 23-24, 42, 79, 94-97, 98-99, 103, 108, 110-112, 119, 120-122, 125-126, 132, 148-150, 153, 161-179, 244, 250-255, 260, 280-281, 292-301, 326-330, 339; federal courts and, ix, x, xi, 13-14, 23, 76, 93-97, 101, 119, 124-126, 143-144, 148, 161, 165, 173, 229, 234, 249, 258, 260, 270, 310-311, 315, 316-317, 319, 323, 327-328, 333, 335; gangs in, 121-126, 145-146, 150-153, 154, 156-158, 180, 188, 195-202, 249-250, 274, 276, 329, 335; health concerns in, 276, 280-281, 282, 300, 302-303; hostage situations in, 109-112, 113-116, 165-166, 182-195, 221-223, 288-291, 298-299; inmate deaths in, 51-52, 65-66, 85, 125, 131-132, 145-146, 148, 154, 155, 156, 157, 159, 180, 196, 197-198, 212, 218, 219, 275-278, 282, 326, 331, 335; lawyers and, 310-311; lease system in, 52-54; legislature and, viii, ix, 19-20, 23, 100, 111-112, 124-126, 214-215, 241, 243, 313, 316-317, 332-333, 338, 339; line squads in, 20, 27-30, 35-47, 88-92, 102, 106, 130; mental illness in, 269-283; naming of, 73; news media and, ix, 13-14, 100, 101, 125, 187, 216, 238, 239, 240, 285-286, 307, 320-322; nursing home care in, 281-283; overcrowding of, 229-230, 234, 282, 326, 329; population of, ix, x, 144, 249, 256, 257-258, 327; pregnancy in, 175; psychiatrists/psychologists of, 271-275, 277, 278, 279; punishment/discipline in, 4, 13, 16, 18, 21-22, 24-26, 32-33, 51-52, 57-59, 63-64, 74, 94-97, 129, 319 (also see death penalty; executions); racial prob-

lems in, 20, 154, 188-189; rehabilitation programs of, viii, 14-16, 21-22, 56, 276-277, 311-320; religion/religious programs in, 14, 176, 238-239, 322-324; riots in, 10-14, 133-141, 149, 156, 330-332; rodeos of, 56; security improvements to, 321-326, 334-336; sex in, 167-178, 251-255, 273, 276, 296; solitary in, 16, 25, 33, 172, 315; strikes in, 66, 74-75, 77-79, 87-97; suicide in, 275-280, 337; tobacco in, 299-301; treatment centers in, 272, 276-278; violence in, 21, 41-42, 59-60, 65-66, 103, 121, 122-126, 127-142, 145-146, 148, 151, 154-159, 161-167, 172, 180, 184, 188-189, 190, 196, 218, 219, 221-222, 288-291, 298, 326-336, 337; vocational training in, 313; wardens of, ix, 7-8, 20-21, 45, 46, 47, 66-67, 71, 73, 79-80, 85-86, 98-101, 119, 120-122, 148-150, 284, 292-293, 296-298, 335, 337; women in, 5, 110-111, 112, 161-179, 212, 235-241, 252-255, 298-299, 328, 330, 335 336, 337; youth in, 5
Procunier, Raymond "The Pro," 148, 166, 180, 186
prohibition, 55-56, 250, 262, 264

R
Ragland, Craig, 184
Rainey, ———, 40-41
Ramsey I and II Units, 49, 54, 102, 115
Ramsey I Unit, 120, 127, 167, 170, 224, 225, 292; hostages, 182-195; psychiatric unit in, 151; shakedown in, 147; violence in, 145-146
Ramsey II Unit, 165-166, 169
Ramsey III Unit, 159, 170, 199, 201, 294-296, 297-298
Ratliff, Marshall, 207-209
Reagan, Nancy, 249
   Ronald, 249
recidivism, 14-16, 21, 76, 312, 313, 319
Redwine, Clarence, 65-66
Reed, Colleen, 232, 233
Reeves, Otis, 27, 28, 31, 32, 33, 41, 96
Rehnquist, Justice William, 258

ABOUT THE AUTHOR

Lon B. Glenn's career in the Texas Department of Criminal Justice began in 1966 when he signed on as a twenty-one-year-old prison guard at the Clemens Unit in Brazoria County. Once the youngest field lieutenant in the prison system, he had the opportunity to work with many of the old-guard force.

Lon would eventually work on five of Brazoria County's six TDCJ prison units. Over the next three decades, the Texas prison system would undergo tremendous change. Lon watched as Texas gradually abdicated all control over its prison system to some California lawyers and the federal courts.

Lon retired after thirty years of service in 1995, serving the last ten years at the rank of warden. Twenty-five of those years of service were on close-custody units.

He spent thirty-five years researching and gathering material for this book, much of it obtained from veteran TDCJ employees and their families. He spent another three years putting the work into written form, eventually cutting the work in half in order to meet publishing requirements.

Lon, currently working on his next book, lives on the Texas Gulf Coast with his wife, Sylvia.